THE AMERICAN ASSOCIATION OF ANATOMISTS, 1888–1987

Essays on the History of Anatomy in America
and a Report on the Membership
—Past and Present

D1193091

Edited by
JOHN E. PAULY

Vice Chancellor for Academic Affairs and Sponsored Research,
Associate Dean of the Graduate School,
Professor of Anatomy,
University of Arkansas for Medical Sciences

THE AMERICAN ASSOCIATION OF ANATOMISTS, 1888–1987

Essays on the History of Anatomy in America
and a Report on the Membership
—Past and Present

Edited by
JOHN E. PAULY

with the assistance of the EDITORIAL COMMITTEE

John V. Basmajian
A. Kent Christensen
William P. Jollie
Douglas E. Kelly

WILLIAMS & WILKINS
Baltimore • London • Los Angeles • Sydney

Editor: Sara A. Finnegan
Copy Editor: Phyllis S. Bergman
Design: Brenda Brienza
Illustration Planning: Wayne Hubbel
Production: Raymond E. Reter

Copyright ©, 1987
Williams & Wilkins
428 East Preston Street
Baltimore, MD 21202, U.S.A.

Printed in the United States of America

Library of Congress Cataloging-in-Publication Data

The American Association of Anatomists, 1888–1987.

Includes bibliographies and index.
1. American Association of Anatomists—History.
2. Anatomy, Human—United States—History.
3. Histology—United States—History. I. Pauly,
John E. (John Edward), 1927–   . [DNLM: 1. American
Association of Anatomists. 2. Anatomy—history—United
States. 3. Societies, Scientific—history—United States. QS 11 AA1 A5]
QM11.A65235 1987   611'.006'073   86-9204
ISBN 0-683-06800-8

86 87 88 89 90   10 9 8 7 6 5 4 3 2 1

CONTRIBUTORS

Tibor Barka, MD
> Professor of Anatomy, Department of Anatomy, Mt. Sinai School of Medicine, New York, New York

John V. Basmajian, MD
> Professor of Medicine, Professor of Anatomy, and Director of Rehabilitation Programs, McMaster University School of Medicine and Chedoke Rehabilitation Centre, Hamilton, Ontario, Canada

Gwen V. Childs (Moriarty), PhD
> Professor of Anatomy, Department of Anatomy, University of Texas Medical Branch, Galveston, Texas

A. Kent Christensen, PhD
> Professor of Anatomy and Cell Biology, Department of Anatomy and Cell Biology, The University of Michigan Medical School, Ann Arbor, Michigan

Carmine D. Clemente, PhD
> Professor of Anatomy, Director of the Brain Research Institute, School of Medicine, The Center for the Health Sciences, University of California, Los Angeles, California

G.E. Erikson, PhD
> Professor of Medical Science, Division of Biological and Medical Sciences, Brown University, Providence, Rhode Island

John W. Everett, PhD
> Professor Emeritus of Anatomy, Duke University School of Medicine, Durham, North Carolina

Sergey Fedoroff, PhD
> Professor and Head, Department of Anatomy, University of Saskatchewan, Saskatoon, Saskatchewan, Canada

James K. Koehler, PhD
> Professor of Biological Structure, Department of Biological Structure, University of Washington School of Medicine, Seattle, Washington

C(harles) P(hilippe) Leblond, MD, PhD
> Professor, Department of Anatomy, McGill University, Montreal, Quebec, Canada

Nicholas A. Michels, PhD
> Late Professor, Department of Anatomy, The Daniel Baugh Institute of Anatomy, Jefferson Medical College, Philadelphia, Pennsylvania

Drew M. Noden, PhD
Professor of Anatomy, Department of Anatomy, New York State College of Veterinary Medicine, Cornell University, Ithaca, New York

Charles E. Oxnard, MB, ChB, PhD, DSc
University Professor, Professor of Anatomy and Cell Biology and of Biological Sciences, Department of Anatomy and Cell Biology, School of Medicine, University of Southern California, Los Angeles, California

George E. Palade, MD
Professor Emeritus, Section of Cell Biology, Yale University School of Medicine, New Haven, Connecticut

Sanford L. Palay, MD
Bullard Professor of Neuroanatomy, Department of Anatomy and Cellular Biology, Harvard Medical School, Boston, Massachusetts

Daniel C. Pease, PhD
Professor, Department of Anatomy, School of Medicine, The Center for the Health Sciences, University of California, Los Angeles, California

Roy R. Peterson, PhD
Professor of Anatomy, Department of Anatomy and Neurobiology, Washington University School of Medicine, St. Louis, Missouri

Keith R. Porter, PhD
Professor and Chairman, Department of Biological Sciences, University of Maryland-Baltimore County, Catonsville, Maryland

Charles H. Sawyer, PhD
Professor, Department of Anatomy, School of Medicine, The Center for the Health Sciences, University of California, Los Angeles, California

B. Scharrer, PhD
Professor Emeritus, Department of Anatomy, Albert Einstein College of Medicine, Bronx, New York

PREFACE

Several attempts have been made to produce a history of the American Association of Anatomists. The first was by the late Dr. Nicholas A. Michels in 1955 when copies of his *The American Association of Anatomists. A Tribute and Brief History* were distributed at the 68th Annual Meeting in Philadelphia, and later published in *The Anatomical Record, 122*:679–714. The Executive Committee recognized the importance of preserving records and appointed a Committee on the History of the Association in 1959, which continued to function until 1972. While he was Secretary-Treasurer (1964–1972), Dr. Russell T. Woodburne edited a volume entitled *American Association of Anatomists. Proceedings of Sessions 1–14. 1888–1900.*

At the 1973 Annual Meeting held in New York, President William U. Gardner appointed Dr. G.E. Erikson the official Archivist-Historian of the Association with the understanding that a history would be written within the next 3 to 5 years. Dr. Erikson interviewed prominent members of the Association, took hundreds of photographs, visited Departments of Anatomy all over the United States and Canada, and collected other background materials needed for the book. The original plan was to write a detailed history of the first 50 years and include a rich appendix of names, facts, and figures that would cover the entire period of the Association's existence. When the book failed to materialize, a decision was made to try a new approach.

An Editorial Committee was formed consisting of John V. Basmajian, A. Kent Christensen, William P. Jollie, Douglas E. Kelly, and John E. Pauly (Chairman). At its first meeting in January 1985, the idea of having a single author write the book was abandoned. Instead, it was decided that prominent anatomists would be invited to write individual chapters about their particular areas of interest. Most of the people asked to contribute accepted the challenge. The Editorial Committee decided on the topics to be covered and established general guidelines as to content and format. The authors were recruited by different members of the Editorial Board, and in retrospect it appears that some of them were not given all the guidelines.

References were supposed to be restricted to no more than one per page of text, but some of the authors were not told this until they had completed their chapters. Unfortunately, their contributions give the impression that other authors failed to cite important papers within their areas. Such is not the case, and the blame for the discrepancy must be placed on members of the Editorial Committee.

The authors of the chapters were asked to submit pictures whenever possible of some of the more prominent contributors to their particular subdiscipline. In most cases the authors themselves have made major contributions, but many of them were reluctant to include their own picture. Therefore, the Editor made a decision to place a picture of each author at the beginning of his or her chapter. Thus, no one can be accused of egotism.

No attempt was made to edit the styles of the authors. Thus, each chapter is different. Some provide insight into the personalities of the individuals being described. This is possible because the authors have known personally many of the major contributors to their fields. Other chapters read more like a regular history. These differences in style should make the book more interesting to read. A certain amount of overlap in content was unavoidable.

The Archivist was asked to write the chapters covering the early history of the Association. When it became apparent that he would not be able to complete this assignment, Dr. Basmajian wrote the section. He used as his references the *American Association of Anatomists. Proceedings of Sessions 1–14. 1888–1900* and the abbreviated history written by Dr. Michels in 1955.

The original title of the book was to have been *The History of the American Association of Anatomists;* however, it really isn't a history of the Association. Instead, it is a collection of essays on the history of the various subdisciplines of anatomy. For this reason the name of the volume was changed to *The American Association of Anatomists, 1888–1987. Essays on the History of Anatomy in America and a Report on the Membership—Past and Present.* Although authors were told to focus on contributions made by members of our own society, it was impossible to tell the story of any particular branch of science without referencing seminal contributions made by scholars from other disciplines.

It is relatively easy to define anatomy in terms of our teaching responsibilities. On the other hand, it is very difficult to list the research interests of anatomists, because as George Washington Corner said, "Anatomy is what anatomists do." Some can be described as gross anatomists, histologists, embryologists, and neuroanatomists; but more accurate descriptions for others might be endocrinologists, molecular biologists, chronobiologists, reproductive biologists, etc. Perhaps the one thing we have in common is an interest in morphology and how structure relates to function. Because of our diverse research interests and limitations of space, it was impossible to include chapters on many subjects. This volume is not meant to be a definitive history of our first 100 years; rather it is a collection of essays or minihistories of some of the subdisciplines that relate to our subject.

Authors were assigned a certain number of pages by the Editorial Committee. Because they were so restricted, many found it necessary to mention only principal discoveries. Thus, it seems only fair to blame the Editorial Committee rather than individual contributors for failure to mention a particular piece of work or investigator. Only the first two chapters really describe the history of the Association as a whole. The *Proceedings* were published in *The American Journal of Anatomy* from 1901 to 1905; beginning in 1906 they became a part of *The Anatomical Record.* In these *Proceedings* the interested reader can find reports of meetings of the Executive Committee, abstracts of papers presented at the Annual Meetings, financial records, and other reports of interest.

Members of the Editorial Committee wish to thank the authors of the individual chapters and Dr. Erikson, who helped many of the contributors by furnishing photographs from his files, information gleaned from his many interviews with members of our Association, and lists and tables of facts and figures he has prepared over the years. Dr. Douglas E. Kelly assisted with the copy editing of the chapters related to cell biology. Finally, special thanks are due Miss Sara Finnegan, President of the Book Division of Williams & Wilkins. Without her help, understanding, and financial assistance this would not have been possible. The entire expense of publishing this volume and mailing it to every member of the American Association of Anatomists was underwritten by Williams & Wilkins. On behalf of the entire membership, the Editorial Committee extends its heartfelt thanks.

Certainly one apology is appropriate. As our Archivist has stated, "some sectors are completely reliable—within the bounds of inevitable human error. Others are incomplete and tentative, though useful approximations. Some faults of omission and commission are remediable with continued research. Others are almost certainly irremediable—from limitations from time, energy and resources or from the simple, stark fact that the evidence is lost forever—a painfully poignant realization for anyone researching the past." Important names have been omitted inadvertently, and certainly the careful reader will find other mistakes. The Editorial Committee made a decision to complete the volume and see that a copy was sent to every member before the 100th meeting of the Association. Thus, it has been necessary to establish a cutoff date and stick to it. Despite the corrections made on the galley proofs, there remain errors that will have to be corrected by future chroniclers of our history. The Editor takes full responsibility for all omissions and commissions of error.

John E. Pauly, PhD

CONTENTS

PART 1

Chapter 1

THE EARLY YEARS

John V. Basmajian

The origins of the American Association of Anatomists probably began informally even before the first official meeting in Washington, D.C., on September 17–18, 1888. The organization named itself the Association of American Anatomists (the name was changed in 1908.) Typical of the record of many such beginnings, our present knowledge of events and actors on that long-ago stage is fragmentary, anecdotal, and largely second-hand. Clearly recorded, however, are the names of those who attended and of the first executive that they elected. In attendance at the inaugural meeting in the lecture room of the Medical Department of Georgetown University were the following 14 anatomists: Dr. Harrison Allen, Philadelphia; Dr. Frank Baker, Washington; Dr. William S. Forbes, Philadelphia; Dr. Augustus C. Bernays, St. Louis; Dr. William W. Gray, Washington; Dr. Horace Jayne, Philadelphia; Dr. Daniel S. Lamb, Washington; Dr. Alexander H.P. Leuf, Philadelphia; Mr. Frederic A. Lucas, Washington; Dr. Washington Matthews, U.S. Army; Dr. George McClellan, Philadelphia; Dr. W.B. Towles, University of Virginia; Dr. Faneuil D. Weisse, New York City; and Dr. Jacob L. Wortman, Washington. It should be noted that most of these individuals were from cities close at hand and almost certainly were primarily physicians or surgeons already in Washington to attend the Congress of American Physicians and Surgeons. Few, if any, were full-time anatomists.

"It was resolved that the object of the society should be the 'advancement of the anatomical sciences.' A constitution was adopted, and the management of the affairs of the Association was delegated to an Executive Committee of which the President and Secretary would be members *ex officio*. The committee was instructed to inform the professors and demonstrators of anatomy in the regular medical schools of the United States and Canada, as well as all others interested in the subject, of the formation and object of the Association and invite them to become members."

The Constitution was a marvel of brevity and clarity:

Section 1. The name of the society shall be the "Association of American Anatomists."

Sec. 2. The Association shall have for its object the advancement of the anatomical sciences.

Sec. 3. The officers of the Association shall consist of a President, two Vice-Presidents, and a Secretary, who shall also act as Treasurer.

Sec. 4. The officers shall be elected by ballot every two years.

Sec. 5. The management of the affairs of the Association shall be delegated to an Executive Committee, consisting of its President, Secretary, and three other members.

Sec. 6. One member of the Executive Committee shall be elected annually.

Sec. 7. The Association shall meet annually, the time and place to be determined by the Executive Committee.

Sec. 8. Candidates shall be proposed in writing to the Executive Committee by a member. Each proposal shall be made at or before the first session of any regular meeting of the Association. The proposal shall state the official position or occupation of the candidate and the character of his investigations. The election shall take place by ballot in open meeting, a two-thirds vote being necessary. Honorary members may be elected, from those, not Americans, who have distinguished themselves in anatomical research

Sec. 9. The annual dues shall be two dollars.

Sec. 10. The rulings of the Chairman shall be in accordance with "Robert's Rules of Order."

Sec. 11. Five members shall constitute a quorum for the transaction of business.

The Association officers were duly elected: President, Dr. Joseph Leidy of Philadelphia (who apparently did not attend the first meeting but was America's outstanding anatomist); First Vice-President, Dr. Frank Baker; Second Vice-President, Dr. Faneuil Weisse; Secretary-Treasurer, Dr. Alexander Leuf (who apparently organized and presided at the founding meeting); and Executive Committee: Drs. W.B. Towles, H. Allen, and B.G. Wilder. The precise minutes of that first meeting are lost. We do know that, as is the practice even today, the small association elected its officers for a couple of years to ensure continuity. Thus Leidy continued as President until his death in April 1891.

At the first meeting, the following six papers were given and discussed:

Dr. A.C. Bernays, St. Louis, Mo. "Some points connected with the formation of the valves and openings of the heart."—Illustrated by diagrams.

Dr. J.L. Wortman, Washington, D.C. "The significance of the hyoid bone in anthropology."—Illustrated by specimens. (Published in The American Anthropologist, Vol. II, 1889, p. 81.)

Dr. Harrison Allen, Philadelphia, Pa. "The bipartite malar bone in the American Indian."—Specimens and remarks. (The paper was incorporated with a clinical lecture on the skull, "Toner" lecture, 1889.)

Dr. A.H.P. Leuf, Philadelphia, Pa. "Case of non-decussation of anterior pyramids in a human female."

Dr. A.H.P. Leuf. "Study of the topography of some human cerebral hemispheres."

Dr. D.S. Lamb, Washington, D.C. "The junction of the eighth costal cartilage with the human sternum."—Specimens and remarks. (Published in The American Anthropologist, Vol. II, 1889, p. 75.)

The affairs of the Association having been left in the hands of the Executive Committee, it was decided to call the next meeting during the Christmas holidays of 1889. An attempt was made to meet at the same time and place as the Society of American Naturalists, since some were members of both societies. But lack of information respecting the plans of the sister society compelled the Association to come to an independent decision, and the committee selected Philadelphia, where accordingly the second meeting was held, December 26–28, 1889.

The Second Annual Meeting proved very "instructive and enjoyable." The Biological Department building of the University of Pennsylvania was put at the disposal of the Association. The members were entertained by the University through Dr. Horace Jayne, and by Dr. J. Ewing Mears; Dr. Harrison Allen and Dr. George McClellan entertained the members of the Association on the evenings of the 26th and 27th, respectively. The mornings and afternoons of two and one-half days were filled with the reading of papers, exhibition of specimens, and discussions. Drs. Leidy and Baker presided alternately. The vacancy in the Executive Committee caused by the resignation of Dr. Towles was filled by Dr. Thomas Dwight. An amended constitution was adopted.

A *Committee on Anatomical Nomenclature* was appointed: Drs. Leidy, Allen, Baker, Stowell, and Wilder. The committee made the following preliminary report at this meeting:

1. That the adjectives DORSAL and VENTRAL be employed in place of *posterior* and *anterior* as commonly used in human anatomy, and in place of *upper* and *lower* as sometimes used in comparative anatomy.

2. That the cornua of the spinal cord, and the spinal nerve roots, be designated as DORSAL and VENTRAL rather than as posterior and anterior.

3. That the costiferous vertebrae be called THORACIC rather than *dorsal.*

4. That the *hippocampus minor* be called CALCAR; the *hippocampus major,* HIPPOCAMPUS; the *pons Varolii,* PONS; the *insula Reilii,* INSULA; *pia mater* and *dura mater,* respectively PIA and DURA.

The Third Meeting was held in Boston, December 29–30, 1890, in the Anatomical Lecture Room of the Harvard Medical School. The Second Vice-President, Dr. Weisse, presided; Dr. Dwight acted as temporary secretary, and Dr. Lamb was elected for the unexpired term. The Executive Committee decided to call the next meeting in Washington, in September 1891. A reception was given for the Association and for the Society of American Naturalists and the American Physiological Society, which were also meeting in Boston at the same time, by Professors H.P. Bowditch, Thomas Dwight, and C.S. Minot, in the Anatomical Museum of Harvard Medical School.

The list of 84 members in the third year includes, among all the MDs, only two persons with both the MD and PhD (Theodore N. Gill of the Smithsonian Institution and George T. Kemp, Associate Director, Department of Physiology and Experimental Therapeutics, Hoagland Laboratory in Brooklyn) and only four PhDs (J. Playfair McMurrich, then of Clark University in Worcester, later at Michigan and Toronto, and President of the Association in 1908–1909; Thomas B. Stowell, Principal of the State Normal and Training School of Potsdam; Othniel C. Marsh, Professor of Paleontology at Yale University; and John A. Ryder, Professor of Comparative Embryology, University of Pennsylvania).

The early years were a northeastern seaboard affair, centered on Washington and the great universities within several hundred miles. There were only 11 members from outside this center of activity: William X. Suddeth, MD, DDS, Professor of Oral Surgery and Pathology at the University of Minnesota; one individual from California; two from the Southwest; four from the Midwest; and three from Canada.

The *Collected Proceedings* of the first three meetings (September 1888 in Washington; December 26–28, 1889, at the University of Pennsylvania in Philadelphia; and December 29–30, 1890, at Harvard University in Boston) include 15 substantial abstracts of the 40 papers that had been presented. Osteology, paleo-anthropology, hematology, neuroanatomy, cytology, and comparative anatomy were the main topics.

The *Fourth Annual Session* of the Association of American Anatomists was held September 23–25, 1891, in Washington, at the Grand Army Hall on Pennsylvania Avenue. In consequence of the death in April of Dr. Leidy, the Association's first President, Dr. Frank Baker of Washington, First Vice-President, acted as president. The meeting learned that the Association had been formally admitted into the Congress of Physicians and Surgeons (from which it withdrew early in the 20th century). A breakdown of the geographical distribution of members was provided. "The four largest numbers are: From Pennsylvania, 19; New York, 14; District of Columbia, 9; and Massachusetts, 7—constituting much more than half the membership; then Virginia, Illinois and Canada, each 3; Maine, Connecticut, Louisiana and California, each 2; New Jersey, Maryland, Tennessee, Missouri, Texas, Ohio, Michigan, Wisconsin, Minnesota, Kansas, Nebraska, Colorado and U.S. Army, each 1."

The Secretary-Treasurer reported: "I have received up to date from dues, $42, which, added to the $230 from Dr. Leuf, makes a total of $272. I have expended for postal cards, stamps and wrappers, $16.32; for telegrams, 91 cents; for transcribing, 50 cents; and for printing, including the printing of the pamphlets, $62.15; making a total expended of $79.88. Balance on hand, $192.12. The amount of dues in arrears is $48. It will be seen that the expenses average about one dollar a member."

Fourteen new regular members, the Association's first honorary member (Daniel J. Cunningham, MD, DSc, LLD, Professor of Anatomy and Chirurgery, University of Dublin), and a new 2-year Executive were elected. Twenty-five papers were read over the 3 days, with a recess on September 24 so that the members of the Congress of Physicians and Surgeons (of which the AAA had become a member) could attend a reception given by the President of the United States. The September 23 session was also shortened to permit the Association to be entertained at the National Zoological Park in the afternoon by Dr. Baker, the Acting President (who was the manager of the Park).

Officers of the year 1891–1892 were Dr. Harrison Allen, Philadelphia, President; Dr. Charles Heitzmann, New York City, First Vice-President; Dr. Theodore N. Gill, Washington, Second Vice-President; and Dr. D.S. Lamb, Washington, Secretary-Treasurer. Executive Committee members were Dr. Burt G. Wilder, Cornell University; Dr. Thomas Dwight, Harvard University; Dr. E.C. Spitzka, New York City—and the President and Secretary, *ex officio.*

At the end of the meeting, the geographical distribution of the 95 members was:

New York	19	United States Army	2
Pennsylvania	19	Maryland	1
District of Columbia	15	Iowa	1
Massachusetts	7	Missouri	1
Illinois	4	Texas	1
Connecticut	3	Wisconsin	1
Virginia	3	Minnesota	1
Canada	3	Kansas	1
Maine	2	Colorado	1
Louisiana	2	Arizona	1
Ohio	2	California	1
Michigan	2	Ireland (honorary)	1

The *Fifth Annual Session* of the Association was held December 27–29, 1892, in the School of Science Hall of the College of New Jersey, Princeton. President Allen presided at the meetings. The following 17 members "were present at some time during the session": Drs. Harrison Allen, Edward D. Cope, Thomas Dwight, Frederick H. Gerrish, Irving S. Haynes, Charles Heitzmann, Charles Luther Herrick, George T. Kemp, Daniel S. Lamb, Charles S. Minot, Henry F. Osborn, George A. Piersol, John B. Roberts, John A. Ryder, E.C. Spitzka, Jacob L. Wortman, and R. Ramsey Wright.

The "Second Preliminary Report" of the Committee on Anatomical Nomenclature of the Association of American Anatomists was received and the following recommendation adopted:

"Other things being equal, we recommend the use of mononyms or single-word terms rather than polyonyms, terms consisting of two or more words."

Twenty-two papers were presented at Princeton, two of them by the energetic President, Harrison Allen, Professor of Comparative Anatomy at the University of Pennsylvania, who also gave the Presidential Address. Subjects included descriptive and developmental osteology, myology, neurophysiology and neurohistology, gross neuroanatomy, splanchnology, physical anthropology, and biostatistics.

By the end of the fifth meeting, the Association had grown to 102 active and two honorary members. The latter were William Anderson, FRCS, Demonstrator of Anatomy at St. Thomas's Hospital and Medical School in London, and Daniel J. Cunningham. Twenty-four states, most with only one or two members, were represented along with Canada (4) and the U.S. Army (3).

The *Sixth Annual Session* of the Association was held May 29 to June 1, 1894, in the Preparatory Department of the Columbian University (now George Washington University), H Street between Thirteenth and Fourteenth, N.W., Washington. The meeting was in conjunction with that of the Congress of American Physicians and Surgeons.

The following officers and members were present: Dr. Allen, President; Drs. Heitzmann and Gill, the Vice-Presidents; Dr. Lamb, Secretary-Treasurer; Drs. Dwight and Gerrish, Executive Committee; Dr. Shufeldt, Delegate to the Congress; and Drs. Baker, Balloch, Browning, Carr, Ferris, Hamilton, Hewson, Mears, Mixter, Moody, Moran, Reyburn, Richardson, Shute, Souchon, and Wilder, Mr. Lucas, and Mr. Moody.

The following excerpts are taken from the report of the Secretary-Treasurer for the 17 months that had elapsed since the Fifth Annual Session at Princeton.

The sixth regular meeting of the Association should have been held in December, 1893, but, in view of the Pan American Medical Congress in Washington, September 5th to 8th, 1893, and the present meeting taking place in May, instead of September, as was anticipated, the Executive Committee decided that a December meeting would be in too close proximity to the others to be successful, and accordingly deferred the meeting to the present time.

Since the last meeting I have collated about 650 names of persons living in the United States and Canada, who are particularly interested in Anatomy. Somewhat over three hundred of this number are professors or demonstrators in medical colleges. Adding our own membership, increases the number to about 750.

In spite of that large potential membership, only 11 new members were added, of whom one was honorary—the distinguished Scotsman, William Turner, Professor of Anatomy at the University of Edinburgh and member of the Royal Scottish Academy. The total active members numbered 107. The three honorary members were leaders in Ireland, England, and Scotland.

The *Seventh Annual Session* of the Association was held in the Medical Department of Columbia College, 437 West Fifty-ninth Street, New York City, December 28–29, 1894. The following officers and members were present: President, Dr. Dwight; Vice-Presidents, Wilder and Shepherd; Secretary-Treasurer, Lamb; Executive Committee, Spitzka and Gerrish, and the *ex officio* members; Allen, Baker, Dwight, and Wilder of the Committee on Anatomical Nomenclature; and Bevan, Bosher, Ferris, Hamann, Heitzmann, C.J. Herrick, Huntington, Moody, and Weisse.

Eleven new members were elected, but a similar number were dropped for persistent nonpayment of dues. Eleven papers were presented, including one by C.J. Herrick. A flavor of the proceedings will be gained from the abstract of his presentation, "The Correlation between Specific Diversity and Individual Variability, as Illustrated by the Eye Muscle Nerves of the Amphibia":

The distinction between such anomalies as must be considered in teratology and that which may be called normal variability, and which is now absorbing so much attention in the biological world, is not an easy one to draw, nor, indeed, is it needful that it be sharply drawn, for the laws found to apply to the regular occurrences of the one will probably hold true *mutatis mutandis* in the more exaggerated cases of the other.

It is a familiar fact, that all of the orbital nerves show the greatest diversity among the various species of the amphibia as to their mode of origin, peripheral courses and terminal relations. The fourth nerve, for instance, is fused with the fifth in Salamandra and Pipa. In tadpoles Dr. Strong describes a small sensory intra-cranial twig. In the frog it terminates in the m. rectus superior. According to Wiedersheim, who also describes it as usually effecting an anastomosis with r. ophthalmicus trigemini, rarely distinct. It is exceedingly variable, the anastomosis, when present, presenting from one to five connecting filaments.

Now, in amblystoma the present writer has found the fourth nerve effecting the typical connection with the superior oblique muscle, and anastomosing with several small and distinct branches of the r. ophthalmicus trigemini. The details of this anastomosis are also extremely variable, as in the frog.

The other eye muscle nerves are quite as irregular in their distribution in the different species of amphibia, and a statistical study of their individual variations would probably prove suggestive.

This great diversity in the distribution of the eye muscle nerves among the various species of amphibia would seem to indicate that this group has passed through a period of great instability phylogenetically considered. There has therefore been less opportunity for cumulative heredity to introduce its conservative factor here than in those organs which, like the brain, have developed in a more continuous and unbroken manner. This weakening of the hereditary forces may be responsible for the individual variability found in these nerves. Such variation is to be expected in all organs now suffering any considerable alteration in the phylogenetic development, whether of retardation or acceleration, as illustrated by the jaws of man and, as has been more recently shown, by the appendix vermiformis.

The *Eighth Annual Session* of the Association was held in the College Hall of the University of Pennsylvania, Philadelphia, December 27–28, 1895, in conjunction with the American Society of Naturalists, American Physiological Society, American Morphological Society, American Psychological Association, and Geological Society of America. The American Folk-Lore Society met at the same time.

Dr. Dwight, President of the Association, presided at the several meetings. Twenty-four AAA members attended. The Committee on Anatomical Nomenclature reported progress on "the complex subject entrusted to them, and expressed the opinion that substantial improvement will result from the work of the Committee of the *Anatomischer Gesellschaft.* . . . Your Committee recommend to anatomists that, other things being equal, terms consisting of a single word each be employed rather than terms of two or more words."

The meeting adopted the following resolution: "That Professors of Anatomy be requested to inform their students concerning the laws upon the subject of anatomical material, and request these students to use their influence with the authorities in their respective places of residence to increase the quantity of anatomical material by making available much that is now withheld, either from neglect or indifference."

An abstract of the Proceedings of the meeting was printed in the January 17, 1896, issue of *Science [III (55)]*; in February 1896 in *The American Naturalist*

(p. 165); and in the same year in *The Journal of the American Medical Association* (*26*:80).

The Presidential Address by Dr. Dwight on "Our Contribution to Civilization and to Science" particularly concerned the procuring of human bodies for dissection, and is quoted in part below.

> It is idle hope, while human nature remains what it is, that aversion to dissection will ever disappear. Our wisest course is to recognize it, and to soften it by removing all just cause of complaint. It should be made clear to the public that dissection can and should be followed by decent burial. I, myself, would go so far as to have the bodies of Protestants and Catholics buried in their respective cemeteries, when the creed of the deceased is known. . . .
>
> I have alluded to the scandal of body-snatching, but an equally great scandal is its cause, the want in many places, of an anatomy act, or the existence of one which the framers and all others know to be inadequate. This state of affairs is in more respects than one an injury to the community. Like a prohibitory law meant to be boasted of on the platform and in the pulpit, but not meant to be inforced (sic), it destroys respect for law. It is the bounden duty of authorities of States, without adequate provision for dissection, to see that it is not practiced. After all, such communities deserve to be treated by surgeons ignorant of anatomy.
>
> Details of law may and must differ with the locality, but a good anatomy act should have the following characteristics: First, it should be just, safeguarding the rights of the poor, and securing decency: next, that it should be mandatory: finally, it should be easy of execution. It is our duty in our several States to do our utmost for the passage of a law that shall advance science, protect the grave and do credit to the community. We have not the excuse of older times, that the question is a new one. In view of our own shortcomings it behooves us to judge them lightly. For my part, I have far more respect for those who opposed dissection on the ground, however mistaken, that it might be displeasing to God, than for those who make it illegal by pandering to the prejudices of the ignorant. Dr. Johnson's advice, "free your mind from cant," is here singularly *a propos*. We cannot boast of our civilization till this is remedied.

The subject of anatomical materials was a constant concern as evidenced by the Report of the Committee on the Collection and Preservation of Anatomical Materials, reprinted in part below from the January 17, 1896, issue of *Science* [*III* (55)].

> (A questionnaire) letter was sent to the professors of anatomy in 148 colleges in the United States, 25 in foreign countries, and 25 copies were sent to the medical journals in this country and abroad. Forty-two replies have been received by the committee containing more or less specific answers to the questions propounded in the circular. An analysis of the replies received presents the following results:
>
> 1. Anatomical material is received wholly under the provisions of the

law in thirty States and countries, in part by law, in seven; and without law, in five.

2. In reply to the second question proposed, fifteen copies of the laws which are in force, have been sent to the chairman of the committee, thirteen of them being the laws of States of this country and two of foreign countries. With regard to the execution of the law, information was given to the effect that the provisions of the law were satisfactorily complied with in ten, fairly so in ten, not satisfactory in twelve, and no replies were given in ten. In eight the provisions of the law were stated to be obligatory, and in six the provisions were optional. In considering the subject of the report so far as it relates to the collection of anatomical material by law, the committee has confined itself to the examination of and report on the anatomical laws of the States of this country.

The answers received to the question of agents employed in accomplishing the preservation of subjects provided information about a large number of agents and their use in various combinations.

An analysis shows that of the agents used carbolic acid stands first, and that it was used not alone but in combination with other agents. Glycerine was reported as an ingredient in the next highest number. It was also employed in combination with other agents. The next in frequency was reported to be arsenic, and this agent was used also in combination. Chloral hydrate and choride of zinc and bi-chloride of mercury come next in the order of use. Alcohol, either pure or in combination, carbonate of potassium, bicarbonate of sodium, chloride of sodium, methyl spirit, formalin, nitrate of potassium, brown sugar, boric acid, were reported as used in numbers varying from four to one. The preservation of subjects by cold storage was reported in five instances. Some of the agents above noted were used in combination to preserve the subject, which has been kept in cold storage after it was placed upon the table for dissection. In one instance the following plan was reported: Injection with carbolic acid one and a half pints, glycerine six pints, with alcohol one and one-half pints. After the injection, directions were given to paint the subject daily for fourteen days with carbolic acid one part to glycerine six parts, and then place it in an air-tight box over a pan of methylated spirits. Perfectly satisfactory results were reported to have been obtained by this method, both as regards the character of the tissues and the absence of odor. Subject keeps indefinitely. Chloride of zinc, a fifty per cent. solution of neutral reaction was reported as an agent used successfully in preserving subjects, but had the objection of unfavorable action on the tissues, causing hardness and change in color. If subject is not required for immediate use it was placed in a saturated solution of salt, forming a strong brine. If immersed for a long time in the brine the subject requires to be soaked in water for a period of twenty-four or forty-eight hours, in order to soften the tissues.

A number of formulae were given, among them Wickersheimer's formula, consisting of three thousand parts of boiling water, one hundred and nine parts of alum, twenty-five parts of chloride of sodium, twelve parts of nitrate of potassium, sixty parts of carbonate of potassium, ten parts of arsenious acid; when cool, filter, and to ten parts of the liquid thus obtained add one part of methylic alcohol and four parts of glycerine.

Van Vetter's formula: Seven parts of glycerine, one part of brown sugar and one-half part of nitrate of potassium.

Langer's formula: One hundred parts of glycerine, fifteen parts carbolic acid, eleven parts of alcohol.

Empersonne's formula: Chloral hidrate (sic) five hundred grains, glycerine two and a-half litres, and distilled water.

Among the formulae reported, arsenic was an ingredient in a large number . . . Carbolic acid appears in a large number of the formulae . . . in most instances in combination with arsenic, some salt of potash or soda or bichloride of mercury. In a few instances it is reported as being used alone.

Bichloride of mercury is also reported as largely used alone or in combination with arsenic, salts of potash or soda, carbolic acid and glycerine . . . Glycerine appears to be a favorite agent, as it forms a part of a large number of formulae. The same may be said, in a very less degree however, with regard to the use of alcohol.

Formalin is reported in two instances, in one of which it was used in connection with the preservation of human subjects, and another in the preservation of an animal. . . . The cost of the formalin was stated to be $1.65 per pound package for a forty per cent. solution.

From 1895 forward the printed records of the scientific meetings become quite voluminous, running to many pages. Topics became broader and deeper, but attendance at the meetings still fell between 28 and 41 until the turn of the century. By 1900 the Association had increased to 128 active members and nine honorary members including European luminaries—L. Ranvier, A. von Koelliker, and Wilhelm His. The membership list of 1902 includes many well-remembered names in American anatomy including Charles R. Bardeen, Lewellys F. Barker, Robert R. Bensley, Albert C. Eycleshymer, Ross G. Harrison, C. Judson Herrick, Ales Hrdlička, G. Carl Huber, Warren H. Lewis, R. Tait McKenzie, J. Playfair McMurrich, Franklin P. Mall, Rudolph Matas, Charles S. Minot, George A. Piersol, and Robert J. Terry. The true scientific attitudes and techniques, already prevailing in Europe, had now taken a firm hold in America, even though many of the practicing anatomists remained pedestrian laboratory instructors who were part-time in the huge number of proprietary medical schools.

The list of 100 meetings of the Association that appears in the Appendix provides some faint evidence of the changes that occurred since the founding of the AAA. It cannot reveal the human dramas, the enthusiasm, the deep concerns, and the growing ambitions within the fledgling society to achieve its aim: "the advancement of anatomical science." No writer has succeeded in capturing the essence of the progress made by American anatomists up to World War II as well as the late Nicholas A. Michels, who had a personal knowledge of both the stage and the *dramatis personae*. His 1955 brochure permitted many of us who were too young to have taken part to catch a glimpse of the people and times. I have selected excerpts from the brochure (very slightly edited) to form the next chapter. It complements and illuminates my account of the early years and provides insights into the activities of the Association and many of its luminaries in the "middle years." Those were the years of the greatest ferment in American biomedical sciences that led to the explosive growth of the past 50 years, chronicled in the chapters in Parts II to IV of this volume.

Chapter 2

"FOR THE ADVANCEMENT OF ANATOMICAL SCIENCE"[1]

Nicholas A. Michels

As is well known, the earliest teaching of anatomy in America was accomplished in proprietary anatomical schools rather than by way of anatomical amphitheaters, like those in various European centers (Pisa, Tubingen, and Padua, 1594), or via "public anatomies," as in England. These were introduced in London by the Barber Surgeon's Company under Thomas Vicary, Chief Surgeon to Henry VIII (whose "sore legge" he treated), and culminated in the erection of an anatomical theater in 1638 known as the Barber's Surgeon's Hall, which functioned until 1785, when it was pulled down. The practice of giving public instruction in anatomy (mostly in winter months) followed the revival of anatomy in the 16th century, occasioned by the publication of Vesalius's *De Humani Corporis Fabrica* at Basel, Switzerland, June 1543, the same year in which the great Pole Copernicus published his *De Revolutionibus*. Their contemporary was the French physician Jean Francois Fernel (1497–1558), who was the first to bring order, learning, and clarity to physiology (1552) and pathology (1554), as opposed to the confusion, ignorance, and obscurity that prevailed in these subjects before his work and writings.

The men who taught anatomy in the United States, for the most part, followed later British methods, especially those of the celebrated English anatomist, John Hunter. Such privately conducted anatomical instruction was given by Dr. Thomas Cadwalader in Philadelphia as early as 1750, and by William Shippen and John Morgan (both students of Hunter) in 1762. Because medical doctors could realize large financial returns from conducting a proprietary school, hybrid varieties of the original type sprang up like mushrooms all over the country, each one worse than

---

[1]This chapter has been excerpted and edited by John V. Basmajian from the brochure, *The American Association of Anatomists: A Tribute and Brief History,* by the late Nicholas A. Michels, The Daniel Baugh Institute of Anatomy, Jefferson Medical College, to commemorate the 68th Session of the AAA held in Philadelphia in 1955 (1955 Anat. Rec., *122*:685–714).

the other. The deplorable conditions were commented upon all over Europe (Osler). Because the individual income of the owner and of the teacher was dependent on the number of medical students enrolled, few proprietary schools established entrance requirements as to previous scientific training, comportment, or character of the applicant. Commonly, a stipulated number of certificates stating courses taken for a year or two and paid for with $100 or $200 was all that was necessary to obtain the medical degree. In some instances, the teaching of the entire medical curriculum was effected by the owner of the proprietary school, with the help of one or two assistants (for instance, at St. Paul Medical College under Dr. A.J. Stone in 1880).

Realizing that something had to be done to better the conditions of medical education in the United States (often effected without clinical training in a hospital), physicians from various parts of the country met at the Academy of Natural Sciences in Philadelphia on May 5, 1847. They organized the American Medical Association (AMA) with the express purpose of devising means to raise the level of American medical education. The Association, after overcoming manifold objections, finally succeeded through the Abraham Flexner report (1910). By closing bad schools and merging others, the number of medical schools in the United States was gradually reduced from an aggregate of 160 (in 1905) to 95 (in 1915) and from 85 (in 1920) to 80 (in 1927). . . .

In the reorganization, betterment, and advancement of medical education and in the furtherance of anatomical research, the American Association of Anatomists played an important and pioneer role. Thus, at the 15th Session of the Association at the University of Chicago (December 31, 1901, to January 2, 1902), Robert J. Terry of the Washington University School of Medicine, St. Louis, discussed "a one-year anatomical course." Participants in this discussion were Warren H. Lewis, Franklin P. Mall, Ales Hrdlička, Charles A. Packer, George S. Huntington, J. Playfair McMurrich, Albert C. Eycleshymer, Charles R. Bardeen, Edward A. Spitzka, C. Judson Herrick, Ross G. Harrison, and G. Carl Huber.

In 1908, the Council of Medical Education of the AMA appointed a committee to outline courses in anatomy, histology, and embryology. That committee was composed of G.A. Piersol, F.P. Mall, I. Hardesty, G.S. Huntington, J.P. McMurrich, A.C. Eycleshymer, T.G. Lee, C.M. Jackson, G.C. Huber, and C.R. Bardeen.

At the 24th Session, held at Johns Hopkins University, December 29–31, 1908, with Professor McMurrich presiding, the Association held its first symposium on experimental embryology. Participants were Conklin, Morgan, Bardeen, Stockard, Warren H. Lewis, Eliot R. Clark, Harrison, Streeter, C.S. Minot, and S. Gage. In his Presidential Address on "Conservatism in Anatomy," McMurrich stated: "If we devote our energies to the graduation of adepts in the art of Medicine, ignorant of the sciences upon which that art must rest, we are failing in our duty; and, similarly, if we overload our students with the facts of Anatomy, without giving them the scientific bases which make the facts intelligible, we are placing their feet upon the highroad to empiricism" (1909 Anat. Rec., 3:23–24).

At the 28th Session of the Association at Princeton University, December 27–29, 1911 (1912 Anat. Rec., 6:181–93), Ross G. Harrison of Yale University gave striking evidence that the type of interest and research in anatomy in the United States could be as profound and ideal as any existent in European centers. Before a symposium on tissue culture, he was the first to demonstrate the genesis and biological significance of the neuron by revealing his discovery that the neuroblast is competent to form a nerve fiber outside of the body when removed from all sources of contamination. Margaret R. Lewis and Warren H. Lewis presented their pioneer work on the use of the hanging-drop method in cultures of chick embryos. President Piersol spoke of the death of Professor Thomas Dwight of Harvard (1911), who was the first to introduce in America the study of anatomy by means of cross sections made from frozen bodies. Thomas G. Lee, pioneer microscopist at Minnesota, was nominated for the post of Vice-President, and Hal Downey, now nationally known as the father of hematology in the United States, was elected a member of the Association.

The Cleveland meeting was held at Western Reserve University from December 30, 1911, to January 2, 1912 (1913 Anat. Rec., 7:91–98). Ross G. Harrison, in his Presidential Address, stated: "Anatomy, amongst the biological sciences, occupies a central position . . . The greatest danger to anatomy, strange to say, lies in the very fact of its practical importance. It is this circumstance that in England and America has threatened, and even now threatens, to make the science entirely subservient to practice."

At the 34th Session, held at the University of Minnesota, December 27–29, 1917 (1918 Anat. Rec., 14:337–456), there was a symposium on "The Teaching of Anatomy and the Inculcation of Scientific Methods and Interest." The participants were C.R. Bardeen, A.G. Pohlman, C.M. Jackson, and G.S. Huntington. Bardeen showed the practical value of roentgenology and fluoroscopy in anatomical studies; Pohlman stated that "no longer did the surgeon hold opera-glass clinics on a dissected cadaver" and that "dissection became a daylight laboratory subject"; Jackson emphasized the elective system in the medical curriculum; and Huntington emphasized the importance of comparative anatomy, inheritance, variation, and evolution in an understanding of human anatomy. In a discussion of Pohlman's paper, Schulte stated: "It is necessary to vitalize the facts of anatomy. To do this we must bring the facts into relation with some biologic process, and here we have at least three at hand. The ontogenetic and the phyletic and the physiologic."

The nation's first medical school, the School of Medicine of the Pennsylvania College, now the University of Pennsylvania, was established in Philadelphia in 1765 by Shippen and Morgan. In 1792, Shippen appointed Dr. Caspar Wistar, a graduate of Edinburgh and student of anatomy at London, as Adjunct Professor of Anatomy in the newly formed school. Following the death of Shippen, Wistar was elected Professor of Anatomy at the University of Pennsylvania in 1808, a position which he held until his death in 1818.

Of the western schools, the University of Michigan was among the first to follow the example of Harvard University in emphasizing a basic scientific instruction for medical students. The leader in this movement was Victor C. Vaughan, later dean of the Medical School at Michigan, who had 269 students in his chemical laboratory in 1878.

Anatomy at Michigan was initially brought to the forefront by Moses Gunn and his roommate, Croydon L. Ford. Leaving Geneva, New York, they went to Ann Arbor, where Gunn established himself as a surgeon and as a teacher in anatomy, ready to instruct prospective medical students privately. He helped organize the medical school and, after being appointed to the chair of surgery, was instrumental in establishing one of the first real university-affiliated hospitals in the United States (1877). It may be noted here that the first hospital in the United

States chartered by the Colonial Assembly was erected in Philadelphia in 1755. A signpost placed at its location (8th and Pine Street) reads: "This is the first hospital in the United States chartered by Colonial Assembly in 1751 'for relief of the sick poor.' Benjamin Franklin and Dr. Thomas Bond were its chief founders. First building erected in 1755 is still used."

To the Michigan school of medicine, at the age of 19, came William Mayo (1880) of Rochester, Minnesota. His father, William Worrall Mayo, had decided that his son should not be trained in a proprietary medical school, as he had been at the Indiana Medical College at LaPorte (1850). Attending Michigan at the same time was Franklin P. Mall of Iowa, who later (1893) became the first Professor of Anatomy at the newly established Johns Hopkins University Medical School (1876). Ford, the roommate of Gunn, taught anatomy to both Mall and Mayo, and Mayo later wrote of Ford that he was "the greatest teacher of anatomy" he had ever heard. After making a dissection, Ford would invariably say, "Now, gentlemen, forget that if you can."

Mall and Mayo were graduates of the same class at Michigan (1883), but how different were their future careers in the critical period of American anatomy! Mall was interested in anatomy primarily as a science. As Professor of Anatomy at Johns Hopkins Medical School, he stood shoulder to shoulder in dignity and importance with William Osler in medicine, William S. Halsted in surgery (who introduced rubber gloves to surgery in 1890), Howard A. Kelly in gynecology, and William Welch in pathology. Mayo studied anatomy solely with regard to its relation to medicine and surgery. Throughout Mall's 24 years in the Department of Anatomy at Hopkins (1893–1917), he waged a successful crusade to get the medical schools of our country to teach anatomy as a basic science and by individual laboratory dissection on the part of the student.

Because of the intimate relationship that existed between the initial teaching of anatomy and medicine and surgery, there was, for a considerable length of time, a grave danger throughout the United States that American anatomy would be handled solely by the Professor of Surgery and assistants from that department, and accordingly studied and taught solely from the practical point of view, i.e., as an adjunct to clinical and surgical subjects.

To be saved as a science, as it was in France with Bichat and in Germany with His and Ludwig, a much stronger foothold for its existence than surgical application and need was required. To gain this foothold in medical education, an astute anatomically inclined group attending the Congress of American Physicians and Surgeons in Washington decided that it was time for those interested in anatomy and its mode of teaching and extent of research to form an association or society. The group assembled at Georgetown University, Washington, and there on September 17, 1888, organized a society with a constitution and named it the "Association of American Anatomists." Initially affiliated with the Congress of American Physicians and Surgeons, the Association withdrew from that organization through a motion made by Bardeen on behalf of the Executive Committee and seconded by Spitzka, at the 21st Session at Columbia University, December 27–29, 1906 (1907 Anat. Rec., *1*:23). Two years later, the original title of the Association was changed by constitutional adoption to "American Association of Anatomists" at the 24th Session at Johns Hopkins, December 29–31, 1908 (1909 Anat. Rec., *3*:68). The committee on revision consisted of Huber, Donaldson, and

Bensley. At this session Dr. J. Parsons Schaeffer of Cornell University (editor of *Morris's Human Anatomy* and for 34 years Professor of Anatomy at The Jefferson Medical College) was elected to membership in the Association.

The newly formed Association held regularly scheduled annual meetings for 14 years. Proceedings of the Association and abstracts of papers presented were published as separate items from year to year. Meetings of the Association held subsequent to 1900 are fully recorded as to abstracts and proceedings in the Association's own journals, the first few being recorded in *The American Journal of Anatomy*, all others in *The Anatomical Record*.

From the days of its formative period, the Association has followed the policy of electing to membership not only professional anatomists, but those individuals who were distinguished in other cognate fields. The following are among the members (244) listed in the first volume of *The Anatomical Record* (pages 96–107, 1907): physicians and surgeons (Barker and Kelly of Hopkins, Blake of Columbia, Dercum of Jefferson, Webster of Rush); pathologists (Howard, Lamb, Leo Loeb, Warthin); physiologists (Burkholder, Carr, Kingsbury); biologists, neurologists, and zoologists (Childs, Coghill, Conklin, Dean, Donaldson, Gage, Guyer, Herrick, Kofoid, Lillie, Locy, McClure, Morgan, Nachtrieb, Osborn, Parker, W. Patten, Streeter, R.M. Strong, and Wilder); anthropologists (Hrdlička); and even an artist (Max Brodel).

Another policy of the Association, constantly followed, has been the election to honorary membership of individuals who merited election on the basis of their accomplishments in anatomical investigative work. Thus, at the 22nd Session, March 28–29, 1907 (1907 Anat. Rec., *1*:95), at the University of Wisconsin, the list of honorary members was composed of S. Ramón y Cajal (Madrid), John Cleland (Glasgow), John D. Cunningham (Edinburgh), Camillo Golgi (Pavia), Oscar Hertwig (Berlin), Alexander Macallister (Cambridge), L. Ranvier (Paris), Gustav Retzius (Stockholm), Carl Toldt (Vienna), Sir William Turner (Edinburgh), and Wilhelm Waldeyer (Berlin). Sir Arthur Keith, Hunterian Professor of Anatomy, College of Surgeons, London, was elected to honorary membership at the 32nd Session, which was held at Yale, December 28–30, 1915 (1915 Anat. Rec., *10*:167), with Huber as President and Stockard as Secretary-Treasurer.

AIMS OF THE ASSOCIATION

In Article 1 of the first formed and adopted constitution, Section 2 states: "The purpose of this Association shall be the advancement of anatomical science." That initial endeavor of the group of individuals who elected Joseph Leidy, the most outstanding scientist in America in his day, as their first President, has been the persistent effort of the Association—an effort (as we all know and are extremely proud of) that has been crowned with success, unsurpassed by that of any other biological scientific society.

The initial and still adhered to motto of the Association, "for the advancement of anatomical science," could not have been better worded. Someone had to have the courage and the ambition to remove anatomy from the position of surgical footstool that it temporarily held in America and bestow upon it the dignity it deserved as the mother of all biological sciences.

Needed for anatomy was, and still is, the liberty and freedom to ramify (in all forms of animal life and in all phases of normal and abnormal morphology and function) in experimental embryology, factors concerned with heredity, favorable and unfavorable environmental influences—in short, freedom to deal with all possible types of form relations and structure, which, biologically considered, are but the expressions and the basis of function. The old. yet ever new, discovery of Charles Darwin, whose *Origin of Species* (1859) and *The Descent of Man* (1871) gave a mighty impetus to modern anatomy, still holds, namely, that structure determines function, as function is dependent on structure, that variation is the most common attribute of organic life, and that by natural selection forms best adapted to particular circumstances survive longest and carry on their kind.

With unparalleled success American anatomy opened vast new fields of medical progress. Anatomy was among the first of all biological sciences to point to what should and eventually will be the essential aim of medical education in the future, i.e., not to stick to curative medicine, to which medical education has for centuries been chained and anchored, but to stress and improve what is needed and wanted most in this modern age, preventive medicine.

With our motto, "for the advancement of anatomical science," American anatomists have justly and boldy entered into and extended the fields of cytology, general physiology, experimental neurophysiology, experimental embryology (theory of progressive differentiation beginning with an organizer; problem of first fetal movements related to function; genetics and transmission of character from gene to gene), experimental psychology and encephalography, experimental histology, endocrinology, biochemistry, hematology, bacteriology, pharmacology, transplantations, regeneration and form regulation, tissue culture, and, more recently, histochemistry and foliative cytology, which is now becoming exceedingly important in the early detection of cancer. As attested by our outstanding contributions to the human race in the elucidation of body structure and function in both health and disease, anatomists have been pioneers, although poorly paid spade diggers, in the respective fields of medical endeavor.

ANATOMY AS A SCIENCE

The arduous task of making American anatomy an independent and far-reaching science was masterfully begun by Joseph Leidy (1823–1891), Professor of Anatomy at the University of Pennsylvania, and first President of the Association. Born in Philadelphia (September 9, 1823), Leidy obtained his doctorate in medicine in 1849 from the University of Pennsylvania. His thesis topic was "The Comparative Anatomy of the Eye of Vertebrate Animals." After 2 years of medical practice, he devoted all of his time to anatomical teaching and nature study, to such an extent that Chapman (1891) wrote of him: "He was an excellent mineralogist, and a botanist without claiming to be either, among the highest living authorities on comparative anatomy and zoology, one of the most distinguished helminthologists and the equal of any paleontologist at home or abroad."

Among the most eminent pioneer teachers of anatomy in the United States were Oliver Wendell Holmes, Thomas Dwight, and Charles Sedgwick Minot of Harvard University. Holmes, the poet-anatomist, held the Parkman Professorship in Anatomy from 1848 to 1883; Dwight held it from 1883 to 1911. Minot's contributions will be discussed later.

It was primarily through the efforts of Franklin P. Mall (1862–1917) and those of his associates that American anatomy obtained a foothold and eventually worldwide recognition and leadership as a science comparable to that held by any European university. The associates of Mall striving for the betterment of American anatomy comprised the members of the first Editorial Board of *The American Journal of Anatomy*: George S. Huntington (Columbia), G. Carl Huber and J. Playfair McMurrich (Michigan), George A. Piersol (University of Pennsylvania), Thomas Dwight and Charles S. Minot (Harvard), Simon H. Gage (Cornell), Lewellys F. Barker (Chicago), and Henry McE. Knower (Johns Hopkins), who acted as Secretary.

Born in Belle Plaine, Iowa (September 28, 1862), Mall, whose father was German, obtained his MD degree from Michigan in 1883 and for 2 years did postgraduate work at Heidelberg and Leipzig (1884–1886) under His and Ludwig. These pioneer and eminent German anatomical investigators left an indelible imprint on the mind of Mall and inspired him in his subsequent manifold anatomical investigations and in his method of teaching anatomy as a science.

At the 21st Session, held at Columbia University, December 27–29, 1906 (1907 Anat. Rec., *1*:23–107), Mall in his Presidential Address, "On Some Points of Importance to Anatomists," courageously advocated the highest development of anatomy as a pure science even in a medical school. He contended that "an anatomical department must include histology, histogenesis, and embryology; in a medical school it must cover vertebrate anatomy in the fullest sense." Mall severely criticized the prevalent policy in the medical schools of this country of *exploiting the chair of anatomy as a steppingstone to surgery.* He stated that "this arrangement may possibly have been beneficial as a training school for surgeons, but it was so bad for anatomy that as a science and as a profession it gradually fell into disrepute among most of the people. . . . It is the duty of the members of this Association to correct this erroneous conception of anatomy by precept and by example. I have full confidence that this can be done with ease." His concluding words were that "we must provide a suitable atmosphere for our investigators" and that "we must have many more productive anatomists. . . . In order to obtain them and to make the efforts of our present investigators more effective, we must use all our influence to bring the greatest opportunities and the best men together. My earnest hope is that those in authority in various communities will recognize that our idea of the scope of anatomy is correct, and that they will seek productive anatomists, when vacancies occur, so that our grand science may be raised to the level it has always held in Europe."

The anatomical interests of Mall culminated in: 1) the establishment of *The American Journal of Anatomy* (1901) and of the *The Anatomical Record* at Johns Hopkins (1906); 2) the use of The Wistar Institute of Anatomy and Biology as a means of publishing results of anatomical and biological research, being eminently aided in this effort by Charles Sedgwick Minot of Harvard (1852–1914), George S. Huntington of Columbia (1861–1927), and Gotthelf Carl Huber of Michigan (1865–1934); 3) the establishment of the Department of Embryology at the Carnegie Institution of Washington (1914), of which Mall was the first Director and which to date (1955) has made 236 contributions to embryology (its present Director is George W. Corner); and 4) the introduction in most American medical schools of the scientific laboratory method in the anatomical instruction of medical students.

Charles Russell Bardeen (1871–1935), a pupil of Mall and a graduate of the first medical class of Johns Hopkins (1897), introduced Mall's method of teaching anatomy at Wisconsin and was the first in the 1890s to correlate for freshman students the anatomy of the dead with that of the living by means of roentgenography and fluoroscopic vision.

Mall's constant plea was "self-education through guidance," meaning that the best way for a medical student to learn anatomy is not through ponderously long lectures and demonstrations, but through the student's own dissections aided by his/her reading of books and atlases, and daily guidance in dissection by a well-trained competent anatomical staff. Mall, in speaking of the importance of the student's own carefully made dissections, said, "Nowhere do we read that the 5,000 questions which were placed before me while a medical student give the 'royal road' to knowledge."

Among the immortal pioneer and outstanding anatomists of the Association is Professor Charles Sedgwick Minot (1852–1914) of Harvard University, from which he obtained his Doctor of Science degree in 1878. As stated by Frederick T. Lewis in his memorial address on Minot, delivered at the 32nd Session at New Haven, December 28–30, 1915 (1915 Anat. Rec., *10*:133–269), Minot probably took the course of gross anatomy with Dr. Oliver Wendell Holmes. After a short experience as Instructor in Oral Surgery and Pathology, Minot was appointed Instructor in Histology and Embryology with full charge in 1883, attaining the rank of full professor in this department in 1892. Having studied with Ludwig at Leipzig, Minot centralized his activities on embryology, firmly convinced from his manifold investigations in this field that human anatomy could best be understood through embryology. In 1890 (according to Lewis), Minot stated that "unless the student betake himself to embryology his anatomy will be no better than a stupid system of mnemonics."

In 1886, Minot designed a rotary microtome, and in 1892, after working on the task for 10 years, published his book (815 pages) on embryology. He was a contributor to the *Manual of Human Embryology,* edited by Keibel and Mall, and published by J.B. Lippincott Co. in 1910. For a time Minot was extremely interested in psychical research and consciousness, but after making several contributions to this subject, he set it aside, very much disillusioned as to its supposed scientific mode of approach.

Minot was one of the founders of *The American Journal of Anatomy* (1901), was on the Editorial Board of *The Anatomical Record* (1906–1908), and was one of the ten original members of the Advisory Board of The Wistar Institute. He was seventh President of the Association (1903–1905), following in the footsteps of Thomas Dwight of Harvard, who was the third President.

At the 31st Session, held at Washington University, St. Louis, December 28–30, 1914 (1915 Anat. Rec., *9*:35–143), G. Carl Huber was President and Charles R. Stockard was Secretary. At this meeting, Huntington in an expression of the profound sorrow felt at the loss of Minot said of him, "Much of the progress of The Wistar Institute of Anatomy originated in his keen executive ability as Chairman of its Advisory Board. He later became most active in establishing and maintaining the eminently valuable relations now existing between the journals and the Publication Department of The Wistar Institute."

In the 1880s, Mall was not alone in his determined effort to make anatomy a pure science, i.e., to make it more than an adjunct to surgery. At Columbia University, George Sumner Huntington (1861–1927), MD, graduate of the College of Physicians and Surgeons (1884), was working vigorously to the same end, i.e., to raise the study and teaching of anatomy to a level comparable with the best of European methods and traditions—an effort to which he gave 35 years of his life as Professor of Anatomy, having been appointed to the chair in 1889.

McClure of Princeton (1865–1955) stated in an address before the 43rd Session of the Association at Vanderbilt, Nashville, Tennessee, April 14–16, 1927 (1927 Am. J. Anat., *39*:355–377), that Huntington was one of the greatest comparative anatomists this country has ever known. For his morphological museum he made over 6,000 exhibits, convinced that by studying the simpler forms of life, the more complex variational type of human anatomy could be better understood. He was always proud of his achievement of making medical students learn anatomy by dissection rather than from textbooks or by didactic lectures. In an article on "The Teaching of Anatomy" published in 1898, Huntington wrote: "The College of Physicians and Surgeons was the first medical school to abandon in 1889 the system universally in vogue at the time of confining didactic instruction in anatomy to lectures to large audiences and to substitute teaching by demonstration of the actual objects to small sections of the class."

Huntington's Presidential Address before the 14th Session of the Association at Johns Hopkins (December 27–28, 1900) was entitled "The Morphological Museum as an Educational Factor in the University System." Therein he stressed the point that "the museum should be a reference library of the student in the widest sense where the undergraduate can review and extend his anatomical knowledge on the hand of the actual object of his study" (1901 Science, *13*).

An ardent admirer and follower of Huntington was Edward Anthony Spitzka (1876–1922), MD, a 1902 graduate of Columbia. Trained under and associated with Huntington for several years, he was called to The Jefferson Medical College (founded in 1825) to promote anatomy as a science, as Huntington had done at Columbia. Of his appointment to professorship, we find recorded (1907 Anat. Rec., *1*:21) the following: "A special significance, however, must attach to the appointment of Dr. E.A. Spitzka as professor of General Anatomy in an independent, or purely professional school, like The Jefferson Medical College, Philadelphia. This school has constantly striven to uphold a high ideal of medical education throughout its previous history, and has equipped its graduates well and practically for their professional careers. So when Jefferson fills the vacant chair, as she has, we have an especially encouraging recognition of the practical value of the type of laboratory organization sketched above."

It was through Spitzka's efforts and during his tenureship of the chair of anatomy (1905–1914) that The Daniel Baugh Institute of Anatomy was founded (1912). It was named in honor of Mr. Daniel Baugh, who graciously provided the funds while a member of the Board of Trustees of The Jefferson Medical College (1896–1921). Spitzka was the editor of one of the first American editions of *Gray's Anatomy* (1913), being assisted in this work by Howard Dehoney and Henry E. Radasch. The publishers of this great work were and still are Lea & Febiger. From Spitzka, who at the 15th Session (Chicago, December 31, 1901, to January 2, 1902) reported on his dissection of the brain of the assassin of President McKinley, came this description of his course in anatomy: "It is a cardinal principle of anatomic teaching that the student learn his anatomy chiefly in the dissecting room and in the section teaching. But the student can be assisted advantageously by a well-equipped study collection, comprising not only preparations of adult human structure, but of comparative and embryonic material as well, arranged to illustrate the unity of plan in vertebrate structure" (1907 Science, 26).

In 1914, J. Parsons Schaeffer of the University of Pennsylvania, Cornell, and Yale was appointed Director of The Daniel Baugh Institute of Anatomy, a position which he held for 34 years (1914–1948). During his directorship an annex building for staff offices and a departmental library were added to the Institute. Since 1948 the possibilities and usefulness of the Institute have been brought to maturity through the development and equipment of several new laboratories for research in neuroanatomy, anthropology, endocrinology, fat and carbohydrate metabolism, tissue culture, histochemistry, experimental surgery, and electron microscopy.

One of Huntington's most prominent associates in teaching at Columbia was Herman von Wecklinger Schulte (1876–1932). Schulte gave the first extensive description of the anatomy of the whale and later became Dean and Professor of Anatomy at Creighton Unviersity; it was from him that the writer (Michels) learned much of the significant work of Huntington at Columbia (1932 Anat. Rec., 55:1–9). Of (local) interest is the fact that Huntington in 1907 gave the valedictory address to the graduating class of The Jefferson Medical College (1907 Science, 26: 233–237), on which occasion he was awarded the LLD degree. Trained in the humanities in Germany, where he had been sent by his mother from the age of 10 to 16 years, Huntington stated in his address, *"Alles Gewordene wird erst verständlich in dem Werden."*

The University of Michigan, the first midwestern medical school to emphasize a basic scientific training for medical students, can always be proud of Gotthelf Carl Huber (1865–1934), one of America's outstanding anatomists. Born the son of a missionary in Hoobly, India, August 30, 1865, he was 4 years old when his family moved to the United States. After obtaining his doctorate in medicine at Michigan (1887), Huber became Assistant Demonstrator in Anatomy for 2 years. With the exception of two periods of training abroad, at Berlin (1891–1892) and at Prague (1895), and a year's leave of absence (as Professor of Embryology at The Wistar Institute, 1911–1912), Huber spent nearly half a century (short of 3 years) in anatomical teaching and research at Michigan. He began his professional career there as Instructor in Histology in 1889, was appointed Professor of Histology and Embryology in 1903, became Professor of Anatomy in 1914, and in 1928 was appointed Dean of the Graduate School. For 14 years he was a member of the Medical Fellowship Board of the National Research Council and its chairman for 8 years.

In the early days at Michigan (1889), histology was part of the physiology course, as was the custom in British schools. Huber made histology and embryology an independent department, and for 20 years conducted it as such, under headships of the Department of Anatomy held by J. Playfair McMurrich (1894–1907) and G.L. Streeter (1907–1914).

Huber played a fundamental and pioneer role in advancing the activities and accomplishments of the AAA. With Mall, Huntington, and Minot he was part of the original Editorial Board of *The American Journal of Anatomy* (1901) and the *The Anatomical Record,* of which he was Managing Editor from 1909 to 1920. As an original member of the Advisory Board of The Wistar Institute (1905), he gave a remarkable amount of time and effort in developing the publication enterprise of the Institute, finally succeeding in making it a functioning concern with uniform format of publications. In the Association, Huber served as Second Vice-President (1900–1901), Secretary-Treasurer (1902–1913), and President (1914–1915).

At the 30th Session [University of Pennsylvania, December 29–31, 1913 (1914 Anat. Rec., 8:69–145)], Harrison was President and Huber was Secretary-Treasurer. At this session the following motion was made by McMurrich and seconded by Bensley: "That this Association accepts with regret the resignation of Dr. G. Carl Huber from the office of Secretary-Treasurer and desires to place on record its high appreciation of his services and its recognition of the prominent part he has taken in bringing the Association to its present prosperous condition and in advancing the cause of Anatomy on this continent both by precept and example."

The address given by Huber in memory of Franklin P. Mall at the 34th Session, held at the University of Minnesota, Minneapolis, December 27–29, 1917 (1918 Anat. Rec., 14:3–17), is a masterpiece long to be remembered in the annals of the Association. Therein he related the slow progressive growth of the Association, stating: "To make fuller expression of anatomic thought, to assist in developing and differentiating work in the anatomical laboratories of our medical schools and the creation of a science of anatomy in America, *The American Journal of Anatomy* was founded." He ended his address with these words: ". . . to the names of Bichat and His, I would add, with your accord, the name of Mall." With the Association's accord, the name of Huber can now be added to the list.

The scientific contributions of Huber are well known, his most outstanding work being the monograph on the avian diencephalon, written with Elizabeth C. Crosby. His studies on nerve regeneration, on the development of the albino rat (at The Wistar Institute), on the histology of the sympathetic nervous system, and on the corda dorsalis are classics that will always be referred to for fundamental information as to existent anatomical structure.

Of George A. Piersol (1856–1924), Professor of Anatomy at the University of Pennsylvania, a volume could be written of his achievements in behalf of the Association and American anatomy. With Mall, Huntington, and Minot, he was on the original Editorial Board of *The American Journal of Anatomy* (1901), on the original Advisory Board of The Wistar Institute (1905), and as early as 1910–1911 was President (tenth) of the Association. In his Presidential Address before the Association's 27th Session at Cornell, Ithaca, December 28–30, 1910 (1911 Anat. Rec., 5:71–86), Piersol reviewed the life work of our first President, Joseph Leidy: "A Self-made Naturalist."

Trained under Koelliker and Fritsch in Germany (1886–1888), Piersol produced the first original outstanding text on human anatomy in America. In this work he was assisted by Dwight of Harvard, McMurrich of Michigan, Hamann of Western Reserve, White of Pennsylvania, and Heisler of Medicochirurgical College, and for work on special subjects by Spiller (central nervous system), Fetterolf (peripheral nervous system), Shumway (eye), Butler (ear), and Addison (microscopic specimens). Piersol's great text on human anatomy comprising over 2,000 plates (1,522 of which were original illustrations based largely on dissections of John C. Heisler and G.G. Davis and on museum specimens of Harvard Medical School and The Wistar Institute) is still a classic. First published in 1907 by J.B. Lippincott Co., it was last reedited by Huber in 1930.

At the 41st Session, held April 6–11, 1925, at Western Reserve, Cleveland (1925 Anat. Rec., 30:67–94), Florence R. Sabin was President and Lewis H. Weed was Secretary. At this meeting W.H.F. Addison presented a resolution regarding the death of George A. Piersol (August 7, 1924, at the age of 68 years) and stated: "He was in continuous touch with progress in his chosen field and assisted in the advancement so noticeable during the past twenty years. In the death of Professor Piersol the Society has lost a member of broad interests and scholarly attainments."

At this point, because of the necessary restriction in length of this brochure, an arbitrary break is made here in recording brief sketches of the life histories and accomplishments of some of the formulators and prominent members of the Association, notably those on the first Editorial Board of *The American Journal of Anatomy*. It is an incumbent hope that someday someone will write in detail the history of the Association, as it should be recorded, in regard to the scientific achievements of its outstanding members, and especially those of the Association Presidents.

ROLE OF THE WISTAR INSTITUTE

A few items, largely unknown to the younger members, are presented to recall the important role played by The Wistar Institute of Anatomy and Biology in furthering the interests of the AAA. Founded as a museum of anatomical specimens by Professor Caspar Wistar while he was Professor of Anatomy at the University of Pennsylvania (1808–1818), it was substantially endowed in 1891 by his grandnephew, General Isaac Jones Wistar (1827–1905), the purpose of the grant ($20,000) being the maintenance of the Wistar Museum. Subequently, a museum and a laboratory were erected by General Wistar, the formal opening of which occurred on May 21, 1894. In a separate Charter from the Commonwealth of Pennsylvania, the University of Pennsylvania incorporated the Institute as an independent foundation set apart from other activities of the University in the pursuit of biological knowledge. The special building for breeding and care of albino rats, now being used throughout the world for research purposes, was erected in 1921 through the generosity of Samuel S. Fels. The installation of press equipment whereby all journals and books could be printed and bound at the Institute was accomplished in 1924, this establishment, thereafter, being known as The Wistar Institute Press.

The creation of The Wistar Institute was a fortunate and effective aid for American anatomy. Of the ten members of its original Advisory Board, organized April 11–12, 1905, with the approval of and in the presence of General Wistar, eight were anatomists and were on the Editorial Board of the first volume of *The American Journal of Anatomy* issued in 1901: Barker, Gage, Huber, Huntington, Mall, McMurrich, Minot, and Piersol. The other two members, Conklin and Donaldson, were zoologists. At yearly intervals, when vacancies occurred, new members were elected to the Advisory Board. Such board members were Milton J. Greenman, Clarence C. McClung, Ross G. Harrison, Clarence M. Jackson, Helen King, Charles R. Stockard, W. Rose, George W. Corner, S. Wright, Philip Smith, George Wislocki, and James Nicholas.

Greenman (1866–1937), for many years the Director of The Wistar Institute (1904–37), recorded these words on April 13, 1925, the 20th anniversary of the organization of the Advisory Board:

The science of Anatomy in America from the time of Shippen to that of Leidy had made but little advancement. In most medical schools the chair of Anatomy was the steppingstone to that of surgery. Not so, however, in the case of the chair of Anatomy of the University of Pennsylvania, where it had become conspicuous by reason of the eminence of its incumbents. Along with the great teacher and investigator, Leidy, came Cope, Harrison Allen and Ryder . . . engaged in researches in comparative anatomy here at the University of Pennsylvania. Leidy used the preparations of the Wistar Museum for demonstrations in his lectures to medical students. Gradually the older preparations had become damaged from use and dust . . . It was at this stage that the Dean of the Medical School, Dr. James Tyson, approached General Isaac Wistar, a grand-nephew of Professor Caspar Wistar for financial assistance to maintain the Wistar Museum.

As stated by Greenman, the conditions and limitations of General Wistar's trust funds (covering an endowment of more than $1.5 million in 1925) are intricate. But these funds made possible what was needed most in America for the advancement of anatomy and biology, i.e., a center for research and facilities for publishing and distributing anatomical and biological journals. With the utmost success The Wistar Institute assumed the publication of the following journals:

1. *The Journal of Morphology,* founded in 1887 and published by Ginn and Co., was the first journal of its kind established in the United States. Suspended for 5 years because of lack of funds, it was assigned to The Wistar Institute by Professor Whitman, its founder, and publication was resumed in February 1908.

2. *The Journal of Comparative Neurology,* founded by C.L. Herrick in 1891, was assigned to The Wistar Institute in 1908 by C. J. Herrick, his brother.

3, 4. *The American Journal of Anatomy* (1901) and *The Anatomical Record* (1906, 1908) were founded by a group of members of the AAA for the express purpose of providing a medium to publish reports of investigative work and society activities. At the Association's 36th Session (U.S. National Museum, Washington, April 1–3, 1920), Plan B, as signed by C.M. Jackson, was adopted, transferring the journals to The Wistar Institute.

The original trustees of the Anatomic Journal Trust (May 9, 1901) were George S. Huntington, Franklin P. Mall, and Charles S. Minot. After the death of Mall and Minot, G. Carl Huber and Henry Donaldson were appointed as trustees. On April 2, 1920, the trustees of the Trust (Huntington, Huber, and Donaldson) transferred the two journals to The Wistar Institute. After the death of Huntington and Huber, Donaldson appointed Stockard and Corner as trustees. Ultimately, the Anatomical Journal Trust Fund (Minot Memorial Fund), amounting to $17,138.05 and last administered by Smith, Patten, and Corner, was terminated at the Association's 61st Session, held at Madison, Wisconsin, April 20, 1948 (1948 Anat. Rec., *101*:428–429), in an official letter read by its last Chairman, George W. Corner. The Association accepted the funds, and for protective purposes was incorporated under the laws of the State of New York.

5. *The Journal of Experimental Zoology* was acquired by The Wistar Institute, December 29, 1932, and Ross G. Harrison was appointed Editor.

In 1911 a sixth publication was created. Known as the *Memoirs of The Wistar Institute* and later changed to the *American Anatomical Memoirs,* it was founded and edited by G.S. Huntington with the purpose of publishing papers too long to be accepted by other journals. In 1917 The Wistar Institute established the Bibliographic Service whereby a library catalog card with author's abstract and name was issued and distributed free of charge. In 1928 the Institute assumed the publication of the *American Journal of Physical Anthropology,* which had been deeded to it by Ales Hrdlička, who founded it in 1918. In 1940 under its present (1955) Director, Edmond J. Farris (appointed in 1938), a depository for motion-picture films of anatomical and biological interest was established at The Wistar Institute. These films, as approved by either a Review Committee of the AAA, American Society of Zoologists, or The Wistar Institute, are listed with explanatory notes in *The Anatomical Record, 120*:167–182,1954.

In each instance in which The Wistar Institute assumed the responsibility of publishing a journal, it formally requested the journal to accept editorial control by electing editors and by outlining a general scientific policy. When *The American Journal of Anatomy* and *The Anatomical Record* were leased to The Wistar Institute in 1908, each member of the AAA received a copy of the two journals under the terms of the dues ($5.00), and when these were increased in 1915 ($6.50), each member received, in addition, a copy of the *Journal of Comparative Neurology* and *Journal of Morphology.* In 1923, the AAA discontinued its method of paying a fixed sum to the Institute from its income dues ($4.50 of $5.00), and the journals thereafter were sold to members at a reduced rate (25%).

In the furtherance of anatomical and biological research in a nationally free and open institute (especially to younger investigators) and in the dissemination through publication of the accomplishments of the AAA and those of cognate societies dealing with anatomy and biology, The Wistar Institute has, by far, surpassed in accomplishments any comparable organization or institute in the entire world. For nearly 50 years The Wistar Institute has loyally fulfilled the purpose for which it was originally established and maintained through grants and inheritances by General Wistar.

The status of these, as evaluated and recorded by Greenman on April 13, 1925, on the occasion of the 20th anniversary of the organization of the Advisory Board of The Wistar Institute (1905–1925), was as follows: "Its total endowment today is $1,666,818.35, and there is yet to be added a residuary estate which will add about two million to the present endowment" (Bulletin No. 6 of The Wistar Institute, p. 39, 1925).

The following are examples of the splendid cooperative work accomplished by The Wistar Institute in behalf of anatomy and biology in America. After the Armistice of World War I had been signed, The Wistar Institute began in 1921 a worldwide free distribution of its journals. This was done largely because of the lack of funds on the part of many universities and institutions in foreign countries to purchase American journals dealing with anatomy and biology. For a time the Institute furnished Japanese and Chinese editions of its journals, every article being preceded by an abstract printed in the Japanese or Chinese language. It also supplied free copies of *The American Journal of Anatomy* and *The Anatomical Record* to each member of organized Chinese anthropology and anatomical associations until 1923. Starting in 1917 an extensive free distribution of copies of its journals was carried out for 3 years in all South American countries. This policy led to the formation in 1918 of a Pan-American edition, in which every article was preceded by an abstract printed in Spanish. Free copies of the journals were also distributed to various centers in Australia, Ceylon, Java, South Africa, and Iceland. According to Greenman, the total subscription value of all free copies distributed in 1921 amounted to $27,435.00. During 1922–1923 the expense of free distribution was paid by the Rockefeller Foundation.

Among the outstanding early books published by The Wistar Institute are *The Rat* by Donaldson (1915–1924) and *Physical Anthropology* by Hrdlička (1919). From 1905 to 1925, according to Greenman, over 50 investigators, as members of the staff or as guests in its laboratories, had published papers from The Wistar Institute.

Through the generosity of Effingham B. Morris, President of The Wistar Institute (1922–1937), a farm with ample housing was deeded to the Institute in 1928. Known as The E.B. Morris Biological Farm, it was used by members and guests of the Institute for research purposes. Through funds donated by Samuel Fels, William Proctor, and Morris, new laboratories were erected on the farm and equipped with facilities for the rearing of standardized rats and amphibia. In 1951, the farm was discontinued and sold. In view of the remarkable accomplishments of The Wistar Institute of Anatomy and Biology over a period of nearly 50 years, when its broad policies were determined by anatomists and zoologists through the Advisory Board, it seems unfortunate that the latter has not been asked to meet and has not been reappointed by the Board of Managers since 1952.

ASSOCIATION JOURNALS

The Wistar Institute publishes the Association journals, but how and by whom were they brought to their present high standard of content? The first volume of *The American Journal of Anatomy* was published from the laboratory of Franklin P. Mall of Johns Hopkins in 1901. Its first Editorial Board was composed of Lewellys F. Barker (Chicago), Thomas Dwight (Harvard), Simon H. Gage (Cornell), G. Carl Huber (Michigan), George S. Huntington (Columbia), Franklin P. Mall (Johns Hopkins), Charles S. Minot (Harvard), George A. Piersol (Pennsylvania), and Henry McE. Knower (Johns Hopkins) as Secretary.

Contributions to a reserve endowment fund were made by individuals from Johns Hopkins and Baltimore, University of Pennsylvania and Philadelphia, Columbia University and New York City, Cornell University, Harvard Medical School, Boston University, University of Chicago, University of Michigan, and Princeton University.

The American Journal of Anatomy

The policy of publishing *The American Journal of Anatomy* by an Editorial Board was continued until March 1921. The last Editorial Board was composed of Bardeen, Donaldson, Gage, Huber, Huntington, McMurrich, Piersol, and Knower as Secretary. Beginning with Volume *29* (May–Nov. 1921), Charles R. Stockard of Cornell University became Managing Editor; the Associate Editors were Clarence M. Jackson (Minnesota), Henry McE. Knower (Cincinnati), Harold D. Senior

(New York), and George L. Streeter (Carnegie Institution). Stockard served as Managing Editor for 18 years, during which period Volumes *29–63* were issued, including the anniversary volume of Simon H. Gage (Vol. *48, 1931*). In 1939 and beginning with Volume *64* (Jan., March, May), George W. Corner of The University of Rochester became Managing Editor; the Associate Editors for this volume were Jackson and Streeter. In the next volume the Associate Editors were Atwell, Sam L. Clark, Cummins, Streeter, and Wislocki. In 1941 Philip E. Smith of Columbia became Managing Editor (Vol. *69*, July, Sept., Nov.); the Associate Editors were Clark, Cummins, Hinsey, Patten, and Wislocki. The present (1955) Managing Editor, Harold Cummins of Tulane University, began his editorial work in 1946 with Volume *79* (July, Sept., Nov.) and has thus far carried the journal to Volume *95*; the Associate Editors were Clark, Mason, Patten, Straus, and Leblond. The latter replaced Hinsey in January 1950 (Vol. *86*).

The Anatomical Record

The first three volumes of *The Anatomical Record* were issued by an Editorial Board. For the first volume (1906–1908), the members of the board were Bardeen (Wisconsin), Donaldson (The Wistar Institute), Dwight (Harvard), Gage (Cornell), Huber (Michigan), Huntington (Columbia), Mall (Johns Hopkins), McMurrich (Toronto), Minto (Harvard), Piersol (Pennsylvania), and Knower as Secretary. The Editorial Board of Volume *2* was composed of Hardesty, Huber, Jackson, Jayne, F.T. Lewis, W.H. Lewis, McClure, Sabin, and Streeter. On the Editorial Board of Volume *3* were Hardesty (Tulane), Jackson (Minnesota), Jayne (The Wistar Institute). Lee (Minnesota), F.T. Lewis (Harvard), W.H. Lewis (Johns Hopkins), McClure (Princeton), Miller (Wisconsin), Sabin (Johns Hopkins), and Streeter (Michigan).

Beginning with Volume *4* (1910), Huber of Michigan became Editing Manager; the Editorial Board was identical with that of Volume *3*. Huber was Managing Editor for 11 years, carrying *The Anatomical Record* from Volumes *4* to *20* (1921), the period of the critical issues of its adolescence.

In 1921, starting with Volume *21* (April–July), John L. Bremer of Harvard University became Managing Editor, serving for 8 years until 1928 (Vol. *38*). From 1928 to 1948, Edward A. Boyden (Illinois, Alabama, and Minnesota from 1931) served as Managing Editor. In this period of 20 years, the longest held by any editor, Boyden, with the help of his Associate Editors, Danforth, Smith, Harvey, Weatherford, Gardner, and Grant, edited Volumes *39* to *101*. The present (1955) Editor of *The Anatomical Record*, Charles M. Goss of Louisiana State University, assumed his post with Volume *102* in 1948; the Associate Editors were Gardner, Greulich, Hoerr, and Hunt.

PART II

Chapter 3

STUDYING CELLS: FROM LIGHT TO ELECTRONS

A. Kent Christensen

One of the exciting quests in which anatomists have been involved over the past century has been the effort to understand the structure and function of cells, an endeavor which has come to be called cell biology. Since cells are the fundamental unit of life, cell biology tends to pervade and underlie the other biological disciplines. Whether one is studying the function of the brain or the development of an embryo, there is need to understand the activity of cells and their organelles at the biochemical and structural levels.

This second section of the book traces the history of cell biology over the past few decades, including the roles that members of the Association have played in these developments. It reflects the excitement of those early years, from the mid-1940s into the 1960s, when the electron microscope opened up a new world of intricate structural organization within cells. It follows the development of cytochemistry, radioautography, immunocytochemistry, and related methods for using light and electron microscopes to derive functional information about cells. Finally, it describes the gradual convergence of structural approaches with biochemical and, more recently, with molecular methodology, giving rise to contemporary cell biology, devoted to understanding the molecular basis of cellular function.

The present chapter provides some background for this section of the book. It begins with the early roots of light microscopy three centuries ago, and follows the major steps that took place in the study of cells. The chapter is not intended as a detailed, scholarly history, but rather as a brief review of how our understanding of cells gradually evolved, and how the conceptual progress frequently depended on technical developments in microscopy.

Some general references that may be consulted for further details on these topics include works by Bradbury (1967), Clay and Court (1932), Ford (1973), Nordenskiöld (1949), and the historical issue (1981) of the *Journal of Cell Biology,* Volume *91* (Number 3, Part 2).

MICROSCOPY BEFORE 1830

Although it had been known since antiquity that a glass sphere could make objects appear larger, the serious use of magnifying glasses to observe nature began in the 1500s. By the end of that century it was found that the image produced by a magnifying glass could be observed with another lens (an eyepiece), leading to the development of compound microscopes. By the mid-1600s, many naturalists, such as Robert Hooke, Marcello Malpighi, Nehemiah Grew, and Jan Swammerdam, were studying animals, plants, and other objects of nature with compound microscopes.

Hooke (1635–1703), who was Curator of the Royal Society of London for 40 years, made careful observations with a sophisticated compound microscope he designed himself. In 1665 he published an extensive work, *Micrographia,* which described his findings. His descriptions extended over a broad range of specimens, and the book was illustrated with striking etchings, including well-known figures of a flea, a louse, the head of a fly, and the sting of a bee, all showing intricate detail. Among his observations was a description of structure within a very thin slice of cork, in which he observed "little Boxes or Cells." This reference is usually cited as the origin of our word for cells.

Malpighi (1628–1694) had a medical degree and taught at universities in Bologna, Pisa, and Messina. He carried out fundamental studies on the microscopic structure of various organs, such as the lung, liver, cerebral cortex, kidney, spleen, and skin. The long list of structures he described for the first time has been commemorated by occasional eponyms such as the malpighian corpuscle (glomerulus) of the kidney and the malpighian layer in the epidermis. He also made extensive microscopic observations on embryonic development (Adelmann, 1966). His descriptions of detailed structure in adult and developing silkworms included what are now called malpighian tubules, the principal organ of excretion in insects. Malpighi was one of the first to carry out broad studies on the microscopic anatomy of plants.

The resolution obtained by microscopes in that era was seriously limited by chromatic aberration. As a result, when an object was viewed with a compound microscope at higher magnification, the fine detail was blurred and appeared as a fuzzy collection of colored fringes. It is a surprising fact that the simple microscope (or magnifying glass consisting of a single lens) was actually less affected by aberrations than the compound microscope, and therefore was capable of higher resolution. Lenses could be ground with great convexity to give high magnification, but their use as a simple microscope was difficult, since it was necessary to hold them very close to the eye, and the object being viewed had to be illuminated (or silhouetted) by very strong light. As a consequence of these difficulties, most of the better microscopists of the period used compound microscopes. Antony van Leeuwenhoek was an exception.

Leeuwenhoek (1632–1723), of Delft in the Netherlands, used simple microscopes to make observations with a resolution that would not be surpassed until the 1830s. His first microscopic observations were made in 1668, after a trip to London in which he may have been influenced by Hooke's *Micrographia.* Leeuwenhoek's lenses, which he taught himself to grind, were small and often almost spherical, some being capable of magnifying almost 300 times. Each lens was mounted in a hole in the middle of a small metal plate. The plate could be held very close to the eye, and by this means a specimen (suspended at the tip of a holder on the other face of the plate) could be viewed. Leeuwenhoek had remarkable ingenuity in arranging specimens for viewing and in devising means of quantitating the size and number of the things he observed. He apparently had exceptionally keen eyes. His observations were communicated to the Royal Society of London in at least 190 letters, and 26 were sent to the Academy of Sciences of Paris. Among the many findings that were reported and often illustrated in these letters were the following: striations of skeletal muscle; red blood corpuscles and measurements of their size, using the size of sand grains as a unit of measurement; circulation of blood in the tail fin of a living eel; spermatozoa of several species; fertilization in frogs and fishes; structure of the lens of the eye; five types of bacteria, described in scrapings from the surface of teeth; five kinds of ciliate protozoa and several flagellate protozoa; and microscopic details of plant-stem cross sections, showing a substantial difference between monocotyledonous and dicotyledonous plants. For an extensive description of Leeuwenhoek's work, see Dobell (1932).

Although there was no fundamental improvement in microscopic resolution for a century or more after Leeuwenhoek, observations continued. By the late 1700s microscopists had described cells in the tissues of plants and animals. Cells were especially obvious in plants, because they were outlined by the wall that forms the cell boundary. However, the resolution of available microscopes was not adequate to see cells clearly, and their nature, significance, and how widely they were distributed in living things remained uncertain. Some microscopists of the era, such as Dutrochet, suggested that cells might be the building blocks of which living things were made. In a sense, then, these individuals could be considered early proponents of the cell theory. Their claims, however, were quite controversial at the time, and could not be supported convincingly with contemporary microscopes.

Even though most microscopists used the compound microscope, the simple microscope still found occasional users as late as the early 19th century. Probably the last of the major findings made with a simple microscope was the discovery of the cell nucleus. In 1833 an English botanist, Robert Brown, described an intracellular structure he had observed consistently within cells of the epidermis in orchids, and which he termed an "areola" or "nucleus." He later showed that a nucleus was also present in a variety of other plant cells.

IMPROVED LENSES LEAD TO THE CELL THEORY

During the late 1700s and early 1800s, a means was developed for greatly reducing the chromatic aberration of microscope lenses, which would bring about a dramatic increase in the effective resolution of light microscopes. The conceptual basis for the improvement was worked out by the Swede Samuel Klingenstierna and later by the Englishman J.J. Lister. The approach was to make a composite lens consisting of two types of glass that exhibited different indices of refraction. The parts of the composite lens were arranged in a manner that allowed one component to cancel most of the chromatic aberrations produced by the other. The result was called an "achromatic" lens, since the colored fringes that had blurred structural detail in earlier lenses were greatly reduced, and the image consequently appeared much sharper. The practical production of the new achromatic lenses for microscopes began in the late 1820s, by microscope makers such as the Frenchman Charles Chevalier (first model, 1825) and the Italian Giovanni Amici (first model, 1827).

Using microscopes equipped with the new lenses, it was possible for microscopists in the 1830s to observe cells with much greater clarity than had been possible before. As a result, notable advances and discoveries occurred rapidly over the 1830s and 1840s. Of the many workers in that period, Matthias Jacob Schleiden and Theodor Schwann had a particular impact on the thinking of the time by their promulgation of the cell theory.

Schleiden (1804–1881), a German botany professor, studied plant cells with the new microscopes. His main article on cells appeared in 1838 and contained a variety of observations on plant cells, including one of the first descriptions of the nucleolus. He synthesized these findings into a hypothesis that was intended to explain how plant cells developed. He maintained that cells developed from nuclei by a gradual process of growth, and that the nuclei in turn arose from nucleoli. Although this central theme of the article later proved to be mistaken, the work had lasting significance because of the importance it ascribed to cells as the functional units of which plants were composed. It was maintained throughout the article that each cell was an independent living entity, and that the organism consisted of a community of cells. This was the essence of the cell theory, and had a substantial effect on subsequent thinking.

Schwann (1810–1882), a German zoologist, was strongly influenced by the work of Schleiden and sought to apply the same insights to animal cells. Schwann published his work on animal cells in 1839, while he was a student with Johannes Müller at the University of Berlin. By studying cells during the embryonic development of animals, Schwann demonstrated the cellular origin of the known tissues, even those in which cells were not apparent in the mature organism (for example, he showed that both the notochord of tadpoles and embryonic cartilage were composed of nucleated cells). This led to the generalization that everything in the animal body was composed either of cells or of cellular products. A further generalization, based on his own work and that of Schleiden, was that the cell was the basic unit of life in all living things, both plant and animal.

With regard to the origin of cells, Schwann accepted the mistaken notion of Schleiden that cells could arise spontaneously in slime, first resembling isolated nucleoli, then becoming similar to nuclei, and finally developing into mature cells. Some other workers disputed this concept at the time. The eventual resolution of this issue came from Rudolf Virchow (1821–1902), who established the principle that cells come only from other cells (i.e., by division).

ERA OF HISTOLOGY

Following the elaboration of the cell theory, there were two or three decades of intensive observations to describe the diversity and organization of cells within the organs of living things. This era of histology provided our basic understanding of how organs are organized.

The histological studies were carried out in most cases with achromatic microscopes, but the methods of specimen preparation were still relatively crude.

Tissues were generally prepared for viewing by microdissection or by maceration (effective sectioning came later), but sometimes were supported between two layers of mica or glass (1791), with a mounting medium of gum arabic (1832) or Canada balsam (1835). The tissue occasionally was stabilized somewhat by fixation with alcohol (1743), chromic acid (1833), or osmium trioxide (1840). Staining was carried out with saffranin (1714), plant infusions (1758), cochineal (1770), or other agents. More sophisticated stains and methods were yet to come.

One of the important conceptual developments in histology was elaborated earlier, without the use of a microscope. Xavier Bichat (1771–1802), a French anatomist and surgeon, perceived during delicate anatomical dissections that the organs of the body were generally composed of several discrete types of materials often arranged in layers, which he called "tissues." Some tissues covered body surfaces, others filled spaces, while others were composed of muscle or were part of the nervous system. Morphologists during the era of histology developed the insights of Bichat into the familiar four basic tissues.

Among the great histologists of this era were Jacob Henle (1809–1885), Rudolf Köller (1817–1905), and Franz Leydig (1821–1905). The textbooks they wrote in the 1850s and 1860s contained much of the basic structural information at the light-microscope level that is taught in histology courses today.

ERA OF CYTOLOGY

Some structures were described within cells during the era of histology, but the methods of specimen preparation in use during that period were generally unsuitable for the study of intracellular detail. Once the main outlines of histological organization within organs had been worked out, the attention of biologists turned more and more toward what was happening within the cells. The 1870s–1890s became an era of cytology.

To make progress in the study of intracellular structures, it was necessary to develop more favorable methods of specimen preparation. Among the new components for fixation were mercuric chloride (1856), osmium tetroxide (1864), and formaldehyde (1892); freeze-drying was first used in 1889. The first true embedding (with infiltration), using alcohol, turpentine, and paraffin, was carried out by Frédericq in 1879; embedding with chloroform and paraffin was introduced by Otto Bütschli in 1881. The first practical microtome for cutting histological sections was that of Wilhelm His in 1870. Various stains and stain combinations were brought into use, for example, basic fuchsin (1863), aniline dyes (red, violet, and purple had been tried by 1860), and hematoxylin (introduced as a stain in 1865 by Bohmer). In the 1880s several manufacturers, especially G. Grubler of Leipzig, developed very highly refined products, and by the turn of the century most of the stains that are routinely used today were available.

The first part of the cell to prove fruitful for cytological research was the nucleus. Although chromosomes had been described earlier, their nature and significance were obscure. These structures seemed to become visible in cells that were capable of dividing, but the mechanism of cell division and the possible role of these small rodlike structures seemed quite mysterious. The pioneering studies of Walter Flemming (1843–1905), Eduard Strasburger (1844–1912), Oscar Hertwig (1849–1922), Theodor Boveri (1862–1915), Edouard van Beneden (1845–1910),

Hermann Fol (1843–1892), and others gradually elucidated the various stages of mitosis, and the detailed behavior of chromosomes, the mitotic spindle, and centrioles during these events. Some of the excitement of this era can be appreciated by reading one of the classic papers of Flemming (1880), which is available in English translation (1965, J. Cell Biol., 25(1):1–69). Although some of the terms are different, the description of mitosis sounds quite modern. The chromosomal events during meiosis in germ cells, as well as nuclear behavior in fertilization, were also gradually worked out by Hertwig, Boveri, van Beneden, Fol, and others.

Beginning in 1886 the Zeiss optical works in Germany started making a series of microscope lenses that had considerably better resolution than achromatic lenses. Based on the theories of image formation formulated by Ernst Abbé a few years earlier, and containing new types of glass, these apochromatic lenses, as they were called, were corrected for chromatic aberration at 3 wavelengths and were also corrected for spherical aberration. The high-power objectives of this series were made to be used with immersion oil of the same refractive index as glass (an idea dating only from 1878). Their resolution approached the theoretical limit for light microscopes, about 0.2 μm, and allowed cytologists to perceive still finer detail within cells.

In contrast to the rapid progress of studies on the nucleus, the observation of cytoplasmic structures proceeded more slowly and usually required much more elaborate methods to preserve them and make them visible.

Occasional descriptions of structures we would now know to be mitochondria appeared here and there in the microscopic literature as early as the 1840s. However, the first study characterizing these structures and showing them to be present in a wide variety of cell types was that of Richard Altmann (1852–1901), published in 1890. Reflecting the conceptual climate of his time, Altmann considered these "bioblasts," as he called them, to be independent entities, constituting the true elementary units of which living matter was composed. This became the granule theory of the nature of protoplasm, which was debated for a decade or so thereafter.

The first description of the Golgi complex appeared in 1898, and was an unexpected dividend from the efforts of Camillo Golgi (1844–1926) to stain neurons by long incubations with osmium tetroxide. In sections of the cerebellum from a barn owl, he noted a network of interconnecting dark lines, which he called a "reticular apparatus," in the cyptoplasm around the nucleus. This was subsequently viewed in other cell types, and came to be known as the Golgi apparatus. Its reality in the living cell was to be a subject of controversy over the next half century.

It had been a common observation for years that there was material in the cytoplasm that stained in the same manner as the chromatin of the nucleus. An extensive description of this basophilic material in a variety of protein-secreting cell types was published in 1899 by Garnier. He believed that the material played an important role in the secretory process, and named it "ergastoplasm." We would agree with that analysis today, since we know that the basophilia is due to ribosomes, either bound to the endoplasmic reticulum or free in the cytoplasm.

As was mentioned above, the centrioles and the general region they occupied in the cell (called the cell center or cytocentrum) was studied extensively by the workers who elucidated the mechanism of mitosis. In addition, centrioles were known to give rise to cilia, which also received a good deal of attention. Ballowitz

(1888) gave microscopic evidence that there were 9–11 subfilaments in a frayed sperm tail, a remarkable observation in view of the 9 + 2 pattern shown decades later by electron microscopy.

In the 1890s it was still considered possible that the nervous system might be an exception to the cell theory, since it had not been conclusively established that all axons and dendrites were derived from nerve cell bodies. The studies of Golgi on cellular staining with osmium tetroxide and metal salts in the nervous system, mentioned above, and the brilliant investigations of Santiago Ramón y Cajal (1852–1934) eventually demonstrated that neural processes were of a cellular nature.

The understanding of cells at the turn of the century was extensively reviewed in the well-known cytological monographs by Oscar Hertwig (1893, 1898), E.B. Wilson (2nd edition, 1907), and Martin Heidenhain (1907, 1911). Many structures we now know to be parts of the living cell had been described in remarkable detail, and in some cases (particularly in the nucleus) a good deal was known about their function.

A HALF CENTURY OF SKEPTICISM

By the turn of the century a mood of skepticism was beginning to set in with regard to many of the results of cytological investigations on the organelles of cells. Most of the work had been done at the resolution limits of the light microscope. For example, the best microscopes could resolve about 0.2 μm, and the average diameter of a mitochondrion was only about 0.5 μm. From our vantage point today we can see that a great many features of the cell as it was described in 1900 were correct. However, at that time there were multiple descriptions and theories, and it was sometimes difficult to distinguish what was meaningful. For instance, major cytologists expended a considerable effort in the 1890s on debating the comparative merits of three different theories about the essential nature of protoplasm: the granule theory (Altmann), the fibrillar theory (Flemming), and the emulsion theory (Bütschli). These speculations may seem unprofitable to us today, but received serious attention at the time. By the turn of the century many cytologists, including E.B. Wilson, were expressing doubts that any of the above three theories were exclusively true, or even that they were verifiable by methods then available.

The possibility of artifact gave rise to serious reservations. It was not certain whether mitochondria, the Golgi complex, and other structures were genuine organelles present and functioning in the living cell or only artifacts produced by the lengthy and laborious cytological procedures that were necessary to demonstrate them (often involving fixation in caustic solutions and long incubations with other noxious agents). Critical papers (for example, Fischer, 1899) pointed out that if fresh egg white, containing protein in solution, was observed under the microscope, it was transparent and showed little or no structure. However, if the egg white was bathed with standard cytological fixatives or with ethanol, routinely used for dehydration, then it became opaque and showed extensive spurious structural patterns, when viewed with the microscope. It was not hard to believe that similar artifactual fabrications might be occurring in the cytoplasm of cells during fixation for light microscopy.

Another major problem was that cytology had reached a point at which efforts to probe the function of organelles by microscopic means had become increasingly difficult. At the same time an era of biochemistry was opening up that offered other approaches to the study of cellular function. There was a developing feeling that morphology had said what it was capable of saying about cells, and that the results, at least with regard to events in the cytoplasm, had not been particularly conclusive or functionally compelling. Morphology seemed to be drifting out of the mainstream, and biochemistry was moving to center stage, a mood expressed in a later comment by Aldous Huxley: "Microscopy really went out of fashion from 1900 until after World War II."

In spite of these reservations, a great deal of worthwhile microscopic research was carried out on cytoplasmic organelles in the years from 1900 to 1950. Organelles were studied in various cell types and in diverse functional states, often utilizing refinements of classical cytological methods. In the 1920s there was a period of supravital staining (Janus green B, methylene blue, neutral red, and others). Many researchers developed cytochemical approaches that sought to localize biochemical function within cells. There were other new approaches. For example, Robert Bensley and Normand Hoerr (1934) in the Anatomy Department of the University of Chicago isolated mitochondria by fractional centrifugation and studied them cytochemically in the pellet.

Further advances involving cytochemistry, radioautography, immunocytochemistry, and other functional approaches with the microscope, which had their roots in the period before 1950, are reviewed in subsequent chapters in this section of the book.

THE ELECTRON MICROSCOPE AND BIOLOGICAL SPECIMENS

Although the first practical electron microscope was constructed in 1931, it was not until the late 1940s that effective means were devised to apply the remarkable resolving power of the instrument to the study of cells.

The theoretical background for electron microscopes dates from 1924, when de Broglie, a French physicist, postulated that electrons had wave properties, and that the wavelength was inversely proportional to the electron velocity. Two years later, Busch showed that a beam of electrons could be focused by magnetic lenses. Transmission electron microscopes were developed in the 1930s, particularly by Knoll, Ruska, and von Borries, and the first commercial instrument appeared in 1939, from Siemens and Halske AG. A scanning electron microscope was shown to be feasible by von Ardenne in 1938. Further progress had to wait for the end of World War II.

But how could the electron microscope be used to study the detailed structure of the cellular organelles that had been matters of uncertainty and controversy for half a century? The fixation routinely used for light microscopy was much too crude for high-resolution work. The beam of electrons could only penetrate a thickness of approximately 0.1 μm (the thinnest light-microscope sections were about 1–2 μm), and the sections would need to be stable under the high vacuum that was essential within electron microscopes. The eventual solution of these problems is described in subsequent chapters.

It is easy to imagine the excitement of the early electron microscopists as they were first able to view the cellular organelles with the power of this new instrument. It disclosed a new world within cells, a world of membranes, of compartmentation, and of intricate organization, only partially anticipated by the cytological investigations of the preceding century. The further chapters of this section review these developments.

ACKNOWLEDGMENTS

This chapter was written while the author was in Paris spending a sabbatical year at the Pasteur Institute. The author would like to thank Dr. Roger du Boistesselin for information on the history of microscopes and histological techniques and Dr. Jean Racadot for helpful discussions and the loan of books. Both Drs. du Boistesselin and Racadot are in the Department of Histology and Embryology, Faculty of Medicine, University of Paris VI, associated with l'Hôpital Pitié Salpétrière in Paris.

REFERENCES

Adelmann, H.B. 1966 Marcello Malpighi and the Evolution of Embryology, Cornell University Press, Ithaca, N.Y.

Altmann, R. 1890 Die Elementarorganismen und ihre Beziehungen zur den Zellen. Veit, Leipzig (2nd edition, 1894).

Ballowitz, E. 1888 Untersuchungen über die Struktur der Spermatozoën, zugleich ein Beitrag zur Lehre vom feineren Bau der contraktilen Elemente. Arch. Mikroskop. Anat. *32*:401–473.

Bensley, R.R., and N. Hoerr. 1934 Studies on cell structure by the freeze-drying method. VI. The preparation and properties of mitochondria. Anat. Rec., *60*:449–455.

Bradbury, S. 1967 The Evolution of the Microscope. Pergamon, Elmsford, New York.

Brown, R. 1833 On the organs and mode of fecundation in *Orchideae* and *Asclepiadeae*. Trans. Linnean Soc. London, *16*:685–745.

Clay, R.S., and T.H. Court. 1932 The History of the Microscope, Compiled for Original Instruments and Documents up to the Introduction of the Achromatic Microscope. Charles Griffin & Co., Ltd., London.

Dobell, C. 1932 Antony van Leeuwenhoek and his "Little Animals." John Bale, Sons & Danielsson, Ltd., London (republished 1960 by Dover Publications, New York).

Fischer, A. 1899 Fixirung. Färbung und Bau des Protoplasmas. Gustav Fischer, Jena, 362 pp.

Flemming, W. 1880 Beiträge zur Kenntniss der Zelle und ihrer Lebenserscheinungen, Theil II. Arch. Mikroskop. Anat. *18*:151–259; English translation, J. Cell Biol., *25*(1,2):3–69.

Ford, B.J. 1973 The Optical Microscope Manual. Past and Present Uses and Techniques. David & Charles, Newton Abbot, England, and Crane, Russak, New York.

Garnier, C. 1899 Contribution à l'Étude de la Structure et du Fonctionnement des Cellules Glandulaires Séreuses. Thesis No. 5. University of Nancy, Nancy.

Golgi, C. 1898 Sur la structure des cellules nerveuses. Du rôle de l'ergastoplasme dans la sécrétion. Arch. Ital. Biol., *30*:60–71.

Heidenhain, M. 1907, 1911 Plasma und Zelle. Section 1 (1907, pp. 1–506), Section 2 (1911, pp. 507–1110). Part of Handbuch der Anatomie des Menschen. K. von Bardeleben, ed. Gustav Fischer, Jena.

Hertwig, O. 1893, 1898 Die Zelle und die Gewebe. Section 1 (1893, pp. 1–296), Section 2 (1898, pp. 1–314). Gustav Fischer, Jena.

Hooke, Robert. 1665 Micrographia: Or Some Physiological Descriptions of Minute Bodies Made by Magnifying Glasses, with Observations and Inquiries Thereupon. J. Martyn and J. Allestry, London (facsimile edition, Culture et Civilization, Brussels).

Nordenskiöld, E. 1949 The History of Biology: A Survey. Tudor Publishing Co., New York.

Schleiden, M.J. 1838 Beiträge zur Phytogenesis. Arch. Anat. Physiol. Wiss. Med., pp. 137–176.

Schwann, T. 1839 Mikroskopische Untersuchungen über die Uebereinstimmung in der Structur und dem Wachsthum der Thiere und Pflanzen. G.E. Reimer, Sandersche Bukhh., Berlin.

Wilson, E.B. 1900 The Cell in Development and Inheritance, 2nd edition. Macmillan, New York.

Chapter 4

THE DEVELOPMENT OF CYTOLOGICAL TRANSMISSION ELECTRON MICROSCOPY

Daniel C. Pease

MICROSCOPE DEVELOPMENT AND EARLY BIOLOGICAL USAGE

Of course the instrument, the transmission electron microscope, had to come before involvement in microtomy. Obviously, too, it took mathematicians, physicists, and engineers to develop the microscope, rather than biologists. However, a Belgian physicist, L. Marton, did take the first electron micrograph of a tissue section as early as 1934 with a prototype microscope. Although his material, from a plant leaf, was fixed with osmium tetroxide, the section was much too thick to yield a useful image. The specimen was also badly fragmented for want of adequate support. Nonetheless, in subsequent reports Marton clearly expressed a vision that electron microscopy would eventually play a seminal role in biomedical research.

It has been remarked that the electron microscope was an inevitable achievement after the French mathematical physicist L. de Broglie in 1924 formulated the hypothesis that electrons could be expected to exhibit wavelike properties. In effect, they would obey optical laws. Accelerated electrons exhibit wavelengths tens of thousands of times shorter than the wavelengths of light; since it is wavelength that ultimately limits the resolving power of any sort of microscope, the advantages of electrons over light for such instrumentation were not overlooked for long.

The first true compound electron microscope of significant resolving power ever built is generally credited to E. Ruska in Germany in 1933, although this claim is slightly obfuscated. The crux of the problem has been that the electron microscope evolved from laboratory studies of the behavior of electrons in what we would now think of as oscilloscopes. Thus, magnetic and electrostatic effects on electron beams were already under investigation in a number of different laboratories before 1933, and it was recognized at least 2 years before then that current flowing through even a simple coil could serve as a weak lens to focus an electron beam. Thus, investigators other than Ruska, including particularly Marton, were in a position to exhibit and describe true compound electron microscopes, partially independently, very shortly after Ruska.

Ruska played an additionally important role in the development of electron microscopes in that he joined the powerful Siemens and Halske Corp. about 1935, and with B. von Borries designed the first and only commercially produced microscope that became available before World War II started, in 1939. By then the threat of war was already present, and the Germans limited the sale of these instruments to their own countrymen and their Axis partners.

At first, the United States lagged behind Europe in the development of electron optical devices, although V.K. Zworykin had started a research and development group at the Radio Corporation of America (RCA) before the war. As a result of his wide-ranging interests in the potentials of electron optics, he lured Marton to the Camden, New Jersey, laboratories in 1938. By that time, Marton had already hand-built three microscopes of successively improved designs. At RCA, he built his fourth, the RCA EM-A, which was originally intended to be the prototype for a production instrument. However, this was not to be, for Marton soon severed his connections with RCA to join the faculty of the Stanford University Physics Department. Meanwhile, in Toronto, in 1935, a group of young investigators and graduate students were assembled by Professor E.F. Burton to design, build, and use electron microscopes there. A successful compound instrument was in operation by 1939. One of Burton's early protégés was James Hillier, who left Toronto and joined RCA early in 1940. There he teamed up particularly with A.W. Vance, an electronics engineer, who was mainly responsible for the development of high-voltage power-supply circuitry for RCA. Together they quickly designed what was to be the first commercial microscope of the Western Hemisphere, produced late in 1940, the RCA EM-B instrument. This served the Allies well in World War II, including major shipments to England and Russia under "Lend-Lease" arrangements.

World War II undoubtedly had profound effects on the course of development of electron microscopy. It almost excluded biological research, for there were so many obvious applications in materials science research that promised direct military usefulness that the demand for instruments far outstripped their availability (about 60 EM-B microscopes were made). In the United States, any corporation or university needed an AA-1 priority from the War Production Board just to get on the waiting list for a microscope. However, this does not mean that no biological research was started. Indeed, even in the prewar years a few biologists had had access to prototype microscopes and had achieved modest, publishable results. Specimen support grids and films had been developed early. Since useful specimens had to be intrinsically thin, it was mainly the microbiologists who could take advantage of the early instrumentation. However, the periodicity of collagen fibers was soon observed independently on both sides of the Atlantic.

During the war, when so few biologists could get near an electron microscope, Keith Porter and Albert Claude at the Rockefeller Institute established liaison with the Interchemical Corp. in New York City. There, an RCA EM-B microscope had been installed under the aegis of E.F. Fullam. Porter had cell cultures to look at, cells grown on supporting films that had flattened themselves so that they turned out to have considerable electron transparency near their edges. In 1944, Porter, Claude, and Fullam had the first good look at cytoplasmic inclusions at electron-microscopic magnifications (Figs. 4.1 and 4.2). Although they used several fixatives for their preparations, osmium tetroxide vapors were recognized as being clearly superior. Since basically they were dealing with whole mounts, they had a somewhat three-dimensional view that helped visualize the reticulum, later to be characterized as being "endoplasmic." Also, during the war, Stuart Mudd, a bacteriologist at the University of Pennsylvania, was instrumental in developing a good working relationship with the RCA laboratories across the river in Camden, New Jersey. This led to the establishment of a National Research Council Fellowship, funded by RCA, to promote biological investigations using the company's facilities. T.F. Anderson became the first recipient. There followed collaboration with a number of other investigators, mainly microbiologists; however, during that period, Anderson, along with G.H. Richards and T.R. Hance, did make an attempt to produce ultrathin sections by cutting wedges. Their work was published in 1942. In Europe, M. von Ardenne in 1939 and F.S. Sjöstrand in 1943 similarly considered cutting wedges, but without producing publishable micrographs. Basically, all of these efforts failed, mainly because of inadequate tissue support.

Finally, the Massachusetts Institute of Technology group, headed by F.O. Schmitt, deserves special comment. As far as I know, these investigators had the only RCA EM-B microscope that was assigned to biologists during the war years. In large measure, this was a result of Cecil Hall's contribution to prototype developments at Toronto, where he had been a graduate student before going first to the Eastman Kodak Research Laboratories and then to MIT. Although later on this laboratory did become quite interested in ultramicrotomy, it was at first concerned mainly with microbiological problems, including virology, and protein structure. All specimens had to be handled as particulate entities, raised in culture or derived from mechanically fragmented tissues and cells.

As the war was drawing to a close, RCA was preparing to manufacture the microscope that was to be the crucial stimulus to American anatomists in particular. Subsequent circumstances gave our AAA group a head start on other biological disciplines, as well as the rest of the world generally. These instruments were marketed as the RCA EMU-Series microscopes, first available in 1944, for about $12,000 (the EM-B originally cost $9,500). They had little competition until the redesigned Siemens "Elmiskop-l" microscope came on the market 10 years later, in 1954. Meanwhile, the Philips-100 microscope was introduced in 1950 and enjoyed considerable popularity in Europe, and with material sciences investigators everywhere, but for various reasons it never met the needs of the cytologists very well.

Younger investigators, who perhaps have never used an RCA EMU microscope, should realize that in spite of all its good qualities, it was introduced lacking at least three features that today would be regarded as absolutely essential. The earliest model (EMU-1) did not even have a biased electron gun, and so lacked the feedback circuitry that now always is to be found stabilizing the electron source and beam. To be sure, that deficiency was quickly corrected in the EMU-2 series microscopes.

A lack of adequate aperturing to screen out stray electrons (thus eliminating most background fog, which otherwise degrades contrast) was a second deficiency, never adequately corrected by RCA in this series of instruments. The most important aperture, of course, is associated with the objective lens of any microscope, and it is taken for granted today that it be externally movable for necessary

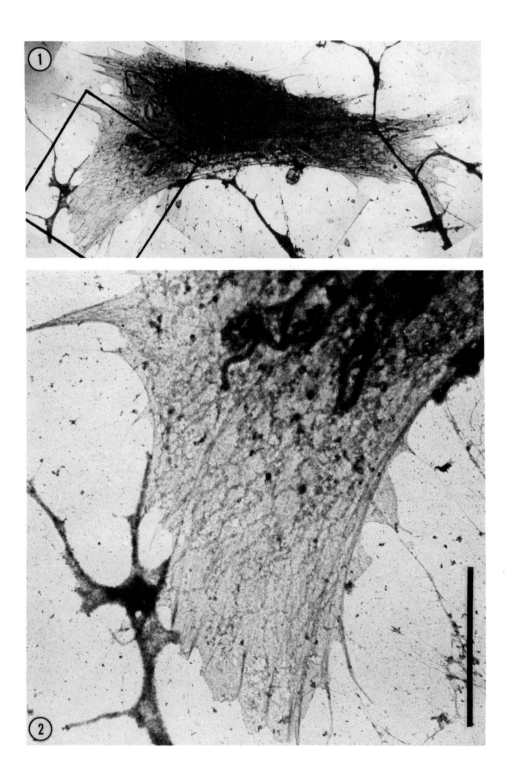

alignment purposes. The early EMU microscopes lacked all aperturing and so inevitably had poor contrast characteristics. Later instruments did incorporate fixed apertures, but not ones that could be externally aligned under operating conditions (a small specialty company, Canalco, Inc. eventually marketed such a device as an accessory).

Finally, in the early EMU microscopes, there was no way to correct the intrinsic astigmatism that inevitably is to be found to some degree in the pole piece of any objective lens. Electromagnetic or electrostatic correction devices are now also taken for granted. Magnetic correction was added to the later EMU instruments, but this was an internal adjustment that could not be corrected under operating conditions. This was not a very satisfactory arrangement until Canalco, Inc. once again came to the rescue with the desirable gadgetry. Thus, there were persistent instrumental design flaws in these microscopes that were serious limitations, even as the cytologists enthusiastically went to work with them.

INITIAL DEVELOPMENT OF ULTRAMICROTOMY

Electron-microscopic cytology, of course, could not be significantly developed until the basic problems of ultramicrotomy were solved. In retrospect, a fundamentally adequate, commercial microtome was unknowingly at hand, unrecognized until 1950 when L.H. Bretschneider in Holland started using it. Curiously, this was one of the oldest of conventional microtomes, the "Cambridge Rocking Microtome," dating back to 1885. However, instead of being developed as an extension of conventional microtomy, ultramicrotomy got off to a bizarre start. This resulted from an erroneous hypothesis of H.C. O'Brien and G.M. McKinley in 1943 that ultrathin sections could only be cut if a knife edge passed through a block at very high speed. Then, presumably, specimen inertia would so restrict strain distribution as to localize it very close to the knife edge. They started with an 8-inch wheel, with a razor blade attached to its perimeter, revolving at 12,500 rpm. The block was pushed into this whirling knife producing a snowstorm of chips and sections of all sorts of thickness. In an effort to improve the sectioning, these investigators later nearly doubled the rotor speed. Still later, in 1946, inspired by these efforts, E.F. Fullam and A.E. Gessler produced a microtome that operated at 57,000 rpm, delivering a cutting speed of 11,000 feet per second! Curiously, a modified version of the latter microtome, but operated at low speed, was the

Figs. 4.1, 4.2. In 1945, Porter, Claude, and Fullam published these micrographs (J. Exp. Med. *81*:233–246), which were the first to show significant *in situ* protoplasmic detail, including what was to become known as the endoplasmic reticulum. To achieve these results, isolated fibroblasts had been allowed to grow and flatten on support films. The cultured cells were then fixed by exposure to osmium tetroxide vapors, and were examined with an RCA-EM-B microscope. These latter instruments constituted the earliest American-made commercial model, first marketed at the end of 1940. They were two-stage microscopes, as were the early RCA-EMU instruments, which followed in 1944. That is to say, these microscopes lacked "intermediate" lenses, and the result was a severe limitation of the useful magnification range without introducing severe distortions. Hence, relatively low magnifications were practical only by combining micrographs like the montage seen in Figure 1. The area included in Figure 2 is outlined in Figure 1. The bar mark in Figure 2 = 1 μm.

Fig. 4.3. This photograph illustrates one of the prototype versions of the "Porter-Blum" single-pass microtome. It can be dated to about 1952, for it is equipped with a glass knife as developed by Latta and Hartmann in 1950. Also, it lacks the mechanical drive mechanism of the first commercial version, available in 1953. The early prototype microtomes of this series were thermally advanced simply by appropriately positioning the goose-necked lamp visible in the picture so as to heat and expand the long specimen-carrier arm. The idea of a thermal expansion microtome drive seems first to have been applied by Newman, Borysko, and Swerdlow in 1949.

instrument employed by Claude in his partially successful pioneering work in ultramicrotomy at the Rockefeller Institute. The latter work was described in a "Harvey Lecture" presented by Claude in 1948. The published report did not actually make its appearance until 1950, however, so that one cannot really date all of the information included. It is clear, however, that Claude was close to developing a practical solution to the difficulties of ultramicrotomy. This led him to express the view that the real problem lay in tissue preservation, not so much in the microtomy.

Meanwhile, this author and R. Baker, aware of the success of double embedding as a means for producing submicron sections for conventional microscopy, set about to exploit this for electron microscopy. They modified the advance mechanism of a Spencer, Inc. rotary microtome so that its nominal unit of advance was 0.4 μm instead of 1.0 μm (Fig. 4.4). Tissue blocks, fixed in osmium tetroxide, were then embedded first in as concentrated Parlodion as possible. This was followed by infiltration with high-melting point paraffin [later carnauba or bayberry waxes, as well as resins, were added to increase the hardness of the embedments (Fig. 4.7)]. Sectioning originally was with specially ground and honed, heavy steel knives. Dry sections were picked up with a fine brush or a hair and transferred by hand to grids, where they were then flattened and stuck down by pressure. Since electron stains had not yet been developed, the paraffin was removed with xylol to create contrast, leaving the Parlodion in place to support the tissue (Figs. 4.5 and 4.6).

The extraction step was unfortunate, for subsequently it became apparent that the residual Parlodion did not provide an adequate support. As a result much fine structure collapsed upon itself, thus producing artifacts that were not originally recognized. Nonetheless, this work, published in 1948, served as a catalyst; for it did demonstrate the feasibility of obtaining electron-translucent tissue sections with modest equipment and with slow-speed cutting. It emphasized two enduring factors that had to be incorporated in a successful technique: first, the need for relatively hard embedments to provide adequate support; and second, the necessity to scale down block size.

Next, in 1949, a major contribution came from a plastics research group at the U.S. National Bureau of Standards, when S. Newman, E. Borysko, and M.

Fig. 4.4.   In 1948, the author and R. Baker reported ultrathin sectioning with a simply modified "Spencer 820" microtome (Proc. Soc. Exp. Biol. Med. *57*:470–474). The alteration reduced its unit of advance by a factor of 10, nominally to 0.1 μm. This was achieved by adding a wedge-shaped fitting to the specimen carriage mechanism as indicated by the heavy arrows in this figure.

Originally, sectioning was with steel knives and without a section flotation trough. Glass knives, as pictured here, were introduced by Latta and Hartmann in 1950, and troughs by Gettner and Hillier the same year. Thus, the modified microtome seen here dates from after that time.

It soon became apparent that section flotation demanded "single-pass" microtomes. These had to be instruments that allowed the block face to contact the knife only during the actual cutting part of the cycle. Thus, the microtome pictured here was also modified to mechanically flip the block holder down and back at the end of its downstroke, and return it to a horizontal position when the upstroke was completed. This was effected by tripping a spring-loaded block holder that was hinged by means of two short knife edges seated in a V-shaped groove as indicated by the arrowhead.

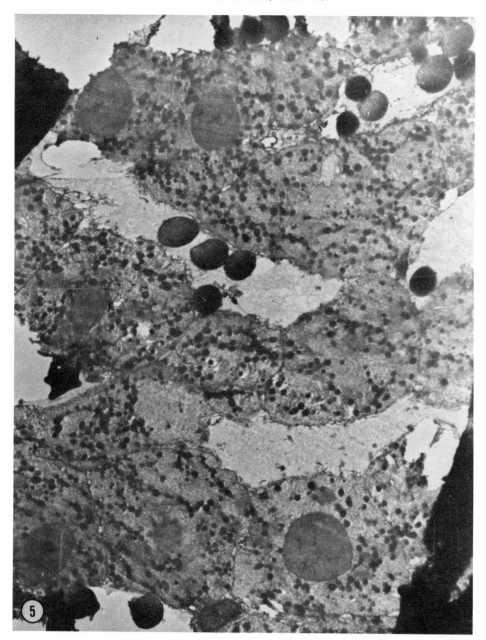

Fig. 4.5.   One of the first series of ultrathin sections made by the author and R. Baker in 1948. The rat liver was fixed in unbuffered osmium tetroxide. It was then double-embedded, first in thick Parlodion, and then with high-melting point paraffin. Dry sections were cut with a heavy steel knife and a modified "Spencer 820" microtome. The dry sections were maneuvered onto a naked grid with a fine brush, and flattened and anchored down by pressure. The paraffin was then removed with xylol, leaving only the permeating nitro-cellulose net as the specimen support. This can be seen here spanning the sinusoidal spaces. In retrospect, this was inadequate support, allowing much fine structure to aggregate. However, at the time it seemed necessary to provide contrast, which was extremely poor in unextracted sections.

Swerdlow introduced polymerized butyl/methyl methacrylate mixtures as an embedding medium. Essentially, all of the key cytological discoveries of the early and mid-1950s were made with such methacrylate-embedded tissues (Fig. 4.8). It should also be noted that these investigators devised a thermal expansion drive for their Spencer microtome, a principle that became popular in later ultramicrotome designs.

In 1950, M. Gettner and J. Hillier formally introduced the idea of floating sections on a water surface, which flattened them and permitted an easy transfer to support grids. Actually, Claude, at the Rockefeller Institute, had been doing this for some time previously, but without publication. A consequent effect of this technical advance was the recognition that only "single-pass" microtomes could be used with a fluid-filled trough. Otherwise, on the return stroke, any section cut was almost certain to be lifted up by the rising block, thus disastrously wetting the block face. This fact set limitations on all future ultramicrotome design efforts.

In these formative years, steel microtome knives seemed inevitable, although obviously unsatisfactory in several respects. The acute edges of disposable razor blades clearly were unduly flexible. Heavy, nondisposable knives had to be honed at least once a day before use, for trough water visibly oxidized their edges even as they were being used. Also, on theoretical grounds, it seemed that at best the crystalline structure of steel could not really be expected to produce a truly uniform edge in terms of the dimensions concerned. Thus, it was a great boon to all of us working at the time when H. Latta and J. Hartmann introduced throwaway glass knives in 1950, a very simple and effective solution to a formidable problem! However, it is amusing to recall the mystique that soon developed in defining and finding the "perfect" strain-free glass that would make ideal fracture edges. The idea developed that very old glass was apt to be better than new glass (I had a prized piece of broken, heavy, plate glass salvaged from a pre-prohibition bar window, still with some old gold lettering on it). The problem, of course, has little significance nowadays.

It can be no surprise that the early 1950s saw quite a number of investigators turning their attention to microtome design. At first, the tendency was to modify existing conventional instruments. Later, ingenious and radically new designs appeared, but only a few actually realized commercial production. There is no space here to review these efforts in any detail. The interested reader can consult excellent reviews by Sitte (1955), Gettner and Ornstein (1956), Porter (1964), and Sjöstrand (1967). Out of this turmoil, however, the remarkably simple but highly effective Porter-Blum microtome emerged as a commercially produced instrument in 1953. The prototype models simply used the heat of a goose-necked lamp to thermally advance the specimen (Fig. 4.3). The manufactured version incorporated a screw- and lever-activated mechanical advance. In fundamental respects, this microtome bore some resemblance to the old Cambridge Rocking microtome. Although recognizing this, Porter insists his instrument was an independent invention. Sjöstrand also developed and marketed an ultramicrotome in Sweden at about the same time. For some years, the latter was the favorite of the Europeans, while the Porter-Blum microtome dominated the American market.

With the availability of RCA EMU microscopes, the Porter-Blum microtome, methacrylate embedding, glass knives, and osmium tetroxide fixation, the stage was set in 1953 for the veritable explosion of cytological investigation that followed. In this development, Porter, more than anyone else, played a key behind-

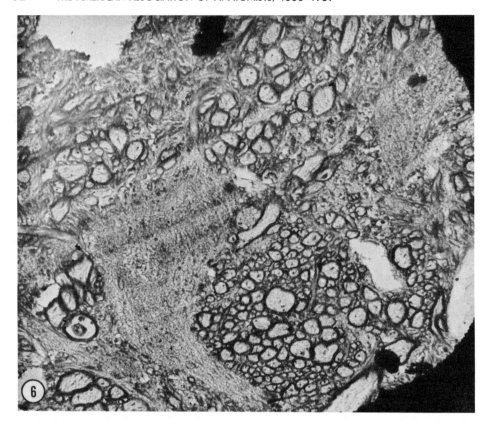

Fig. 4.6. This figure illustrates rat cervical spinal cord tissue, which was sectioned by the author and R. Baker a few months after the liver tissue of Figure 5, in 1949. The preparative technique was basically the same as that of Figure 5 with the improvement in sectioning due, perhaps, to a harder block achieved by adding carnauba wax to the embedding paraffin, and also more effective steel knife sharpening. There was no special staining or support film. The section was a little too thick to demonstrate substructure in the myelin, but did show that an extracellular compartment was virtually nonexistent in central nervous system neuropil.

the-scenes role as a highly effective ambassador and diplomat to the administrative leaders of the National Institutes of Health (NIH) and the National Science Foundation (NSF). He was able to convince them that the time had come when we had the tools at hand for a truly pervasive breakthrough, at least as important to cytology as the late 19th-century development and improvement of conventional microscopy and microtomy had been to histology. With the logic and leverage he could muster, Porter succeeded in loosening purse strings in Washington, and before long the establishment of new, biologically oriented electron microscope laboratories became commonplace in universities all over America, as well as within NIH itself. This having been accomplished, it was inevitable that the first flowering should be particularly within the province of anatomists and anatomy departments. Whereas originally it had been the Rockefeller Institute and MIT laboratories that had dominated the struggling growth of cellular fine structure, within a few years time, in the mid-1950s, clones, rapidly expanding from these sources, sprang up all around the country. In this expansion, first the Department of Anatomy at the University of Washington, under the leadership of Stanley Bennett, deserves special recognition as a training center, and then later the NIH laboratory directed by Sanford Palay and the Harvard Department of Anatomy chaired by Donald Fawcett.

Organizations played an educational role. First was the Electron Microscope (sic) Society of America, which had its origin at a somewhat informal meeting in Chicago in 1942, and for its first decade was dominated by physicists, engineers, chemists, and materials scientists. In its second decade, its annual meetings did serve as an increasingly important forum for interested biologists, but still with considerable emphasis upon technical developments and instrumentation. The American Association of Anatomists, with its Wistar journals partly controlled by the Association, was therefore the main stage for substantive cytological presentations for a while. Thus, the 1952 AAA meeting included a demonstration of "Palade's pickle," the slightly alkaline, veronal acetate-buffered, 1% osmium tetroxide solution that was to be the commonly used fixative for histological electron microscopy for the next decade. Table 1 statistically suggests the role played by the Association, but does not do justice to the opportunities for the interchange of ideas and information that were very important at that time. I well

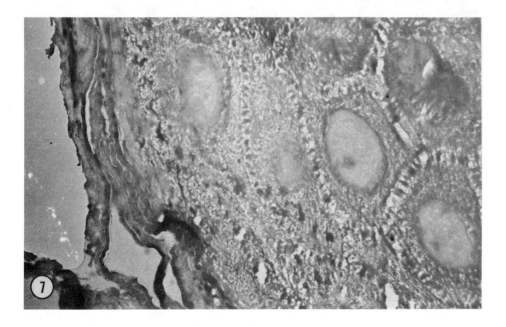

Fig. 4.7.   This section of human "thin" skin was prepared in 1950, from a block hardened by "triple embedding," adding a hard resin from a chloroform solution after infiltrating the specimen with nitrocellulose (chloroform precipitates nitrocellulose from ether-alcohol). The chloroform was then removed by infiltrating with a molten hard wax mixture. A flotation trough and support films were being used at this time, but sectioning was still with an especially sharpened steel knife. Subsequently, this author turned to methacrylate embedding, which had been introduced by Newman, Borysko, and Swerdlow in 1949.

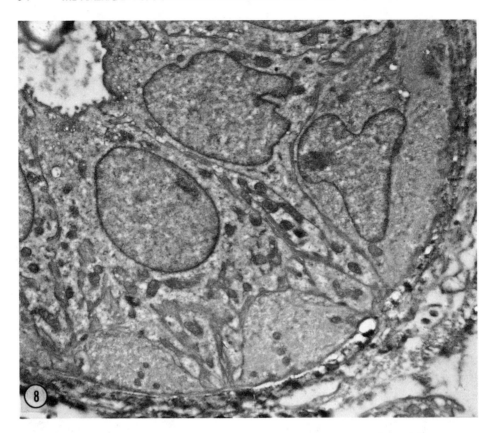

Fig. 4.8. A 1953 methacrylate-embedded section of a sweat gland from a rat footpad. Fixation was with Palade's veronal-buffered osmium tetroxide, introduced in 1952. Highly acidic phosphotungstic acid was also being used as a stain at the time, which greatly increased the density of collagen and basal lamina material, but was only marginally useful for most other tissue components. The relatively low contrast generally observed in micrographs of this period was due partly to inadequate stains and partly to the lack of objective lens aperturing in the RCA-EMU series microscopes of those early years.

remember the excitement of the annual meetings of those years, where the electron microscopists usually could be identified carrying black folders of 8 × 10 micrographs. At the banquets, we huddled at corner tables and talked so vociferously as to probably annoy our neighbors. They were heady times, and fortunate were the individuals of the generation that experienced them.

In fact, most of the truly basic discoveries relating to the fine structural features of cells were achieved in the 1950s with the technology as so far defined. There were international congresses of electron microscopy in London in 1954 and in Berlin in 1958, and a regional congress at Stockholm in 1956. Further, there was an important 1956 international "Conference on Tissue Fine Structure" at Arden House, Harriman, New York, organized by Porter and uniquely subsidized by NIH. By that time, Porter and Bennett had also launched the *Journal of Biophysical and Biochemical Cytology,* later to become the *Journal of Cell Biology.* Early volumes had a decidedly morphological direction, largely concerned with cytological fine structure. These publications provide a fascinating overview of the

Table 1

The annual meetings of the AAA played an important and expanding role in the dissemination of cytological information derived from electron microscopy during the critical decade of the 1950s, as this chart shows. During that period it was not the policy of the AAA to publish abstracts of all demonstrations; consequently, these presentations were quite significantly underrecorded. In 1960, the AAA annual meeting was held jointly with the VII International Congress of Anatomists, which, not surprisingly, resulted in a marked increase in the number of papers and demonstrations (*). During this decade, too, the editorial boards of the anatomical journals associated with the AAA consistently accepted and published a fair proportion of reports based on electron microscopy.

Year	AAA Annual Meetings		Journals	
	Platform papers	Demonstration abstracts	Anat. Rec.	Am. J. Anat.
1951	1	3	4 (v. 109–111)	2 (v. 88–89)
1952	6	7	6 (v. 112–114)	0 (v. 90–91)
1953	10	10	7 (v. 115–117)	4 (v. 92–93)
1954	12	8	4 (v. 118–120)	3 (v. 94–95)
1955	12	15	7 (v. 121–123)	3 (v. 96–97)
1956	14	14	6 (v. 124–126)	1 (v. 98–99)
1957	18	14	6 (v. 127–129)	3 (v. 100–101)
1958	27	10	4 (v. 130–132)	7 (v. 102–103)
1959	36	10	2 (v. 133–135)	2 (v. 104–105)
1960	98*	22*	8 (v. 136–138)	4 (v. 106–107)

electron-microscopic accomplishments of the era. Rather than being critical of shortcomings, one has to be impressed by the extraordinary achievements that occurred that were forever to change our notions of cell structure and set the stage for the developments of cell biology as we know them today.

Keeping up with this explosion of both substantive biological work and technical knowledge quickly became a full-time professional occupation. This was greatly aided by the New York Society of Electron Microscopists' publication of *The International Bibliography of Electron Microscopy*. This covered all aspects of the subject so that the first comprehensive volume, dealing with the period from 1950 to 1955, was able to include 4,054 entries, while the second volume, from 1956 to 1961, expanded astonishingly to 11,238 references. Publication unfortunately then ceased when the sheer quantity of new reports became overwhelming.

The explosion of biological knowledge derived from electron microscopy also inevitably led to the necessity for a new, specialized association. Porter became the central figure identified with the founding of the American Society for Cell Biology, which held its first meeting in 1961. Originally, this society was dominated by morphologists, and the AAA should take pride in the fact that it originally was a major part of its root system. Indeed, cell biologists should never be allowed to forget that knowledge of cellular fine structure constitutes the very foundation of their discipline.

THE DEFINITIVE TECHNICAL REVOLUTION

From its first use, as early as 1949, it was realized that there were curious problems associated with methacrylate as an embedding medium. Polymerization itself not uncommonly, but seemingly haphazardly, sometimes produced "explosion damage." This was later attributed to polymerization expanding with discrete fronts from relatively widely separated centers, thus pushing cellular components about. Individual cells might be swollen and cytomembranes broken. Cytoplasm could have a flocculent look with "empty" patches. To some extent, successful efforts were made to counter this with various "seeding" techniques, particularly including partial prepolymerization before tissue infiltration.

A second problem with methacrylate concerned its partial volatilization in an electron beam. The organizational pattern of fine structural elements, such as the triple-layered appearance of cytomembranes, was then apt to disappear as support was lost and collapse occurred at macromolecular levels. This eventually led to a suggestion that divinyl benzene be added to the polymerization mixture to cross-link the methacrylate. This worked well. However, this and related agents are now recognized as being highly carcinogenic substances, so it is fortunate that other cross-linked embedments came into being at about the same time. The new generation of embedments deliberately cross-linked either epoxy or polyester monomeric components. The resulting plastics then did not decompose during electron bombardment.

Prototype experiments with epoxies were first reported by O. Maaløe and A. Birch-Anderson in 1956, but it remained for A.J. Glauert, G.E. Rogers, and R.H. Glauert later in the same year to introduce the first practical epoxy embedment, using "Araldite M." This was an English-made resin which turned out to be slightly but significantly different from its American counterpart. This initially caused confusion and frustration on this side of the Atlantic, because the British successes were not generally duplicated here. It was not until John Luft introduced Epon 812 as the resin of choice that cytologists worldwide had an easily obtainable and reasonably reliable epoxy embedment. Although Luft did not formally publish his Epon protocol until 1961, word-of-mouth information about it was available at least as early as 1959, and Luft was generous in supplying those who asked with typewritten copies of his protocol.

Meanwhile, A. Ryter and E. Kellenberger (1958) in Switzerland successfully developed a cross-linked polyester resin, Vestopal W, with many of the same properties for embedding purposes as the epoxies. For a while this became quite popular in Europe, but was never used much in the United States because of the difficulties of importing it directly from Geneva.

The microtomy story cannot be ended here, however, for the development of the cross-linked embedments immediately led to another problem. These non-volatilizing plastics, constituting the background material of any section, had very nearly the same electron density as the organic biological materials that one wanted to visualize. It became imperative to develop and rely on differential, heavy metal stains to observe specimens. Except for phosphotungstic acid (and osmium tetroxide introduced as a fixative), these hardly existed in the early 1950s, nor were they particularly necessary with methacrylate sections; for as volatilization occurred during electron bombardment, the specimen image became visible with generally good contrast against an increasingly brighter background. It was almost like watching a photographic print being developed.

This is not to say, of course, that numerous investigators had not explored a long list of easily available heavy metal compounds, generally with little demonstrable success. M.L. Watson, in 1957, published the most exhaustive of these studies, which included lead "hydroxide." This was the one electron stain that serendipitously turned out to be highly effective with the cross-linked embedments, particularly following pretreatments with osmium tetroxide and uranyl acetate. The active stain was by no means simple lead hydroxide, which is highly insoluble. The original, somewhat elaborate, formulation proved to be extremely susceptible to lead carbonate precipitates, both during its preparation and its use. It was so sensitive, in fact, that this led to the publication of a number of ingenious strategies to exclude carbon dioxide during all processing steps. A fully satisfactory solution to the dilemma was not forthcoming until the lead was chelated, first by G. Millonig in 1961 with tartrate, and more successfully in 1963 by E. Reynolds, who substituted citrate.

Originally, the most serious biological problem encountered was how best to fix tissue to preserve fine structure. It proved to be the last major problem to be resolved. Although buffered osmium tetroxide served cell biologists very well for a critical decade, it gradually became apparent that it was often destructive at macromolecular levels of observation when it was used as a primary fixative (formaldehyde was known to be completely inadequate when used by itself, and the other conventional fixatives of light microscopy had quickly proved to be disastrous). The big break came in 1963 when D. Sabatini, K. Bensch, and R. Barrnett demonstrated the virtues of glutaraldehyde. First and foremost, because it was a dialdehyde, it had excellent cross-linking properties, particularly with proteins, yet the enzymatic properties of many proteins were not destroyed, indicating the survival of much native structure. Also, it could readily be perfused (unlike osmium tetroxide); and when this was done, preservation patterns were generally uniformly good. It could be used with a variety of buffers and salt solutions, as well as be successfully blended with formaldehyde, which increased the rate of fixative penetration (Karnovsky, 1965). *En-bloc* secondary fixation with osmium tetroxide and/or uranyl salts often proved to be additionally effective and particularly advantageous when used as a prelude to the alkaline lead stains.

Thus, in 1963, the keystone that supports our present technology of ultramicrotomy was finally put in place. The stones that built the arch were laid by many investigators, a high proportion of them American. A good number were identifiable as anatomists, but they included also those in related disciplines, particularly pathology. Some of the seminal contributions were mechanical, others required chemical expertise. Thus, the highly successful end result of a 15-year technological journey coordinated very diverse skills toward a common end. The methodology, even in its developmental phases, had permitted anatomists, in particular, to go on to make the fundamental morphological discoveries of cellular fine structure that are an integral part of our modern biology.

SUGGESTED READINGS

Transmission Electron Microscopes

Burton, E. F., and W.H. Kohl 1946 The magnetic electron microscope. In: The Electron Microscope, 2nd edition. Reinhold, New York, Chapter 17, pp. 207–219.

Hawkes, P.W. 1985 The beginnings of electron microscopy. In: Advances in Electronics and Electron Physics, Suppl. 16. P.W. Hawkes, ed. Academic Press, Orlando, pp. 1–633.
Marton, L. 1968 Early History of the Electron Microscope. San Francisco Press Inc., San Francisco (also W. Heffer & Sons, Ltd., Cambridge, England), pp. 1–56.
Mulvey, T. 1967 The history of the electron microscope. Proc. R. Microsc. Soc., *2*:201–227.
Reisner, J. H. 1981–1983 Reflections. Electron Microsc. Soc. Am. Bulls., *11–13*:10–19.

Ultramicrotomes and Ultramicrotomy

Claude, A. 1948 Studies on cells: morphology, chemical constitution, and distribution of biochemical functions. Harvey Lect. *43*:1921–1964.
Gettner, M., and L. Ornstein. 1956 Microtomy. In: Physical Techniques in Biological Research. G. Oster and A. Polister, eds. Academic Press, New York, Vol. 3, Chapter 13, pp. 627–668.
Pease, D.C. 1964 Introductory remarks to chapters. In: Histological Techniques for Electron Microscopy, 2nd edition. Academic Press, New York, pp. 1-379.
Pease, D.C., and K.R. Porter. 1981 Electron microscopy and ultramicrotomy. J. Cell Biol., *91*(3): 287s–292s.
Porter, K.R. 1964 Ultramicrotomy. In: Modern Developments in Electron Microscopy. B. M. Siegel, Ed. Academic Press, New York, Chapter 4, pp. 119–145.
Sitte, H. 1955 Ein einfaches Ultramikrotom für hochauflösende elektronenmikroskopische Untersuchungen. Mikroskopie, *10*: 365–396.
Sjöstrand, F.S. 1967 The preparing of thin specimens for electron microscopy. In: Electron Microscopy of Tissues and Cells. F. S. Sjöstrand, ed. Academic Press, New York, Vol. 1, Chapter 9, pp. 222–310.

Early Achievements

Conference on Tissue Fine Structure. 1956 J. Biophys. Biochem. Cytol. (Suppl.), *2*:1–154.
Electron Microscopy: 1956 Proceedings of the Stockholm Conference (1st European Regional Conference). F. S. Sjöstrand and J. Rhodin, eds. Almqvist and Wiksell, Stockholm, 1957, pp. 1–355.
Proc. 3rd Int. Conf. Electron Microscopy, London, 1954, R. Microsc. Soc., London, 1956, pp. 1–705.
Proc. 4th Int. Conf. Electron Microscopy, Berlin, 1958. Springer-Verlag, Berlin, 1960, Vol. 2, Biol. Med., pp. 1–639.

Chapter 5

ELECTRON MICROSCOPY OF
CULTURED CELLS

Keith R. Porter

Some of the older anatomists will remember that the possibility of viewing cells or sections of cells with the electron microscope seemed very remote during the first few years that instruments were available. The problem was one of specimen thickness, and if biological objects such as bacteria and even cilia were too thick for beam penetration and resolution of detail, one could hardly expect to view the interior of whole tissue cells. The cutting of sections substantially thinner than 1μm was not ordinarily possible with the microtomes available in the 1940–1945 period. The success that was eventually attained might have come sooner had not World War II consumed brains and energy that might have been applied to the various technological problems encountered.

During part of this early period in electron microscope (EM) design and manufacture, the author was attempting to follow the *in vitro* transformation of cells to malignancy, much as Wilton Earle was doing successfully at NIH. As everyone who has grown and observed cells *in vitro* knows, they have a tendency to spread out to extreme thinness, apparently in an attempt to cover as much of the substrate as possible. They are beautiful for light microscopy and microphotography, as many of the early publications will attest (Lewis, 1923; Richardson, 1934). Although not a peer among the microscopists of that time, I was experienced enough to perceive that such diaphanous cells might be suitable for electron microscopy, at least in their thinner margins. An opportunity, when it came, to use the only RCA-EMB in New York City was quickly seized. The instrument in prospect was housed in the laboratories of Interchemical Corporation located on the west side of Manhattan at 45th Street. It was operated by Ernest Fullam, a graduate in microscopy from Cornell. Albert Claude had been using the microscope at the invitation of Albert Gessler, Director of Research at Interchemical. Claude's purpose was to get images of the microsome fraction he was isolating from chicken tumors and chick embryo tissues. We were allowed to bring specimens to the instrument after regular working hours when Fullam was available to help us. The preparation of adequate specimens was, at first, a discouraging process, but not totally so. I found that most cells able to grow *in vitro* would grow on Formvar[1]-coated coverslips and that the Formvar film could be peeled from a glass surface and transferred under water to the EM grids then in use.[2] When the grid, held between the points of watchmaker's forceps, was removed from the water and drained on filter paper, the Formvar film stretched over and adhered to the grid surface. The technique required a steady hand as well as determination and endurance. Approximately 50% of the specimens were satisfactory (Porter et al., 1945; Porter, 1953).

The reader can well imagine that fixation to preserve faithfully the structure of the cells seemed a serious problem. However, as it turned out, we could not have been more fortunate. In a paper published much earlier by Strangeways and Canti (1927), it was shown convincingly that OsO_4 produced the least obvious distortion of any of the several fixations they tried. Furthermore, it could be applied as a "vapor" from a 2% solution. All one had to do was to invert the coverglass with live cells in place over a well slide containing two or three drops of the osmium solution. Watching the cells during fixation included some hazards for the observer, but not ordinarily bad enough to impair one's sight for more than a couple of days. Since essentially no observable change in the cells resulted from the fixation, the watching step in the procedure was soon abandoned. As everyone now knows, this fixation has the added advantage of "staining" the specimen, in that some organelles reduce the OsO_4 more actively than others, and osmium scatters electrons very actively.

When the time came to put the specimen into the electron microscope, not much of worth was expected. To our everlasting delight, however, the first specimen was surprisingly good and served to introduce the observers to more structural information than had been expected or could be interpreted (Fig. 5.1).

These initial successes introduced a first-phase in the application of electron microscopy to cell biology, and during the years that immediately followed, we attempted to exploit the techniques that combined tissue culture and electron microscopy. It became suddenly feasible to look at cells derived from tumors to observe whether virus-like particles might be present. Since Murphy's[3] laboratory had had a long-standing interest in chicken tumors that could be transmitted by filter-passing agents (Chicken Tumor 1) (Claude and Murphy, 1933), it was our first interest to look at a couple of these. Chicken Tumor 1 (later known as the Rous sarcoma) was the first target, and Claude and I succeeded in getting images of some cells from this tumor (Claude et al., 1947).[4] We found, not unexpectedly, numerous virus-sized particles (70 nm). These were scattered somewhat randomly throughout the cytoplasm. More or less simultaneously we looked at cells from another chicken tumor (C.T. 10) with characteristics that set it apart from Chicken Tumor 1. It was relatively slow growing and compact. Here the cells also contained virus-like particles, which were frequently in compact patches (crystalline arrays).

---

[1] A polyvinyl formal sold by the Shawinigan Products Corporation, New York.

[2] These were grids punched from sheets of stainless steel cloth used by photoengravers.

[3] James B. Murphy was chief of the laboratory for cancer research at Rockefeller Institute.

[4] By 1947 the Rockefeller Foundation had purchased an RCA-EMU and had it installed in space rented from the Rockefeller Institute. It was cared for by E.G. Pickels who, in turn, allowed us to use it.

These were among the first EM observations ever made on virus-infected cells, and while they were not startling in any major respect, they did show what could be done. No striking pathology of the tumor cells was evident as virus-related.

In this same period, cancer biologists were interested in mouse mammary tumors that could be transmitted by the Bittner milk factor. With Lynn Thompson, a postdoctoral fellow in the laboratory, we cultured epithelial sheets from mammary tumors and transferred them to grids as in other instances (Porter and Thompson, 1948). Here, also, virus-like particles were found and studied for size and other characteristics. In this study we made use of the "shadowing" techniques that had been introduced by Williams and Wyckoff (1946). The procedure highlighted the virus particles and made their identification somewhat easier. It should be noted parenthetically that this technique, and the brilliance it brought to virus studies, did much to give electron microscopy respectability in the biomedical world.

About this same time, Thompson and I examined cells grown from a rat sarcoma known as 4337 (Porter and Thompson, 1947). Since the causative agent here had not been identified as virus-like, this was doubly exciting. Particles were found but not with virus-like characteristics. In retrospect, they were probably coated endocytic vesicles associated with the rapid turnover of the cell surface in tumor cells.

These studies involving cultured cells and electron microscopy did not exhaust

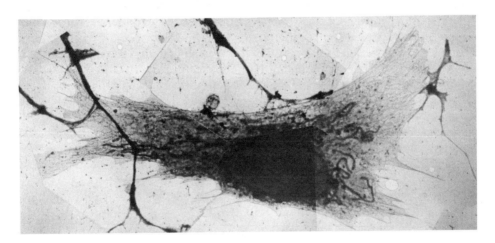

Fig. 5.1. Electron micrograph of a fibroblast-like cell cultured from an explant of gizzard derived from a 14-day-old chick embryo. The nucleus is obviously too thick for penetration of low-energy electrons (60-kv beam), but the cytoplasm is mostly thin enough, especially at the margins of the cell. The dense strands outside the cell are non-myelinated nerve fibers. Of these, a growth cone is shown in contact with the cell at the bottom of the image. The mitochondria are easily identified as are also portions of the lacelike ER. It was necessary with the RCA-EMB to take the cell in several micrographs and then piece them together. Microscopes of that era were not equipped to take low-power, high-resolution images. For fixation, the cell, in balanced salt solution (Locke's), was exposed to vapors of OsO_4 from a 2% solution of the compound for 45 min. It was then washed for 30 min in distilled water. During this latter period, portions of the Formvar film with cells attached were transferred to steel grids. The density of the specimen is in part provided by the osmium, which acts as a stain as well as a fixative. $\times$ 1,600.

the possibilities of the approach by any means. There were, however, other interests competing for research and microscope time. In large measure these focused on the assembly of collagen and fibrin filaments.

In this connection it became important to observe fibroblasts in the act of putting down collagen fibers. George Pappas was my collaborator in this effort (Porter and Pappas, 1959). Together and separately we were of one mind after extensive culturing of chick fibroblasts and electron microscopy by the then-established techniques. The relationship of the extracellular fibers and what appeared as intracellular stress fibers convinced us that the fibroblast is intimately associated in orienting the assembly of the collagen fibrils. This made sense at the time and still does. That the fibroblast and related cell types of the connective tissue synthesize collagen is well established. But, for some reason, 30 years ago it was not recognized that connective tissue comprises organized populations of fibroblasts and that those have the capacity to exert control over the disposition and orientation of collagen fibers.

THE ENDOPLASMIC RETICULUM

In the earliest micrographs of cultured cells, it was possible always to identify a lacelike component in the cytoplasm that could not be readily identified with any equivalent in the light-microscope image. It was not easy to see in some of the early micrographs. This was not due to any limitation of the microscope but resulted instead from the presence around it of some electron-scattering matrix or ground substance. Later, we learned to get rid of this by simply fixing the cells overnight in vapors of OsO_4. While active initially in "fixing" the matrix, the OsO_4 subsequently undid the fixation and rendered that part of the cell soluble in the balanced salt solution used to bathe the cells during fixation. It was this fortuitous action that gave us a better image of all the membrane-limited structures in the cytoplasm. We learned from such preparations, and micrographs of them, that this lacelike component was limited by a membrane, because in the dried preparation we could identify small folds in its surfaces. Thus, the lacelike component came to be recognized as a complex vacuolar system. Its position in the endoplasm and its reticular structure in these thinly spread cultured cells led us to call it the endoplasmic reticulum or ER (Porter and Kallman, 1952).

Before the thin sections of pancreas cells (among others) had enabled Palade (1955) to find the little particles now called ribosomes, we had come to the conclusion (slowly and with some pain) that the endoplasmic reticulum had the same configuration as the basophilic component (Porter, 1953) and that it ought to be identified with what Garnier (1900) had seen in protein-secreting cells and called the ergastoplasm (work plasma). It was simultaneously pictured by Mathews, then a student of E.B. Wilson's at Columbia.[5] Now, of course, it is known to exist in general forms of which the two commonest are the rough (RER) and the smooth (SER, without ribosomes), which is involved in some instances in monitoring the concentration of intracellular free calcium.

---

[5] The Mathews study was surprisingly good for its time, but received less than the attention it deserved (Mathews, 1899).

Preparing cultured cells for electron microscopy never achieved great popularity among electron microscopists. It was a procedure for the few with some degree of finger dexterity. It was, however, better than nothing and did have some influence on what followed. For example, the fixation with OsO_4 was good and owed its quality in part to the fact that the cells were in balanced salt solution while exposed to the vapors of OsO_4. "Buffered osmium," subsequently recommended as a fixative for intact tissues, owed some of its credentials to the cultured-cell experience. The observation that prolonged exposure to OsO_4 resulted in an extraction of practically everything from the cell except membranes helped to gauge the quality of image one wanted from thin sections of tissue blocks. Then also, cultured cells as useful objects for studies in cell biology have certain limitations that are not shared by tissue cells fixed *in situ*.

CUTTING THIN SECTIONS

In the period between 1948 and 1953, the emphasis was on sectioning and how, if ever, one was going to get sections thin enough for electron penetration. For a discussion of this interesting topic, the reader is referred to Pease's chapter in this book and to Pease and Porter (1981) in that special issue of the *Journal of Cell Biology* that celebrates its 25th year as a successful journal. Neither of these is definitive in recording accurately all of the facts and this account will not, in this respect, be any different. The author was intimately involved with the design and production of *the* successful model and feels entitled to set the record straight on two or three accounts.

First, any similarity the MT-1 bears to the Cambridge Rocking microtome is simply accidental. We never had one of the Cambridge instruments in the laboratory at Rockefeller, and I have never seen one. Second, the comment on the origins of the MT-1 in the popular Alberts et al. text (1983) is utterly false. Fritjof Sjöstrand never designed a microtome bearing the slightest resemblance to the MT-1. Actually, the microtome he put together, initially for his own use, was very similar to the instrument that Claude and Fullam designed and built around 1949. Finally, as I noted in a video recording of my early life,[6] edited by Mary Bonneville, the MT-1 owed at least one of its design features, the rocking arm, to an instrument that Stan Bennett was developing in his laboratory when I was there in the summer of 1952. Stan and I did enough that summer with a then-popular Spencer rotary to realize that thin sections could be obtained, and that a microtome of simple design, if produced, would be extremely popular. The first preliminary models were very crude, but good enough to prove the point. Joseph Blum, an excellent instrument maker, then at Rockefeller, added the gimbal, for universal motion of the bar, and a mechanical advance. We had a microtome (Porter and Blum, 1953)! Incidentally, no patents were taken out on the instrument until Blum went to work for Ivan Sorvall, Inc. No royalties were ever distributed to the designers. We were working at that time in an institution (Rockefeller) that was operated for the benefit of mankind.

---

[6] Available for viewing upon request to M. Bonneville.

HIGH-VOLTAGE MICROSCOPY

As far as cultured cells were concerned, they took a back seat to microtomy and thin sections for about 20 years. It was not until high-voltage microscopes became available that one could again dream of looking at intact (whole) cells and of obtaining, additionally, three-dimensional images recording their fine structure.

There are several reasons why this became important and why cultured cells offered new possibilities. For one thing, the culturing itself was much easier than in 1944. The conditions required for successful culturing were improved with the availability of commercial media, sterile plasticware, and antibiotics. In addition, completely defined media were on the shelf and needed only double-distilled water to make them useful, with greatly expanded experimental possibilities. Not insignificant, also, was the recognition by anatomists that the thin section was a very small fragment of the cell and that to gain an appreciation of organization in cells one needed to see the depth dimension of the entire living unit. Serial thick sections, much easier to produce than thin sections, became uniquely valuable for computer-aided graphics. Finally, we found that cells could be grown on gold grids covered with Formvar and evaporated carbon.

Hence, in the new regimen cells are grown on the grids, fixed in glutaraldehyde and OsO_4, deprived of water in anhydrous acetone, and dried by the critical point method. Alternatively, they can be instantaneously frozen at liquid nitrogen temperatures and dried while frozen at $-95°C$. The way is opened for a wealth of new investigation into not only structure but also structural changes associated with cell motion or intracellular translocations. Specific antigens in or on the cells can be identified with gold-labeled antibodies, and the genesis of viruses relative to cell structure is simple to follow.

It seemed to us, for several reasons, that the cell matrix could not be a soup lacking the capability of controlling the non-random disposition of organelles. The uniform size and shape of cells of the same kind seemed to require the existence of a unit structure in the cytoplasm, a structure in which the better known filaments of the cytoplasm are contained, and in which organizational information is expressed.

For these and essentially only these reasons, we acquired a 1 Mev electron microscope. It proved to be no disappointment. Instead it has, for years, turned out excellent images in large numbers. (Fig. 5.2). It is a shared facility supported by grants from the Biotechnology Resources Program at NIH. As such, it is available to anyone who has an appropriate project. There have been many users, some anatomists, some pathologists, and some cell biologists. The down-time has been minimal. If one studies the papers that have emerged from data collected with the microscope, one is bound to be impressed. That more might have been done with a more highly organized approach is not denied. It should, however, be remembered that it is only one installation and that capabilities in terms of micrograph numbers do not go up with the voltage.

We have used the high-voltage electron microscope (HVEM) to explore the cytoplasmic ground substance, also called the cytoplasmic matrix (cytomatrix for short). This includes, for some students, all of the filamentous components as well as the obvious strands (microtrabeculae, 10–30 nm in diameter) that interconnect the filaments and the membrane-limited components of the cytoplasm. This system appears to comprise a vast three-dimensional network or lattice (the micro-

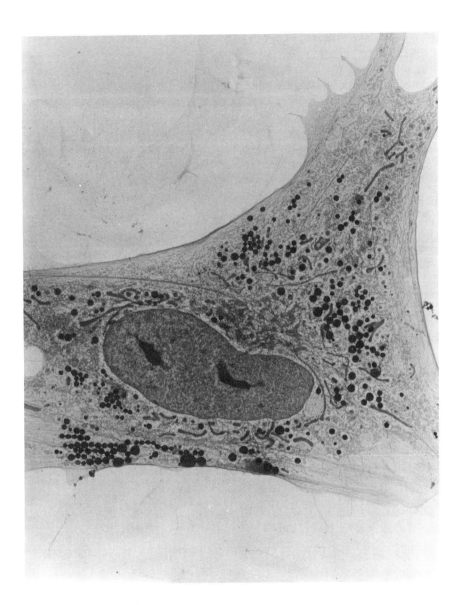

Fig. 5.2. A low-magnification image of a whole fibroblast cultured from an explant of lung tissue from a 14-day-incubated chick embryo. It is evident that the high-energy electrons (100 kv) are better able to penetrate the nucleus and other parts of the cell than was true of the 60-kv beam. The cell center is just left of the nucleus in a shallow hof. Other components of the cytoplasm tend to adopt a radial arrangement relative to the center. Mitochondria, stress fibers, and lipid granules are easily identified. In places the lacelike configuration of the ER can be seen. Other fine structure at this low magnification is difficult to discern. Fixation was with glutaraldehyde (15 min) followed by OsO_4, a 1% water solution, for 5 min. Comparison of this image with the cell in Figure 5.1 illustrates the improvement achieved with the higher voltage instrument. × 3,000.

trabecular lattice, MTL) that contains the better known components of the cytoplasm (Porter et al., 1983). It can be regarded as a unit structure with its center of organization in the cytocentrum or centrosome, i.e., two centrioles and a population of dense bodies (microtubule organizing centers or MTOCs) that initiate microtubule assembly. It divides the cytoplasm into two phases, one protein-rich and the other water-rich. The former supports and accounts for the distribution of microtubules, microfilaments, and ribosomes; the latter is thought to provide for the diffusion of small molecule metabolites and the maintenance of intracellular homeostasis. The system is dynamic in the sense that it is constantly changing locally, and on the larger scale it is thought to be responsible for the relatively macroscopic motion of larger organelles, such as parts of the ER, lysosomes, and endocytic vesicles. In chromatophores, a related form of the lattice participates in the rapid motion of pigment granules.

These observations and speculations obviously open to view and experimentation a newly identified component of the cytoplasm. There is a suggestion of its activity available to the viewer in video-recorded images of living cells, but more research is required to understand and use this light-microscope adjunct to the electron-microscope picture.

One is always concerned lest one is investigating artifacts from some step in the preparation of the specimen. Great care has been taken to control the conditions of fixation and drying and additionally to avoid the use of chemical fixatives, as well as critical point drying, by freezing the cells at liquid nitrogen temperatures and drying from the frozen state with the specimen at $-95°C$. The images and dimensions are basically the same regardless of the procedure. Acceptance of the system as genuine would be easier if there were some evidence of order in the disposition of trabeculae relative to microtubules where they would seem to represent membrane-associated proteins (MAPs). However, in cells, there is nothing of the sort that one finds in the disposition of spokes in axenomes of cilia and flagella, structures that in their dimensions closely resemble microtrabeculae.

There is no appropriate place to end this story. The technology that has been introduced over the last four decades will doubtless grow and expand in what it can achieve. Instrumentation, especially associated with light microscopy, is improving enormously, and it looks as if the living cell will again enjoy a period of popularity such as it has not enjoyed since 1945. Any anatomist thinking of going into biochemistry should think again.

REFERENCES

Alberts, B., D. Bray, J. Lewis, M. Raff, K. Roberts, and J.D. Watson 1983 Molecular Biology of the Cell. Garland Publishing, Inc., New York, p. 158.

Claude, A., and J.B. Murphy 1933 Transmissible tumors of the fowl. Physiol. Rev., *13*:246–275.

Claude, A., K.R. Porter, and E.G. Pickels 1947 Electron microscope study of chicken tumor cells. Cancer Res. *7*:421–430.

Garnier, C. 1900 Contribution a l'etude de la structure et du fonctionnement des cellules glandulaires sereuses. Du role de l'ergastroplasme dans la secretion. J. Anat. Physiol. 36:22

Lewis, W.H. 1923 Amniotic ectoderm in tissue cultures. Anat. Rec. 26:97–118.

Mathews, A. 1899 The changes in the structure of the pancreas cell. A consideration of some aspects of cell metabolism. J. Morphol. (Suppl.), *15*:171–222

Palade, G.E. 1955 A small particulate component of the cytoplasm. J. Biophys. Biochem. Cytol., 1:59–68.

Pease, D.C., and K.R. Porter 1981 Electron microscopy and ultramicrotomy. J. Cell Biol., 91:287s–292s.

Porter, K.R. 1953 Observations on a submicroscopic basophilic component of cytoplasm. J. Exp. Med., 97:727–750.

Porter, K.R., M. Beckerle, and M. McNiven 1983 The cytoplasmic matrix. In: Modern Cell Biology. B.H. Satir, ed.; Vol. 2: Spatial Organization of Eukaryotic Cells. J.R. McIntosh, ed. Alan R. Liss, Inc., New York, pp. 259–302.

Porter, K.R., and J. Blum 1953 A study in microtomy for electron microscopy. Anat. Rec., 117:685–710.

Porter, K.R., A. Claude, and E.F. Fullam 1945 A study of tissue culture cells by electron microscopy; Methods and preliminary observations. J. Exp. Med., 81:233–246.

Porter, K.R., and F.L. Kallman 1952 Significance of cell particulates as seen by electron microscopy. Ann. N.Y. Acad. Sci., 54:882–891.

Porter, K.R., and G.D. Pappas 1959 Collagen formation by fibroblasts of the chick embryo dermis. J. Biophys. Biochem. Cytol. 5:153–166.

Porter, K.R., and H.P. Thompson 1947 Some morphological features of cultured rat sarcoma cells as revealed by the electron microscope. Cancer Res., 7:431–438.

Porter, K.R., and H.P. Thompson 1948 A particulate body associated with epithelial cells cultured from mammary carcinomas of mice of a milk-factor strain. J. Exp. Med., 88:15–24.

Richardson, K.C. 1934 Golgi: Apparatus and other cytoplasmic structures in normal and degenerate cells in vitro. Arch. Exp. Zellforsch., 16:100–115.

Strangeways, T.S.P., and R.G. Canti 1927 Living cell in vitro as shown by dark-ground illumination and changes induced in such cells by fixing reagents. Q. J. Microsc. Sci., 71: 1–14.

Williams, R.C., and R.W.G. Wyckoff 1946 Applications of metallic shadow-casting to microscopy. J. Appl. Phys., 17:23–33.

Chapter 6

FREEZE-FRACTURE IN ULTRASTRUCTURE RESEARCH: A HISTORICAL PERSPECTIVE

James K. Koehler

The use of freezing as a possible method of preserving cells and tissues for structural investigations was already shown to be feasible by the work of Altmann (1890) almost a century ago. Gersch (1932) and his followers, among others, made very significant contributions to the solution of histological and histochemical studies because of the retention of chemical activities after freeze fixation. After the advent of the electron microscope, it was natural that investigators attempted to extend such freezing methods to the fine-structure level. It was immediately obvious that whereas an ice crystal viewed in a cell at 0.1-μm resolution in a light microscope was, at worst, slightly annoying, in the electron microscope at 1 nm, it was disastrous. Except for a few dedicated and persistent groups of investigators (Bernhard and LeDuc, 1967; Christensen, 1971), the use of freeze-fixation approaches was temporarily shelved in favor of more traditional chemical fixation for fine structural studies. In the past decade or so, methods such as freeze-substitution, freeze-drying, and particularly cryoultramicrotomy have enjoyed a significant renaissance due to greatly improved fast-freezing methods and instrumentation (DuBochet et al., 1983).

During the past two decades, however, it has been the results of work done with the freeze-fracture method that have made the most significant advances in the area of cell biology. The method derives this status largely from the fact that it involves the examination of biological material while it is in the deeply frozen state. The cells are not partially thawed or intervened with in order to infiltrate, stain, or otherwise treat the material at temperatures that could cause recrystallation of ice. This fact makes freeze-fracture qualitatively different from most other methods and allows us in this brief historical sketch to concentrate on this procedure rather than to attempt to include other cryotechniques in the discussion. This is not meant to imply that these other approaches are not equally important or interesting, or that it is not appropriate, where possible, to correlate the results of freeze-fracture work with such approaches as well as conventional electron microscopy.

HISTORICAL DEVELOPMENT

The pioneering work of Cecil Hall (1950) in the physics and optics of electron microscopy included the initial suggestion of freeze-etching as a specimen-preparation procedure. Thirty-five years ago, Hall reasoned that the sublimation of ice from frozen material followed by a replication process could produce a replica for examination at electron optical resolution. Hall not only supplied the idea, but carried out some interesting initial experiments involving inorganic crystal morphology. Merryman and his coworkers in the mid-1950s introduced more sophisticated instrumentation for fracturing specimens *"in vacuo"* and studied various forms of ice structure. Russel Steere (1957) published the first successful freeze-fracture study of biological material in his work on tobacco mosaic virus. Steere used an instrument of his own design, which involved cutting the frozen specimen in the vacuum, and he developed a prototype of a commercial machine that (highly modifed) is still being marketed.

Although these early experiments were interesting, they were considered by most fine-structure workers as minor and rather esoteric embellishments to conventional preparative methods. New and exciting discoveries of cytological detail were being made by such conventional methods almost on a daily basis in the 1950s and 1960s, so that new technologies such as freeze-fracture were by no means immediate successes or even of general interest to the ultrastructural community. The work of Hans Moor (Fig. 6.1) and his associates in Switzerland,

Fig. 6.1.   Hans Moor.

Fig. 6.2.   Daniel Branton.

however, put freeze-fracture and freeze-etching on the "cell biological map" beginning with a major publication in 1961. This paper described a rather elaborate instrument that performed freeze-fracture and freeze-etchng in a rapid, precise, and highly reliable fashion. This machine was basically a heavy-duty, high-vacuum evaporator fitted with a controlled freezing stage for the specimen and a liquid nitrogen-cooled microtome similar to the Porter-Blum design. This prototype developed into the Balzer's machine in the mid-1960s and evolved into the second and third generation instruments still marketed by that company. The biological studies initiated in this early paper and in subsequent papers from Moor's group were remarkable in the wealth of new detail shown, particularly focusing on yeast cell fine structure. Structures involved in the yeast cell wall and attached membrane, which had not been seen by other methods, were visualized.

By the mid-1960s, numbers of additional workers had adopted the freeze-fracture approach as an adjunct to conventional methods of fine-structure research. Haggis (1961) and Bullivant and Ames (1966) had separately developed simplified procedures for freeze-fracture and carried out initial studies on red blood cells showing, among other details, the ubiquitous membrane-associated particles that were to become such an integral component of the fluid mosaic hypothesis of the plasma membrane. Daniel Branton (Fig. 6.2) and I both spent some time in Hans Moor's laboratory in 1961–1962, becoming familar with freeze-fracture methods and other aspects of the institute directed by Dr. A. Frey-Wyssling. We both returned to the United States hoping to develop freeze-fracture laboratories to explore our respective interests in cell biology.

The Membrane Splitting Hypothesis

Although freeze-fracture work was well underway in a number of laboratories by the mid-1960s, several problems concerning interpretation existed that made definitive explanations of the observations difficult or impossible. Many of us were so infatuated by the unique quality of the images of cells created by freeze-fracture that such interpretative problems did not inhibit our productivity, even though we often had little that was meaningful to say about the results.

Two problems were of particular importance and occupied the experimental expertise of several groups. The first, and most significant, of these questions concerned the problem of determining precisely where the fracture plane traversed the specimen during preparation, when a membranous structure was encountered by the scalpel or razor blade. The latter half of the 1960s saw an animated debate on this topic, especially between the Moor and Branton groups. Moor consistently took the position that the surface (inner and outer) of the membrane was revealed by the fracturing process, whereas Branton became convinced that membranes were split down the hydrophobic center. I do not intend to go into all of the pros and cons generated during those years, since they were well documented in an earlier review for those that might be interested (Koehler, 1968). However, it is instructive to summarize briefly the points mentioned in Branton's landmark paper (1966), in which he expounds his view of membrane splitting.

1) When single membranes that have been cross-fractured and also show *en-face* views are carefully analyzed, the face view seems to be continuous with the center of the cross-fractured membrane.

2) When etched and nonetched images of cells are examined, it appears that membrane faces show little, if any, change upon etching, whereas nonfacial structures become progressively pitted. Branton reasoned that this nonetchable feature was consistent with the lipoidal face created by splitting the membrane, whereas the hydrophilic surfaces should be etchable.

3) Particles such as those on certain plastid surfaces or rough endoplasmic reticulum were generally not visualized after freeze-fracturing, presumably because such surfaces were not revealed by the process.

These and similar arguments made by Branton and his coworkers were intriguing and correlated with a good deal of other data on membrane structure, but were, nevertheless, indirect in nature. At the time, some of Moor's arguments seemed equally logical, such as the finding of fine filaments that appeared to connect the membrane "surface" to the cell walls of various bacterial and yeast cells.

Indirect evidence favoring the idea of membrane splitting mounted after Branton's initial paper on the subject; finally, work with surface labels on red blood cells provided definitive, direct evidence that membrane splitting did indeed occur, at least in this system. That evidence was forthcoming in two papers published in the same issue of the *Journal of Cell Biology,* just 50 pages apart. The first of these reports (Pinto da Silva and Branton, 1970) illustrated the appearance of rabbit red blood cells before and after labeling the surface covalently with ferritin. Ferritin, although roughly spherical in shape, is much larger than the usual membrane-associated particles seen after fracturing membranes and could be easily detected on the deep-etched surface of the red blood cells, but not on the faces created after ordinary freeze-fracture. Thus, subliming away the ice from the true membrane surface exposed structures attached to it. Tillack and Marchesi (1970), a few pages later, described similar experiments using human red blood cells to which F-actin had been linked. The simplest and, undoubtedly, the correct interpretation of these experiments was that the fracturing process cleaved membranes at a level other than the surface and that the faces so produced provided for the first time extended views of the interior of biological membranes.

The second interpretational problem, alluded to earlier, concerns the nature and location of the membrane-associated particles seen on virtually all animal and plant cell membrane faces. The particle question was further confounded by a number of reports that claimed they were artifacts created in the high vacuum by the condensation of impurities or water vapor. Such condensation artifacts can be created by improper technique or faulty equipment; however, they can always be differentiated from the *bona fide* particles by several criteria. The question of the location of these structures is, of course, related to the problem just discussed concerning the locus of the fracture plane in the membrane. Up to the time of the labeling experiments just described, Moor and his coworkers held a rather conservative view of membrane structure. The finding of particulate components associated with their images of membrane faces suggested a surface location to correlate with the earlier hypotheses of proteins coating the bilayer. Branton and others, including Weinstein and Bullivant (1967), had more liberal ideas concerning membrane modulations and felt that the particles might represent material intercalated into or even through the bilayer. Thus, the labeling studies demonstrated not only the locus of the fracture plane but also positioned the intramembranous particles, as the name implies, to the hydrophobic region of the bilayer.

Freeze-Fracture in the Modern Era

The clarification of questions concerning the location of membrane cleavage during freeze-fracturing and the intramembranous orientation of the membrane-associated particles set the stage for increased interest in and use of freeze-fracture technology in the early 1970s. The advent of commercial versions of the Moor-inspired instrument by the Balzer's High Vacuum Co. and Steere's machine by Denton Vacuum allowed a number of laboratories to utilize freeze-fracture to attack specific biological problems without becoming involved in developing instrumentation of their own. For the first time it was possible to visualize, at high resolution, the internal organization of cellular membranes. The developmental and physiological processes that occupied much of the experimental work of membrane biologists was now open to very detailed morphological analysis just short of the molecular level. Experiments during the next few years by Marchesi, Steck, Branton, and others using the red blood cell as a model showed that at least some of the intramembranous particles are protein in nature and intercalate into or span the bilayer. The discovery of spectrin was a biproduct of such studies. This type of analysis has been brought to a high level of precision in a series of studies on the membrane of the purple bacterium. These studies by Fisher and Stoeckenius (1977) have shown that the particles observed by freeze-fracture in this membrane are complexes of bacteriorhodopsin arranged in a precise crystalline array. Diffraction analysis has provided further details concerning the conformation of these structures. Approximately 7 molecules, each having as many as 12 alpha helical chains, combine in the complex to constitute the freeze-fracture particle. Studies such as these have set a pattern for the analysis of membrane proteins and glycoproteins by combining the use of freeze-fracture and protein chemical techniques to characterize the orientation and locus of various membrane activities. Such studies have also formed one of the major sources of evidence in support of the fluid mosaic model of the cell membrane.

Many other specific cellular organelles and membrane specializations became a focus for freeze-etch experimentation during the decade of the 1970s. A complete discussion or even listing of these studies is far beyond the charge of this short essay, but a few highlights should be mentioned. Although there was significant interest and work going on in the area of cell junctional biology, freeze-fracture provided the ideal morphological tool to examine these membrane specializations. Extensive *en-face* views of junctional connections provided information that would have been virtually impossible to obtain in other ways. For example, the interconnected strand appearance of tight junctions could not have been guessed at using conventional sections. Representative key papers that should be mentioned in this area include those of Staehelin et al. (1969), Goodenough and Revel (1970), and Gilula (1974).

Friend's work (1982, for example) has shown the incredible degree of structural differentiation present within the plasma membrane of the spermatozoon, whereas Karnovsky's group has used freeze-fracture to advantage in the analysis of membrane modulations of immune cells and cells in culture. Heuser et al. (1979) have demonstrated that "conventional" freeze-fracture preparations probably come with their own set of artifacts by using their ultrarapid freezing methods with unfixed and uncryoprotected specimens. With this approach, Heuser and co-workers have visualized membrane fusion phenomena in a number of systems including synaptic vesicles and cortical granules in oocytes.

A number of offshoots of the freeze-fracture approach have appeared that also are worthy of mention. Fisher (1976) has used the concept of membrane splitting to actually prepare and analyze "half membranes" of cells by freezing and cleaving between layers of glass. Pinto da Silva et al. (1981), whose name was mentioned earlier in conjunction with surface-labeled red blood cells, has recently developed a very interesting combination of freeze-fracture and conventional sectioning techniques. In this procedure called "fracture label," it is possible to specifically label internal membrane components and to visualize their localization using electron-microscopic markers.

In conclusion, perhaps one of the most important results of work done during the past two decades has not yet been mentioned. In the overwhelming majority of cases, freeze-fracture observations have generally confirmed views of the cell and its organelles that were generated using conventional techniques involving fixation, dehydration, and other procedures that might have resulted in massive artifactual changes. Freeze-fracture and the concept of membrane splitting have, however, greatly refined our notions of how cells are constructed and how they work and, in some cases, have provided evidence of structures that would previously not have been imagined.

REFERENCES

Altmann, R. 1890 Die Elementarorganismen und ihre Beziehungen zur den Zellen. Veit Publishers, Leipzig.

Bernhard, W., and E.H. Leduc 1967 Ultrathin frozen sections. I. Methods and ultrastructural preservation. J. Cell Biol., *34*:757–771.

Branton, D. 1966 Fracture faces of frozen membranes. Proc. Natl. Acad. Sci. U.S.A., 55:1048–1056.

Bullivant, S., and A. Ames 1966 A simple freeze-fracture replication method for electron microscopy. J. Cell Biol., 29:435–557.

Christensen, A.K. 1971 Frozen thin sections of fresh tissue for electron microscopy with a description of pancreas and liver. J. Cell Biol., 51:772–804.

Dubochet, J., A.W. McDowall, B. Menge, E.N. Schmid, and K.G. Lickfield 1983 Electron microscopy of frozen hydrated bacteria. J. Bact., 155:381–390.

Fisher, K.A. 1976. Analysis of membrane halves: Cholesterol. Proc. Natl. Acad. Sci. U.S.A., 73:173–177.

Fisher, K.A., and W. Stoeckenius 1977 Freeze-fractured purple membrane particles: Protein content. Science, 197:72–74.

Friend, D.S. 1982 Plasma membrane diversity in a highly polarized cell. J. Cell Biol., 93:243–249.

Gersch, I. 1932 The Altmann technique for fixation by drying while freezing. Anat. Rec., 53:309–337

Gilula, N.B. 1974 Junctions between cells. In: Cell Communication. R.P. Cox, ed. John Wiley & Sons, New York, pp. 1–29.

Goodenough, D.A., and J.P. Revel 1970 A fine structural analysis of intercellular junctions in the mouse liver. J Cell Biol., 45:272–290.

Haggis, G.H. 1961 Electron microscope replicas from the surface of a fracture through frozen cells. J. Biophys. Biochem. Cytol., 9:841–852.

Hall, C.E. 1950. A low temperature replica method for electron microscopy. J. Appl. Phys., 21:61–62.

Heuser, J.E., T.S. Reese, M.J. Dennis, Y. Jan, L. Jan, and L. Evans 1979 Synaptic vesicle exocytosis captured by quick freezing and correlated with neurotransmitter release. J. Cell Biol., 81:275–300.

Koehler, J.K. 1968 The technique and application of freeze-etching in ultrastructure research. In: Advances in Biological and Medical Physics. J.H. Lawrence and J.W. Gofman, eds., Academic Press, New York, Vol. 12, pp. 1–84.

Moor, H., K. Muhlethaler, H. Waldner, and A. Frey-Wyssling 1961 A new freezing ultramicrotome. J. Biophys. Biochem. Cytol., 10:1–13.

Pinto da Silva, P., and D. Branton. 1970 Membrane splitting in freeze-etching. J. Cell Biol., 45:598–605.

Pinto da Silva, P., C. Parkinson, and N. Dwyer 1981 Fracture-label: Cytochemistry of freeze-fractured faces in the erythrocyte membrane. Proc. Natl. Acad. Sci. U.S.A., 78:343–347.

Staehelin, A.L., T.M. Mukherjee, and A.W. Williams 1969 Freeze-etch appearance of the tight junctions in the epithelium of small and large intestine of mice. Protoplasm, 67:165–184.

Steere, R.L. 1957 Electron microscopy of structural detail in frozen biological specimens. J. Biophys. Biochem. Cytol., 3:45–60.

Tillack, T.W., and V.T. Marchesi 1970 Demonstration of the outer surface of freeze-etched red blood cell membranes. J. Cell Biol., 45:649–653.

Weinstein, R.S., and S. Bullivant 1967 The application of freeze-cleaving techniques to studies on red blood cell fine structure. Blood, 29:780–789.

Chapter 7

REFLECTIONS ON HISTOCHEMISTRY: THE PAST FIFTY YEARS

Tibor Barka

"There are several ways in which to lay out a little garden; the best way is to get a gardener."[1]

—*But who is the "gardener" of histochemistry?*

Writing this short contribution commemorating the 100th anniversary of the American Association of Anatomists from the vantage point of a histochemist has not been easy. Either the memory or the distance is too short to allow either accuracy or complete objectivity. What follows is thus a highly personal view; for omissions[2] and commissions only the author can be blamed, although the generous suggestions of many of his colleagues[3] are gratefully acknowledged.

I had the privilege of knowing many of the leading histochemists of our time who made or are making significant contributions to the field. I wish I could intersperse this brief essay with historical anecdotes, anecdotes that, like details of a Flemish tapestry, would convey the spirit of times passed, and the aspirations and frustrations of those who contributed substantially to the development of histochemistry and to its present appreciation as an important, constantly evolving methodology.

The premise of this brief account is that the scientists who developed and applied the histochemical methods have made lasting contributions to biology and

---

[1]Ĉapek, K., ed. 1984 The Gardener's Year. The University of Wisconsin Press, Madison, p. 1.

[2]I have made no attempt to provide an extensive bibliography, which can be found, on each topic, in the reviews cited, as well as in the texts of Glick (1949), Barka and Anderson (up to 1962), Thompson (1966), Geyer (1973), the series edited by Hayat (1974–1977), and, above all, in the new edition of Pearse (1980, 1985).

[3]P.J. Anderson, R.J. Barrnett, E.P. Benditt, H.S. Bennett, D. Glick, N.S. Halmi, C.P. Leblond, M.J. Karnovsky, F.H. Kasten, and B.V. Scharrer.

medicine. Many of these were anatomists, and, in the realm of science that recognizes no national boundaries, many were Americans.

From its early days, histochemistry had many definitions. Its objective to reveal the chemical nature of cellular and subcellular structures and tissue components as a basis toward an understanding of normal and altered functions has been a common element of all definitions. Within this broad interpretation, histochemistry encompasses not only microscopic and electron-microscopic histochemistry and immunocytochemistry, but also the application of microchemical and varied physical methods to localize and quantify chemically recognized substances in morphologically defined structures. What follows is based on such a broad definition.

No matter how brief, a historical review of histochemistry should neither glorify nor justify the discipline; rather, it should attempt to put it into the broader perspective of biological sciences. Histochemistry, like any other discipline or methodology, has its limitations. Critical texts, beginning with Lison's *Histochimie Animale. Méthods et Problèmes,* published in 1936, and culminating with Pearse's comprehensive fourth edition of *Histochemistry. Theoretical and Applied* (1980, 1985), have amply discussed these limitations or pitfalls (a word histochemists like to use, particularly when it applies to their colleagues' work); and I have no intention of being boringly repetitious here. I share Pearse's view, who considers histochemistry ". . . more a technology than a science," which "stands or falls . . . by its applicability to other disciplines" (Pearse, 1980). Judged by this criterion alone, histochemistry now occupies a rather illustrious position. It permeates a great many areas of biology, fully justifying Gomori's 1952 statement: "There is every indication that histochemistry is emerging now as an independent discipline with its own theoretical background, methods, and special problems, just as was the case with biochemistry shortly after the turn of the century." Yet there are few objective measures to assess the impact of histochemistry. Pearse (1980) quotes a citation analysis[4] indicating that during the period of 1961–1972 five of the 29 most-cited books in biochemistry and biomedicine were histochemical.[5] This statistic is rather flattering for histochemistry, notwithstanding the fact that, in general, methodological texts (books and papers) enjoy a higher frequency of citations. But does this diminish their impact?

Although histochemistry has its own theoretical background, it developed as a borderline discipline, borrowing from morphology, analytical chemistry, biochemistry, physics, immunology, etc. Developers and practitioners of histochemistry came from diverse disciplines and were trained in various fields. They were botanists, anatomists, pathologists, practicing clinicians, virologists, immunologists, and so on. In a way, histochemists are amateurs, in the true sense of the word. But aren't we all?[6]

Histochemistry is not entirely a new discipline; its origin goes back to empirical staining methods (Sandritter and Kasten, 1964; Pearse, 1968; Clark and Kasten, 1983). But major developments took place during the past 50 years, the second half of AAA's existence, and particularly after World War II, when Europe

---

[4]1974 Current Contents, *1*:80.

[5]Pearse, 1969; Lillie, 1965; Gomori, 1952; Barka and Anderson, 1963; Jensen, 1962.

[6]Borrowing from the title and closing words of the delightful play "Aren't We All?" by F. Lonsdale, performed recently and inimitably on Broadway by Rex Harrison and Claudette Colbert.

and Japan were recovering from the devastations of war. In these developments American scientists, including many anatomists, have played eminent roles. A great deal of the history of histochemistry can be equated with the history of the development of methods. The development of techniques and instrumentation is of fundamental importance in the progress of science. This is generally acknowledged by all experimental scientists as individuals, but, paradoxically, not when they act as a group in an advisory capacity to granting agencies.

Of the early contributions of anatomists to histochemistry, the isolation of mitochondria from guinea pig liver by Bensley and Hoerr in 1934 stands out. Perhaps equally important was the use of Janus green B for the supravital staining of mitochondria (reviewed by Cowdry, 1953), which helped to establish the non-artifactitious nature and universal cellular occurrence of mitochondria. In this early work on mitochondria, Arnold Lazarow, Bensley's gifted student, who went on to have a distinguished career in anatomy, has played an active part (Lazarow and Cooperstein, 1953). The importance of the work of Bensley and his coworkers is hardly diminished by Bensley's reluctance to accept the mitochondrion as a cell organelle.[7] His pioneering work using differential centrifugation techniques has been continued by many others (Dounce, 1950), leading to the Nobel Prize for Claude, DeDuve, and Palade in 1974.

Although somewhat outside the mainstream of histochemistry in his later years, Gersh was most active in histochemistry for several decades. Back in 1932 in the Department of Anatomy at the University of Chicago, he made practical the freeze-drying technique, dormant since 1890, when Altmann first described it (Gersh, 1932). Gersh remained an ardent advocate of the freeze-drying technique, particularly as applied to the histochemical demonstration of nucleic acids and proteins, although his enthusiasm was not universally shared by histochemists. Gersh also has the distinction of having written, so far as I know, the first review on histochemistry in America that covered the progress in the field that took place after the publication of Lison's work in 1936 (Gersh, 1941). One should not leave this era without acknowledging a young French anatomist, Charles Leblond (see his chapter in this volume), who published, with his teacher Giroud, several papers on the histochemical localization of vitamin C (e.g., Giroud and Leblond, 1934, 1935, 1936).

Ralph Lillie, one of the most distinguished histochemists of our time, estimated that no one had greater influence on histochemistry in the present century than George Gomori (Lillie, 1957). The publication, in 1939, of Gomori's classical paper on the histochemical demonstration of alkaline phosphatase activity is, together with the independent publication of the same method by Takamatsu (1939), a cornerstone in the history of histochemistry. However, his contributions and influence go far beyond this, and his textbook *Microscopic Histochemistry. Principles and Practice* (1952) remains an exemplary critical contribution. Gomori, who achieved the rank of Professor in Medicine in 1949 at the University of Chicago Medical School, was an 'amateur' histochemist who liked to call himself "a tool maker." Original, highly intelligent, critical, he was also a scholar

---

[7] Bensley, as an honorary member of the Histochemical Society addressing a symposium in 1953, remarked that there is "a tendency to erect the mitochondria to the dignity of an organelle or cell organ. This is a blunder. Mitochondrial substance is expendable." This remark should remind us that only the Pope is infallible!

of classical Greek and the New Testament. Earl Benditt related to me that in the home of Gomori, on the occasion of the meeting of the Histochemical Society, Lillie and Gomori had a friendly 'contest' in classical Greek to the amazement and amusement of those present.

Alas, I never met Gomori, who died in 1957 at the age of 53. I had only an exchange of letters with him concerning our early method of quantifying the alkaline phosphatase technique by introducing a radioactive isotope into the final reaction product. Gomori quoted our work, published originally in Hungarian (Barka et al., 1951, 1952) in his book, an indication that he never lost contact with his motherland and mother tongue. At the time of sizable research teams, scientific empire-builders, entrepreneurs, and multi-multi-authored publications, Gomori stands out as a loner; he had no coworkers, no immediate students, and no successor. He is the sole author of most, if not all, of his numerous publications. He had, however, as already indicated, a great impact and true influence on histochemistry with his original contributions and unfailing critical attitude.

It would be difficult to say who was directly influenced by Gomori, but Earl Benditt, in the Pathology Department at the same school, was one of them. Benditt has published studies on enzyme kinetics (Benditt and Arase, 1958), the effect of proteases (Benditt and French, 1953), and mast cells (Benditt and Arase, 1959; Lagunoff and Benditt, 1961) before turning to other topics not closely related to histochemistry. Gomori's interest was not restricted to histochemistry. His aldehyde-fuchsin staining had wide use among those interested in the endocrine pancreas, and conversations with Gomori led Nicholas Halmi to develop the Halmi staining method for the pituitary gland (Halmi, 1952) that was widely used for the distinction of adenohypophyseal cell types before the advent of immunocytochemistry.

In the 1950s, histochemistry indeed became popular. One of the most active centers of anatomists who recognized the potential of histochemistry in studying physiological problems was the Department of Anatomy at Harvard Medical School, led by George Wislocki. Members of this group and students of Wislocki who made numerous contributions to "pure" and "applied" histochemistry include H. Stanley Bennett, Edward W. Dempsey, Helene W. Deane, Russell J. Barrnett, and Helen Padykula. (A few of their early representative papers include: Dean and Dempsey, 1945; Dempsey and Singer, 1946; Dempsey and Wislocki, 1946, 1947; Deane, 1947; Dempsey, 1948; Padykula, 1952; Barrnett, 1953; and Padykula and Herman, 1955). In 1951, Bennett and his coworkers introduced mercury orange as a specific sulfhydryl stain, one of the first reagents explicitly designed for histochemical localization (Bennett and Watts, 1958); and, inspired by a young pathologist, George Haas (Bennett, personal communication), described the application of phenylhydrazine for the demonstration of reactive groups in a comprehensive paper on the adrenal cortex of the cat (Bennett, 1940). The orientation of Wislocki and several of his students is perhaps best characterized by the term "physiological histochemistry," coined by Dempsey and Wislocki (1946) in analogy with "histophysiology."

In developing and applying microscopic histochemical techniques, pathologists and anatomists were in the forefront. McManus (1946) described the periodic acid-Schiff reaction, and, in 1960, he and Mowry authored a book on microtechnical and histochemical techniques to encourage the use of these methods in routine pathology. A towering figure in histochemistry was Ralph Lillie, also a pathologist. He represented the natural combination of an empirical histologist and a highly versed histochemist. His long, productive life and numerous contributions have been well recounted by Kasten (Clark and Kasten, 1983). Lillie's text *Histopathologic Technic and Practical Histochemistry* [the last, fourth edition written with Harold Fullmer (1976), an able histochemist himself] is a standard book in histopathological laboratories. An account of this era of histochemistry would not be complete without mention of two other practicing pathologists: Max Wachstein, who first used potassium tellurite for the histochemical demonstration of dehydrogenase activity in 1949 and who described a widely used method for ATPase (Wachstein and Meisel, 1957), and Samuel Spicer, who with his prodigious productivity has been making significant contributions, particularly in the field of carbohydrate histochemistry, application of lectins, and, more recently, immunocytochemistry. Anatomists, and others whose contributions to histochemistry during this period ought to be acknowledged, include L.F. Belanger, D. Bodian, G. Bourne, Y. Clermont, W. Doyle, V.M. Emmel, W.H. Fishman, H. Koelle, H. Koening, C.P. Leblond, A.B Novikoff, M. Singer, and L. Weiss. Detailed accounts of their contributions can be found in Pearse's thorough text (1968, 1972).

The introduction of azo-dye methods in 1944 by Menten et al., allowing the development of reliable techniques for a number of hydrolytic enzymes, marks another turning point in the history of histochemistry. Major contributions to enzyme histochemistry, but also to many other areas of histochemistry, were made by Arnold Seligman, surgeon by profession and histochemist by vocation, and by his coworkers. Seligman, who with his irrepressible intellectual curiosity and creativity, turned to his lifetime preoccupation, histochemistry, even in his last research effort. He developed chemotherapeutic agents against prostatic cancer to be administered to himself, based on histochemical data on prostatic acid phosphatase (Serrano et al., 1976). He was a remarkable scientist indeed. The search for improving existing histochemical methods and efforts to develop new ones resulted in a series of new substrates, reagents, tetrazolium salts, etc. that were synthesized by Seligman and his coworkers, including the gifted organic chemist K.C. Tsou; it also resulted in entirely new principles, such as the first indigogenic method for esterase (Barrnett and Seligman, 1951).[8]

With the development of new enzyme substrates and with the application of histochemical methods to anatomical and pathological problems, M.S. Burstone, who was trained as a dentist and worked at NIH, earned a distinguished place in the history of histochemistry. His book, *Enzyme Histochemistry and Its Application in the Study of Neoplasms* (1962), attests to his deep involvement with enzyme histochemistry and the underlying chemistry.

It required no great insight on our part when we (Barka and Anderson, 1963) wrote. . . . "Since the biochemist is now operating at the molecular level and the anatomist is concerned with subcellular structure, the future development of histochemistry must inevitably be in these directions." Although the extension of microscopic histochemistry to the ultrastructural level was a logical development, numerous problems of preservation of structure, chemical composition, and enzymatic activity, and of finding methods of increasing contrast of specific components to be demonstrated, had to be solved. In this process electron microscopists

---

[8]The indoxyl methods were later developed extensively by Holt in England, who described the indigogenic principle independently in 1952 (Holt, 1958).

and histochemists learned from each other. Although perhaps the most important biological information came from the application of enzyme and immunocytochemical electron-microscopic methods, ultrahistochemistry of carbohydrates, nucleic acids, protein end-groups, and lipids also provided valuable data (reviewed by Scapelli and Kanczak, 1965, and Pearse, 1972).

The development of electron-microscopic histochemistry to its present level resulted from contributions by numerous scientists in America, Europe, and Japan. In this development, the introduction of glutaraldehyde by Sabatini et al. (1963, 1964) and the fixative of Karnovsky (1965b) were of major importance.

Although the first application of an electron-microscopic enzyme histochemical method was reported from the Karolinska Institute in Stockholm (Sheldon et al., 1955; Brandes et al., 1956), American histochemists were in the forefront of developing and exploiting this relatively new methodology. A list, far from complete, of pioneers in this field includes R.J. Barrnett, L. Ornstein, G. Palade, A.M. Seligman, A.B. Novikoff, M.J. Karnovsky, D. Pease, and J.S. Hanker. Representative publications are: Barrnett and Palade, 1957, 1958; Ornstein, 1957; Essner and Novikoff, 1958, 1962; Barrnett, 1959; Tice and Barrnett, 1962a,b; Hanker et al., 1964; Seligman et al., 1967; Beard and Novikoff, 1969; and, of course, those of their coworkers. The development and early history up to 1964 of electron-microscopic histochemistry were ably reviewed by Scarpelli and Kanczak (1965), as well as in the series edited by Hayat (1974–1977), and may be consulted for additional references. Since electron-microscopic histochemistry is but an extension of light-microscopic histochemistry, it is no wonder that many prominent electron-microscopic histochemists left a no less distinguished mark on light-microscopic histochemistry (e.g., the introduction of the 3′,5′-diaminobenzidine, the ferricyanide acceptor methods, and the detection of sites of H_2O_2 production with cerium ions by Karnovsky and his coworkers (Karnovsky, 1965a; Graham and Karnovsky, 1966; Briggs et al., 1975).

We (Barka and Anderson, 1963) have defined histochemistry "as a collective term, applied to those techniques that aim at the microscopic (and now electron-microscopic) localization of chemical compounds within the cell and tissue, which are therefore direct and nondestructive." Distinctively, we used the term cytochemistry for "microchemical methods applied to minute amounts of tissues, cells, or groups of cells for direct or statistical correlation with cellular morphology." The terms histochemistry and cytochemistry have been frequently used interchangeably; we now prefer the general use of histochemistry for both groups of techniques, which, in their objectives and concepts, are quite similar.

The chemical analyses of morphologically defined tissue samples that provide information not readily obtained by microscopic histochemical methods were pioneered by Linderstrøm-Lang (1939) at the Carlsberg Laboratories in Copenhagen. Introduced to this new and exciting methodology, David Glick became an original and highly productive histochemist, as well as an ardent promoter of quantitative histo- and cytochemistry. An appreciation of his extensive contributions to histochemistry may be obtained by reading his reflections, "Fifty Years with Histochemistry and Cytochemistry" (1985), which includes his complete bibliography. Equally important contributions to this field were made by Oliver Lowry and his students (Lowry and Passoneau, 1963, 1972). Although neither Glick nor Lowry was trained in morphological sciences, they fully appreciated the principle of structural-chemical-functional correlation that is the basis of histo-chemistry.

Accurate quantification in histochemistry had long been achieved, even before the application of microchemical methods. I am referring to the fundamentally important work of Caspersson, who developed the ultraviolet micro-spectrophotometric method as early as 1936. Since that time a continuous stream of important findings and improvements in instrumentation came from Caspersson and his coworkers (Caspersson, 1950). Cytophotometry, as the method became generally known, developed rapidly after the war as a branch of histochemistry. Impetus to quantitate the Feulgen reaction to measure the DNA content of the cell led not only to the modification of the Schiff reagent (Kasten, 1967) and to the development of new instruments, but also to theoretical considerations of micro-spectrophotometry. Arthur Pollister at Columbia University and Hewson Swift at the University of Chicago were the leaders in this field (Pollister and Ornstein, 1955; Swift and Rasch, 1956). It was in Pollister's laboratory that a graduate student, Leonard Ornstein, developed the theory of the two-wavelength method allowing for the correction for distributional error in microspectrophotometry (1952).[9]

The cytophotometric techniques were the forerunners of microfluorometric (e.g., for DNA) and microspectrofluorometric (e.g., for biogenic amines) methods, and more recently of flow cytometric techniques with the capability of cell or particle (e.g., chromosomes) sorting based on multiparameter analysis. The impor-tance of these methods in research in biology, immunology, medicine, and other fields is now widely recognized, although their potential is far from being ex-hausted.

One of the most widely used and important methods of experimental biology in this century is polyacrylamide gel electrophoresis developed by Leonard Orn-stein and Baruch J. Davis at the Cell Research Laboratory at Mount Sinai Hospital in New York City in the 1950s (Ornstein, 1964; Davis, 1964). Attempts to find new embedding media applicable to enzyme cytochemistry and immunocytochemistry led to polyacrylamides, but the spark of genius that from there turned to the conceptual and practical development of discontinuous ("disc") electrophoresis remains a mystery. To describe the environment and the laboratories where disc electrophoresis and many other ideas were 'born' would require a Sinclair Lewis [e.g., the use of hexazonium pararosanilin as an excellent coupler in azo-dye methods (Davis et al., 1959; Davis, 1959) that allowed us to develop a reliable, popular method for the demonstration of acid phosphatase activity (Barka and Anderson, 1962), and the electron histochemical demonstration of cholinesterase activity (Lehrer and Ornstein, 1959)]. The Cell Research Laboratory of Mount Sinai in the 1950s was a remarkable place, where from his tiny hole of an office Paul Klemperer, a retired giant of pathology, overlooked a seemingly chaotic laboratory teeming with activity—a laboratory subsequently swept away by the lack of support from unresponsive administrators and short-sighted granting agen-cies.

Polyacrylamide gel electrophoresis allowed the ready application of histo-

---

[9] The method was independently described in the same year by Patau.

chemical methods to the detection of isoenzymes (or isozymes), separated by electrophoresis, without recourse to their elution. The zymogram technique was pioneered by the anatomist Robert Hunter, who with his coworkers used the method for the characterization of esterases (Hunter and Markert, 1957; Markert and Hunter, 1959). I applied this technique in 1961 to characterize isozymes of liver acid phosphatases (Barka, 1961).

An explosive growth of histochemistry occurred with the introduction of immunohistochemical (or immunocytochemical) techniques, beginning with Albert Coons' classical work (Coons et al., 1942). With the rapid progress in cloning and sequencing structural genes and hence establishing the primary structures of proteins coded by such genes, with the increase in our understanding of the tertiary structure and antigenicity of proteins and other molecules, and with the relative ease by which site-specific polyclonal and monoclonal antibodies can be produced, the potential of localizing immunocytochemically molecules of biological importance appears limitless. However, technical and conceptual problems remain, and we would be well-advised to keep our perspectives, as we are so delightfully reminded by Chargaff: "When listening to all these wonderful papers at this Symposium, from which it appeared to me that almost all the riddles of life were riddles no longer, I began to dream of what might have gone on at an International Congress of Pure and Applied Alchemy held sometime in the 15th Century. What was said there I could not reproduce; but I am sure of one thing: no one got up and said he could not make gold."[10] Anyhow, the history and contributions of immunocytochemistry are covered in another chapter of this book.

There are several other areas of histochemistry, such as the application of various optical techniques, electron probe x-ray microanalysis, *in situ* hybridization, etc., that I have not mentioned. A historical review of their development and contributions should probably be left for the year 2087.

Anatomy is a broad discipline and a viewpoint. Histochemistry has contributed in a significant way to the anatomical sciences, as did anatomists to histochemistry. The Histochemical Society and *The Journal of Histochemistry and Cytochemistry* have been important for catalyzing and critically fostering the development of histochemistry. The idea of establishing the Society originated with Lillie, Leblond, and Dempsey during a luncheon chat (Lillie, 1962). Of the past 32 presidents of the Society, 15 were anatomists/cell biologists, with George Wislocki being the first president. A great number of anatomists were officers of the Society, or served as editors or as members of the editorial board of the Journal. And, of course, other learned societies and journals with participation of anatomists were intimately involved with progress in histochemistry.

Histochemistry represents but one of the many techniques applicable to biological problems, and data obtained by using histochemical techniques have to be properly integrated with information provided by other methods if we are to understand complex phenomena. Thus, while it is proper to ask how the present concept(s), for example, of cellular immunology, or neuroendocrinology, or even of the nature and functioning of a cell organelle developed historically, and in this context include the contributions of histochemists, it would be rather self-serving

---

[10]Chargaff, E. 1957 Base composition of deoxypentose and pentose nucleic acids in various species. In: A Symposium on the Chemical Basis of Heredity. W. D. McElvoy and B. Glass, eds. The Johns Hopkins Press, Baltimore, p. 521.

to narrow our focus to histochemistry alone. Fundamental problems in biology are not solvable; only the level of inquiry and our interpretations are shifted. "In science, there is always one more Gordian knot than there are Alexanders."[11] The unflattering truth is that in science no one made a "discovery" that would not have been made, at some time, by someone else by using the same or a different approach, method, or reasoning.[12]

With this philosophical caveat, what follows is a short, partial, and fragmentary list of areas to which, I believe, histochemistry and histochemists have made significant contributions. Some of these areas have been reviewed recently (Stoward and Polak, 1981).

Histochemists, primarily Caspersson and Brachet, were the first to implicate RNA in protein synthesis, pointing out the presence of high concentrations of RNA in cells synthesizing large quantities of proteins (Caspersson, 1950; Brachet, 1959). Application of microspectrophotometric methods has contributed to the establishment of DNA constancy. The relatively new *in situ* hybridization techniques allowed the analysis of gene expression at the single-cell level and the direct chromosomal localization of selected genes. Autoradiographic techniques were most important in analyzing DNA replication and the cell cycle, and to establish, as the work of Leblond has shown so eminently, the dynamic nature of cellular and tissue components (Schultze, 1969).

There are many areas of cell biology in which the progress has been greatly accelerated by histochemists and the application of their armamentarium. Examples are the present concept of the structure and function of lysosomes, to which, among others, Alex Novikoff (1961) and Werner Straus (1967) have made notable contributions, and the mechanism of phagocytosis (Karnovsky and Robinson, 1981). Without the application of histochemical (e.g., Novikoff and Goldfischer, 1961) and immunocytochemical techniques, the functions of the Golgi complex or the structure and function of the cytoskeleton and its contractile elements would be less completely understood. The present status of endocrinology (and particularly neuroendocrinology) owes much to histochemists (Scharrer, 1981). The establishment of the concept of a diffuse neuroendocrine system (Pearse, 1977) and the entire area of gut hormones (Polak and Bloom, 1983) are closely connected, if not dependent on, contributions by histochemists. Present day concepts of neurobiology have been greatly influenced by the histochemical and immunocytochemical demonstration of neurotransmitters, biogenic amines, and the enzymes involved in their synthesis in discrete regions of the brain and in the nervous system in general. Finally, it is difficult to envision the rapid progress in immunolgy, and particularly in cellular immunology, without the availability and application of immunocytochemical methods.

Histochemistry, now the most cited discipline in biomedical literature, insidiously invaded a multitude of fields. It is now routinely applied in hematology (e.g., Ornstein and Ansley, 1974), in the diagnosis and classification of lymphoreticular tumors (Isaacson and Wright, 1983), and in the diagnosis of tumors, storage

---

[11]Chargaff, E. 1978 Heraclitean Fire: Sketches from a Life before Nature. The Rockefeller University Press, New York, p. 116.

[12]This is in sharp contrast to art, as pointed out by Chargaff (See Footnote 11). "The Testament" or the A major "Trout" quintet would not exist had François Villon and Franz Schubert, respectively, not created them.

diseases, and diseases of muscle, kidney, nervous system, etc. (Zugibe, 1970; Filipe and Lake, 1983; Polak and Van Noorden, 1983; DeLellis, 1981, 1984). As an experimental tool, its application extends from anatomy, immunology, and virology to molecular biology and organ physiology. Scientists who subscribe to the viewpoint that structure and function are inseparable, anatomists at heart, all have contributed to its present state of development and appreciation. In this brief essay, I have taken a broad view of anatomy and histochemistry. A narrower interpretation of histochemistry and anatomy would be contradictory to my optimistic view of the future of both of these disciplines.

REFERENCES

Barka, T. 1961 Studies on acid phosphatase. I. Electrophoretic separation of acid phosphatases of rat liver on polyacrylamide gels. J. Histochem. Cytochem., 9:542–547.

Barka, T., and P.J. Anderson 1962 Histochemical methods for acid phosphatase using hexazonium pararosanilin as coupler. J. Histochem. Cytochem., 10:741–753.

Barka, T., and P.J. Anderson 1963 Histochemistry. Theory, Practice and Bibliography. Hoeber Medical Division, Harper & Row, New York, pp. 1–660.

Barka, T., S. Szalay, Z. Pósalaky, és. L. Kertész 1951 Quantitative histokémiai phosphatáse meghatározás radioaktive ólom felhasználásával. Kisérletes Orvostud. 1–7.

Barka, T., S. Szalay, Z. Pósalaky, and L. Kertész 1952 Quantitative histochemical determination of phosphatase by means of radioactive lead. Acta Anat., 16:45–53.

Barrnett, R.J. 1953 The histochemical distribution of protein-bound sulfhydryl groups. J. Natl. Cancer Inst., 13: 905–925.

Barrnett, R.J. 1959 The demonstration with the electron microscope of the end-products of histochemical reactions in relation to the fine structure of cell. Exp. Cell Res. (Suppl.), 7: 65–89.

Barrnett, R.J., and G.E. Palade 1957 Histochemical demonstration of the sites of activity of dehydrogenase systems with the electron microscope. J. Biophys. Biochem. Cytol., 3: 577–588.

Barrnett, R.J., and G.E. Palade 1958 Applications of histochemistry to electron microscopy. J. Histochem. Cytochem., 6: 1–12.

Barrnett, R.J., and G.E. Palade 1959 Enzymatic activity in the M band. J. Biophys. Biochem. Cytol., 6: 163–170.

Barrnett, R.J., and A.M. Seligman 1951 Histochemical demonstration of esterases by production of indigo. Science, 114:579–582.

Beard, M.E., and A.B. Novikoff 1969 Distribution of peroxisomes (microbodies) in the nephron of the rat. J. Cell Biol., 42:501–518.

Benditt, E.P., and M. Arase 1958 Enzyme kinetics in a histochemical system. J. Histochem. Cytochem., 6: 431–434.

Benditt, E.P., and M. Arase 1959 An enzyme in mast cells with properties like chymotrypsin. J. Exp. Med., 110:451–460.

Benditt, E.P., and J.E. French 1953 Histochemistry of connective tissue: 1. The use of enzymes as specific histochemical reagents. J. Histochem. Cytochem., 1:315–320.

Bennett, H.S. 1940 The life history and secretion of the cells of the adrenal cortex of the cat. Am. J. Anat., 67:151–228.

Bennett, H.S., and R.M. Watts 1958 The cytochemical demonstration and measurement of sulfhydryl groups by azo-aryl mercaptide coupling, with special reference to mercury orange. In: General Cytochemical Methods. J.F. Danielli, ed. Academic Press, New York. Vol. 1, pp. 317–374.

Bensley, R.R. 1953 Symposium: The structure and biochemistry of mitochondria (Address). J. Histochem. Cytochem., 1:179–182.

Bensley, R.R., and N. Hoerr 1934 The preparation and properties of mitochondria. Anat. Rec., 60:449–455.

Brachet, J. 1959 The Biological Role of Ribonucleic Acids (Sixth Weizmann Memorial Lecture Series). Elsevier Publishing Co., Amsterdam, pp. 1–144.

Brandes, D., H. Zetterqvist, and H. Sheldon 1956 Histochemical techniques for electron microscopy: Alkaline phosphatase. Nature, *177*:382–383.

Briggs, R.T., M.L. Karnovsky, and M.J. Karnovsky 1975 Cytochemical demonstration of hydrogen peroxide in polymorphonuclear leukocytes by a new cytochemical method. J. Cell Biol., *67*:566–586.

Burstone, M.S. 1962 Enzyme Histochemistry and Its Application in the Study of Neoplasms. Academic Press, New York, pp. 1–621.

Caspersson, T.A. 1950 Cell Growth and Cell Function. A Cytochemical Study. W.W. Norton & Co., Inc., New York, pp. 1–158.

Clark, G., and F.H. Kasten 1983 History of Staining, 3rd edition. Williams & Wilkins, Baltimore, pp. 1–304.

Coons, A.H., H.J. Creech, R.N. Jones, and E. Berliner 1942 The demonstration of pneumococcal antigen in tissues by the use of fluorescent antibody. J. Immunol., *45*:159–170.

Cowdry, E.V. 1953 Historical background of research on mitochondria. J. Histochem. Cytochem., *1*: 183–187.

Davis, B.J. 1959 Histochemical demonstration of erythrocyte esterases. Proc. Soc. Exp. Biol. Med., *101*:90–93.

Davis, B.J. 1964 Disc electrophoresis—II. Method and application to human serum proteins. Ann. N.Y. Acad. Sci., *121*:404–427.

Davis, B.J., L. Ornstein, P. Taleporos, and S. Koulish 1959 Simultaneous preservation of intracellular morphology and enzymatic or antigenic activities in frozen tissues for high resolution histochemistry. J. Histochem. Cytochem., *7*:291–292.

Deane, H.W. 1947 A cytochemical survey of phosphatases in mammalian liver, pancreas and salivary glands. Am. J. Anat., *80*:321–359.

Deane, H.W., and E.W. Dempsey 1945 The localization of phosphatases in the Golgi region of intestinal and other epithelial cells. Anat. Rec., *93*:401–417.

DeLellis, A.D. (ed.) 1981 Diagnostic Immunocytochemistry. Masson Publishing USA, Inc., New York, pp. 1–347.

DeLellis, R.A. (ed.) 1984 Advances in Immunocytochemistry. Masson Publishing USA, Inc., New York, pp. 1–364.

Dempsey, E.W. 1948 The chemical cytology of endocrine glands. Recent Prog. Horm. Res., *3*:127–153.

Dempsey, E.W., and M. Singer 1946 Observations on the chemical cytology of the thyroid gland at different functional stages. Endocrinology, *38*:270–295.

Dempsey, E.W., and G.B. Wislocki 1946 Histochemical contributions to physiology. Physiol. Rev., *26*:1–27.

Dempsey, E.W., and G.B. Wislocki 1947 Further observations on the distribution of phosphatases in mammalian placentas. Am. J. Anat., *80*:1–33.

Dounce, A.L. 1950 Cytochemical foundations of enzyme chemistry. In: The Enzymes. Chemistry and Mechanism of Action. J.B. Sumner and K. Myrback, eds.. Academic Press, New York, Vol. 1, pp. 187–266.

Emmel, V.M. 1945 Alkaline phosphatase in the Golgi zone of the absorbing cells of the small intestine. Anat. Rec., *91*:39–47.

Essner, E., and A.B. Novikoff 1962 Cytological studies on two functional hepatomas. Interrelations of endoplasmic reticulum, Golgi apparatus, and lysosomes. J. Cell Biol., *15*: 289–312.

Essner, E., A.B. Novikoff, and B. Masek 1958 Adenosinetriphosphatase and 5-nucleotidase activities in the plasma membrane of liver cells as revealed by electron microscopy. J. Biophys. Biochem. Cytol., *4*:711–716.

Filipe, M.I., and B.D. Lake, eds. 1983 Histochemistry in Pathology. Churchill Livingstone, Edinburgh, pp. 1–349.

Gersh, I. 1932 The Altmann technique for fixation by drying while freezing. Anat. Rec., *53*: 309–337.

Gersh, I. 1941 Recent developments in histochemistry. Physiol. Rev., *21*:242–266,.

Geyer, G. 1972 Ultrahistochemie. Gustav Fischer Verlag, Stuttgart, pp. 1–478.

Giroud, A., and C.P. Leblond 1934 Etude histochimique de la vitamine C dans la glande surrénale. Arch. Anat. Microsc., *30*:105–129.

Giroud, A., and C.P. Leblond 1935 Localization élective de l'acide ascorbique ou vitamine C (cortex surrénal, testicule, corps jaune, hypophyse). Arch. Anat. Microsc., *31*:111–142.

Giroud, A., and C.P. Leblond 1936 L'acide ascorbique dans les tissues et sa detection. Hermann & Co., Paris, pp. 1–47.

Glick, D. 1949 Techniques of Histo- and Cytochemistry. Interscience, New York, pp. 1–531.

Glick, D. 1985 Fifty years with histochemistry and cytochemistry. J. Histochem. Cytochem., *33*:720–728.

Gomori, G. 1939 Microtechnical demonstration of phosphatase in tissue sections. Proc. Soc. Exp. Biol. Med. *42*:23–26.

Gomori, G. 1952 Microscopic Histochemistry. Principles and Practice. University of Chicago Press, Chicago, pp. 1–273.

Gomori, G., and E.P. Benditt 1953 Precipitation of calcium phosphate in the histochemical method for phosphatase. J. Histochem. Cytochem., *1*:114–122.

Graham, Jr., R.C., and M.J. Karnovsky 1966 The early stages of absorption of injected horseradish peroxidase in the proximal tubules of mouse kidney: Ultrastructural cytochemistry by a new technique. J. Histochem. Cytochem., *14*:291–302.

Halmi, N.S. 1952 Differentiation of two types of basophils in the adenohypophysis of the rat and the mouse. Stain Technol., *27*:61–64.

Hanker, J.S. 1975 Oxidoreductases. In: Electron Microscopy of Enzymes. Principles and Methods, MA. Hayat, ed. Van Nostrand Reinhold Co., New York, Vol. 4, pp. 1–139; Vol. 1, pp. 1–204 (1973).

Hayat, M.A., ed. 1974a Electron Microscopy of Enzymes. Principles and Methods. Van Nostrand Reinhold Co., New York, Vol. 2, pp. 1–158.

Hayat, MA., ed. 1974b Electron Microscopy of Enzymes. Principles and Methods. Van Nostrand Reinhold Co., New York, Vol. 3, pp. 1–175.

Hayat, M.A., ed. 1975 Electron Microscopy of Enzymes. Principles and Methods. Van Nostrand Reinhold Co., New York, Vol. 4, pp. 1–277.

Hayat, M.A., ed. 1977 Electron Microscopy of Enzymes. Principles and Methods. Van Nostrand Reinhold Co., New York, Vol. 5, pp. 1–220.

Holt, S.J. 1958 Indigogenic staining methods for esterases. In: General Cytochemical Methods. J.F. Danielli, ed. Academic Press, New York, Vol. 1, pp. 375–398.

Hunter, R.L., and C.L. Markert 1957 Histochemical demonstration of enzymes separated by zone electrophoresis in starch gels. Science, *125*:1294–1295.

Isaacson, P., and D.H. Wright 1983 Immunocytochemistry of lymphoreticular tumours. In: Immunocytochemistry. Practical Applications in Pathology and Biology. J.M. Polak and S. Van Noorden, eds. John Wright and Sons, Ltd., Bristol, pp. 249–273.

Kahn, M.A. 1976 Histochemical characteristics of vertebrate striated muscle: A review. Prog. Histochem. Cytochem., *8*(4):1–48.

Karnovsky, M.J. 1965a. The localization of cholinesterase activity in rat cardiac muscle by electron microscopy. J. Cell Biol., *23*:217–232.

Karnovsky, M.J. 1965b. A formaldehyde-glutaraldehyde fixative of high osmolarity for use in electron microscopy. J. Cell Biol., *27*:137A–138A.

Karnovsky, M.J., and J.M. Robinson 1981 Contribution of oxidative cytochemistry to our understanding of the phagocytic process. In: Histochemistry: The Widening Horizons. P.J. Stoward and J.M. Polak, eds. John Wiley & Sons, New York, pp. 47–66.

Kasten, F.H. 1967 Cytochemical studies with acridine orange and the influence of dye contaminants in the staining of nucleic acids. Int. Rev. Cytol., *21*:141–202.

Koelle, G.B. 1963 The use of histochemistry in pharmacological studies. In: Methods for the Study of Pharmacological Effects at Cellular and Subcellular Levels. O.H. Lowry and P. Lindgren, eds. Macmillan Co., New York, Vol. 5, pp. 5–15. (Proceedings of the First International Pharmacological Meeting, August 22–25, 1961, General Editor: Borje Uvnas.)

Lagunoff, D., and E.P. Benditt 1961 Histochemistry. Histochemical examinations of chymotrypsin-like esterases. Nature, *192*:1198–1199.

Lazarow, A., and S.J. Cooperstein 1953 Studies on the enzymatic basis for the Janus green B staining reaction. J. Histochem. Cytochem., *1*:234–241.

Lehrer, G.M., and L. Ornstein 1959 A diazo coupling method for the electron microscopic localization of cholinesterase. J. Biophys. Biochem. Cytol., 6:399–406.

Lillie, R.D. 1957 George Gomori 1904–1957. J. Histochem. Cytochem., 5:203.

Lillie, R.D. 1962 History of the Histochemical Society, its origin and development, with lists of past and present officers and members. J. Histochem. Cytochem., 10:123–126.

Lillie, R.D., and H.M. Fullmer 1976 Histopathologic Technic and Practical Histochemistry, 4th edition. McGraw-Hill Book Co., New York, pp. 1–942

Linderstrøm-Lang, K. 1939. Distribution of enzymes in tissues and cells. Harvey Lect., 34:214–245.

Lison, L. 1936 Histochimie Animale. Méthodes et Problèmes. Gauthier-Villars, Paris, pp. 1–320.

Lowry, O.H., and J.V. Passonneau 1963 The application of quantiative histochemistry to the pharmacology of the nervous system. In: Methods for the Study of Pharmacological Effects at Cellular and Subcellular Levels. O.H. Lowry and P. Lindgren, eds. Macmillan Co., New York, Vol. 5, pp. 173–180. (Proceedings of the First International Pharmacological Meeting, August 22–25, 1961, General Editor: Borje Uvnas.)

Lowry, O.H., and J.V. Passonneau 1972 A flexible system of enzymatic analysis. Academic Press, New York, pp. 1–291.

Markert, C.L., and R.L. Hunter 1959 The distribution of esterases in mouse tissues. J. Histochem. Cytochem., 7:42–49.

McManus, J.F.A. 1946 Histological demonstration of mucin after periodic acid. Nature, 158:202.

McManus, J.F.A., and R.W. Mowry 1960 Staining Methods. Histologic and Histochemical. Paul B. Hoeber, Inc., New York, pp. 1–423.

Menten, M.L., J. Junge, and M.H. Green 1944 Distribution of alkaline phosphatase in kidney following the use of histochemical azo dye test. Proc. Soc. Exp. Biol. Med., 57:;82–86.

Novikoff, A.B. 1961 Lysosomes and related particles. In: The Cell. Biochemistry, Physiology, Morphology. J. Brachet and A.E. Mirsky, eds. Academic Press, New York, Vol. 2, pp. 423–488.

Novikoff, A.B., A. Albala, and L. Biempica 1968 Ultrastructural and cytochemical observations on B-16 and Harding-Passey mouse melanomas. J. Histochem. Cytochem., 16:299–319.

Novikoff, A.B., and S. Goldfischer 1961 Nucleosidediphosphatase activity in the Golgi apparatus and its usefulness for cytological studies. Proc. Natl. Acad. Sci. U.S.A., 47:802–810.

Ornstein, L. 1952 The distributional error in microspectrophotometry. Lab. Invest., 1:250–262.

Ornstein, L. 1957 "Osmiophilia", fact or fiction. J. Biophys. Biochem. Cytol., 3:809–811.

Ornstein, L. 1964 Disc electrophoresis—I. Background and theory. Ann. N.Y. Acad. Sci., 121:321–349.

Ornstein, L., and H.R. Ansley 1974 Spectral matching of classical cytochemistry to automated cytology. J. Histochem. Cytochem., 22:453–469.

Padykula, H.A. 1952 The localization of succinic dehydrogenase in tissue sections of the rat. Am. J. Anat. 91:107–145.

Padykula, H.A., and E. Herman 1955 Factors affecting the activity of adenosine triphosphatase and other phosphatases as measured by histochemical techniques. J. Histochem. Cytochem., 3:161–195.

Patau, K. 1952 Absorption microphotometry of irregular shaped objects. Chromosoma, 5:341–362.

Pearse, A.G.E. 1968 Histochemistry. Theoretical and Applied, 3rd edition. Little, Brown and Co., Boston, Vol. 1, pp. 1–759.

Pearse, A.G.E. 1972 Histochemistry. Theoretical and Applied, 3rd edition. Williams & Wilkins, Baltimore, Vol. 2, pp. 1–1518.

Pearse, A.G.E. 1977 The diffuse neuroendocrine system and the APUD concept: Related "endocrine" peptides in brain, intestine, pituitary, placenta, and anuran cutaneous glands. Med. Biol., 55:111–125.

Pearse, A.G.E. 1980 Histochemistry. Theoretical and Applied, 4th edition; Vol. 1, Preparative and Optical Technology. Churchill Livingstone, London, pp. 1–439.

Pearse, A.G.E. 1985 Histochemistry. Theoretical and Applied, 4th edition; Vol. 2, Analytical Technology. Churchill Livingstone, Edinburgh, pp. 1–1055.

Polak, J.M., and S.R. Bloom 1983 Immunocytochemistry of regulatory peptides. In: Immunocytochemistry. Practical Applications in Pathology and Biology. J.M. Polak and S. Van Noorden, eds. John Wright and Sons, Ltd., Bristol, pp. 184–211.

Polak, J.M., and S. Van Noorden 1983 Immunocytochemistry. Practical Applications in Pathology and Biology. John Wright and Sons, Ltd., Bristol, pp. 1–396.

Pollister, A.W., and L. Ornstein 1955 The photometric chemical analysis of cells. In: Analytical Cytology. Methods for Studying Cellular Form and Function, 2nd edition. R.C. Mellors, ed. McGraw-Hill Book Co., New York, pp. 431–518.

Sabatini, D.D., K. Bensch, and R.J. Barrnett 1963 Cytochemistry and electron microscopy. The preservation of cellular ultrastructure and enzymatic activity by aldehyde fixation. J. Cell Biol., 17:19–58.

Sabatani, D.D., F. Miller, and R.J. Barrnett 1964 Aldehyde fixation for morphological and enzyme histochemical studies with the electron microscope. J. Histochem. Cytochem., 12:57–71.

Sandritter, W., and F.H. Kasten, eds. 1964 100 Years of Histochemistry in Germany. F.K. Schattauer-Verlag, Stuttgart, pp. 1–140.

Scarpelli, D.G., and N.M. Kanczak 1965 Ultrastructural cytochemistry: Principles, limitations and applications. Int. Rev. Exp. Pathol., 4:55–126.

Scharrer, B. 1981 Neuroendocrinology and histochemistry. In: Histochemistry. The Widening Horizons of Its Applications in the Biomedical Sciences, P.J. Stoward and J.M. Polak, eds. John Wiley & Sons, Chichester, pp. 11–20.

Schultze, B. 1969 Autoradiography at the cellular level. In: Physical Techniques in Biological Research, 2nd edition. A.W. Pollister, ed. Academic Press, New York, Vol. III, Part B, pp. 1–301.

Seligman, A.M., J.S. Hanker, H. Wasserkrug, H. Dmochowski, and L. Katzoff 1965 Histochemical demonstration of some oxidized macromolecules with thiocarbohydrazide (TCH) or thiosemicarbazide (TSC) and osmium tetroxide. J. Histochem. Cytochem., 13:629–639.

Seligman, A.M., R.E. Plapinger, H.L. Wasserkrug, and J.S. Hanker 1967 Ultrastructural demonstration of cytochrome oxidase activity by the Nadi reaction with osmiophilic reagent. J. Cell Biol., 34:787–800.

Serrano, J.A., W.A. Shannon, N.J. Sternberger, H.L. Wasserkrug, A.A. Serrano, and A.M. Seligman 1976 The cytochemical demonstration of prostatic acid phosphatase using a new substrate phosphorylcholine. J. Histochem. Cytochem., 24:1046–1056.

Sheldon, H., H. Zetterqvist, and D. Brandes 1955 Histochemical reactions for electron microscopy: Acid phosphatase. Exp. Cell Res., 9:592–596.

Stoward, P.J., and J.M. Polak, eds. 1981 Histochemistry. The Widening Horizons of Its Applications in the Biomedical Sciences. John Wiley & Sons, Chichester, pp. 1–293.

Straus, W. 1967 Lysosomes, phagosomes and related particles. In: Enzyme Cytology. D.B. Roodyn, ed. Academic Press, London, pp. 239–319.

Swift, H., and E. Rasch 1956 Microphotometry with visible light. In: Physical Techniques In Biological Research; Vol. III, Cells and Tissues. G. Oster and A.W. Pollister, eds. Academic Press, New York, pp. 354–400.

Takamatsu, H. 1939 Histologische und biochemische Studien über die Phosphatase. I. Histochemische Untersuchungsmethodik der Phosphatase und deren Verteilung in verschiedenen Organen and Geweben. Trans. Jap. Pathol. Soc., 29:492–498.

Thompson, S.W. 1966 Selected Histochemical and Histopathological Methods. Charles C Thomas, Springfield, pp. 1–1639.

Tice, L.W., and R.J. Barrnett 1962a Fine structural localization of adenosine triphosphatase activity in heart muscle myofibrils. J. Cell Biol., 15:401–416.

Tice, L.W., and R.J. Barrnett 1962b The fine structural localization of glucose-6-phosphatase in rat liver. J. Histochem. Cytochem., 10:754–762.

Wachstein, M. 1949 Reduction of potassium tellurite by living tissue. Proc. Soc. Exp. Biol. Med., 72:175–178.

Wachstein, M., and E. Meisel 1957 Histochemistry of hepatic phosphatases at a physiologic pH. Am. J. Clin. Pathol., 27:13–23.

Zugibe, F. T. 1970 Diagnostic Histochemistry. C.V. Mosby Co., St. Louis, pp. 1–366.

Chapter 8

RADIOAUTOGRAPHY: THE ROLE PLAYED BY ANATOMISTS IN THE DEVELOPMENT AND APPLICATION OF THE TECHNIQUE

C(harles) P(hilippe) Leblond

In 1895, Henri Becquerel found that a fragment of uranium ore placed next to a photographic plate caused a shadow-like image to appear on the developed plate, and he concluded that uranium produced mysterious rays capable of activating photographic emulsion. Such "radioactive" rays were later shown to be produced by other substances, particularly polonium and some lead isotopes. When one of these substances was injected into an experimental animal, sections of tissues placed in contact with a photographic plate elicited a photographic image, that is, a radioautograph (also called autoradiograph) (Gross and Leblond, 1946).[1] Thus, Antoine Lacassagne in 1924 localized polonium in the intestinal wall and lymph nodes of the rabbit (reviewed in the above reference along with other early works).

That radioactive atoms could be used in living organisms as "tracers" of stable atoms of the same element was realized by Georg deHevesy in 1923. By placing a solution of radioactive lead isotope in contact with the roots of the horse-bean *(Vicia faba)*, he observed the passage of lead to the leaves and fruit of the plant (deHevesy, 1940). In this work, he detected the radioactive lead with a gold leaf electroscope but, years later, he mentioned to the writer his regret not to have

---

[1] The reasons why the term "radioautography" is preferred to "autoradiography" for the detection of radioactive elements by photographic emulsion are as follows. The term "autoradiography" is a compound word including the term "radiography." This term is defined as a picture produced by an x-ray beam that has passed through an object. Since this object, for instance a bone examined after a fracture, is located between the source of radiation and the emulsion, it appears white in the emulsion; that is, it is seen as a *negative* image. In contrast, when radioactive elements are detected in sections, the object under study is itself the source of the radiation that influences the emulsion. The black image thus produced is a photographic *positive*. It may be referred to as an autograph, that is "the reproduction of form or outline of anything by an impression from the thing itself" (*Oxford English Dictionary,* 1975). Hence, the author called it initially a "radioactive autograph." Later, on the advice of an editor, he condensed these two words into "radioautograph." The procedure is often called "autoradiography," but "radioautography" is the correct term.

localized it by radioautography. On a less serious note, legend has it that he suspected his landlady of serving him recycled hash for dinner. One day, behind her back, he spiked his uneaten hash with radiolead and, when hash was served him again, he pocketed a sample and found that it activated his electroscope. The story goes that the landlady evicted him when she was confronted with the evidence.

Tracing substances such as polonium and lead was of little interest to biologists. In 1934, Irène and Frédéric Joliot discovered that radioactivity could be artifically induced by bombardment with the alpha rays of polonium. Soon thereafter, physicists learned to prepare two radioactive elements of great interest to biologists, phosphorus 32 and radioiodine 128.

In 1937, the author took a position at the newly built Laboratoire de Synthèse Atomique in Paris under the guidance of Antoine Lacassagne and Frédéric Joliot. He joined forces with a brilliant chemist, Pierre Süe, to make use of the radioiodine 128 produced by exposure of ethyl iodide to the neutrons arising from radon-beryllium. This iodine had only a 25-min half-life, but its initial radioactivity was strong enough to be detected for 6 or 7 half-lives, that is, about 3 hr. To complete experiments within that time, Süe managed in 20–30 min to transform the crude radioiodine into clean sodium iodide; this was then injected intravenously into rats or guinea pigs, which were sacrificed 10 min later; the thyroid gland was then removed and tested for radioactivity. The gland was found to accumulate radioactive iodine (Leblond and Süe, 1940). This observation led, a few years later, to the treatment of hyperactive thyroids by high doses of radioiodine.

In the experiments with Süe, radioautography was also attempted by rapidly drying frozen sections of thyroids containing radioiodine and placing them on photographic plates. But not enough radioactivity was left to affect the emulsion. This failure was painful. Who could have thought at the time that, within the next 20 years, radioautography would become the tool by which an intense dynamism was detected in cells and cell components?

RADIOAUTOGRAPHIC TECHNIQUES

After the 1940 Battle of France, the author came to North America, where cyclotrons made it possible to obtain radioiodine 130, which has a 12.6-hr half-life, and radioiodine 131, which has an 8-day half-life. With these isotopes, thyroid radioautography became possible. This was done by a simple "contact technique." A photographic plate was clamped in tight contact with a glass slide bearing the radioactive tissue section; after allowing a period of exposure sufficient for the radioactive emission to produce a photographic effect, the plate was separated from the slide, developed, and fixed as in ordinary photography. To assign any photographic darkening to definite sites within the section, it was necessary to realign plate and section meticulously under the microscope. This aligning was cumbersome so that, in practice, the resolving power of the technique was not much better than 100 μm, that is, one could not distinguish with certainty two sources of radioactivity closer than 100 μm.

Nevertheless, the contact technique was used to test the theory of thyroid function that was popular at the time. This theory was that the functional stages of thyroid cells differed in different follicles: 1) follicles with tall columnar cells would be at a stage when colloid is secreted to the lumen; 2) follicles with cuboidal cells would be at the subsequent stage when colloid is absorbed and released to the circulation; and finally 3) follicles with flattened cells would be at a resting, inactive stage. When the thyroid of animals injected with radioiodine 130 was radioautographed by the contact technique, it was found that, contrary to expectation, the entering iodine was incorporated into the colloid of all follicles, whether they were lined by tall, cuboidal, or flat cells (Leblond, 1943). The conclusion of this and subsequent studies was that all follicles, even though they might function at different rates, were continually incorporating iodine into the colloid (Nadler and Leblond, 1955).

The contact technique was not satisfactory, except for work on large specimens or for the detection of radioactive spots on gels or paper chromatograms (Gross et al., 1950). In January 1946, the author returned to McGill University from service overseas with the Free French Army and was joined by Léonard Bélanger (Fig. 8.1) returning from service with the Canadian Air Force; they attempted to improve the contact between tissue section and emulsion. After a few unsuccessful tests, they met on a Montreal street a physicist, Pierre Demers, who specialized in the study of photographic emulsions. He advised as follows: "Take Eastman-Kodak lantern slides; place them in tepid water for a few minutes to induce the emulsion to swell and soften; then scrape off the emulsion into a beaker, where at about 32° it will liquefy; finally, use a brush to paint the emulsion at the surface of the section."

This "coating technique" provided intimate contact between section and emulsion; it was applied to sections of thyroids from rats given ^{131}I-iodide and to sections of jaws and bones from mice given ^{32}P-phosphate. After exposure and development of the emulsion, images were obtained with a tenfold improvement in resolution (Bélanger and Leblond, 1946), which later, with the advent of nuclear emulsion and appropriate isotopes, will be almost a hundredfold. The enthusiasm at the time may be felt from a description of the event by Bélanger (1965) nearly 20 years later: "It was on a bright and crisp Saturday of February 1946 that a striking radioautographic record was first seen over the tissue. It reminded me of the biblical story of a message written in letters of fire on the wall of the palace of the wicked Assyrian king. But the imprint in the photographic emulsion was not recording a message of doom, but one by which to understand life."

Other procedures were later proposed, in particular the "stripfilm technique," by which an emulsion film is floated over the section (Pelc, 1947). Meanwhile, the painting of the emulsion on the section-bearing slide was simplified when photographic firms provided bulk emulsions that could be melted. The slides could then be directly dipped into the emulsion. This "coating technique" was flexible enough for adaptation to many situations; eventually it prevailed over the old contact technique as well as over the stripfilm technique.

Work by a group of four anatomists, the mathematically inclined Norman Nadler (Fig. 8.2), the imaginative Jack Gross, the technically skilled Rita Bogoroch (Fig. 8.4), and the author, led to the conclusion that a better resolution demanded thinner tissue sections, thinner photographic emulsion coats, and no interspace between them (Gross et al., 1951). Later, Beatrix Kopriwa (Fig. 8.5), who became one of the best specialists in the field and eventually trained a number of North American radioautographers, introduced detailed improvements in the technique. In particular, she devised a semiautomatic "coating instrument" that made it

Fig. 8.1. Léonard F. Bélanger (deceased, 1986), with whom the author developed the integration of emulsion and section, known as the "coating technique" of radioautography. Later, he became Professor and Chairman of the Department of Histology at the University of Ottawa, Ottawa, Canada. Over the years, Léonard Bélanger made use of radioautography to reveal the dynamic features of bone and tooth components.

Fig. 8.2. Norman J. Nadler, who did a mathematical analysis of the conditions under which radioautography is carried out and thus helped devise optimal conditions for success. He also worked out methods for the quantitation of radioautographic reactions. He is Associate Professor of Anatomy at McGill University in Montreal, Canada.

Fig. 8.3. Richard C. Greulich, who investigated ^{14}C-bicarbonate radioautographs and collaborated with the author in demonstrating that all cells in the body synthesize protein. Later he investigated tooth formation. He is Scientific Director at the National Institute on Aging and Director of the Gerontology Research Center, Francis Scott Key Medical Center, in Baltimore, Maryland.

possible to control the thickness of the emulsion coat (Kopriwa, 1966). In this regard, one of the key advantages of radioautography is the possibility to quantitate reactions by counting the number of silver grains per unit area over reactive histological structures. To be reliable, however, counts must be carried out over emulsion coats of reproducible thickness. This is made possible by the use of the coating instrument of Kopriwa.

The radioautographic technique developed in many directions. First, new isotopes appeared: carbon 14 in the form of bicarbonate, sulfur 35 in the form of sulfate and hydrogen 3, or tritium in the form of water. These substances could be administered as such for radioautography, but they were mainly used after being synthesized into an endless variety of compounds, such as amino acids, sugars, nucleotides, etc., which were then administered and traced through the body. In particular, the introduction of the hydrogen isotope, tritium, was a technical milestone in the story of radioautography (Fitzgerald et al., 1951). The advantage of this isotope is due to the energy of its beta rays (averaging 0.018 Mev), which is lower than that of other useful isotopes; the beta rays of ^{32}P have a mean energy of 1.710 Mev, that is almost 100 times that of tritium. Since the length of the path of beta rays is related to their energy, those from tritium will have a very short path and, therefore, affect the emulsion in close vicinity to the source. As a result, resolution is good.

An important development was the application of radioautography at the electron microscope (EM) level in the 1960s. This was done in many laboratories, particularly those of Elizabeth Hay (Fig. 8.6) in Boston, Steve Pelc in England, Lucien Caro in New York, Philippe Granboulan in Paris, and Miriam Salpeter (Fig. 8.8) in Ithaca. The early work of these investigators, particularly the use of a celloidin film, introduced by Miriam Salpeter for the support of the sections during coating with emulsion, was reported at a symposium held in Montreal in 1965 (Leblond and Warren, 1965). A few years later, Beatrix Kopriwa combined the best elements in the published procedures, as well as her own experience, to devise the technique routinely used in this and many other laboratories (Kopriwa, 1973). The resolution of the EM procedures was systematically evaluated by Miriam Salpeter (1981), who measured the scatter of silver grains around artificially prepared radioactive lines. The results provided an index of resolution that was particularly useful for investigation of linelike structures (e.g., plasma membrane), as in the case of locating receptors at the cell surface with the help of radioactive ligands (Bergeron et al., 1985; Bergeron and Posner, 1985), as mentioned below.

Over the years, there have been numerous applications of the radioautographic technique, so numerous that several books have been published on the subject in English (Rogers, 1973) and one in Japanese. Hence in this review, only two major findings will be mentioned in some detail, that is, the demonstration of the continuous renewal of many cell types, using the intestinal epithelium as an example, and the evidence of a continuous renewal of tissue components, using protein as an example. In the final section, a few recent developments will be briefly mentioned.

RENEWAL OF CELLS

Two anatomists, G. Bizzozero in Italy and R.R. Bensley in Chicago, suggested in the 1890s that epithelial cells undergo renewal in stomach (Bizzozero, 1893;

Fig. 8.4. In this picture, Rita Bogoroch is shown preparing a radioautograph in 1948 using an early modification of the "coating technique" that she had devised. While Léonard Bélanger and the author initially used a brush to apply the melted emulsion on slides, she obtained a more even distribution of the diluted emulsion by depositing it with an eye dropper, as shown here. Later, however, the slides were simply dipped in melted emulsion.

Fig. 8.5. Beatrix Kopriwa devised a semiautomatic instrument to dip the slides into melted emulsion. As a result, the thickness of the emulsion coat on the sections could be controlled. She also helped in standardizing the methods for light-microscopic and electron-microscopic radioautography. She is Head of the Radioautography Division and Associate Professor of Anatomy at McGill University in Montreal, Canada.

Bensley, 1898) and intestine (Bizzozero, 1892). Thus, Bizzozero (1892) reasoned that the number of mitotic figures in intestinal crypts was such that the columnar cells arising from the mitoses must migrate out of the crypts to the villus surface. In the following years, German histologists generally interpreted crypt mitoses as a response to damage, which provided cells for the regeneration of the epithelium (Patzelt, 1936). In 1946, however, Catherine Stevens and the author observed that mitoses were present at all times of day in the absence of detectable epithelial damage in rat small intestine; they counted the proportion of dividing cells, worked out a simple method to measure mitotic duration, and calculated that the epithelium of small intestine was renewed in less than 2 days. This renewal of the intestinal epithelium was described as a continuous, physiological event (Leblond and Stevens, 1948). When Catherine Stevens presented these findings at a meeting of the AAA, the gentlemen who taught histology at the time at the University of Western Ontario rose to say, "This is too silly for words," and sat down. In view of such reaction, direct proof was needed! Radioautography provided it. With the use of various labeled DNA precursors that were incorporated into cells about to divide, e.g., ^{32}P-phosphate initially (Leblond et al., 1948), ^{14}C-adenine later (Walker and Leblond, 1958), and finally ^{3}H-thymidine (Leblond and Messier, 1958), it was found that the cells arising from mitosis in the crypts rapidly migrated to the villus wall, ascended the length of the villus, and were lost at its tip.

Columnar cells have a remarkable life story, which the author has worked out with Hazel Cheng (Fig. 8.7) and Gabriel Altmann (Fig. 8.12). These cells arise from stem cells displaying typical embryonic features (many free ribosomes, open-network nucleolus, etc.); they gradually differentiate as they ascend the crypt and enter a villus (Cheng and Leblond, 1974a); they reach maturity in the mid-villus region and, when approaching the villus tip, show various signs of degeneration, including an atrophic nucleolus (Altmann and Leblond, 1982). In fact, columnar cells in a few days go from birth to old age following a sequence comparable to that extending over a whole lifetime in stable cells, such as those of kidney (Leblond, 1981).

The loss of cells from the villus tip is explained by Altmann as follows. He finds that the ability of columnar cells to synthesize protein is markedly decreased in the villus tip region. Moreover, the injection of protein inhibitors into rats causes villus cells to desquamate rapidly. He consequently proposes that, under normal conditions, the decrease in the synthesis of protein by columnar cells approaching

Fig. 8.6. Elizabeth Hay, working with Jean Paul Revel, developed one of the first effective techniques for electron-microscopic radioautography. The photograph shows her in 1961 when they worked out the technique. In 1963 they published the first electron-microscopic demonstration of the intracellular pathway of newly synthesized proteins. She is Chairman of the Department of Anatomy, Harvard University, Boston, Mass.

Fig. 8.7. Hazel Cheng, who showed a remarkable skill in the application of light-microscopic and electron-microscopic radioautography to specific problems of the gastrointestinal tract. She is Associate Professor of Anatomy at the University of Toronto in Toronto, Canada.

Fig. 8.8. Miriam Salpeter, who played a crucial role in working out a basic step in the technique for electron-microscopic radioautography, which has been adopted universally. She also devised a method to assess the resolution obtainable with various isotopes. She is Professor and Chairman, Section of Neurobiology and Behavior, Division of Biological Sciences, Cornell University, Ithaca, New York.

the villus tip induces their degeneration and eventual desquamation (Altmann, 1976).

All the cells in the intestinal epithelium undergo renewal. Mucous and entero-endocrine cells migrate along with columnar cells from crypt to villus (Cheng, 1974a; Cheng and Leblond, 1974b), whereas Paneth cells turn over within the crypt base (Cheng et al., 1969; Cheng, 1974b) in a manner analyzed by Hazel Cheng and Matthew Bjerknes in the Department of Anatomy at the University of Toronto (Bjerknes and Cheng, 1981).

These various studies are generally based on the use of the DNA precursor, ^{3}H-thymidine—a major tool in cell biology. Of its numerous applications to studies of cell renewal, let us also mention the timing of male germ cell development. In the rat, the cycle of the seminiferous epithelium has been measured at 12 ± 0.2 days and the whole spermatogenesis at about 48 days (Clermont et al., 1959). In man, Yves Clermont has estimated that the cycle takes 16 ± 1 days, while spermatogenesis occupies 74 ± 4 days (Heller and Clermont, 1964).

The use of ^{3}H-thymidine radioautography has made it possible to classify cell populations into three categories (Leblond, 1964):

1) static cell populations, whose cells do not take up ^{3}H-thymidine in the adult and, therefore, do not undergo division (e.g., the neurons of cerebral cortex and retina;

2) expanding cell populations, in which the number of labeled nuclei gradually decreases with age to a low value in the adult, and, therefore, cell addition continues, but at a decreasing rate (e.g., in liver, kidney, and a majority of organs);

3) renewing cell populations, in which the number of labeled nuclei remains high throughout life, that is, new cells are continually being supplied, but the cell addition is balanced by an equivalent loss (e.g., most epithelia, particularly those of testis, intestine, and stomach, as well as hemopoietic tissues).

RENEWAL OF TISSUE COMPONENTS

In the early 1950s, an anatomy graduate student in the author's laboratory, Richard Greulich (Fig. 8.3), injected carbon 14 in the form of ^{14}C-bicarbonate (Greulich and Leblond, 1953). Meanwhile, in the course of a summer spent by the author with Newton Everett (generally known as Ben Everett) at the University of Washington in Seattle, the incorporation of the amino acid methionine labeled with sulfur 35 was examined (Leblond et al., 1957). In both cases, all the cells of the body became labeled soon after a single injection. Since both lines of evidence pointed to the label being in proteins, it was concluded that all cells of the body were continually synthesizing proteins (Fig. 8.9). Around 1950, this conclusion was heretical, since it was widely believed that only the cells of a few organs, particularly liver and pancreas, made protein; and the widespread radioautographic reactions were generally shrugged off as artifacts. In the ensuing years, however, the objections diminished and, when the conclusion was fully confirmed with ^{35}S-methionine in 1957, the public response was: "Everyone knows that all cells synthesize proteins."

The origin of the proteins appearing in cells was examined by George Palade and collaborators in acinar pancreatic cells. They assigned the synthesis to ribosomes (Siekevitz and Palade, 1958) and later provided evidence that newly formed proteins migrated from ribosomes through the Golgi apparatus to zymogen granules (Siekevitz and Palade, 1960). However, the evidence was based on cell fractionation and not considered decisive by all workers in the field. Hence, several laboratories used radioautography to reexamine the problem. Thus, in 1963, Hershey Warshawsky (now a leader in dental research) was the senior investigator in a light-microscopic radioautographic study of pancreatic acini after injection of ³H-leucine. The label first appeared over the basophilic base of the

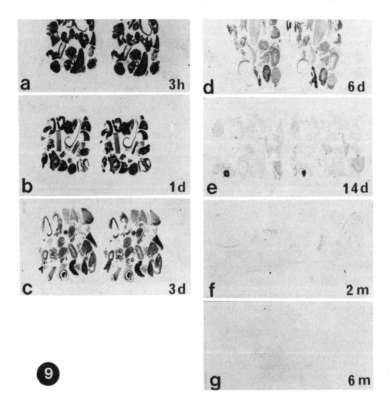

Fig. 8.9. When substances such as ³H-methionine, ¹⁴C-bicarbonate, or ¹⁴C-glucose are injected into young animals, all cells become labeled, as these various labels find their way into newly synthesized protein. However, the label is eventually lost, indicating that proteins turn over.

This figure represents photographs of whole histological slides bearing unstained radioautographs from rats given 30 μCi of ¹⁴C-glucose at the age of 3 days, and sacrificed from 3 hr to 6 months later. Exposure has been equal in all cases.

Three hours after the injection (a), an intense blackening outlines the shape of the various organs and tissues. By 1 day (b), there is a slight decrease in the intensity of the reactions, indicating some loss of labeled material, presumably as a result of secretion or turnover. At later intervals (c and following), the intensity of the reactions progressively decreases. By 14 days (e), reactions are weak, except for a black spot due to the presence of radioactivity in the lens, a unique structure in which proteins do not seem to turn over. At 2 months (f), very little radioactivity is retained in organs and tissues, with the exception of line reactions in bone and dentin. At 6 months (g), the decrease in dentinal reactions is due to wear of the tooth surface and in bone reactions is due to resorption processes.

In conclusion, proteins and other substances are rapidly synthesized in all tissues of young animals, but they turn over eventually in nearly all sites.

cells, where the rough endoplasmic reticulum (rER) was known to be located, and peaked over the Golgi region 30 min later and over secretory granules by 4 hr (Warshawsky et al., 1963). With the use of EM radioautography after ^{3}H-proline injection in 1963, Jean-Paul Revel and Elizabeth Hay examined the biogenesis of collagen in chondrocytes. The label appeared in the rER, migrated to the Golgi apparatus, and was carried by secretory vesicles to the extracellular space (Revel and Hay, 1963). The next year, the same sequence was described in EM radioautographs of pancreatic acini after ^{3}H-leucine injection by Huberta van Heyningen at McGill (1964) and Lucien Caro and George Palade at the Rockefeller Institute (1964).

Why do secretory proteins pass through the Golgi apparatus? It had been shown in 1950 that the Golgi region was frequently stained by the periodic acid-Schiff technique (Leblond, 1950) and, presumably, contained glycoprotein. To find out whether sugars were processed in this region, labeled glucose was injected and EM radioautographs of intestinal goblet cells were prepared. The label directly appeared in the Golgi apparatus (Neutra and Leblond, 1966) where, presumably, sugars were incorporated into glycoprotein side chains. When a similar experiment was done with other labeled sugars (Whur et al., 1969), galactose was also taken up into the Golgi apparatus, but mannose was incorporated into the rER. Since, within carbohydrate side chains, mannose was known to be located close to the protein chain and galactose far from it, it was concluded that the addition of sugars began in the rER, but was continued and presumably completed in the Golgi apparatus (Whur et al., 1969).

With the use of another sugar incorporated into the Golgi apparatus, ^{3}H-fucose, as marker of glycoproteins, the author observed with Gary Bennett (Fig. 8.11) that these substances ended in different sites (Leblond and Bennett, 1977). They may be carried outside the cell by secretory granules, or they may be incorporated into the surface membrane of the cell, or they may remain within the cell and pass into lysosomes. In neurons, however, a different pathway was observed after ^{3}H-leucine injection. This study was in collaboration with Bernard Droz (Fig. 8.10). Newly synthesized protein was seen to enter the axon hillock and flow down the axon at a rate estimated at 1.5 mm per day (Droz and Leblond, 1963). This work demonstrated what is now known as the "slow axoplasmic flow." Later, Bernice Grafstein (1967) found that some labeled material migrated at least ten times faster. This was described as "rapid axoplasmic flow" by Raymond Lasek (1970), who made important contributions to this field. Tracing the axoplasmic flow by radioautography soon became a routine technique, by which neuroanatomists could identify the pathway followed by axon bundles in the nervous system.

RECENT DEVELOPMENTS

Among the applications of the radioautographic technique in recent years, three will be mentioned: 1) the identification of antibody binding to tissue sections or free cells; 2) the recognition of ligands binding to cell surface receptors; and 3) the assignment of a messenger RNA to the cell producing it, as done by hybridization with the corresponding cDNA.

Fig. 8.10. Bernard Dröz, who, during a stay at McGill University, carried out the radioautographic experiments that provided the first direct evidence of the flow of proteins down the axon. He is Director of the Institute of Histology at the Medical School of the University of Lausanne, Lausanne, Switzerland.

Fig. 8.11. Gary Bennett, who is using radioautography to investigate the synthesis of carbohydrate side chains in glycoproteins, as well as the intracellular migration of these substances. He is Professor of Anatomy at McGill University in Montreal, Canada.

Fig. 8.12. Gabriel Altmann, who is making skillful use of radioautography to examine the behavior of intestinal epithelial cells. He is Associate Professor of Anatomy at the University of Western Ontario in London, Ontario, Canada.

Fig. 8.13. Dennis G. Osmond, who applies radioautography to the solution of basic problems regarding the role of bone marrow lymphocytes in immunity. He is Chairman of the Department of Anatomy at McGill University, Montreal, Canada.

Identification of Antibodies

To locate an antigen, antibodies directed against it may be labeled by radioiodine, ^{125}I, and applied to sections in which the presence of the antigen is suspected; the site at which the antibodies are bound to the antigen is then detected by radioautography (Paiement and Leblond, 1977). Dennis Osmond (Fig. 8.13) has used such an approach to identify the B lymphocytes produced in massive numbers by mammalian bone marrow. Since B cells secrete an immunoglobulin, IgM, and deposit it at their own surface, anti-IgM antibodies should bind at this surface. If these antibodies are labeled with radioiodine, the cells that carry them may be identified in radioautographs (Osmond, 1980). Dennis Osmond has followed the development of B lymphocytes in the bone marrow by an ingenious double-labeling experiment. 1) The age of the cells is evaluated by repeated injections of ^{3}H-thymidine over 1 to 84 hr, in which case labeled nuclei are recognized by the small size and compactness of the overlying group of radioautographic silver grains (due to the low energy of the beta rays from tritium). 2) The presence of IgM antibodies at the surface of the cells is assessed from the uptake of ^{131}I-labeled anti-IgM antibodies, in which case labeled cells are recognized by the wide scattering of the silver grains they produce (due to the high energy of the beta and gamma rays from ^{131}I). Accordingly, the cells taking up thymidine or IgM antibodies or both can be identified. The work led to the conclusion that IgM molecules are not produced by young B cells, but appear and increase progressively in density as these cells mature (Osmond and Nossal, 1974).

Cell Surface Receptors

Radioiodine labeling of circulating hormones has been the method of choice to observe their uptake by cell surface receptors in target organs. For example, to locate insulin receptors, a physiological dose of ^{125}I-insulin is injected intravenously; tissues are fixed within minutes and processed for radioautography. The label then appears along the cell surface of target organs. Thus, John Bergeron and coworkers have demonstrated that, 2 min after injection of labeled insulin, the label appears at the surface not only of liver cells, a known target of the hormone, but also of cells without known relation to insulin, such as the intestinal epithelium (Bergeron et al., 1985; Bergeron and Posner, 1985). Later, the receptor with the labeled insulin bound to it is endocytosed; after spending about 20 min within the cell, receptor and insulin separate; the insulin gradually disappears, while the receptor returns to the cell surface (Bergeron et al., 1985).

Hybridization

Single strands of DNA combine with strands of RNA arranged in a complementary sequence—a property that is the basis for *in situ* hybridization (Budd and Pansky, 1985). One application of this property is the localization of specific mRNA sequences in tissue sections with the help of the corresponding cDNA probe. For example, to detect whether the cells of a certain tissue, such as pancreas or pituitary, produce insulin, sections of this tissue are exposed to insulin-cDNA (which has been labeled previously) and are then radioautographed. Any cell taking up the label contains material capable of hybridizing with the insulin-cDNA, that is the mRNA responsible for the synthesis of insulin. Cells containing such mRNA have thus been observed not only in the Langherans islet cells of pancreas, as expected, but also in some pituitary cells, which, presumably, are insulin producers (Budd and Pansky, 1985).

CONCLUSIONS

Radioautography has had applications in many different fields, but the main result of its use has been to reveal an unsuspected dynamism of cells and cell components.

With the exception of embryology, morphological sciences tend to give a static picture of the body. Radioautography, on the other hand, reveals the sites where cells and molecules arise, as well as their eventual migration away from these sites. As a result, histological sections of organs formerly believed to be static are shown by radioautography to be involved in movements of cells and molecules that may be traced over long periods of time. One may say therefore that radioautography has introduced the time dimension into histology (Leblond, 1965).

REFERENCES

Altmann, G.G. 1976 Factors involved in the differentiation of the epithelial cells in the adult rat small intestine. In: Stem Cells of Renewing Cell Populations. A.B. Cairnie, P.K. Lala, and D.G. Osmond, eds. Academic Press, New York, pp. 51–66.

Altmann, G., and C.P. Leblond 1982 Changes in the size and structure of the nucleolus of columnar cells during their migration from crypt base to villus top in rat jejunum. J. Cell Sci., *56*:83–99.

Bélanger, L.F. 1965 Opening address. In: The Use of Radioautography in Investigating Protein Synthesis. C.P. Leblond and K.B. Warren, eds. Academic Press, New York, pp. 1–6.

Bélanger, L.F., and C.P. Leblond 1946 A method for locating radioactive elements in tissues by covering histological sections with a photographic emulsion. Endocrinology, *39*:386–400.

Bensley, R.R. 1898 The structure of mammalian gastric glands. Q.J. Microsc. Sci., *41*: 361–389.

Bergeron, J.J.M., J. Cruz, M.N. Khan, and B.I. Posner 1985 Uptake of insulin and other ligands into receptor-rich endocytic components of target cells: The endosomal apparatus. Ann. Rev. Physiol., *47*:383–403.

Bergeron, J.J.M., and B.I. Posner 1985 Insulin-receptor interactions in vivo. A cell biological approach. In: Polypeptide Hormone Receptors. B.I. Posner, ed. Marcel Dekker Inc., New York, pp. 137–156.

Bizzozero G. 1892 Ueber die schlauchförmigen Drüsen des Magendarmkanals und die Beziehungen ihres Epithels zu den Oberflächenepithel der Schleimhaut. Arch. Mikrosk. Anat., *40*:325–375.

Bizzozero, G. 1893 Ueber die schlauchförmigen Drüsen des Magendarmkanals und die Beziehungen ihres Epithels zu den Oberflächenepithel der Schleimhaut. Arch. Mikrosk. Anat., *42*:82–152.

Bjerknes, M., and H. Cheng 1981 The stem cell zone of the small intestinal epithelium. I. Evidence from Paneth cells in the adult mouse. Am. J. Anat., *160*:51–63.

Budd, G.C., and B. Pansky 1985 *In situ* DNA-mRNA hybridization as a microscopic cytochemical tool. Bull. Microsc. Soc. Can., *13*:5–13.

Caro, L.G., and G.E. Palade 1964 Protein synthesis, storage and discharge in the pancreatic exocrine cell. An autoradiographic study. J. Cell Biol., *20*:473–482.

Cheng, H. 1974a Origin, differentiation and renewal of the four main epithelial cell types in the mouse small intestine. II. Mucous cells. Am. J. Anat., *141*:481–502.

Cheng, H. 1974b Origin, differentiation and renewal of the four main epithelial cell types in the mouse small intestine. IV. Paneth cells. Am. J. Anat., *141*:521–536.

Cheng, H., and C.P. Leblond 1974a Origin, differentiation and renewal of the four main epithelial cell types in the mouse small intestine. I. Columnar cell. Am. J. Anat., *141*:461–480.

Cheng, H., and C.P. Leblond 1974b Origin, differentiation and renewal of the four main epithelial cell types in the mouse small intestine. III. Enteroendocrine cells. Am. J. Anat., *141*:503–520.

Cheng, H., J. Merzel, and C.P. Leblond 1969 Renewal of Paneth cells in the small intestine of the mouse. Am. J. Anat., *126*:507–526.

Clermont, Y., C.P. Leblond, and B. Messier 1959 Durée du cycle de l'épithélium séminal du rat. Arch. Anat. Microsc. Morphol. Exp., *48*:37–55.

deHevesy, G. 1948 A review. Cold Spring Harbor Symp. Quant. Biol., *13*:129–150.

Droz, B., and C.P. Leblond 1963 Axonal migration of proteins in the central nervous system and peripheral nerves as shown by radioautography. J. Comp. Neurol., *121*:325–346.

Fitzgerald, P.J., M.L. Eidinoff, J.E. Knoll, and E.B. Simmel 1951 Tritium in radioautography. Science, *114*:494–498.

Grafstein, B. 1967 Transport of protein by goldfish optic nerve fibers. Science, *157*:196–198.

Greulich, R.C., and C.P. Leblond 1953 Radioautographic visualization of radiocarbon in the organs and tissues of newborn rats following administration of C^{14}-labeled bicarbonate. Anat. Rec., *115*:559–586.

Gross, J., R. Bogoroch, N.J. Nadler, and C.P. Leblond 1951 The theory and methods of the autographic localization of radio-elements in tissues. A.J.R., *65*:420–458.

Gross, J., and C.P. Leblond 1946, 1947 Histological localization of radioactive elements. A review. Can. Med. Assoc. J., *57*:102–122.

Gross, J., C.P. Leblond, A.E. Franklin, and J.H. Quastel 1950 Presence of iodinated amino acids in unhydrolyzed thyroid and plasma. Science, *111*:605–608.

Heller, C.G., and Y. Clermont 1964 Kinetics of the germinal epithelium in man. Recent Prog. Horm. Res., *20*:545–575.

Kopriwa, B.M. 1966 A semiautomatic instrument for the radioautographic coating technique. J. Histochem. Cytochem., *14*:923–928.

Kopriwa, B.M. 1973 A reliable, standardized method for ultrastructural electron microscopic radioautography. Histochemie, *37*:1–17.

Lasek, R. 1970 Axonal transport of proteins in dorsal root ganglion cells of the growing cat: A comparison of growing and mature neurons. Brain Res., *20*:121–126.

Leblond, C.P. 1943 Localization of newly administered iodine in the thyroid gland as indicated by radio-iodine. J. Anat., *77*:149–152.

Leblond, C.P. 1950 Distribution of periodic acid-reactive carbohydrates in the adult rat. Am. J. Anat., *86*:1–50.

Leblond, C.P. 1964 Classification of cell populations on the basis of their proliferative behavior. Natl. Cancer Inst. Monogr., *14*:119–150.

Leblond, C.P. 1965 The time dimension in histology. Am. J. Anat., *116*:1–28.

Leblond, C.P. 1981 The life history of cells in renewing systems. Am. J. Anat., *160*:113–158.

Leblond, C.P., and G. Bennett 1977 Role of the Golgi apparatus in terminal glycosylation. 1st Int. Cong. Cell Biology, *1*:326–336.

Leblond, C.P., N.B. Everett, and B. Simmons 1957 Sites of protein synthesis as shown by radioautography after administration of S^{35}-labelled methionine. Am. J. Anat., *101*:225–271.

Leblond, C.P., and B. Messier 1958 Renewal of chief cells and goblet cells in the small intestine as shown by radioautography after injection of thymidine-H^3 into mice. Anat. Rec., *132*:247–259.

Leblond, C.P., and C.E. Stevens 1948 The constant renewal of the intestinal epithelium of the albino rat. Anat. Rec., *100*:357–378.

Leblond, C.P., C.E. Stevens, and R. Bogoroch 1948 Histological localization of newly formed desoxyribonucleic acid. Science, *108*:531–533.

Leblond, C.P., et P. Süe 1940 Passage de l'iode radioactif (I^{128}) dans la thyroïde stimulée par l'hormone thyréotrope de l'hypophyse. C.R. Soc. Biol. (Paris), *133*:543.

Leblond, C.P., and K.B. Warren 1965 The Use of Radioautography in Investigating Protein Synthesis. Academic Press, New York.

Nadler, N.J., and C.P. Leblond 1955 The site and rate of the formation of thyroid hormone. Brookhaven Symp. Biol., 7:40–60.

Neutra M., and C.P. Leblond 1966 Synthesis of the carbohydrate of mucus in the Golgi complex, as shown by electron microscope radioautography of goblet cells from rats injected with 3H-glucose. J. Cell Biol., 30:119–136.

Osmond, D.G. 1980 Production and differentiation of B lymphocytes in the bone marrow. In: Immunoglobulin Genes and B Cell Differentiation. J.R. Battisto and K.L. Knight, eds. Elsevier North Holland, Inc., Amsterdam, pp. 135–158.

Osmond, D.G., and R.J. Nossal 1974 Differentiation of lymphocytes in mouse bone marrow. II. Kinetics of maturation and renewal of antiglobulin-binding cells studied by double labeling. Cell. Immunol., 13:132–145.

Paiement, J.M., and C.P. Leblond 1977 Localization of thyroglobulin antigenicity in rat thyroid sections using antibodies labeled with peroxidase or radio-iodine 125I. J. Cell Biol., 74:992–1015.

Patzelt, V. 1936 Der Darm. In: Handbuch der mikroskopischen Anatomie des Menschen. W. von Möllendorf, W. Handl, eds. Springer, Berlin, Vol. 5, pp. 1–448.

Pelc, S.R. 1947 Autoradiographic technique. Nature, 160:749–750.

Revel, J.P., and E.D. Hay 1963 An autoradiographic and electron microscopic study of collagen synthesis in differentiating cartilage. Z. Zellforsch., 61:110–144.

Rogers, A.W. 1973 Techniques of Autoradiography, 2nd edition. Elsevier, Amsterdam.

Salpeter, M.M. 1981 High resolution autoradiography. In: Techniques in Cellular Physiology. P.F. Baker, ed. Elsevier/North Holland Scientific Publishers Ltd., Dublin, Ireland, pp. 1–45.

Siekevitz, P., and G.E. Palade 1958 A cytochemical study on the pancreas of the guinea pig. I. *In vivo* incorporation of leucine-1-C14 into the proteins of cell fractions. J. Biophys. Biochem. Cytol., 4:557–566.

Siekevitz, P., and G.E. Palade 1960 A cytochemical study on the pancreas of the guinea pig. V. *In vivo* incorporation of leucine-C14 into the chymotrypsinogen of various cell fractions. J. Biophys. Biochem. Cytol., 7:619–632.

Walker, B.E., and C.P. Leblond 1958 Sites of nucleic acid synthesis in the mouse visualized by radioautography after administration of C14-labeled adenine and thymidine. Exp. Cell Res., 14:510–531.

Warshawsky, H., C.P. Leblond, and B. Droz 1963 Synthesis and migration of proteins in the cells of the exocrine pancreas as revealed by specific activity determinations from radioautographs. J. Cell Biol., 16:1–24.

Whur, P., A. Herscovics, and C.P. Leblond 1969 Radioautographic visualization of the incorporation of 3H-galactose and -mannose by rat thyroids *in vitro* in relation to the stages of thyroglobulin synthesis. J. Cell Biol., 43:289–311.

van Heyningen, H.E. 1964 Secretion of protein by the acinar cells of the rat pancreas, as studied by electron microscopic radioautography. Anat. Rec., 148:485–498.

Chapter 9

THE BEGINNINGS OF IMMUNOCYTOCHEMISTRY

Gwen V. Childs (Moriarty)

The impending birth of immunohistochemistry was heralded in 1930 by the announcement that one could link azo-dyes to antibodies without damaging their biological ("agglutinating") activity (Reiner, 1930). Marrack (1934) was the first to use these compounds to stain typhoid and cholera bacterial cells, and he reported that agglutinated bacteria were colored pink or red if the antiserum had been conjugated to the dye.

These findings helped to provide inspiration to a young medical student at Harvard, Albert H. Coons. In 1934, his interest in the field was sparked by stimulating courses in bacteriology and immunology conducted by Hans Zinsser and a summer research program in immunology in John Enders' laboratory. The inspiration that led him to develop the stains did not occur until after graduation, however, while he was on a 6-month holiday in Berlin (Coons, 1961). There he spent afternoons walking the streets, "talking to people in cafes and trying to improve his halting German."

One afternoon, on one of his walks, he was thinking of the microscopic lesion characteristic of rheumatic fever, the Aschoff nodule. It had been assumed that it formed as the result of a reaction involving streptococcus and circulating antibodies or hypersensitive cells. He reasoned, however, that this could only be proved by somehow demonstrating the antibody or the antigen microscopically in the lesion. When he returned to an internship at Harvard with its heavy clinical load, he had only a few spare hours to work with the antibodies and azo-dyes. Fortunately for him (and the field), he was given a small fund by Dr. George Minot for the purchase of chemicals. At the same time, Minot urged him to apply for a research fellowship instead of continuing his clinical investigations. Thus, his research career and the development of immunocytochemistry were launched.

The following year, Dr. Enders agreed to let him work in his laboratory as a Research Fellow, stating that "labeled antibodies might not answer the rheumatic fever question, but they should provide a general procedure for locating antigens in tissues and cells; they obviously would have application to countless problems" (Coons, 1961).

During the first phases of his work, Coons repeated Marrack's studies. His results were similar; however, he concluded that the reaction was too faint to be suitable. Thus he sought another dye molecule. At this same time, two innovative Harvard chemists, Drs. Hugh Creech and Norman Jones, were linking fluorescent compounds to proteins; they agreed to couple some anthracene isocyanate to antipneumococcal antiserum. When the bacteria were stained, the agglutinated clumps were brilliantly fluorescent in ultraviolet light (Coons et al., 1941).

The next step involved the application of fluorescein isocyanate, made by a graduate student, Ernst Berliner, and conjugated to antibody by Creech. Their intent was to apply the compound to tissues; however, for this they needed a fluorescence microscope. Coons then turned to his former histology professor, Dr. Allan Grafflin, who was in the process of assembling a fluorescence apparatus to be attached to a Zeiss photomicroscope. When he learned of Coons' problem, Grafflin hastened the construction of the unit, and the first immunocytochemically stained tissues were viewed (Coons et al., 1942). Thus, while immunologists and chemists were responsible for the early development of immunocytochemistry, the technique itself could not have come to full fruition without the cooperation and fluorescence equipment built by an anatomist.

The subsequent decades proved that Enders' original prediction was correct. Weller and Coons introduced the more sensitive indirect method in 1954. As the field of electron microscopy was being developed, it became clear that electron-opaque labels were needed; the next forefront of activity was focused on these labels along with better conjugation methods that preserved antibody activity. In 1959, Singer described the first ferritin-antibody conjugates and showed that the reaction could be detected at the electron-microscopic level by the micellar structure of the ferritin molecule. The conjugate was applied to the cells before embedding and sectioning—thus, the first "preembedding stain" was born (Singer and McLean, 1963). These early conjugates were not applied successfully to embedded ultrathin sections, however, because they were adsorbed readily by the hydrophobic surfaces of the plastic.

Another approach for immunoelectron microscopy was to label antibodies with heavy metals. Thus the prototype of the current colloidal gold stains was conceived. In 1961, the use of mercury to label antibodies for electron-microscopic stains was described by Pepe (1961a,b). During the early 1960s, a group led by Dr. Ludwig Sternberger sought additional ways to label antibodies with metals that would avoid damage to antigen-reactive sites and reduce nonspecific adsorption of the conjugates to plastic-embedded sections. Labeling procedures were developed with purified antibodies complexed to the specific antigen. After conjugation, the antigen-antibody complex was dissociated leaving purified antibodies with binding sites free for tissue antigen. Both uranium-labeled (Sternberger et al., 1963, 1965) and ferritin-labeled (Striker et al., 1966) antibodies were prepared in this way.

Sternberger and his colleagues found that the use of these purified labeled antibodies prevented their nonspecific adsorption to the plastic; however, the embedded antigens were inaccessible to the antibodies. They therefore developed an "etching" reagent for methacrylate sections that allowed more intense staining. Thus, the first "postembedding stains" were introduced in 1965.

This group also reported that the uranium labeling technique produced a weak stain, and hence they began to develop ways of intensifying the reaction so that it could be better quantified (Sternberger et al., 1966). Their work might have been continued; however, it was quickly shifted when the new, more promising label, horseradish peroxidase, appeared. It was this sudden turn of events that led to their discovery of the peroxidase-antiperoxidase complex (PAP) several years later. Before discussing this further, let us turn to the story of the development of enzyme-labeled antibodies.

The first application of enzyme cytochemistry to immunocytochemistry was done by Ram and his colleagues, who were experienced in the production of ferritin-antibody conjugates (Ram et al., 1963). They had reasoned that the high molecular weight of ferritin precluded its penetration into tissue and therefore were seeking smaller molecules. They initially conjugated acid phosphatase to antibody and found that the enzyme reaction product could be localized at the site of the antigen (Ram et al., 1966).

At the same time, Graham and Karnovsky (1966) were developing cytochemical methods for the localization of peroxidase. During that year, the method was used by Nakane and Pierce (1966) and Avremeas and Uriel (1966) to localize the first immunoperoxidase stains. The peroxidase-antibody conjugates were more stable than acid-phosphatase conjugates, and hence the stains were more reliable. This technological breakthrough also produced a stain that was permanent and could be used at both light- and electron-microscopic levels (Nakane and Pierce, 1966, 1967).

Nakane continued the pioneering studies of the peroxidase conjugates and showed that the application of different substrates produced different colored reaction products. This clever approach allowed the application of multiple stains to localize different antigens in the same section (Nakane, 1968). By the late 1960s he and his colleagues had also shown that the immunoperoxidase stain could be applied to methacrylate-embedded ultrathin sections that were etched with the same solutions developed by Sternberger and his colleagues (Kawarai and Nakane, 1970). In a subsequent report, the use of hydrogen peroxide was added to the list of etching agents after it was discovered that it allowed one to reveal antigenic sites in epoxy-embedded material.

After the initial introduction of the peroxidase-labeled antibodies, it became clear that improvements were needed in the conjugation methods to increase the yield of labeled antibodies (Nakane and Kawaoi, 1974). Pioneers in the field continued to work on the problem of improved conjugation methods as well as methods designed to conjugate Fab fragments to enzymes (Kraehenbuhl et al., 1971).

Meanwhile, two other groups of workers elected to approach the problem differently. They reasoned that the peroxidase molecule could be used as an antigen to make antiperoxidase antibodies that could then be applied sequentially in a four-step immunocytochemical stain, thereby avoiding the direct conjugation of label to the first or second antibody. The new "unlabeled antibody" or "bridge" technique was presented at the same meeting of the Histochemical Society by both groups (Sternberger and Culculis, 1969; Mason et al., 1969).

It was this course of action that led Sternberger's group to discover the PAP complex. It was recognized that the antiperoxidase in the unlabeled antibody stains must be purified in order to achieve maximal sensitivity. Their attempts at affinity-column purification resulted in the loss of high-affinity antibodies. Thus, they began to purify the antiperoxidase by adding peroxidase in mild excess to form soluble complexes. During the course of this addition, they discovered that the PAP complex formed a stable ring that most often contained 3 molecules of peroxidase and 2 molecules of antiperoxidase. The extra peroxidase in the complex made it more reactive as a staining solution, and the use of purified antiperoxidase promoted the desired increase in sensitivity. The technique and its first applications as a light-microscopic stain were published in 1970 by Sternberger et al.

The enthusiasm for immunoperoxidase methods grew rapidly in the 1970s. The first major front of activity was focused initially on the light-microscopic differentiation of cell types in the anterior pituitary gland. Pioneering contributors included Nakane, Baker, Spicer, Mason, and Phifer. Collectively, they showed the feasibility of applying single and double immunoperoxidase stains to differentiate and study the various pituitary cell types. The prominent anatomist, Dr. Burton L. Baker, showed that the results from immunocytochemical stains correlated favorably with data obtained from tinctorial methods and also demonstrated that the stained cells responded, as expected, to various experimental manipulations like castration (Baker, 1970).

There were some surprises in the field, however. We have a long-standing caveat about the first application of immunocytochemistry to any tissue that states, "the technique will often tell you more than you wanted to know about the antigenic sites." This prediction was certainly true in some of the initial studies of the pituitary, when two groups published the exciting news that both gonadotropins could be stored in the same cells in rats (Nakane, 1968) or humans (Phifer et al., 1973), and that melanocyte-stimulating hormone was stored in the same cells that contained adrenocorticotropic hormone (ACTH) (Phifer et al., 1972). The strangest finding was reported by our group when we discovered that a subpopulation of pituitary cells stored two chemically unrelated hormones, ACTH and follicle-stimulating hormone (FSH) (Moriarty and Garner, 1977).

The earliest impact of these immunocytochemical studies was to negate the long-standing "one cell-one hormone theory" held for many endocrine cell types. Thus, the concept of the production and storage of multiple hormones in the same cell was introduced. It has since been confirmed many times by anatomists studying neural and endocrine cells types throughout the body.

The earliest electron-microscopic immunoperoxidase techniques were developed in the 1970s after the introduction of methods by Nakane's group. The rate of development was heightened in 1968 when two beginning graduate students in anatomy were challenged simultaneously with the same thesis problem (designed to solve the heated controversy about the identity of the cell that produced ACTH). At The University of Iowa, I was assigned this problem by Dr. N.S. Halmi, and the same challenge was assigned to Phyllis Bowie by Dr. E. Rennels at the University of Texas. During the subsequent 4 years, both of us were attracted to the immunoperoxidase method and, in independent studies, we applied it successfully to solve the controversy (Moriarty and Halmi, 1972; Bowie et al., 1973). Dr. Halmi and I were particularly fortunate because we had obtained some PAP complex from Dr. L.A. Sternberger and were able to report that it produced a more intense, reliable stain than the early peroxidase-antibody conjugates. Thus, we showed that the PAP complex was a highly sensitive immunocytochemical tool for use at the electron-microscopic level (Moriarty and Halmi, 1972; Moriarty et al., 1973).

Another major front of activity was in the brain and spinal cord. Groups of workers led by Knigge, Elde, Zimmerman, Reis, Hökfelt, Petrusz, and Baker applied both immunoperoxidase and immunofluorescence techniques to the brain to identify cell bodies, fiber tracts, and terminals. The papers by workers from these groups are too numerous to reference in this brief review. The application of the techniques to nervous tissue at the electron-microscopic level was further developed by a young pioneering neuroanatomist, Dr. Virginia Pickel, who devised a preembedding method that is being used widely today (Pickel et al., 1975).

As the studies with immunoperoxidase techniques proliferated, new ways of coupling antibodies to label were developed. One of the most sensitive means was pioneered by groups led by Bayer and Wilchek (1976), Heitzmann and Richards (1974), and Guesdon et al. (1979), who applied the avidin-biotin system in their stains. They attached the small biotin molecule successfully to antibodies and then applied peroxidase-labeled avidin conjugates to localize the biotin. The major advantage of this system was the high affinity of the avidin for the biotin (dissociation constant $- 10^{-15}$ M) that resulted in stronger, more rapid linkages and more sensitive stains. A very sensitive modification of this technique that employs avidin-biotin peroxidase complexes was introduced by Hsu et al. in 1981.

Meanwhile, many prominent anatomists and cell biologists recognized that peroxidase was not without its drawbacks, since the reaction product diffused readily. This rendered it less suitable for precise electron microscopy. The development of colloidal gold labeling techniques (Faulk and Taylor, 1971) was a promising answer to the problem. The technique advanced rapidly when pioneers discovered that one could produce different sizes of gold molecules and thereby label more than one antigen in the same section (Frens, 1973; Geoghegan and Ackerman, 1977). The beauty of the technique was enhanced by the fact that it could be applied along with routine heavy metal counterstains to allow the study of organelle structure.

Modern day anatomists now have a wide choice of immunocytochemical methods that can be applied to answer their questions. The introduction of the colloidal gold technique has stimulated many to substitute these labels for the immunoperoxidase stains at the electron-microscopic level. Immunoenzyme and immunofluorescence stains, however, are still used widely at the light-microscopic level; their value as antigen mapping tools is unquestioned. The technology has continued to surprise workers with discoveries that show the ubiquity of certain antigens in different tissues, as well as many unusual combinations of antigens that appear to be produced by the same cell or stored in the same secretory granules.

Thus, in 1939, when Coons recognized that labeled antibodies were needed to unlock the secrets behind the formation of the Aschoff lesion, he began an approach to a type of question that can only be answered by immunohistochemistry. The technology that has developed over the past 56 years is now providing a base for the development of other ways of identifying functional sites in cells. These include the localization of mRNA activity with labeled cDNA or anti-sense mRNA probes, or the study of receptors with labeled ligands. Pioneering anatomists of today are seeking to combine these newer techniques with immunocytochemistry in order to obtain a more complete view of cell receptivity and function.

REFERENCES

Avremeas, S., and J. Uriel 1966 Methods de marquage d'antigens el de'anticorps avec des enzymes et son application en immunodiffusion. Acad Sci. Paris, *262*:2543–2545.

Baker, B.L. 1970 Studies on hormone localization with emphasis on the hypophyses. J. Histochem. Cytochem., *18*:1–8.

Bayer, E.A., E. Skutelsky, D. Wynne, and M. Wilchek 1976 Preparation of ferritin-avidin conjugates by reductive alkylation for use in electron microscopic cytochemistry. J. Histochem. Cytochem., *24*:933–939.

Bowie, E.P., G. Williams, M. Shiino, and E.G. Rennels 1973 The corticotroph of the rat adenohypophysis: A comparative study. Am. J. Anat., *138*:499–520.

Coons, A.H. 1961 The beginnings of immunofluorescence. Presidential Address to the American Association of Immunologists. J. Immunol., *87*:499–503.

Coons, A.H., H.J. Creech, and R.N. Jones 1941 Immunological properties of an antibody containing a fluorescent group. Proc. Soc. Exp. Biol. Med., *47*:200–202.

Coons, A.H., H.J.Creech, R.N. Jones, and E. Berliner 1942 The demonstration of pneumococcal antigen in tissues by the use of fluorescent antibody. J. Immunol., *45*:159–170.

Faulk, W.P., and G.M. Taylor 1971 An immunocolloid method for the electron microscope. Immunochemistry, *8*:1081–1083.

Frens, G. 1973 Controlled nucleation for the regulation of the particle size in monodisperse gold suspensions. Nature Phys. Sci., *241*:20–22.

Geoghegan, W.D., and G.A. Ackerman 1977 Absorption of horseradish peroxidase, ovomucoid, and anti-immunoglobulin to colloidal gold for the indirect detection of concanavilin A, wheat germ agglutinin and goat anti-human immunoglobulin G on cell surfaces at the electron microscope level: A new method, theory and application. J. Histochem. Cytochem., *25*:1187–1200.

Graham, R.C., and M.J. Karnovsky 1966 The early stages of absorption of injected horseradish peroxidase in the proximal tubule of mouse kidney: Ultrastructural cytochemistry by a new technique. J. Histochem. Cytochem., *14*:291–302.

Guesdon, J.L., T. Terynck, and S. Avremeas 1979 The use of avidin-biotin interaction in immunoenzymatic techniques. J. Histochem. Cytochem., *27*:1131–1139.

Heitzmann, H., and F.M. Richards 1974 Use of the avidin-biotin complex for specific staining of biological membranes in electron microscopy. Proc. Natl. Acad. Sci. U.S.A. *71*:3537–3539.

Hsu, S.M., L. Raine, and H. Fanger 1981 The use of avidin-biotin-peroxidase complex (ABC) in immunoperoxidase techniques. A comparison between ABC and unlabelled antibody PAP procedures. J. Histochem. Cytochem., *29*:577–580.

Kawarai Y., and P.K. Nakane 1970 Localization of tissue antigens on the ultrathin sections with peroxidase-labeled antibody method. J. Histochem. Cytochem., *18*:161–165.

Kraehenbuhl, J.P., P.B. DeGrandi, and M.A. Campiche 1971 Ultrastructural localization of intracellular antigen using enzyme-labeled antibody fragments. J. Cell Biol., *50*:432–445.

Marrack, J. 1934 Nature of antibodies. Nature, *133*:292–293.

Mason, T. E., R.F. Phifer, S.S. Spicer, R.S. Swallow, and R.D. Dreskin 1969 New immunochemical localizing technique for intracellular antigens. J. Histochem. Cytochem., *17*:190.

Moriarty, G.C., and L.L. Garner 1977 Immunocytochemical studies of cells in the rat adenohypophysis containing both ACTH and FSH. Nature, *265*:356–358.

Moriarty, G.C., and N.S. Halmi 1972 Electron microscopic study of adrenocorticotropin-producing cells with unlabeled antibodies and soluble peroxidase-antiperoxidase complex. J. Histochem. Cytochem., *20*:590–603.

Moriarty, G.C., C.M. Moriarty, and L.A. Sternberger 1973 Ultrastructural immunocytochemistry with unlabeled antibodies and the peroxidase antiperoxidase complex. A technique more sensitive than radioimmunoassay. J. Histochem. Cytochem., 21:825–833.

Nakane, P.K. 1968 Simultaneous localization of multiple tissue antigens using the peroxidase-labeled antibody method: A study on pituitary glands of the rat. J. Histochem. Cytochem., 16:557–560.

Nakane, P.K., and A. Kawaoi 1974 Peroxidase-labeled antibody. A new method of conjugation. J. Histochem. Cytochem., 22:1084–1091.

Nakane, P.K., and G.B. Pierce 1966 Enzyme labeled antibodies. Preparation and application for the localization of antigens. J. Histochem. Cytochem., 14:929–931.

Nakane, P.K., and G.B. Pierce 1967 Enzyme-labeled antibodies for the light and electron microscopic localization of tissue antigens. J. Cell Biol., 33:308–318.

Pepe, F. A. 1961a The use of specific antibody in electron microscopy. I. Preparation of mercury-labeled antibody. J. Biophys. Biochem. Cytol., 11:515–520.

Pepe, F.A. 1961b The use of specific antibody in electron microscopy. II. The visualization of mercury labeled antibody in the electron microscope. J. Biophys. Biochem. Cytol., 11:521–531.

Pickel, V.M., T.H. Joh, and D.J. Reis 1975 Ultrastructural localization of tyrosine hydroxylase in noradrenergic neurons of brain. Proc. Natl. Acad. Sci. U.S.A., 72:659–663.

Phifer, R.F., A.R. Midley, and S. Spicer 1973 Immunohistologic and histologic evidence that follicle stimulating and luteinizing hormones are present in the same cell types in the human pars distalis. J. Clin. Endocrinol., 36:125–142.

Phifer, R.F., D.N. Orth, and S.S. Spicer 1972 Immunohistologic evidence that melanocyte stimulating hormone (MSH) and adrenocorticotropin (ACTH) are produced in the same human hypophyseal cells (abstr.) IV Int. Endocrine Congress, Washington, D.C., June 18–24.

Ram, J.S., P.K. Nakane, D.G. Rawlinson, and G.B. Pierce 1966 Enzyme-labeled antibodies for ultrastructural studies. Fed. Proc., 25:732.

Ram, J.S., S. Tawde, G.B. Pierce, and A.R. Midgley 1963 Preparation of antibody-ferritin conjugates for immuno-electron microscopy. J. Cell Biol., 17:673–675.

Reiner, L. 1930 On the chemical alteration of purified antibody-proteins. Science, 72:483–484.

Singer, S.J. 1959 Preparation of an electron-dense antibody conjugate. Nature, 183:1523–1525.

Singer, S.J., and J.D. McLean 1963 Ferritin-antibody conjugates as stains for electron microscopy. Lab. Invest., 12:1002–1008.

Sternberger, L.A., and J.J. Cuculis 1969 Method for enzymatic intensification of the immunocytochemical reaction without the use of labeled antibodies. J. Histochem. Cytochem., 17:190 (abstr.).

Sternberger, L.A., E.J. Donati, J.J. Cuculis, and J.P. Petrali 1965 Indirect immunouranium techniques for staining of embedded antigens in electron microscopy. Exp. Mol. Pathol. 4:112–125.

Sternberger, L.A., E.J. Donati, J.S. Hanker, and A.M. Seligman 1966 Immuno-Diazothioether-Osmium Tetroxide (Immuno-DTO) technique for staining embedded antigen in electron microscopy. Exp. Mol. Pathol. (Suppl.), 3:36–43.

Sternberger, L. A., E.J. Donati, and C.E. Wilson 1963 Electron microscopic study on specific protection of isolated Bordetella Bronchiseptich antibody during exhaustive labelling with uranium. J. Histochem. Cytochem., 11:48–58.

Sternberger, L.A., P.H. Hardy, Jr., J.J. Cuculis, and H.J. Meyer 1970 The unlabeled antibody enzyme method of immunohistochemistry. Preparation and properties of soluble antigen-antibody complex (horseradish peroxidase-antihorseradish peroxidase) and its use in identification of spirochetes. J. Histochem. Cytochem., 18:315–333.

Striker, G.E., E.J. Donati, J.P. Petrali, and L.A. Sternberger 1966 Postembedding staining for electron microscopy with ferritin-antibody conjugates. Exp. Mol. Pathol. (Suppl.) 3:52–58.

Weller, T.H., and A.H. Coons 1954 Fluorescent antibody studies with agents of varicella and herpes zoster propagated in vitro. Proc. Soc. Exp. Biol. Med., 86:789–794.

Chapter 10

CELL FRACTIONATION

George E. Palade

GENERAL CONSIDERATIONS

Cell fractionation has played an important role in the development of cell biology, a field of research that—by its nature and by its initial "budding site"— can be considered a branch of the anatomical or morphological sciences. It proved to be a remarkably vigorous branch in the historical context of the past four decades of work and progress in basic biomedical sciences.

The introduction of cell fractionation procedures in cell research coincided within a few years in time with the introduction into the same field of another powerful technique, i.e., transmission electron microscopy. It was an unusually happy coincidence, since the two technologies are in some respects complementary. Together they became the main motive force in the early, spectacular development of cell biology.

The basic approach in cell fractionation is to start with fresh cells, tissues, or organs; to rupture cell membranes by physical forces (i.e., shearing or hypotonic shock); to release subcellular particulate components undamaged into an appropriate medium; and to sort them out of the resulting tissue brei or tissue homogenate by taking advantage of some of their distinct features or properties. At the beginning and for a long while, these distinct features were general physical parameters, such as size and specific gravity (density), and the sorter was a centrifugal field generated by a variety of centrifuges with a variety of rotors. It was a good, initial choice, for many subcellular components are indeed different in size and density. Fractionation was obtained by subjecting the homogenate to differential centrifugation (or velocity sedimentation) in which particle separation depends essentially on the product of these two parameters.

In time and as it often happens, the starting premises proved to be overoptimistic. Many subcellular components are membrane-bound compartments and their membranes are also affected by shearing forces, which cause partial losses of content and membranes (Scheele et al., 1978), although on a much more limited scale than is the case with the plasmalemma. We learned, therefore, that in cell fractionation we must reckon with leakage and relocation artifacts. These artifacts are substantial, but far from being so large as to invalidate the approach. Moreover, in many cases, the sorting of subcellular components by velocity sedimentation proved to be either impossible or unsatisfactory. Hence, other centrifugal procedures or entirely different approaches had to be envisaged and applied. Limitations were recognized as cell fractionation became more widely used; once identified, they acted—in fact—as an impulse for further technical improvements, as well as a corrective for the interpretation of the experimental data yielded by procedures then available.

Cell fractionation and electron microscopy depended on one another in a number of ways. Since cell fractionation had preceded by a few years the introduction of electron microscopy in cell research, initial efforts were centered on the isolation of components visible by light microscopy, such as nuclei, mitochondria, and secretion granules. But soon electron microscopy provided a wealth of new structural information on subcellular organization. It demonstrated characteristic structural details within already known components, like mitochondria and nuclei, and it uncovered the existence of a number of structural entities previously unknown or vaguely perceived, such as the endoplasmic reticulum and ribosomes, to mention only a few. Electron microscopy soon became the required procedure for confirming the identity and checking the morphological integrity of the components of already available fractions (e.g., the mitochondrial fraction), and for identifying the main intracellular source of already existing fractions (i.e., the microsomes). Moreover, it acted either as a guide or final check for procedural modifications and refinements needed to separate additional cell fractions enriched in, or representative of, newly discovered subcellular components such as polysomes, coated vesicles, lysosomes, and peroxisomes.

In this interplay, the unique, salient contribution of cell fractionation was to make possible quantitative, biochemical studies of subcellular components. In time, cell biologists and biochemists took advantage of this possibility on a large scale; their studies succeeded in building a substantial link beween anatomy, more precisely structural cytology, and biochemistry. It was this integrated approach based on structural findings as starting premises, followed by the isolation in mass of subcellular components in corresponding cell fractions and by their biochemical and functional analysis, that made the field of cell biology particularly fertile.

As techniques for the isolation and characterization of macromolecules, especially proteins and nucleic acids, improved rapidly and dramatically, and as subcellular components, membranes, ribosomes, and a wide variety of other macromolecular assemblies became amenable for study at the level of molecular and macromolecular interactions, cell biology and molecular biology merged into a continuous body of knowledge based on common concepts and a common set of technologies. Cell fractionation has played an important role in this merger and at present, in a simplified or refined form, it is still an integral part of the set of common technologies mentioned above. It is often buried at the very base of many current research projects, but it is still there supporting more elaborate technological developments of more recent vintage.

This continuous body of knowledge, which should be properly named cellular and molecular biology, could be compared to a bridge which, like its equivalents in civil engineering, has two bridgeheads: one in traditional anatomical-morphological sciences and the other in equally traditional biochemistry. The cautious and careful have stayed close to the bridgeheads because the ground around them has been consolidated over centuries by the work of their predecessors. The bold and venturesome have ventured on the bridge itself from both directions, because they believed that there was where the action was going to be. They did not worry about the young age and in some respects the still untested solidity of the bridge. As in the old Latin proverb, fortune favored the bold[1]: the bridge proved to be strong enough to support the intense, occasionally frantic activities of whole armies of explorers.

A SHORT HISTORY

Pioneers and Explorers

The earliest recorded attempts at cell fractionation are ascribed to F. Mischer (1871), who separated nuclei from leukocytes and used them as a starting preparation for the isolation of nucleic acids, and to O. Warburg (1913), who found that O_2 uptake was concentrated in particles sedimented by centrifugation from cell lysates. Later on, a more systematic approach to cell fractionation began in this country in two different laboratories: one in the Department of Anatomy at the University of Chicago, where the protagonists were R. Bensley, N. Hoerr, and A. Lazarow, and the other at the Rockefeller Institute for Medical Research (now the Rockefeller University) in New York, where the work was carried out by a single man, Albert Claude.

Preparatory versus Analytical Approach

The approach of the Chicago group was essentially preparatory: the aim was to isolate mitochondria (Bensley and Hoerr, 1934). Claude's approach was basically analytical and therefore significantly different. The purpose was to resolve a tissue homogenate, usually prepared from liver, into a standard series of fractions, to study the distribution of chosen compounds or activities in each and all fractions, and to account for the activity of the initial homogenate by the sum of the activities recovered in the fractions derived from it (Claude, 1943, 1947).

Claude's fractionation protocol was simple. From a tissue homogenate prepared usually in an isotonic saline solution, four fractions [nuclear, large granules, small granules (later called microsomes), and a final supernate] were separated by differential centrifugation in three successive runs. Claude concentrated his work on the last three fractions, because the first one was too heavily contaminated with cell debris. At the beginning, the distribution of chemical elements and general, "nonspecific" compounds (proteins, phospholipids, nucleic acids) was studied but soon, in collaboration with G. Hogeboom and R. Hotchkiss, the scope of the investigations was considerably enlarged to include specific enzymes of the Krebs cycle and respiratory electron transport chain. They were found to be concentrated in the large granule fraction (Hogeboom et al., 1946). Claude was particularly cautious: he was assuming that this fraction contained other particulates (perhaps secretion granules) besides mitochondria and therefore preferred a de-

[1] *Audaces fortuna juvat.*

scriptive, noncommittal term ("large granule fraction") for the preparation. The small granules or microsomes proved to be rich in phospholipids and nucleic acids (RNA), and at the beginning their discovery led to many intriguing questions and speculations about their possible relations to "plasmagens," which—at the time—were postulated to be cytoplasmic genes. Virus particles were of similar calculated size and of comparable gross chemistry. Besides, Claude (1943) had found these small particles in control homogenates in his attempts to isolate in mass the virus of the Rous sarcoma.

The Chicago group stuck to the preparatory approach, identified the isolated particles as mitochondria on the basis of their staining by classical procedures (Altmann's acid fuchsin), and localized cytochrome oxidase in them (Lazarow, 1943). But after this promising beginning, the work came practically to an end. Claude had the advantage of a more biochemically oriented environment, which made possible the collaboration with Hotchkiss. Moreover, his early interest in electron microscopy gave him a broad vista. He knew that there were many other structures within cells that could be isolated and studied. In fact, he assumed that the microsomes were derived from the "lace-like reticulum" (the first description of the future endoplasmic reticulum) that he, Porter, and Fullam had found by electron microscopy in cultured cells (Porter et al., 1945). Incidentally, Claude (1943, 1947–1948) also used a preparatory approach to isolate melanine granules from melanomata, a secretion granule fraction from pancreas, and chromatin threads from leukemia cells.

Saline versus Sucrose Solutions

In Claude's original procedure, the use of 0.15 M NaCl solution as homogenization medium often led to extensive particle aggregation that reduced yields and interfered with subsequent separation. It was in relation to this issue that his approach was modified by Hogeboom, Schneider, and myself by introducing a sucrose (nonelectrolyte) solution for tissue homogenization. In hypertonic sucrose (0.88 M), the vast majority of the particles in the large granule fraction proved to be mitochondria, which, upon isolation, retained their characteristic morphology (rods and grains) and their stainability with procedures considered specific in the cytology of the period (Hogeboom et al., 1948). These results showed clearly that Claude's "large granule fraction" was a mitochondrial fraction and that sucrose solutions were more reliable as homogenization media than their saline counterparts. Sucrose became the preferred ingredient for tissue homogenization media, but hypertonic solutions were soon replaced by an isotonic solution after Schneider (1948) and Lehninger (1964) found that the former inhibited certain mitochondrial enzyme activities. In time, isotonic sucrose solutions were further modified by buffers and additives introduced in concentrations low enough not to induce particle aggregation. With or without such additives, sucrose solutions are still in use today.

New Protagonists and Major Improvements

In the 1950s, after Claude's departure from the Rockefeller Institute, work on cell fractionation was continued vigorously in an increasing number of laboratories, among which the most prominent were those of Hogeboom and Schneider at

NIH and of de Duve at the University of Louvain (Leuven) in Belgium. Both groups expanded the inquiry to many other enzymic activities in the "classical" four fractions, and both groups repeatedly stressed the importance of the analytical approach, which step by step generated the current picture of functional specialization of subcellular components.

In the 1950s, de Duve's group undertook a systematic analysis of the parameters of cell fractionation by differential centrifugation and arrived at the conclusion that the power of resolution of the procedure was quite low (de Duve and Berthet, 1954; de Duve et al., 1959). In Claude's original protocol, this shortcoming was partly mitigated by repeatedly washing each isolated fraction. To improve the separation of different classes of subcellular particles, a number of different approaches were tried in de Duve's and other laboratories active in the field. The ideal solution appeared to be centrifugation to equilibrium (or isopycnic sedimentation) in a continuous density gradient generated by mixing two solutions of different sucrose concentrations (de Duve et al., 1959). The resolving power of such gradients was quite impressive: particles of different density came to rest as distinct bands at rather precise positions within the gradient. This improvement in resolution led rapidly to the widespread use of the procedure. Sucrose density gradients proved to have, in fact, enough resolution to separate macromolecules (Hogeboom and Kuff, 1954) and macromolecular assemblies. Moreover, velocity sedimentation in continuous density gradients was soon shown to resolve remarkably well ribosomes and polysomes of increasing sizes, and was used extensively for this particular purpose. A shortcut of the procedure was the use of discontinuous density gradients, which concentrated particles of comparable density at interfaces, thereby facilitating their collection. But such gradients could (and often did) yield mixed particle populations unless judiciously constructed.

Density gradients, however, introduced problems of their own. Long centrifugal runs are required to reach isopycnic conditions, since concentrated sucrose solutions are highly viscous. The most important drawback, however, is damage (leakage and fragmentation) incurred by certain particles, such as mitochondria, at the high hydrostatic pressure generated during long centrifugal runs at high speed (Wattiaux et al., 1971). The present trend is to construct isosmotic density gradients with Percol or mixtures of sucrose and dextrans, which obviate such damage and in addition require shorter centrifugation times because of their inherent low viscosity. High density-low viscosity gradients can also be constructed with substituted carbohydrates such as metrizamide and nokadozol.

Modified Rotors and Modified Particles

Gradient centrifugation required modified rotors to allow sedimentation along the axis of the tubes, as achieved in swinging bucket rotors, or along the radii of a rotor modified to minimize artifacts introduced by wall effects, which develop when particles hit and stick to the walls of centrifuge tubes. Such zonal rotors were initially introduced by N. Anderson (1966). A fully automated version for loading and unloading specimens and gradients was constructed by Beaufay (1966), whose rotor has been extensively used by de Duve's group.

Yet, notwithstanding gradients and modified rotors, certain classes of biochemically distinct particles proved to be difficult to separate from other particles of similar density. To solve this problem, the particles themselves had to be modified by different procedures. For instance, the administration of a non-degradable detergent (Triton WR1339) to living animals resulted in its accumulation in hepatocytic lysosomes, whose density was thereby sufficiently reduced to make possible a satisfactory separation from mitochondria (Wattiaux et al., 1963). After displacing the lysosomes by this modification, a reasonably homogeneous peroxisomal fraction could be obtained by prolonged centrifugation in hypertonic media (Leighton et al., 1968) (peroxisomal membranes are permeable to sucrose). The density of membrane-bound particles can be shifted (to higher densities) by digitonin treatment if the cognate membrane has a high cholesterol content (Thines-Sempoux et al., 1970). In this way, plasmalemma-derived and Golgi-derived vesicles can be partially separated from endoplasmic reticulum-derived microsomes. More recently, overloading of Golgi elements with lipoprotein particles was used to increase the yield of Golgi fractions (Ehrenreich et al., 1973), and uptake of peroxidase-tagged ligands was used to isolate vesicular carriers (Courtoy et al., 1982) whose density was increased by a peroxidatic reaction carried out on the starting preparations.

Morphological Correlates

As already discussed, initial attempts to isolate mitochondrial fractions were guided by morphological criteria such as shape, size, and staining reactions considered "specific" at that time in light-microscope cytology. Later on, when characteristic structural features were uncovered by electron microscopy, these features became structural markers used for assessing cell fractions in terms of homogeneity and particle preservation. The mitochondrial cristae, for instance, replaced Altmann's or Janus green staining.

It was such a structural marker, namely the attached ribosomes, which made possible the identification of the rough-surfaced endoplasmic reticulum of intact cells as the main intracellular source of Claude's microsomes. The final work was done by P. Siekevitz and myself (Palade and Siekevitz, 1956a, b), but suggestive evidence had been obtained before by other investigators (Slautterback, 1953). Structural markers also guided the isolation of coated vesicle fractions (Pearse, 1975) and, to some extent, that of Golgi fractions (Ehrenreich et al., 1973).

In the morpological survey of cell fractions, attempts were generally made to examine systematically the entire depth of the pellets representing the fractions, primarily because different particles are not homogeneously distributed in the depth of these pellets. The result of such surveys was a qualitative assessment of the composition of the fractions. A procedure for the quantitative morphological analysis of cell fractions was worked out by Baudhuin and Berthet (1967), who collected fractions on filters (to obtain random distributions) and applied morphometric procedures to quantitate the different types of particles present in the fraction under study. The procedure was extensively used for studying particle distribution in fractions derived from continuous density gradients, and good agreement was found between morphometric and biochemical data. An attempt was also made to correlate morphometric data obtained on intact liver tissue with morphometric and biochemical data derived from liver homogenates and cell fractions (Bolender et al., 1978). The results were in reasonably good agreement except for outer mitochondrial membranes, which were lost from mitochondrial fractions and transferred as simple vesicles to the microsomal fractions.

Markers and Distributions

A comprehensive review of the evolution of centrifugal procedures as applied to cell fractionation has been written by de Duve (1971). It should be consulted by readers interested in a more detailed discussion of this topic than presented in this essay. In that review, and especially in a subsequent paper (1975), de Duve presented the basic postulates that have guided the work of his laboratory. One of them, defined as the "postulate of single location," assumes that a given compound or enzyme activity is restricted in its distribution to a single type of particle for which it can be used as a marker. Particle recovery in a fraction can, therefore, be calculated from the percent recovery of the cognate marker from the homogenate. Moreover, the degree of contamination of a given fraction can be calculated from its content of markers for other fractions. The marker concept has been extensively used not only in guiding refinements in cell fractionation procedures, but also and quite generally in characterizing cell fractions of interest in applied experimental work. It has been and still is obviously useful, as long as the limit of stringency with which it is applied does not try to approach 100%. At present we realize that precursors for plasmalemmal proteins or lysosomal enzymes, for instance, must be found in microsomal and Golgi fractions, not as contaminants, but as *bona fide* components in transit from their site of synthesis to their site of final functional residence. A comparable, but not identical, situation appears in the case of recycling vesicular carriers.

The other postulate assumes that particles in a given class are biochemically homogeneous, but not necessarily physically identical. Hence, they will appear as relatively broad distributions rather than sharp bands in a gradient. For this reason, a more realistic presentation of experimental data should take the form of distribution of markers in standard gradients rather than in isolated cell fractions. One may assume that perhaps other sorting procedures may resolve the distribution patterns in distinct, nonoverlapping fractions.

New Fractions

In the early 1970s, attempts were made to complete the inventory of cell fractions by filling in a few obvious missing entries, of which the most prominent was a fraction representing the Golgi complex. The first success in this direction was obtained by Morré and his collaborators, who guided their efforts by morphological markers (Morré et al., 1970). They were followed shortly thereafter by Fleischer and Fleischer (1970), who defined an enzymic marker for their Golgi fraction, namely galactosyltransferase, and later on by Ehrenreich et al. (1973) and Bergeron et al. (1973), who resolved the Golgi complex into a series of subfractions. By now, quite a number of variants of these procedures have been published. The isolation of coated vesicle fractions (Pearse, 1975) belongs also to the same period.

At present it is quite clear that the inventory is far from complete, notwithstanding the success in isolating Golgi fractions. Certain cell organs, among which the Golgi complex is an outstanding example, appear to be clusters of bio-chemically distinct subcompartments, and certain cellular membranes, such as the plasmalemma, have structurally and biochemically differentiated domains. In fact, attempts to obtain representative fractions of differentiated plasmalemmal domains have already been done or are in progress (e.g., Roman and Hubbard, 1984). In addition, cells in general use large numbers of different types of vesicular carriers, but corresponding cell fractions have been isolated only for a single type of such carriers, i.e., the secretion granules of exocrine and endocrine cells (Castle et al., 1975; Cameron and Castle, 1984).

Fractions Resolved into Subfractions

Many cell fractions, notably the nuclear, mitochondrial, and microsomal frac-tions, have been used as starting preparations for a systematic dismantling of the corresponding cell organs into the membranes, particles, and soluble components they contain. The outstanding example is the subfractionation of mitochondria (Lehninger, 1964); quite far advanced is the dismantling of microsomes into attached polysomes, membranes, associated molecules (or particles), and cister-nal content. And still not far from the starting base is similar work on Golgi, lysosomal, and peroxisomal fractions. The relevant literature is vast. It provides deep insights into the organization and function of the corresponding cell organs and has been one of the main contributors to the construction of the bridge mentioned earlier in this essay. A review of this area is, however, beyond the intentions of the present exercise. In many cases we are still in the midst of relevant analytical work, and in most cases we are too close to the biochemical bridgehead alluded to earlier in this paper. A structurally oriented reader may find that I already went too far in that direction.

It should be mentioned, however, that this type of analytical work has been complemented by reconstituting functional systems from previously isolated parts. Again, the outstanding examples come from work on mitochondria and micro-somes.

Other Separation Procedures

It should be clear from the preceding sections that centrifugal fields, used in combination with appropriate modifications of centrifuges and rotors, suspension media, and particles, have been remarkably useful in generating over the past 40 years an impressive body of knowledge on the chemistry and function of sub-cellular components. The corresponding technology has been developed to dif-ferent degrees in different areas. For instance, differential centrifugation is still the standard procedure for the isolation of mitochondrial fractions. Their study has generated all that we know at present about mitochondrial function and bio-genesis. More refined procedures had to be worked out for the separation of lysosomal, peroxisomal, Golgi, and plasmalemmal fractions; rather elaborate tech-niques had to be developed for the isolation of coated vesicles. In the meantime, other means of separation have been tried, based again on general physical parameters. For instance, free flow electrophoresis has been applied successfully for the isolation of cell types (Hannig and Zeiller, 1969) and classes of subcellular components (Heidrich et al., 1970), and more recently endosomes (Merion and

Sly, 1983). In addition, countercurrent distribution procedures were introduced for the isolation of subcellular components by Albertsson (1960). So far, however, these separatory techniques have been used on a much more limited scale than different types of centrifugal separations.

All particle sorting procedures discussed or mentioned so far rely on physical, nonspecific parameters of a simple (size, density, surface charge) or relatively subtle (surface solubility) nature. It is probable that we have obtained from methods that depend on nonspecific physical parameters as much, or nearly as much, as they can yield. Perhaps at this time we should consider other means of sorting, based on specific biochemical interactions between specific macromolecules at the surface of the particles and specific ligands insolubilized at the surface of a sorting matrix. The interacting pair can be represented by a lectin "receptor" and a lectin, or an antigenic determinant and its antibody. This type of separation was applied to microsomes by Kawajiri et al. (1977) and expanded to Golgi fractions by Ito and myself (1978), who, in addition, devised a procedure for the visualization of the immunoadsorbed particles or vesicles at the surface of the polyacrylamide beads used to insolubilize the sorting antibodies. In a more recent development, fixed *Staphylococcus aureus* cells were used as immunoadsorbent (Merisko et al., 1982) to isolate coated vesicles and clathrin cages.

This new approach has been used more and more widely over the past few years. It has been applied for the isolation of vesicles derived from the biliary domain of the hepatocytes' plasmalemma (Roman and Hubbard, 1984), for sorting plasmalemmal membranes from synaptic vesicles (Miljanich et al., 1982), and more recently for resolving coated vesicle fractions in functionally distinct classes (Pfeffer and Kelly, 1985). It is doubtful that the same kind of resolution could be obtained by using physical parameters for sorting, and it seems reasonable to assume that separation by immunoadsorption (or immune separation) may provide the means needed to advance the analytical inquiry on cell organs past levels at which morphological markers are no longer available, biochemical markers may have limitations, and physical parameters no longer work. Sorting vesicular carriers, differentiated domains, and microdomains of the plasmalemma and Golgi subcompartments represent proper targets for these new procedures. They may also help in obtaining from cultured cells relevant fractions for proper characterization as well as for the reconstruction of *in vitro* systems from cleaner preparations than are now in use. Centrifugal cell fractionation procedures have been developed for large amounts of starting material, and have rarely been applied successfully to cultured cells usually available in small amounts.

A Note of Thanks to Evolution

It would be a serious mistake to assume that the vast body of information secured and the depth of insight attained in our understanding of cellular organization can be explained only by the fortunate choice of our procedures and the incisive character of our experimental protocols. We should recognize that our recent spectacular successes are explained to a very large extent by the unusually sturdy character of the pieces of cellular equipment we describe as cell organs. Although made of perishable materials, they are so well constructed that they withstand cell disruption, "liberation" in foreign media non-iso in practically any way, and tumbling in high speed centrifuges for hours or days on end. At the end of this ordeal, they emerge still capable of displaying not only simple enzymatic activities, but also complex reactions involving the well-integrated activity of scores or hundreds of components, as in oxidative phosphorylation, mRNA translation, gene transcription, protein targeting and translocation across microsomal and mitochondrial membranes, transport of ions and metabolites, and signal transduction across the membrane of plasmalemma-derived vesicles. Moreover, some subcellular particles, like mitochondria, come out of the ordeal of cell fractionation with part of their regulatory mechanisms still intact. It is this sturdiness of cell organs that has allowed us to go rapidly beyond a catalogue of their biochemicals to a recognition of their specialized functions. We may assume that we owe this unexpected bonus to the stringency of selection in early cellular evolution through which only the toughest constructs have survived. This means that we can look at cell fractionation as a lesser ordeal than evolution. Be it as it may, a note of thanks to evolution is in order for all users of cell fractionation procedures.

REFERENCES

Albertsson, P.A. 1971 Partition of Cell Particles and Macromolecules: Distribution and Fractionation of Cells, Viruses, Microsomes, Proteins, Nucleic Acids, and Antigen-Antibody Complexes in Aqueous Polymer Two-Phase Systems. John Wiley & Sons, New York.

Anderson, N.G. 1966 The development of zonal centrifuges and ancillary systems for tissue fractionation and analysis. Natl. Cancer Inst. Monogr., *21*.

Baudhuin, P., and J. Berthet 1967 Electron microscope examination of subcellular fractions. II. Quantitative analysis of the mitochondrial population isolated from rat liver. J. Cell Biol., *35*:631–648.

Beaufay, H. 1966 La Centrifugation en Gradient de Densité: Application a l'Étude des Organites Subcellulaires. Centrick, Louvain.

Bensley, R.R., and N.L. Hoerr 1934 Studies on cell structure by the freezing-drying method: VI. The preparation and properties of mitochondria. Anat. Rec., *60*:449–455.

Bergeron, J.J.M., J.H. Ehrenreich, P. Siekevitz, and G.E. Palade 1973 Golgi fractions prepared from rat liver homogenates: Biochemical characterization. J. Cell Biol., *59*:73–88.

Bolender, R.P., D. Paumgartner, G. Losa, D. Muellener, and E.R. Weibel 1978 Integrated stereological and biochemical studies on hepatocytic membranes. I. Membrane recoveries in subcellular fractions. J. Cell Biol., *77*:565–583.

Cameron, R.S., and J.D. Castle 1984 Isolation and compositional analysis of secretion granules and their membrane subfraction from the rat parotid gland. J. Membr. Biol., *79*:127–144.

Castle, J.D., J.D. Jamieson, and G.E. Palade 1975 Secretion granules of the rabbit parotid gland: Isolation, subfractionation, and characterization of the membrane and content subfractions. J. Cell Biol., *64*:182–210.

Claude, A. 1943 Distribution of nucleic acids in cell and morphological constitution of cytoplasm. Biol. Symp., *10*:111–129.

Claude, A. 1947–1948 Studies on cells: Morphology, chemical constitution, and distribution of biochemical functions. Harvey Lect., *43*:121–164.

Courtoy, P.J., J. Quintart, and P. Baudhuin 1982 Shift in the equilibrium density of subcellular organelles containing peroxidase using the diaminobenzidine procedure. J. Cell Biol., *95*:424(abstr.)

de Duve, C. 1971. Tissue fractionation: Past and present. J. Cell Biol., *50*:20D–55D.

de Duve, C. 1975. Exploring cells with a centrifuge. Les Prix Nobel, 142–160.

de Duve, C., and J. Berthet 1954 The use of differential centrifugation in the study of tissue enzymes. Int. Rev. Cytol., *3*:225–275.

de Duve, C., J. Berthet, and H. Beaufay 1959 Gradient centrifugation of cell particles. Theory and applications. Prog. Biophys. Biophys. Chem. 9:325–369.

Ehrenreich, J.H., J.J.M. Bergeron, P. Siekevitz, and G.E. Palade 1973 Golgi fractions prepared from rat liver homogenates. I. Isolation procedure and morphological characterization. J. Cell Biol., 59:45–72.

Fleischer, B., and S. Fleischer 1970 Preparation and characterization of Golgi membranes from rat liver. Biochim. Biophys. Acta, 219:301–319.

Hannig, K., and K. Zeiller 1969 Zur auftrennung und characterisierung immunekompetenter zellen mit hilfe der trägerfreien ablenkungselektrophorese. Hoppe Seylers Z. Physiol. Chem., 350:467–472.

Heidrich, H.G., R. Stahn, and K. Hannig 1970 The surface charge of rat liver mitochondria and their membranes: Clarification of some controversies concerning mitochondrial structure. J. Cell Biol., 46:137–150.

Hogeboom, G.H., A. Claude, and R.D. Hotchkiss 1946 The distribution of cytochrome oxidase and succinoxidase in the cytoplasm of the mammalian liver cell. J. Biol. Chem., 165:615–629.

Hogeboom, G.H., and E.L. Kuff 1954 Sedimentation behavior of proteins and other materials in a horizontal preparative rotor. J. Biol. Chem., 210:733–751.

Hogeboom, G.H., W.C. Schneider, and G.E. Palade 1948 Cytochemical studies of mammalian tissues. I. Isolation of intact mitochondria from rat liver: Some biochemical properties of mitochondria and submicroscopic particulate material. J. Biol. Chem., 172:619–635.

Ito, A., and G.E. Palade 1978 Presence of NADPH-cytochrome P-450 reductase in rat liver Golgi membranes: Evidence obtained by immunoadsorption method. J. Cell Biol., 79:590–597.

Kawajiri, K., A. Ito, and T. Omura 1977 Subfractionation of rat liver microsomes by immunoprecipitation and immunoadsorption methods. J. Biochem. (Tokyo), 81:779–789.

Lazarow, A. 1943 Chemical structure of cytoplasm as investigated in Professor Bensley's laboratory during the past 10 years. Biol. Symp. 10:9–26.

Lehninger, A.L. 1964. The Mitochondrion: Molcular Basis of Structure and Function. W.A. Benjamin, New York.

Leighton, F., B. Poole, H. Beaufay, P. Baudhuin, J.W. Coffey, S. Fowler, and C. de Duve 1968 The large-scale separation of peroxisomes, mitochondria, and lysosomes from the livers of rats injected with Triton WR-1339. Improved isolation procedures, automated analysis, biochemical and morphological properties of fractions. J. Cell Biol., 37:482–513.

Merion, M., and W.S. Sly 1983 The role of intermediate vesicles in the adsorptive endocytosis and transport of ligand to lysosomes by human fibroblasts. J. Cell Biol., 96:644–650.

Merisko, E.M., M.G. Farquhar, and G.E. Palade 1982 Coated vesicle isolation by immunoadsorption on Staphylococcus aureus cells. J. Cell Biol., 92:846–857.

Miljanich, G.P., A.R. Brasier, and R.B. Kelly 1982 Partial purification of presynaptic plasma membrane by immunoadsorption. J. Cell Biol., 94:88–96.

Mischer, F. 1871 Hoppe Seylers Med. Chem. Untersuch. 4:441.

Morré, D.J., R.L. Hamilton, H.H. Mollenhauer, R.W. Mahley, W.P. Cunningham, R.D. Cheetham, and B.S. le Quire 1970 Isolation of a Golgi apparatus-rich fraction from rat liver. I. Method and morphology. J. Cell Biol., 44:484–491.

Palade, G.E., and P. Siekevitz 1956a Liver microsomes: An integrated morphological and biochemical study. J. Biophys. Biochem. Cytol., 2:171–200.

Palade, G.E., and P. Siekevitz 1956b Pancreatic microsomes: An integrated morphological and biochemical study. J. Biophys. Biochem. Cytol., 2:671–690.

Pearse, B.M.F. 1975 Coated vesicles from pig brain: Purification and biochemical characterization. J. Mol. Biol., 97:93–98.

Pfeffer, S.R., and R.B. Kelly 1985 The subpopulation of brain coated vesicles that carries synaptic vesicle proteins contains two unique polypeptides. Cell, 40:949–957.

Porter, K.R., A. Claude, and E.F. Fullam 1945 A study of tissue culture cells by electron microscopy: Methods and preliminary observations. J. Exp. Med., 81:233–246.

Roman, L.M., and A.L. Hubbard 1984 A domain-specific marker for the hepatocyte plasma membrane. III. Isolation of bile canalicular membrane by immunoadsorption. J. Cell Biol., *98*:1497–1504.

Scheele, G.A., G.E. Palade, and A.M. Tartakoff 1978 Cell fractionation studies of guinea pig pancreas—Molecular redistribution of exocrine proteins during tissue homogenization. J. Cell Biol., *78*:110–130.

Schneider, W.C. 1948 Intracellular distribution of enzymes. III. The oxidation of octanoic acid by rat liver fractions. J. Biol. Chem., *176*:259–266.

Slautterback, D.B. 1953 Electron microscopic studies of small cytoplasmic particles (microsomes). Exp. Cell Res., *5*:173–186.

Thines-Sempoux, D., M. Wibo, and A. Amar-Costesec 1970 Action de la digitonine sur les microsomes et les membranes plasmiques du foie de rat. Arch. Int. Physiol. Biochim., *78*:1012–1013.

Warburg, O. 1913 The oxygen-using granules of liver cells and the oxygen respiration in the Berkefeld filtrates of aqueous liver extracts. Arch. Ges. Physiol., *154*:599–617.

Wattiaux, R., S. Wattiaux-De Coninck, and M.F. Ronveaux-Dupal 1971 Distribution d'enzymes mitochondriaux apres centrifugation isopycnique d'une fraction mitochondriale de foie de rat dans un gradient de saccharose: Influence de la pression hydrostatique. Arch. Int. Physiol. Biochim. *79*:214–215.

Wattiaux, R., M. Wibo, and P. Baudhuin 1963 Influence of the injection of Triton WR-1339 on the properties of rat-liver lysosomes. In: CIBA Foundation Symposium on Lysosomes. A.V.S. De Reuck, ed. Churchill Ltd., London, pp. 176–196.

PART III

Chapter 11

THE CONTRIBUTIONS OF EMBRYOLOGISTS TO THE AMERICAN ASSOCIATION OF ANATOMISTS

Drew M. Noden

When the American Association of Anatomists was founded, the discipline of embryology was still a descriptive science burdened by causal links with phylogeny, as promulgated by Haeckel, and built upon the germ-layer doctrine of Von Baer. The anatomy faculty of most medical colleges included one or more embryologists, who typically received their training in medical anatomy and histology in Europe. In addition, gross anatomists and, later, histologists frequently examined and gave reports about embryonic material. Human embryology was a core course in medical morphological sciences, comparative embryology was largely a subdiscipline of zoology, and developmental mechanisms had not yet emerged as an independent field of research.

The 20th century has seen these dogmas discredited and traditions fade, and many specialized subdisciplines have emerged. This is due in large part to new discoveries that have been described at the meetings of the American Association of Anatomists. Over 4,800 oral reports, demonstrations, and posters announcing the results of descriptive and experimental embryological research have been presented at these annual sessions.

Equally important in bringing about these changes are the motivations and character of the many morphologists who have publicly shared their ideas and data at the AAA meetings. No brief overview can do justice to these contributors, the range of developmental topics, and the scope of techniques that constitute the proceedings of this Association. In preparing this review I have attempted to identify some of the prominent anatomists whose research interests have included developmental problems, and also those scientists whose contributions to embryology have had significant impact upon the subsequent teaching of, or research in, this discipline.

Assessing the impact that embryologists have had upon the AAA is an impossible task—like choosing the one vital organ that is most necessary to sustain life. Which is the valid measure? Is it that slightly over 20% of all the papers presented

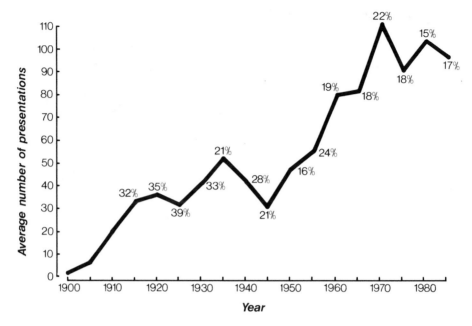

Fig. 11.1. Number of presentations made at Annual Meetings of the American Association of Anatomists and their percentage of the total program.

at the annual meetings during these 100 years have dealt with animal development (Fig. 11.1)? Is it that 18 of the first 23 Presidents of the Association published papers on embryological topics? Is it that the founders of the *Journal of Morphology* in 1887 (C.O. Whitman, E.P. Allis, Jr.) and *The American Journal of Anatomy* in 1901 (F.P. Mall, C.S. Minot, G.S. Huntington, H. McE. Knower) all were keenly interested in embryology?

The following discussion is organized along two broad lines: descriptive embryology and organogenesis, and experimental embryology. No attempt has been made to be inclusive, but rather to provide a glimpse of some of the researchers who have laid the foundations for contemporary vertebrate developmental biology.

DESCRIPTIVE EMBRYOLOGY AND ORGANOGENESIS

Among the early leaders of the Association, two stand out for their contributions to descriptive embryology. Charles S. Minot (1852–1914) began his scientific career as an entomologist and received a doctorate from Harvard for studies on the physiology of muscular contraction. During several years of study in Leipzig with Ludwig and Leuckhart and in Wurtzburg under Semper, Minot learned the emerging methods of tissue preservation and staining. This training served as a basis for the many significant technical innovations in microtomy that Minot would later develop. During this period he also embraced a more disciplined approach to science than he believed was practiced at most American universities.

Following his appointment in 1880 as Lecturer in Embryology at Harvard Medical School, Minot built one of the strongest embryology teaching and research programs of the time. His texts, *Human Embryology* (1892) and *Laboratory*

Textbook of Embryology (1903), set a new standard for thoroughness and accuracy. Most developmental details in these texts were verified through personal observations that Minot and his students, including F.T. Lewis, made. Minot's collection of nearly 2,000 vertebrate embryos, all catalogued and sectioned, remains a valuable asset for current embryologists, along with the Carnegie collection, B.M. Patten's series at the University of Michigan, and the Cornell Embryo Collection (primarily domestic species) established by B.F. Kingsbury and H. Adelmann in Ithaca.

Given Minot's view of orderliness in embryogenesis, it is not surprising that he embraced the germ-layer concept. Referring to observations reported shortly before the turn of the century by Julia Platt, a student of C.O. Whitman's at Chicago, and by Goronovitch and Klaatsch in Europe that ectoderm-derived neural crest cells formed craniofacial skeletal structures, Minot (1901) stated, "It is true that attempts are made from time to time to upset the validity of this fundamental (germ layer) doctrine, but they have hitherto failed to find support or recognition from any leading embryologist, and I deem these attempts unworthy of serious consideration." This debate continued until extirpation and transplantation studies in the 1920s confirmed Platt's conclusions, although some, for example Gavin de Beer, remained skeptical for another two decades.

Frederick T. Lewis (1875–1952) brought to the study of embryology the eye and artistic talents needed to transform two-dimensional images into elegant three-dimensional wax plate and graphic reconstructions. These were first introduced in Minot's 1903 laboratory text, and later he contributed several chapters for Keibel and Mall's *Manual of Human Embryology* (1910, 1912). Lewis presented his observations and reconstructions of the development of the caudal vena cava, stomach and midgut, coelom, and mesenteries at Association meetings between 1910 and 1921, but his interest in this type of research waned toward the end of this period. He became disenchanted because such gross approaches offered little hope of revealing the mechanisms underlying morphogenesis or explaining the etiology of malformations.

Lewis turned his attentions to detailed analyses of cell geometry, carefully reconstructing plant and animal cells and constructing mathematical descriptions of their complex but, he believed, geometrically regular shapes. While a causal relation between cell shape change and morphogenesis is now a proven feature in gastrulation, neurulation, and organogenesis, Lewis' proposals usually were not seriously considered by the embryologists of his time.

Franklin P. Mall (1862–1917), together with W.K. Brooks, F.R. Sabin, and others, established at Johns Hopkins the preeminent program in embryology in this country at the turn of the century. Prior to receiving his appointment at Johns Hopkins in 1893, Mall studied with Wilhelm His and K. Ludwig in Leipzig. His discovery that the thymus is derived from pharyngeal pouch endoderm, not visceral cleft ectoderm, contradicted the ideas of His but they both agreed that Mall's observation was correct. Keibel and Mall's *Manual of Human Embryology* combined for the first time the formalism of the German school of embryology with the pragmatism of the American school. Like Minot's earlier text, much of the material was based on detailed studies of new specimens. In 1913 Mall founded the Department of Embryology at the Carnegie Institute of Washington.

In addition to being instrumental in the training of many leading embryologists, including R.G. Harrison, W. Lewis, and G.L. Streeter, Mall shared

Minot's belief in the need to upgrade the quality of medical education in America. In particular, he argued that clinical education should be performed by full-time university faculty engaged in teaching and research, an idea that did not gain broad academic support until after his death.

Before expanding upon the research of embryologists, a few of the many important contributions by anatomists who were primarily known for their work in areas other than animal development need to be mentioned. Two past AAA Presidents who yielded occasionally to the allure of the embryo were Herbert M. Evans (1892–1971) and Edward A. Boyden (1886–1976). Evans was a student of Mall's who, during a long career at Berkeley, made significant discoveries on the control of estrous cycles and the role of vitamin E. Among his embryological contributions were a description of the formation of intraembryonic blood vessels in the pig and the chick and, later, together with G.W. Bartelmez, an elegant description of a 7-somite human embryo.

Boyden, who spent most of his career at the University of Minnesota, is primarily known for his work on the functional morphology of the gallbladder and on pulmonary anatomy. However, throughout his long research career he returned to the embryo, presenting papers on visceral arch anatomy, cloacal formation, gut closure and histogenesis, and the development of pulmonary branching patterns.

Detailed morphological studies of early human development have been a consistent feature of the Annual Meetings of the Association. Following in the tradition of Mall was George L. Streeter (1873–1948), whose name is synonymous with the staging of human embryos. A regular contributor at the Annual Meetings from 1906 through 1942, and President from 1926 to 1928, Streeter focused especially on the development of sense organs in human embryos, and later on the formation of extraembryonic structures.

Specimens in the Carnegie Collection also drew the attention of George W. Corner (1889–1981), another Johns Hopkins graduate, and George W. Bartelmez (1885–1967). Bartelmez, who studied under C.O. Whitman at Chicago, was one of the first embryologists not trained in a medical anatomy department who participated actively in the Association meetings. The research for his dissertation was an examination of the orientation of the pigeon blastodisc *in ovo*. Soon he became interested in neurulation, describing the process in several vertebrate classes; this culminated in his collaboration with H.M. Evans. Later, he studied cyclic changes in the primate endometrium. All three of these embryologists served as President of the AAA.

The tradition of careful descriptive analyses of mammalian embryos was taken up by a new generation of embryologists beginning in the 1920s. Most notable were Leslie B. Arey, whose *Developmental Anatomy* became the most popular textbook of embryology of its day; C. Heuser, who made many definitive observations on human and non-human primate embryos and their extraembryonic membranes; and Bradley M. Patten (1889–1971). In addition to authoring texts on pig and chick embryology, Patten's *Foundations of Embryology* became the standard reference for vertebrate embryology outside of the medical curriculum. Patten presented many of his studies on cardiogenesis, neurogenesis, and congenital malformations at the AAA meetings during the 1930s and 1940s.

These prolific authors were followed by many embryologists who generally were more specialized. For example, M. Moss presented a series of studies describing the growth of the skull, while P. Gruenwald focused most of his attention and writing upon congenital malformations of the limb and axial skeleton. The curatorship of the Carnegie collection passed to Ronan O'Rahilly, who has described in detail the development of the human hand and the early formation of caudal skull and cervical structures.

Most non-morphologists view anatomy as a discipline bereft of controversy. Insiders, of course, realize that structural analyses frequently provide contradictory results. This is especially true during embryogenesis, when tissue primordia may move great relative distances before revealing their true identity.

A very heated debate, formalized in 40 platform presentations, continued during the first two decades of this century. This concerned the source of vascular endothelial cells and lymphatic vessels. One side, led by Minot and Florence R. Sabin (1871–1953), a member of the Johns Hopkins anatomy faculty and the first woman elected President of the Association (1924–1926), supported the angioblast or continuous growth theory proposed previously by Wilhelm His. This postulated that all intraembryonic vascular endothelial cells are derived from extraembryonic precursors that develop in the yolk sac.

In contrast, the local origin theory claimed that intraembryonic mesenchyme forms most or all of the endothelial tissues in the body. George S. Huntington of Columbia University and Charles F.W. McClure (1865–1955) of Princeton, both of whom served as AAA President, argued in favor of this hypothesis.

Sabin, who was primarily concerned with the origin of lymphatics, and H.M. Evans based their claims on the results of intraembryonic injection of India ink. In addition, Eliot Clark directly observed the invasion of lymphatic cords into the tail of a frog larva.

The local origin proponents initially supported their position with descriptive observations. A well-documented report presented by F.T. Lewis in 1910 was claimed as supporting evidence by both sides. Lewis described the presence of endothelial vesicles within the mesenchyme adjacent to lymphatic vessels; some of these vesicles were later found by John L. Bremer, one of his students, to be connected to the parent vessel by epithelial cords. But whether the vesicles arose independently *in situ* and later fused with a larger vessel, or budded off from that vessel, remained unresolved.

Apparent resolution of this controversy occurred as a result of two experimental analyses. In 1914, A.M. Miller and J.E. Whorter reported the results of surgically isolating the trunk of a chick embryo from the extraembryonic area opaca. Despite this insult, primitive intraembryonic blood vessels formed. The following year Charles R. Stockard (1879–1939), a pioneer in the field of teratology and President of the Association from 1928 to 1930, found that fish embryos with chemically induced depletions of most major blood vessels still developed local networks of vascular capillaries.

The angioblast group surrendered, at least with regard to hemal endothelium, and the controversy has been largely forgotten. However, a critical reading of this literature indicates that the issue of vascular and lymphatic vessel origins remains unresolved, which is surprising given the many labeling techniques currently available to embryologists.

EXPERIMENTAL EMBRYOLOGY

Experimental embryology encompasses both the methodological and philosophical approaches that distinguish this discipline. The former typically involves a mechanical, chemical, or other form of perturbation upon the organism or some of its cells. Philosophically, the field aims at defining causal relations by documenting how cells and organisms respond to applied alterations. This discipline and the Association of American Anatomists were both conceived in the late 1880s, and struggled for several years before gaining widespread and enthusiastic acceptance.

By the turn of the century, experimental embryology was well established in this country, although the principal focus was upon invertebrate systems. An exception to this was a young scientist who trained at Johns Hopkins (PhD, 1894) with the comparative embryologist William K. Brooks and later with Mall, and who studied for several years in Germany, receiving an MD from Bonn in 1899. His name, of course, is Ross G. Harrison (1870–1959).

Harrison was the first American embryologist to combine the observational skills of an anatomist with mechanistic approaches espoused by the new experimentalists. His appointment as Professor of Comparative Anatomy at Yale in 1907 also represented a deliberate decision to escape from the confines of the traditional medical anatomy department, although he retained close friendships with his former colleagues at Hopkins.

Harrison's first presentation at an AAA meeting occurred in 1900, shortly after he returned from Bonn. This was a description and discussion of the presence of a vestigial tail in a human infant, which he published in greater detail the following year (Harrison, 1901). There followed on an almost annual basis a series of presentations describing the development of chimeric embryos, the effects of spinal cord extirpation, growth of neural tissues *in vitro,* and the results of limb transplantation in urodele embryos. In 1908, Harrison organized a Symposium on Experimental Embryology at the AAA annual meeting held that year in Baltimore. The occasion also served as a reunion, since Harrison, Conklin, and Morgan had been students together at Johns Hopkins. Included on the program were:

Edwin G. Conklin, Princeton University. "Experiment as Applied to the Organization and Early Differentiation of the Egg."

Thomas H. Morgan, Columbia University. "The Effects Produced by Centrifuging the Egg before and during Development."

Charles R. Bardeen, University of Wisconsin. "Variations in Susceptibility of Developing Organisms to X-rays at Different Periods of Development."

Charles R. Stockard, Cornell Medical School. "The Artificial Production of One-Eyed Monsters and Other Defects Which Occur in Nature, by the Use of Chemicals."

Warren H. Lewis, Johns Hopkins University. "The Experimental Production of Cyclopia in Fish Embryos *(Fundulus heteroclitus)."*

Eliot R. Clark, Johns Hopkins University. "The Tail of the Living Frog Larva as a Field for the Experimental Study of Growing and Functioning Lymphatics."

Ross G. Harrison, Yale University. "The Experimental Method as Applied to the Study of the Development of the Nervous System."

George L. Streeter, University of Washington. "Experimental Observations on the Development of the Amphibian Ear Vesicle."

Charles S. Minot, Harvard Medical School. "On the Blood-Destroying Function of the Mesenchyma."

Simon H. Gage and Susan P. Gage, Cornell University. "Coloration of the Milk and Staining of the Fat in Suckling Rats Where Sudan III Was Fed to the Mother."

There is no record of the reaction by the assembled anatomists to this intense infusion of experimental biology. Harrison was by nature nondemonstrative, soft-spoken, and reflective. Yet, the data he presented at this symposium must have excited even the most skeptical listener, since they dealt directly with a major issue in neuroanatomy—the cellular organization of the nervous system. Here was absolute proof that isolated embryonic spinal cord fragments could be maintained and would differentiate outside the embryo in an appropriate medium, and that from these tissues there grew out axons capped by growth cones similar to those described in fixed material by Ramón y Cajal. These early explantation and transplantation experiments opened new vistas for exploration of fundamental problems in neurogenesis and development. Harrison was elected President of the AAA in 1911.

Another measure of Harrison's outstanding abilities is the trail of significant contributions left by his students. In his memorial remarks, J.S. Nicholas lists 40 anatomists who trained with Harrison at Yale. Those who remained active in the Association include:

E. Adams (Mount Holyoke)	J. Oppenheimer (Bryn Mawr)
W. Ballard (Dartmouth)	J. Piatt (Pennsylvania)
R. Blount (Galveston)	R. Reyer (West Virginia)
H. Burr (Yale)	W. Schultz (New Hampshire)
W. Copenhaver (Columbia)	J. Schwind (Cincinnati)
S. Detwiler (Columbia)	F. Swett (Duke)
E. Hall (Louisville)	W. Spoffard (Syracuse)
D. Hooker (Pittsburgh)	E. Van Campenhout
C. Hutchinson (Jefferson)	(Louvain)
J. Nicholas (Yale)	C. Yntema (Syracuse)

Beginning in 1916 with presentations by Samuel R. Detwiler (1890–1957) and Davenport Hooker (1887–1965), both of whom served as Presidents of the AAA, and continuing into the 1970s, over 140 presentations have been made at the Association meetings by these students. Many second and third generation scientific progeny of these Harrison students are now active in the Association.

The contributions of Detwiler were especially important to the emerging field of neuroembryology. He perfected the use of extirpation and heterotopic transplantation of limb primordia, of segments of immature spinal cord, or of somite anlagen to investigate the effects of changed spatial relations on nerve outgrowth and limb function, neuroblast aggregation and proliferation, and vertebral development. Later, he returned to his first area of interest, the anatomy and development of the reptilian and amphibian retina. The last presentation Detwiler sponsored at the Association meetings was in 1954. This was an analysis of the role of spinal cord-somite interactions in vertebral chondrogenesis and was coauthored by Howard Holtzer.

Surprisingly missing from Nicholas' list are Frances Dorris and Graham Du-Shane, both of whom made important contributions to our knowledge of the origin of vertebrate pigment cells. Also omitted is Leon S. Stone, who performed an exhaustive series of transplantation experiments defining the contributions of placodes and the neural crest to lateral line and cranial sensory ganglia, before turning his attentions to problems of eye and ear development.

Comparable experimental analyses on avian embryos were initiated by Benjamin H. Willier, who worked in the laboratory of Frank R. Lillie at the University of Chicago. In 1924, Willier described for the first time the technique of chorio-allantoic grafting, which was soon adopted by Ernst Van Campenhout, Mary E. Rawles, and Dorothea Rudnick. During the 1930s, Rawles presented several papers on the use of this method to assess the developmental potential of small pieces of chick blastula and gastrula tissue excised from various regions of the blastodisc.

In 1932, Viktor Hamburger came to Lillie's laboratory, bringing with him an arsenal of microsurgical techniques perfected in Spemann's laboratory in Freiburg. Soon coelomic grafts and limb bud transplantations became routine in the hands of these skilled investigators. Rawles and Willier reported the results of xenoplastic transplantations using tissues that contained pigment cell precursors. These experiments elegantly defined the relative roles of the integument and melanocytes in pigment pattern expression in birds. Similar techniques were used by John Saunders, Jr., Edgar Zwilling, and, later, John Fallon to identify the roles of somatic mesoderm and overlying surface ectoderm in controlling the outgrowth and cranio-caudal polarization of developing avian limbs. Their results were reported at the Association meetings beginning in 1956.

A whole embryo culture method that supports avian development during the gastrula and neurula stages was first reported by Nelson Spratt of the University of Minnesota in 1942. By placing small carbon particles on the exposed surface of the epiblast, Spratt was able to refine the avian fate maps established previously by Pasteels.

Through the efforts of Douglas E. Kelley, Allen C. Enders, and Bruce Carlson, a Morphogenesis Club was established in 1977. This group organizes a symposium, supported by the Association, which is presented at the annual meetings. The purpose of this forum is to provide a greater focus on morphological problems in development that are of interest to the membership of the AAA and that will attract a broader audience to the meetings. Topics presented thus far include biophysical aspects of morphogenesis, the development of teratocarcinomas, neuronal interactions in development, and the neural crest.

CLOSING REMARKS

Rarely does one stop and review the presentations in their area of specialization made over a 100-year period, and having done so I am left with conflicting impressions. First is a curiosity as to the fate of all those contributors who presented interesting new data and never again participated in embryological research. Next is an excitement, mixed with frustration, at discovering many important, exciting results that were presented but not published in more detailed form. Data based on amphibian researches that parallel many of the avian embryonic mapping experiments currently being conducted were found in many issues.

Finally, there is a renewed appreciation for the great tradition that is embryology/developmental biology, and the profound contributions that have been made by so many dedicated scientists through their participation in the American Association of Anatomists.

REFERENCES

Harrison, R.G. 1901 On the occurrence of tails in man, with a description of the case reported by Dr. Watson. Johns Hopkins Hosp. Bull., *12*:96–101.

Keibel, F., and F.P. Mall, eds. 1910 Manual of Human Embryology. J.B. Lippincott Co., Philadelphia, Vol. 1.

Keibel, F., and F.P. Mall, eds. 1912 Manual of Human Embryology. J.B. Lippincott Co., Philadelphia, Vol. 2.

Minot, C.S. 1892 Human Embryology. William Wood, New York.

Minot, C.S. 1901 The embryologic basis of pathology. Science, *13*:481–498.

Minot, C.S. 1903 A Laboratory Textbook of Embryology. P. Blackiston's, Philadelphia.

Chapter 12

A CENTURY OF NEUROANATOMY IN AMERICA: 1888–1987

Sanford L. Palay

During the past hundred years, neuroanatomy has been a prominent focus of investigation by American anatomists. Growing along with the American Association of Anatomists, the numbers of American neuroanatomists are now so great and their activities are so diverse that a summary of their research and even the mention of all their names is beyond the compass of this brief essay. At the very outset, I offer apologies to my contemporaries for its inadequate treatment of the modern scene and the seemingly capricious highlighting of certain names instead of others. The purpose of this article is to pass in review some of the great figures in American neuroanatomy during the first half century of the Association, thus setting the stage for the extraordinary expansion of neuroanatomy that has occurred during the second half century. The major themes of the first epoch have been largely superseded by new concerns of the second epoch. We are no longer exercised about grand dogmas and incontestable laws; we are able to tolerate more ambiguity and particularity or specificity. We have a greater appreciation of the ingenious and variable in nature. Although the major problems now are still fundamentally what they were a century ago, our emphasis and the way we cast the questions have shifted as new techniques have become available and have given rise to new insights that necessarily shape our view of the nervous system. A generation that is aware of the ultrastructure of synapses and the localization of multiple neuroactive substances cannot ask whether the neurofibrillae are the essential conducting elements of the nervous system. Yet, the major problem is still the morphological and functional organization of the nervous system of any particular animal, and the necessary corollaries of this theme are the questions: how does it develop? and how is it maintained? Everything that neuroanatomists do can be subsumed under these headings.

The founders of American neuroscience, Clarence Luther Herrick and Charles Judson Herrick, became members of the Association of American Anatomists during its first decade. Prominent European neuroscientists were elected honorary members in the early years, for example, Ranvier and von Kölliker in 1897 and both Retzius and Waldeyer in 1903. Golgi was made an honorary member in 1903 and Ramón y Cajal in 1905, before they were awarded the Nobel Prize in 1906. At the end of the 19th century and during the first few years of the 20th century, a number of men in their thirties joined the Association and over succeeding years became leaders in the developing field of neuroanatomy. The first group included G.C. Huber, Ross Harrison, George Coghill, Henry H. Donaldson, Adolf Meyer, L.B. Johnston, Lewellys F. Barker, Oliver S. Strong, and George Parker. During the next decade they were joined by S. Walter Ranson, Frederick Tilney, and Albert Kuntz. The next generation, becoming members just before and during World War I, included George Bartelmez, Jesse Conel, Elizabeth Crosby, Marion Hines, Olof Larsell, James Papez, A.T. Rasmussen, and Lewis Weed. Just listing their names is to compile an honor roll of American neuroanatomists, all born before 1890, who reached their efflorescence in the first 30 years of the 20th century and contributed signally to the high development that neuroscience enjoys today.

Clarence Luther Herrick (1858–1904) founded the *Journal of Comparative Neurology* in 1891 and thus established comparative neuroanatomy as a peculiarly American science. He wrote and illustrated many of the first issues and filled them out with letters he had received and science notes from abroad. He had a broad-ranging vision of neurology as encompassing everything concerning the nervous system from straightforward gross anatomy to experimental psychology and psychiatry. He sensed the ferment in all biological sciences that was going on in Europe in the 1880s, and he wanted to induce this excitement in America. He had ambitious plans (described in William F. Windle's book, 1979), which were unfortunately derailed by his recurrent battles with tuberculosis and ultimately his death at an early age. From the beginning he was ably assisted by his younger brother, Charles Judson Herrick (1868–1960), who took over the management of the Journal after the first year and filled much of the early issues with his own writings. It was C.J. Herrick who made the Journal viable, and after supporting it out of his own pocket for almost two decades, he was able to convey it to The Wistar Institute as a gift in good fiscal condition.

Early in his career, C.J. Herrick conceived the idea that one could learn the principles of organization of the vertebrate nervous system by studying an animal that displayed no specialized features, that had a brain of which all the parts appeared to be in balance—a generalized brain. He chose the tiger salamander *Ambystoma tigrinum* as such an animal and spent the major part of his life studying the organization and pathways of its brain with Golgi and myelin stains. In the end he had to admit that his basic premise was flawed, that even the apparently simple brain of a salamander was too complex for one man's lifetime of investigation. C.J. Herrick, like his brother, also studied the brains of fishes, especially their visual and gustatory pathways. But he was not an experimentalist; in fact most of the sections he studied were prepared by colleagues who lent him their material. In his long life, he had time to develop his thoughts on evolution and philosophy and to write books on the brains of rats and men as well as those of fishes and salamanders. Among C.J. Herrick's students were Elizabeth Crosby, Marion Hines, and David Bodian.

John Black Johnston (1868–1939), a contemporary of the Herrick brothers, wrote a seminal book *The Nervous System of Vertebrates,* which was published in

1906 and laid out the fundamental plan of the nervous system as expressed in a series of longitudinal functional columns in the brain stem. Johnston rationalized the components of the cranial nerves on the basis of his studies on the brains of fishes. His doctoral dissertation at the University of Michigan was a classic study of the brain of the sturgeon *Acipenser,* which he regarded as a "primitive generalized type." Johnston's career moved into administration after he became a professor at the University of Minnesota. In 1914 he became Dean of the College of Science, Literature, and the Arts and no longer found time for publishing works on neuroscience, although he was a prolific contributor to the literature on education.

George E. Coghill (1872–1941) was a student of C.L. Herrick from 1897 to 1900 while the latter was President of the new University of New Mexico. He had early decided to study the mind as a biological problem, rather than a metaphysical entity. Under Herrick's tutelage he learned neuroanatomy and the scientific point of view, which he then applied to his doctoral thesis (from Brown University) on the cranial nerves of the tiger salamander *(A. tigrinum).* He and C.J. Herrick became fast friends. In 1904 he settled on his life's work, which was to follow the growth of a typical, generalized vertebrate from premotile stages to adulthood and to correlate the successive stages in the development of structure with the concomitant changes in behavior. Coghill found that local reflexes differentiated out of a total pattern of behavior as the brain and spinal cord differentiated, and he concluded that behavior consists not of a concatenation of reflexes but of a progressive refinement and evolution out of gross undifferentiated movement. Coghill's correlated studies had a profound effect during the 1930s on the biological interpretation of psychological issues. He spent most of this period at The Wistar Institute in Philadelphia, and he served as President of the American Association of Anatomists in 1932–1934. Plagued by ill health in his later years, he never completed the planned summary of his observations and thinking.

A younger member of this generation, and an excellent example of the deepening self-confidence of American neuroscientists during the first quarter of the 20th century, was Stephen Walter Ranson (1880–1942). Ranson was a student of J.B. Johnston at the University of Minnesota, where he became deeply interested in the nervous system, stimulated by Donaldson's book on the growth of the brain. After receiving his PhD in 1905 at the University of Chicago and his MD at Rush Medical School in 1907, he became an Assistant in Anatomy at Northwestern University. Like C.L. Herrick, J.B. Johnston, and many others, he spent the mandatory year or two in Germany and returned to this country to become Chairman of Anatomy at Northwestern. In 1924 he went to Washington University in St. Louis as Professor of Neuroanatomy, a position in which his teaching responsibilities were sufficiently subordinated to his research. In 1928 he was enticed back to Northwestern to become director of the Institute of Neurology, a position in which he could devote himself entirely to his research. For the next 14 years he was America's preeminent neuroscientist. His accomplishments were outstanding for their combination of neuroanatomy with neurophysiology, but they coincided with what must in retrospect be regarded as a period of decline in neuroanatomy and neurohistology.

In the early part of his career, Ranson introduced a useful pyridine silver method, which Cajal (according to E. Horne Craigie) regarded as an unimportant variation of his own silver method. In any case, with this method Ranson made a careful study of the nerve fibers entering the spinal cord through the dorsal rootlets. He demonstrated the unmyelinated fibers in the sensory nerves and showed how they became segregated into the lateral fascicle of the rootlets and entered the tract of Lissauer. While at Washington University he was instrumental in reviving the use of the Horsley-Clarke apparatus for making prescribed and repeatable lesions in the brains of experimental animals, and at Northwestern his successful studies of the physiology and anatomy of the hypothalamus and midbrain opened the way for neuroendocrinology and the understanding of the central regulatory mechanisms. By carefully placing small lesions in the hypothalamus of dogs, Ranson and his coworkers were able to dissect the pathway for regulating body temperature and thus demonstrated the critical role of the hypothalamus in integrating visceral and somatic functions. His team of collaborators showed that the neural link between the hypothalamus and the posterior pituitary was necessary for the regulation of water excretion and that diabetes insipidus could be produced experimentally by severing that link. He was, of course, wrong in considering the posterior pituitary as a gland innervated by descending fibers from the hypothalamus and in denying even the possibility that the nerve cells in the hypothalamus could themselves be the source of the secretion, but his work (fully reported in a classic monograph by C. Fisher, W.R. Ingram, and S.W. Ranson, 1937) proved that the hypothalamohypophysial pathway carries the regulating impulses for water metabolism and thus paved the way for the recognition of neurosecretion and its role more than a decade later. Although Ranson was aware of the concept of neurosecretion, which had been introduced by Ernst Scharrer in 1928 and elaborated during the late 1930s, he could not take it seriously. It is symptomatic of the low esteem in which neuroanatomy was held during these decades, that even Ranson's intense pursuit of the integration between structure and function, as represented by concurrent anatomical and physiological investigation of the hypothalamus, did not permit him to appreciate the ultimate integrative concept of the nerve-gland cell. Neuroanatomy was a science of location of function, not an expression of dynamic events.

In 1920 Ranson published his famous and durable textbook, *Anatomy of the Nervous System,* which was the first textbook of neuroanatomy in English expressly written for medical students. Previously students pieced together their knowledge from gross anatomy texts. The book went through seven editions in his lifetime, and two more editions were prepared by Sam L. Clark after Ranson's death. For more than two decades it was the only textbook of neuroanatomy used in American medical schools. It was an extremely detailed descriptive text, and although it contained clinical case histories, it made almost no allusions to physiology. A comparison of even the seventh edition, the last to be prepared by Ranson, with a current textbook such as *Principles of Neuroscience* by Kandel and Schwartz demonstrates dramatically how fundamentally the subject has altered during the past 40 years. Among the students of Ranson who became prominent neuroscientists were Sam L. Clark, Walter R. Ingram, Horace Magoun, and William F. Windle.

In contrast to Ranson, we may set his self-effacing contemporary James W. Papez (1883–1958), who was trained at the University of Minnesota and spent most of his career at Emory University and Cornell University in Ithaca. Papez has had an enormous influence on neuroanatomy, neurophysiology, and psychiatry, stemming almost entirely from his recognition of a potential circuit linking the hypothalamus and the cortex. Papez saw that a circuit of projections could be constructed from the mamillary body by way of the mamillothalamic tract to the anterior nucleus of the thalamus to the cingulate gyrus to the entorhinal cortex to the hippocampus and thence by way of the fornix back to the mamillary body. Although this Papez circuit has had to be modified by recent discoveries which make it appear less and less relevant as well as viable, it was an important ingredient in the development of the concept of the limbic system as the neural substrate for emotion and memory, which gained currency after World War II.

We should also include in this generation a number of other influential neuroanatomists whose compass was more restricted. One of these, Olof Larsell (1886–1964), was a student of Ranson at Northwestern and spent almost all of his career at the University of Oregon in Portland. Larsell devoted himself to the comparative anatomy of the cerebellum, from the study of which he devised the classical scheme of ten transverse lobules for all birds and mammals. The scheme allowed comparisons to be made between comparable regions of the cerebellum in different species despite the enormous variation in the pattern of lobulation. His monumental book on the evolution of the cerebellum was completed after his death by his friend, Jan Jansen. Elizabeth Crosby (1888–1983) was a student of C.J. Herrick at the University of Chicago and spent most of her career at the University of Michigan. She achieved early eminence with her thesis on the brain of the alligator. She devoted a large part of her investigative career to the analysis of the pathways controlling eye movement from the cortex to the midbrain. Crosby always emphasized the comparative approach to neuroanatomy that she had learned from her association with Herrick and G.C. Huber. She was largely responsible for completing and editing the monumental two-volume work *The Comparative Anatomy of the Nervous System of Vertebrates, Including Man* (Ariens Kappers, Huber, and Crosby), which appeared in 1936. Among her students and close associates were Russell T. Woodburne, Clement A. Fox, Tryphena Humphrey, and Edward Lauer.

The next generation of American neuroanatomists, born at the turn of the century and the first decade of the 20th century, is not much larger than the first, pioneering group. As representatives we may take William F. Windle and Horace Magoun, both students of Ranson. Windle (1895–1985) had a varied career as a teacher, investigator, and administrator. Early on he became interested in the development of the central nervous system and began a study of the differentiation of nerve fiber bundles and nuclear groups in the brain stem in correlation with the development of behavior. His studies led him to the conclusion that in mammals, at least, simple reflexes appeared first and were gradually assimilated into complex behavior as the animal developed, a conclusion directly opposite to that drawn by Coghill from his observations on amphibians. The establishment, consisting of C.J. Herrick and the developmental biologists of the day, who restricted themselves almost entirely to amphibian embryos as experimental subjects, reacted very negatively to this clear challenge by a young upstart. Although this controversy never was resolved, Windle attempted to support his view by analyzing the factors that control the onset of respiratory movements in the chick. An outgrowth of this work was a long series of studies with many collaborators on the effects of perinatal anoxia on the brain. Concurrently with these investigations Windle carried on an intensive examination of the factors promoting regeneration in the peripheral and central nervous systems. Windle thrived on controversy, and his papers, reviews, monographs, and symposia served to stimulate interest and much research.

Perhaps more important for the development of neuroanatomy in America were Windle's administrative achievements. He became chairman of the Department of Anatomy at the University of Pennsylvania in 1947 and in the space of 4 years transformed it into the most active center of neuroanatomical research in the country. In 1951, after a brief interlude in the pharmaceutical industry, he undertook to establish the Laboratory of Neuroanatomical Sciences at the National Institute of Neurological Diseases and Blindness (as it was then called) in Bethesda. This event marked the beginning of the upsurge in neuroanatomical research that characterizes the last half of the 20th century. In the Laboratory of Neuroanatomical Sciences, Windle emphasized investigation of his favorite topics, regeneration and perinatal asphyxia, but he also promoted studies on the auditory pathway, fine structure, and neuropathology. The impetus and the protection that he afforded during the 1950s, not only at the National Institute but also in international symposia and conferences, brought neuroanatomy into the fore again as it had been at the beginning of the century and rekindled the excitement and vitality that the advent of new methods justified.

In 1959 Windle established a new journal, *Experimental Neurology,* to serve as a vehicle for experimental work to complement the mainly anatomical reports favored by the *Journal of Comparative Neurology* and the electrophysiological work in the *Journal of Neurophysiology.* In his long career at several institutions, Windle had many students and close associates whom he influenced greatly and whose careers he fostered. Among them were Ruth Rhines, William W. Chambers, Chan-Nao Liu, James M. Sprague, Carmine D. Clemente, Grant Rasmussen, Jan Cammermeyer, Lloyd Guth, Sanford L. Palay, Milton Brightman, James B. Ranck, and C. Murphy Combs.

Horace W. Magoun is another student of Ranson who played an important role in the development of neuroanatomy in the middle of this century. When Windle left the Institute of Neurology at Northwestern University in 1946, Magoun succeeded to the directorship. Subsequently he was called to the University of California at Los Angeles where he became the founding director of the Brain Research Institute in 1950. During the 1940s and 1950s Magoun mounted an intensive study of the reticular formation, a long-neglected region of the brain stem. Together with Ruth Rhines and then with the physiologist Giuseppe Moruzzi, Magoun formulated the concept of a multisynaptic, diffuse ascending system of nuclei and fiber tracts in the core of the brain that regulated the activity of the cerebral cortex—the reticular activating system. This proposal led to a flood of papers and monographs on the structure and function of the reticular formation, including a careful analysis by Alf Brodal and his collaborators of the nuclear patterns and complex interconnections of the cells in the reticular formation, which showed that this mysterious region was neither diffuse nor particularly mysterious. These studies initiated either by Magoun or in reaction to his imaginative proposals are the direct antecedents to the current understanding of parallel ascending pathways centered on the locus ceruleus and the raphe nuclei and characterized by specific transmitter chemicals.

It must be clear from this selection of capsule biographies that the principal locus of neuroanatomical investigation in America from the end of the 19th century to the middle of the 20th century lay in the Midwest, specifically in the universities in the vicinity of Chicago, Minneapolis, and Ann Arbor. The number of investigators was small, the techniques at their disposal were severely limited, and the problems that they could solve were correspondingly restricted in scope. Indeed, by the 1930s confidence in the value of neuroanatomy for understanding the organization of the nervous system seems to have reached a low point in America.

The construction of atlases parceling the cerebral cortex into progressively smaller and more numerous subfields, which began in Germany with Meynert and reached its zenith with the atlases of the Vogts and of von Economo and Koskinas, seemed to have become an end in itself and held little attraction for American neuroanatomists. The antipathy to this apparently endless morphological subdivision of the cortex coincided with an analogous reaction against cerebral localization of function that gathered force in psychology and clinical neurology in the 1930s and 1940s. For example, G. von Bonin and P. Bailey, agreeing with K.S. Lashley on the generalization of function in the cerebral cortex, published a book in which they blurred the cytoarchitectonic boundaries and asserted that the gradual shifting in cellular density and lamination from place to place did not permit the minute parceling pursued by the Vogts and their collaborators. As physiological experiment (with its own severe but disregarded limitations) did not substantiate different functions for so many different areas, it was thought that the anatomical distinctions must be considered either fanciful or of no account.

The dispute between the neuronists and the reticularists, which had raged in Europe since the 1890s' aroused little or no interest in Americans, who were quite convinced by the arguments of Cajal and the evidence of neurophysiology. In fact, Americans had contributed decisive evidence (as far as light microscopy could be decisive) to the controversy (see below) and did not feel that the issue required any further debate.

Furthermore, because of the limitations of the methods available, the analysis of connections between the parts of the central nervous system had reached an impasse during the first quarter of the century. Tracing techniques based on myelin sheath stains in normal animals allowed only the larger tracts and fibers to be followed and then only to the region where the myelin sheaths stopped and the fibers dispersed. Experimental chromatolysis, pioneered in the 1890s by Nissl, could be applied with confidence only to some large nerve cells, and the degenerative fiber techniques such as the Marchi method were notoriously unreliable as well as restricted to large fibers. The silver methods also provided only the most general overview of trajectories, and once a fiber bundle dispersed into the neuropil, the terminus of the fibers became ambiguous. The most detailed and most secure methods were the several variants of the Golgi method, but they were so erratic in practice that very few neuroanatomists had the patience to learn and use them. Besides, since the early work of Cajal it was well known that they could be applied successfully only to the brains of fetal or infantile subjects. Therefore, even successful preparations gave only an unreliable view of immature nervous systems. By 1950 hardly any Americans had any experience with the Golgi method; Clement Fox and Grant Rasmussen among the older investigators and the Scheibels and Kent Morest among the younger were just about the only practitioners of the art in the country. Even so expert a Golgi-ist as Rafael Lorente de Nó, the youngest surviving student of Cajal, had long since turned to physiology, convinced that there was no future in neuroanatomy. What was needed for neuroanatomy to progress again were new methods and a new approach to morphology.

In view of this loss of confidence in its methods and in the value of its results, neuroanatomy was left largely to neurophysiologists, who attempted to trace functional circuits in the brain by means of implanted electrodes and evoked potentials. Applying strychnine to the cortex was one technique whereby hidden connections could be uncovered. The successes of Ranson and his school fostered a drift of neuroanatomists from morphology to physiology, so that they were more at home in the American Association of Physiologists than in the American Association of Anatomists. In addition, important contributions of anatomists to the triumphant analysis of the reproductive cycle, the complex relationships of the pituitary gland, and the other major discoveries of endocrinology, all reported voluminously at the annual meetings, made the remaining neuroanatomists feel less welcome.

In April 1947, at the annual meeting of the American Association of Anatomists in Montreal, a handful of young neuroanatomists decided to do something about the low estate of neuroanatomy. In order to promote the anatomical study of the nervous system, they agreed to form the Cajal Club, which would meet annually as a forum for exchanging information and ideas, in a socially supportive milieu. The original group consisted of Wendell J.S. Krieg, E. Horne Craigie, Pinckney J. Harman, Clement Fox, R. Frederick Becker, George Clark, James Graves, David S. Jones, Anthony A. Pearson, Duncan C. Hetherington, Arthur J. Jansen, Grant L. Rasmussen, Charles Berry, and Talmage Peele. It is interesting to note that the majority were Midwesterners. The original impetus was provided by Krieg, who called the first meeting and continued as a leader for many years. But the main force that held the club together during its first two decades was Pinckney J. Harman, who served as secretary-treasurer (or, in the playful jargon of the Club, the Apical Dendrite) until his death in 1966. At first the club was purely informal and social, but in a few years, as the number of adherents slowly grew, a formal program of papers and lectures became traditional. Since 1950 the meetings have always been held on the day before the opening session of the annual meeting of the American Association of Anatomists, and as interest in neuroanatomy revived during the 1960s, the Cajal Club became a more and more important attraction to the Association meeting, with formal symposia, foreign visitors, and an annual Pinckney Harman Prize Lecture, attended by hundreds of interested anatomists. The vision of the founders has been amply justified and realized.

The founding of the Cajal Club was prescient, as technical advances were in the offing that would transform neuroanatomy into one of the most vital sciences of the 20th century and the largest single contributor to the annual meetings of the American Association of Anatomists. By 1975 fully half of the papers presented at the annual meetings dealt with some aspect of neuroanatomy. What happened during the postwar period to effect this change? The first event was the rise of neurocytology and the second was the discovery of physiological marking techniques for tracing connections in the nervous system. Neither of these was brand-new and both grew out of the halting progress of the previous century, but the development of new techniques, and especially the new understanding that accompanied them, reinforced the appeal of neuroanatomy for increasing numbers of students who became neuroanatomists during the 1960s and 1970s.

In America the principal precursor of modern neurocytology was Ross G.

Harrison (1870–1959), who invented tissue culture in order to observe directly the growth of nerve fibers (1907). He showed that the axon was not a pluricellular construction but the growing process of a single neuroblast, thus disproving all the variants of the cell-chain theory that originated with Schwann in 1839. Harrison's embryological experiments on anuran embryos during the first two decades of the 20th century proved that "each axon arises as the outgrowth of a single ganglion cell" and that the associated Schwann cells were merely accessory structures. So well accepted is this concept now that it is difficult to believe the passion with which it was resisted even into the 1920s and how often experimental studies had to be repeated until it was generally credited.

One of Harrison's postdoctoral fellows at Yale in 1932 was Paul A. Weiss, who had trained in Vienna as an engineer and had come to New Haven to learn experimental embryology from the master. Weiss made signal contributions to analytical embryology, particularly to the analysis of factors that regulate nerve growth and the matching of the peripheral distribution with the central nervous system. His work and his eminence in this field led naturally to his being asked during World War II to explore methods for improving the regenerative efficacy of injured nerves. In the course of this study, conducted in collaboration with Helen B. Hiscoe, Weiss demonstrated that chronic constriction of a nerve results in the accumulation of axoplasm proximal to the point of constriction and atrophy distally. Reasoning from the analogy of the effect of a dam thrown across the channel of a river, Weiss interpreted his experiments as demonstrating that in the normal nerve fiber axoplasm continuously flows from the cell body, where it is produced, down the axon to its endings; the axon normally is in a state of perpetual growth. This idea, together with the correlation of protein synthesis with RNA-containing, basophil cytoplasm by Caspersson, Hyden, and others, soon gained general acceptance as a working hypothesis. Droz and Leblond demonstrated by autoradiography that radioactively labeled amino acids were taken up by nerve cells in injected ganglia and appeared quickly in the nucleus, then successively in the Nissl substance, in the Golgi apparatus, and finally in the processes. Later Raymond Lasek performed a very careful study of the rates of movement of radioactively labeled protein as a wave front of label down the axon.

In a short time Weiss's axoplasmic flow became transformed into axoplasmic transport, an energy-dependent variety of protoplasmic streaming, requiring ATP, microtubules, a host of associated proteins, and intricate structure-function inter-relationships. In the process, the nerve fiber has become transformed in imagery from a static silver-impregnated wire into the living, dynamic, cellular structure it should have been from the beginning. The development of new microscopic optics and techniques of illumination with enhanced contrast provided increasingly satis-fying visual documentation in time-laspe movies of axoplasmic transport in action. All of this new morphological evidence brought together the diverse lines of investigation into normal development, nerve regeneration, and the mature ner-vous system. The nervous system is seen as structurally and chemically, as well as physiologically, dynamic and constantly changing. We accept this idea as so banal now as not to need expression. It is hard to imagine a time when it did not represent the general consensus. It derives from Paul Weiss and his experiments with constricted nerves only 40 years ago.

A different aspect of neurocytology concerns the intimate interrelations be-tween nerve cells, an unresolved problem inherited from the time of Cajal. Cajal insisted that each nerve cell is an independent functional, embryological, and morphological entity, and that it relates to other cells only by contact, not by protoplasmic continuity. In more modern terms this idea, the Neuron Doctrine, essentially means that each nerve cell is enclosed in its own cell membrane. This is not the place to review the vexatious controversy that dogged this idea. As mentioned above, most American neuroanatomists were convinced of its truth by the mid-1920s. In fact several Americans contributed importantly to the documentation supporting the Neuron Doctrine. For example, George Bartelmez (1885–1967) showed before World War I that the cytoplasm of the Mauthner cell in the goldfish was separated from the cytoplasm of the large club endings impinging upon it by a distinct synaptic plate. The same problem was taken up again in the 1930s by David Bodian, who, although a student of C.J. Herrick, actually worked more closely with Bartelmez. With cytological stains and his own copper-protargol method, he showed that the neurofibrillae in the endings do not continue into the cytoplasm of the postsynaptic cell, from which the axoplasm is separated by a synaptolemma. Furthermore, a pioneering freeze-dry study of neurofibrillae in motor cells and large nerve fibers by Normand Hoerr (1902–1958) demonstrated that neurofibrillae are real structures, not artifacts of chemical fixation, a subject that George Parker had debated in a famous review of 1929. Again, it must be noted that these important studies took place at the University of Chicago under the aegis of R.R. Bensley.

The morphological solution to the controversy over the synapse could not be achieved until the advent of electron microscopy and the development of adequate techniques for preparing nervous tissue for it. In 1953, the author working with George E. Palade at the Rockefeller Institute (as it was then called) characterized the fine structure of the Nissl substance in the neuronal soma and identified electron microscopically the synaptic junction in the central nervous system and the neuromuscular junction in the periphery. They presented a preliminary report on their findings at a meeting of the Electron Microscopy Society of America in October of that year and a more detailed report at the Galveston meeting of the American Association of Anatomists in April 1954. These early reports, elaborated in more extended papers subsequently, clearly demonstrated the cleft between the two synaptic partners, thus confirming Cajal's Neuron Doctrine and laying to rest the dispute of a century. In addition, however, the first reports disclosed the internal architecture of the synaptic terminal and its partner. In the terminal, mitochondria, tubules of the smooth endoplasmic reticulum, and clusters of synaptic vesicles were described. Attached to both the pre- and postsynaptic membranes were tufts of dense fibrillar material, and often the synaptic cleft was occupied by a sheet of dense fibrillar material. Shortly afterward, the findings were confirmed by Eduardo De Robertis and H. Stanley Bennett and then by many others. Improved techniques since then have resulted in the disclosure of much more detail, and many refined distinctions can now be made. From the beginning the idea was proposed that the synaptic vesicles are the morphological counterparts of the quanta of transmitter released into the synaptic cleft upon axonal excitation, as demonstrated by the physiological studies of Sir Bernard Katz and his collaborators. This "vesicle theory" is a speculation that has still not been proved. Although it has been seriously challenged by Israel and his colleagues in France, it still has many adherents. That is for the future to resolve. The discovery of the fine structure of the synapse was the final piece of evidence that reified the conception of the nerve cell as a secretory entity. Thus the concept of neurosecretion merged into the mainstream of neuroanatomy (see Chapter 17).

The fine structure of the synapse was not the only contribution of electron microscopy to neuroanatomy, nor even the first. The intensive examination of nerve cells in different parts of the nervous system and in different species rapidly disclosed the essential cytological features of the nerve cell body, its nucleus, Nissl substance, Golgi apparatus, neurofilaments, microtubules, and multifarious inclusions. In a few years every part of the neuron was recognized and described, along with variations and alterations with age and disease. Dendrites were differentiated from axons; the axon hillock and initial segment of the axon were distinguished from the definitive axon; and the nodes of Ranvier were distinguished from all other parts. Dendritic thorns were recognized and a wide variety of synaptic types were described. The difficulties in tracing parts of a cell as complicated in shape and as varied in size as the nerve cell were formidable in the small samples and ultrathin sections of electron microscopy. The really rapid progress made in the 1950s and 1960s is a testament to the value of the basic information accumulated by light microscopy in the preceding century. As methods improved, it became possible to describe in detail the fabric of the nervous system in different parts of the brain and to begin to relate architecture to function. After some initial confusion, the supporting cells, the neuroglial cells, were recognized and sorted out and their relations to nerve cells could be studied. The structure of the myelin sheath, which was the first biological problem to be solved by electron microscopy (H. Fernandez-Moran, Betty Ben Geren, David Robertson, and later Daniel Pease and Henry Webster), gradually gave up its secrets. Its formation in the central nervous system posed additional obstacles, which were overcome in the embryological studies of Alan Peters and Richard and Mary Bunge. By the end of the 1960s, Alan Peters, S.L. Palay, and H. de F. Webster published a book on the fine structure of the nervous system which marked the coming of age of neurocytology. The subject continued to grow, and a greatly expanded second edition was published in 1976.

One important effect of the successes of electron microscopy was the restoration of confidence in the Golgi method. Electron microscopy showed conclusively that the impregnation with silver chromate in this method lay inside the nerve cell (W. Stell, V. Chan-Palay) and that, although the precipitate might result in some dimensional distortion, the image produced by the Golgi method is remarkably faithful to the form of the original living cell. For example, the form of dendritic spines in the two methods is quite consistent. Electron microscopy validated the existence of dendritic spines and showed that they are sites for synaptic junctions, a matter that had been in dispute on the basis of light microscopy alone. Knowing that the Golgi method is reliable after all stimulated an upsurge in Golgi studies correlated with electron microscopy. Finally, even ways of combining both techniques in the same preparation were found.

The second event that transformed neuroanatomy after World War II was the introduction of a regressive silver stain that selectively marks degenerating fibers—the Nauta method. Walle J.H. Nauta, after being trained in the Netherlands and Switzerland, immigrated into the United States in the early 1950s. In 1954 he published the first of several variants of a method based on the Laidlaw silver stain that allowed him to trace degenerating axons into the neuropil close to the region of their termination. Although the method was superseded about 15 years later by the Fink-Heimer modification, which labeled regions where terminals were degenerating, these methods produced a revolution in the practice of tracing connections in the central nervous system. The new methods made feasible a much more detailed analysis of connections than had ever been possible before. Complex connections, such as those between the thalamus and the cortex, between the various basal ganglia, between the vestibular and the oculomotor nuclei, became amenable to study and were dissected by these methods. There were, however, severe limitations. The methods depended upon the size and location of carefully placed lesions. It is nearly impossible to make exactly reproducible lesions in different animals. Therefore the ensuing degeneration was variable in extent from animal to animal. In addition, the most serious limitation was introduced by fibers arising outside the lesion and merely passing through it and could not be avoided in making lesions. Consequently neuroanatomists eagerly turned to two new methods that became available at the beginning of the 1970s.

The first of these methods was based upon the work of Raymond Lasek showing that tritiated amino acids were incorporated into proteins by nerve cell bodies and transported down the axon to its terminals. Axoplasmic transport, rather than degeneration products, offered a means to label the terminals of nerve fibers arising from known cell bodies. These connections between regions of the nervous system could be traced in detail by injecting radioactive amino acids into small specified regions of gray matter, such as nuclei or cortical areas, and subsequently preparing autoradiographs of serial sections of the brain. The method was brought to a high level of refinement by 1972, when Max Cowan, David Gottlieb, Anita Hendrickson, Joseph L. Price, and Thomas Woolsey published their detailed study, showing that it is a reliable technique for locating projections from nerve cells in the site of injection. The detail that can be derived from the autoradiographic method is largely determined by the size of the injection site, and fibers of passage are not considered a serious problem.

The second method was developed at about the same time and because it depends upon retrograde axoplasmic transport it complements the autoradiographic method. This second technique originated from the observation that vesicles in nerve endings can be labeled by the uptake of a foreign protein injected into the terminal distribution of a nerve fiber. Time-lapse cinematography of living nerve fibers in tissue culture or in surviving nerves *in vitro* showed that granules and other particles migrate up the axon in a retrograde direction toward the cell body. Kristensson and Olsson injected horseradish peroxidase (HRP) into skeletal muscles, such as the gastrocnemius muscle or the tongue, and found that the corresponding motor cells in the central nervous system were labeled by the enzyme transported retrogradely along their axons.

The idea of using this enzyme and retrograde axoplasmic transport for tracing fiber connections in the central nervous system was initiated in 1972 by Jennifer and Matthew LaVail, who used it to demonstrate the projections of the isthmo-optic nucleus to the retina (by intraocular injection) and the projection of retinal ganglion cells upon the optic tectum (by injections into the tectum) in chicks. The HRP method became widely used, often in coordination with orthograde transport of injected amino acids and autoradiography. But it was soon discovered that HRP is not reliably restricted to intact nerve fibers, and the fiber-of-passage problem again became troublesome. A variety of other proteins have come into use, for example, HRP conjugated to certain lectins such as wheat germ agglutinin or *Phaseolus vulgaris* leucoagglutinin, which can be used for tracing by orthograde transport and which appear to be more specific than HRP alone.

In addition, various fluorescent dyes have been introduced as tracers, primarily by Kuypers and his colleagues, and are widely used in this country. The variety of marker substances is now broad and the methods are constantly undergoing refinement. As a result, the amount of data collected concerning connections has expanded enormously. The details of connectivity of almost any region of the central nervous system in any one species is now well beyond the memory capacity of any one neuroanatomist. All this information will have to be committed to a computer system that will codify and correlate and allow retrieval on demand.

In the past few years, histochemistry and immunocytochemistry have been developed into still other fruitful neuroanatomical techniques. These methods make it possible to characterize a pathway according to its chemical signature, for example, a catecholamine pathway or a cholinergic pathway. Although these particular methods have been pioneered by European investigators (e.g., Eranko, Hillarp, Falck, Shute, and Lewis), American neuroanatomists have been very active in exploiting them to analyze the nervous system. Immunocytochemistry has provided a powerful tool for differentiating nerve cells and nerve fibers or endings that may appear alike in all respects, yet display differing chemistry. These methods vastly increase the level of detail that must be taken into account when analyzing the organization of the nervous system. Among the more prominent investigators in this field are Victoria Chan-Palay, Virginia Pickel, Robert Y. Moore, Ann Graybiel, Margaret Wong-Riley, Floyd Bloom, Robert Elde, and a host of others.

Perhaps the most interesting result of these new chemical approaches is the recognition that individual nerve cells can contain more than one neuroactive substance, thus overthrowing the former dogma that a nerve cell can have only one neurotransmitter. Although the functional significance of this discovery is still to be determined, it certainly enlarges the repertoire of individual cells and increases the modes by which they can influence the activity of their postsynaptic partners. These neuroactive agents must exert their influence through the activation of quite precise and highly regulated mechanisms, which are currently under investigation by pharmacologists and molecular biologists. For the purposes of neuroanatomy, however, an exciting prospect for the future lies in the fact that the co-existence of multiple transmitters vastly increases the options available to both the pre- and postsynaptic elements and thus exquisitely refines the conditions which result in the initiation of a nerve impulse in any particular nerve cell.

Thus the two strains of contemporary neuroanatomy converge and reinforce each other. Fine structure and living cytology provide the tools for tracing connections and uncovering the architectural design of the nervous system. Chemistry, physiology, and morphology interlock as interdependent aspects of its structural principles.

ACKNOWLEDGMENT

I am grateful to Dr. G.E. Erikson, Archivist of the American Association of Anatomists, for kindly providing the biographical data and analytical listings used in this essay.

SUGGESTED READINGS

Ariens Kappers, C.U., G.C. Huber, and E.C. Crosby 1936 The Comparative Anatomy of the Nervous system of Vertebrates, Including Man. Macmillan, New York.
Bartelmez, G. 1915 Mauthner's cell and the nucleus motorius tegmenti. J Comp Neurol 25:87–128.

Ben Geren, B., and J. Raskind 1953 Development of the fine structure of the myelin sheath in sciatic nerves of chick embryos. Proc Natl Acad Sci USA *39*:880–884.

Bodian, D. 1937 The structure of the vertebrate synapse. A study of the axon endings on Mauthner's cell and neighboring centers in the goldfish. J Comp Neurol *68*:117–145.

Chan-Palay, V., and S.L. Palay, eds 1982 Cytochemical Methods in Neuroanatomy. Alan R. Liss, New York.

Coghill, G.E. (1914–1936) Correlated anatomical and physiological studies of the growth of the nervous system of Amphibia. Parts I to XII: J Comp Neurol *24*:161–233, 1914; *26*:247–340, 1916; *37*:37–69, 1924; *37*:71–120, 1924; *40*:47–94, 1926; *41*:95–152, 1926; *42*:1–6, 1926; *45*:227–247, 1928; *51*:311–375, 1930; *53*:147–168, 1931; *54*:327–358, 1933; *64*:135–167, 1936.

Cowan, W.M., D.I. Gottlieb, A.E. Hendrickson, J.L. Price, and T.A. Woolsey 1972 The autoradiographic demonstration of axonal connections in the central nervous sytem. Brain Res *37*:21–51.

Donaldson, H.H. 1895 The Growth of the Brain. Walter Scott, London.

Fisher, C., W.R. Ingram, and S.W. Ranson 1938 Diabetes Insipidus and the Neuro-Humoral Control of Water Balance: A Contribution to the Structure and Function of the Hypothalamico-Hypophyseal System. Edwards Bros., Ann Arbor.

Harrison, R.G. 1907 Observations on the living developing nerve fiber. Anat Rec *1*:116–118.

Harrison, R.G. 1924 Neuroblast versus sheath cell in the development of peripheral nerves. J Comp Neurol *37*:123–205.

Hoerr, N.L. 1936 Cytological studies by the Altmann-Gersh freezing-drying method. III The preexistence of neurofibrillae and their disposition in the nerve fiber. Anat Rec *66*:81–90.

Horne Craigie, E. 1981 What kind of man was Santiago Ramón y Cajal? Proc Cajal Club *3*:13–28.

Johnston, J.B. 1906 The Nervous System of Vertebrates. Blakiston, Philadelphia.

LaVail, J.H., and M.M. LaVail 1972 Retrograde axonal transport in the central nervous system. Science *176*:1416–1417.

Larsell, O. (Jansen, J., ed) 1967 The Comparative Anatomy and Histology of the Cerebellum from Myxinoids through Birds. University of Minnesota Press, Minneapolis.

Larsell, O. 1970 The Comparative Anatomy and Histology of the Cerebellum from Monotremes through Apes. University of Minnesota Press, Minneapolis.

Larsell, O. (Jansen, J., ed—with chapters by H.K. Korneliussen and E. Mugnaini) 1972 The Comparative Anatomy and Histology of the Cerebellum; The Human Cerebellum, Cerebellar Connections, and Cerebellar Cortex. University of Minnesota Press, Minneapolis.

Lasek, R. 1968 Axoplasmic transport in cat dorsal root ganglion cells: As studied with [³H]-LL-leucine. Brain Res *7*:360–377.

Magoun, H.W. 1952 The ascending reticular activating system. Res Publ Assoc Res Nerv Ment Dis *30*:480–492.

Nauta, W.J.H., and P.A. Gygax 1954 Silver impregnation of degenerating axons in the central nervous system. A modified technique. Stain Technol *29*:91–93.

Palay, S.L. 1956 Synapses in the central nervous system. J. Biophys Biochem Cytol 2:193–202.

Papez, J.W. 1937 A proposed mechanism of emotion. Arch Neurol Psychiatr *38*:725–734.

Parker, G. 1929 The neurofibril hypothesis. Rev Biol 4:155–176.

Peters, A., S.L. Palay, and H. deF. Webster 1970 The Fine Structure of the Nervous System. Harper & Row, New York (2nd edition published by Saunders, Philadelphia, 1976).

Ranson, S.W. 1920 The Anatomy of the Nervous System. Saunders, Philadelphia.

von Bonin, G., and P. Bailey 1947 The Neocrotex of *Macaca mulatta*. University of Illinois Press, Urbana.

Weiss, P.A., and H.B. Hiscoe 1948 Experiments on the mechanism of nerve growth. J Exp Zool *107*:315–396.

Windle, W.F. 1979 The Pioneering Role of Clarence Luther Herrick in American Neuroscience. Exposition Press, Hicksville, New York.

Chapter 13

GROSS ANATOMY: CONTRIBUTIONS OF FIVE AMERICAN ANATOMISTS DURING THE FIRST CENTURY OF THE ASSOCIATION

Carmine D. Clemente

Shortly after the first meeting of the Association of American Anatomists (as it was initially named) in Washington, D.C., in September 1888, it was decided to invite certain distinguished anatomists from foreign countries to become honorary members in the Association. The first of these was Professor Daniel John Cunningham, the brilliant Irish anatomist of Trinity College at the University of Dublin. A number of other renowned anatomists were soon added, so that by 1898 the Association could boast of having on its rolls, in addition to Cunningham, such outstanding anatomists as Karl Gegenbauer from Heidelberg, Wilhelm His of Leipzig, A. von Koelliker of Würtzburg, Alexander Macalister of Cambridge, L. Ranvier of the College de France in Paris, William Turner from the University of Edinburgh, and a few years later Camillo Golgi and S. Ramón y Cajal. During the previous 133 years, i.e., from the time that the University of Pennsylvania accepted the first medical students to be trained in the Americas in 1765, very few American anatomists had distinguished themselves to quite the same extent as these honorary foreign members. The opening statement made by Professor Charles Sedgwick Minot of Harvard during his Presidential Address at the Association meeting in December 1904 emphasized this point. He said, "The science of anatomy, although one of the oldest of all sciences, was long neglected in America, and taught only in a routine fashion by professors who had little or no thought for the promotion of the science or any aim higher than teaching a certain number of established facts in gross anatomy to the maximum possible number of students." Although Minot did go on to say that during the previous generation a few pioneers in anatomy in America had contributed important discoveries, he failed to mention any, but did praise the German anatomist Wilhelm His, who had died that year, as "the greatest anatomist of his time" (Minot, 1904).

Certainly one American anatomist who, at the birth of the Association, could be compared with the great professors in Great Britain and Europe was JOSEPH LEIDY (Fig. 13.1), who for nearly 40 years held the Professorship of Anatomy at the University of Pennsylvania. Leidy was a natural scientist who could have as readily been appointed a professor of zoology or botany or even of geology, since his knowledge and scientific contributions in each of these disciplines was both broad and profound. Born in Philadelphia in September 1823, about three months before President James Monroe issued his famous Monroe Doctrine, Joseph Leidy was totally a 19th-century "renaissance man." He was as much at ease discussing the extinct mammals of the Dakotas and Nebraska or the freshwater rhizopods of North America as he was in lecturing on the anatomy of the human body which, in fact, he did for decades to medical students in Philadelphia.

Leidy received a medical degree from the University of Pennsylvania in 1844 by presenting a thesis entitled "The Comparative Anatomy of the Eye of Verte-brated Animals." He had shown an extraordinary skill and knowledge in the natural sciences even as a young boy, and by the time he was 10 years old he had composed a book of drawings of shells accompanied by both scientific and common names. It was his stepmother (Leidy's mother died before his first birthday) who urged him to become a physician and an anatomist. After graduating from medical school, Leidy tried to build a private medical practice, but he failed because his interests were in science and not in clinical medicine. He then accepted an appointment as a Demonstrator of Anatomy at the Franklin Medical College in Philadelphia and in 1848 visited Europe in the company of Dr. William Edmonds Horner, who was then Professor of Anatomy at the University of Pennsylvania. Shortly thereafter, he became the prosector to Professor Horner. During Horner's terminal illness, Leidy was made Lecturer in Anatomy (1852–

Fig. 13.1. Joseph Leidy (1823–1891).

1853) and upon Horner's death in 1853 he was appointed to the Chair of Anatomy at the University of Pennsylvania at the age of 30. For the next 38 years in this position and likewise for 45 years as officer of the Philadelphia Academy of Natural Sciences, Leidy's scientific contributions flowed continuously during the second half of the 19th century. According to William Keith Brooks (1907), the Henry Walters Professor of Zoology at the Johns Hopkins University during the first decade of this century, Leidy's "character was simple and earnest and he had such a modest opinion of his own talents and his work that the honors and rewards that began to come to him in his younger days, from learned societies in all parts of the world, and continued to come for the rest of his life, were an unfailing surprise to him." A few years after his appointment at Pennsylvania, Leidy (1861) published a widely used treatise in gross anatomy, which was subsequently redone in a second edition in 1889. Leidy's book appeared only 3 years after Henry Gray published the first edition of his anatomy text in England. Often compared with *Gray's Anatomy,* Leidy's book was characterized as "one of the best works ever offered (up to that time) to the medical profession on the subject."

Leidy served as a surgeon in the Satterlee United States Army General Hospital in Philadelphia during the Civil War. During this service he performed many autopsies that were subsequently reported in the *Medical and Surgical History of the War of the Rebellion*. In addition to his appointment as Professor of Anatomy at the University of Pennsylvania, he was for 15 years (1870–1885) Professor of Natural History at Swarthmore College, Director of the Department of Biology at the University of Pennsylvania, and President of the Academy of Natural Sciences in Philadelphia between 1881 and 1891 (Chapman, 1891; Brooks, 1907; Osborn, 1913).

As was true of many gross anatomists of that time and today, Joseph Leidy's most important scientific contributions were made in other fields. Thus, he was the first to describe the cysts of *Trichina spiralis* in pork and thereby showed for the first time the means by which these parasites gain access to the human body. Further, his contributions to vertebrate paleontology have characterized him as the founder of that discipline in America, and yet other biologists point to his work in the field of protozoology. Among his 600 (or more) published works, there were, however, a number of important contributions to gross anatomy, in addition to his own textbook on the subject. In 1849 he was the editor of the first American edition (from the fifth English edition) of *Quain's Textbook of Human Anatomy*. He published studies on the anatomy of the human larynx, the comparative anatomy of the liver, the evolutionary history of articular cartilages, and the intermaxillary (incisive) bone in the human embryo (Joseph Leidy Commemorative Meeting, 1924).

It was not surprising that upon its establishment the Association of American Anatomists in 1888 elected Professor Leidy as its first President and 50 years later in 1938 struck a handsome medallion with Leidy's likeness on the front, and the words "To celebrate fifty years of achievement, 1888–1938" on the back. Among many honors, Leidy received an honorary LLD from Harvard University and in 1863 was appointed one of the founding members of the National Academy of Sciences (Osborn, 1913). Leidy's death in 1891 came only 3 years after the Association of American Anatomists was established. At about this time or slightly earlier were born four American anatomists who would in the decades ahead contribute significantly to the field of gross anatomy: Edward Allen Boyden, born in 1886; Oscar Vivian Batson and Barry Joseph Anson, both born in 1894; and Jacob Parsons Schaeffer, born earlier in 1878.

EDWARD ALLEN BOYDEN (Fig. 13.2) published important papers in the fields of embryology and gross anatomy for 63 years in the 20th century. His first paper (Boyden and Rand, 1913) described the inequality of the two eyes in regenerating planarians and his final research contribution (Boyden, 1976) dealt with the development of the lung in the pig-tail monkey, *Macaca nemestrina*. In between these two, Dr. Boyden published over 180 other major papers, many of which related to the comparative anatomy and physiology of the gallbladder as well as the anatomy of the sphincter of Oddi, the structure of the lung and variations in the human bronchopulmonary segments, and, in later years, the prenatal development and postnatal maturation of the lungs.

Boyden was born in Bridgewater, Massachusetts, in 1886. His father was the President of Bridgewater State Teachers College as had been his father's father. The young Boyden graduated from this school in 1907 and enrolled at Harvard, from which he received a bachelor's degree in 1909 and master's degree in 1911. The following academic year, 1911–1912, was spent in the laboratory of the world-renowned embryologist Franz Keibel, at the anatomical institute in Freiburg (Breslau). The year abroad focused Boyden's interest toward embryology and anatomy, and away from zoology, and upon returning to Harvard he received the

Fig. 13.2. Edward Allen Boyden (1886–1976).

PhD in Medical Science in 1916. Professor Keibel's influence on Boyden was quite profound and, indeed, throughout Boyden's life his interests and ability to apply embryological observations to an understanding of adult gross anatomy resulted in the publication of developmental papers during every period of his career. Thus, in 1922, he published a thorough paper on the development of the cloaca in birds (Boyden, 1922); in 1932, he wrote on congenital absence of the kidney in the human embryo (Boyden, 1932); in 1954, with L.J. Wells, he described the development of the bronchopulmonary segments in human embryos (Boyden and Wells, 1954); and, in the 1970s, he described the developing bronchial arteries in the fetus (Boyden, 1970), as well as the development of the fetal lung in both man and subhuman primates (Boyden, 1975, 1976).

As distinguished as Boyden's studies in embryology were, however, he will be especially remembered for his research on the gallbladder and the extra-hepatic biliary ducts, as well as his work on the segmental anatomy of the lungs. By the early 1920s it was known that the gallbladder concentrates hepatic bile from seven to ten times; and, although investigators realized that when the gallbladder contracted, the sphincter of Oddi relaxed, what was not known was the nature of the stimulus that initiated gallbladder contraction. Boyden in 1923 showed that the gallbladder in cats could be emptied by a meal consisting of egg yolk and cream and that the most effective component was the egg yolk (Boyden, 1923). Further, in 1926 Boyden showed that the gallbladder in a fasting animal could be induced to contract by injecting intravenously into that animal 10 ml of arterial blood from a cat that was digesting egg yolk (Boyden, 1926). Ivy and Oldberg (1928) discovered that an extract from the duodenal mucosa, recognized as cholecystokinin, when injected intravenously, could lead to evacuation of the gallbladder in dogs. Boyden's early work, thus, was seminal in pointing to the importance of humoral substances in the regulation of the extrahepatic biliary tract (Boyden, 1953).

In the early 1940s, Boyden, then a mid-career scientist, commenced working on the detailed anatomy of the lung. As was described in a tribute to him in *The Anatomical Record* on the occasion of his 68th birthday (Goss, 1954), the commencement of his studies on the lung was stimulated by a request from his colleagues in the Department of Surgery at Minnesota to discuss the anatomy of segmental pneumonectomy at a surgical staff conference. From 1945 until his death 31 years later in 1976, Boyden published (many with colleagues such as J. Francis Hartmann, J. Gordon Scannell, Franklin R. Smith, C.J. Hamre, Ronald M. Ferry, L.J. Wells, R.J. Johnson, and D.H. Tompsett) nearly 50 papers, chapters, and other full-length articles on the anatomy of the lung. A number of these articles dealt with the pulmonary structure in subhuman primates; however, Dr. Boyden's most important contributions in this field analyzed the development and maturation of the bronchovascular and segmental lung patterns, and he and his colleagues (in several publications) described variations of the general segmental patterns in hundreds of adult human lungs.

Upon receiving his PhD in 1916, Boyden was appointed an Instructor of Comparative Anatomy at Harvard. Three years later he was promoted to Assistant Professor. In 1926, he moved to the University of Illinois where he stayed for 3 years, and in 1929 he was appointed Professor and Chairman of the Anatomy Department at the University of Alabama. Two years later he went to Minneapolis, where he was initially appointed Professor of Anatomy in 1931 and Chairman of the department in 1940. He was to remain at Minnesota until 1954 when he "retired." At age 68 he moved to Seattle, where he served as a Visiting Professor of Anatomy in the Department of Biological Structure at the University of Washington Medical School for 2 years, after which (in 1956) he was appointed Research Professor, a position he was to hold for an additional 20 years! During this latter period he annually taught gross anatomy to the medical class at the University of Washington and he continued his research program. Among the many honors that Dr. Boyden received was his recognition as an Honorary Fellow in 1961 by the American College of Chest Physicians, and in 1974 he was made Honorary Fellow of the International College of Surgeons. In addition, he received in 1970 the first Henry Gray Award of the American Association of Anatomists, and he was President of the Association in 1956–1957. At the age of 90, Dr. Boyden died while actively at work in the laboratory (Smith, 1977).

OSCAR VIVIAN BATSON (Fig. 13.3) was born in Sedalia, Missouri, on November 10, 1894. This small city of about 20,000 people is located on the central plains, about 150 miles due west of St. Louis and about 75 miles east and slightly south of Kansas City. Batson was the valedictorian of his high school class and throughout his life demonstrated a keen and quick wit and was a fount of information in clinical anatomy. He was highly intellectual, extremely eloquent, and

Fig. 13.3.   Oscar Vivian Batson (1894–1979).

possessed an organized mind, making him an outstanding teacher and lecturer throughout his life. He attended the University of Missouri where he received his bachelor's degree in 1916. He remained at Missouri as a medical student in the 2-year program, and completed his preclinical basic science courses in 1918, at which time he was granted a master's degree in Anatomy. Continuing his medical education, Batson was admitted as a third-year student at St. Louis University School of Medicine. Upon completion of his clinical clerkships, he graduated with the MD degree in 1920. It was at Missouri, however, that Batson came under the influence of Dr. Eliot Round Clark, who was the head of the gross anatomy course, and it was there he decided that if it were possible he would combine a career in clinical medicine and in anatomy.

Upon graduation Dr. Batson went as an Instructor to the Anatomy Department at Wisconsin for a year and then he accepted an appointment at the University of Cincinnati in 1921. He was to stay at this school for 7 years, but during that time he was promoted to full professor when he was only 32 years of age. Meanwhile, E.R. Clark had been appointed Chairman of the Anatomy Department at the University of Pennsylvania, and a professorial position in Anatomy became available in the Graduate School of Medicine at that school (Deuschle, 1980). Probably no better qualified person in the United States than Dr. Batson could have been selected for the instruction of anatomy to physicians during their residency period. As was stated by John W. Everett (1975) during the presentation of the Henry Gray Award to Dr. Batson at the annual meeting of the AAA in 1975 in Los Angeles, "To his students and associates he came to be known for his vast knowledge of comparative and human anatomy with the addition of a down-to-earth clinical experience, a pungent wit, a flair for the dramatic and an unequaled clarity of exposition." He was to remain at Pennsylvania for 38 years until his retirement in 1965.

It is not possible because of space limitations to describe in detail all of the contributions that Dr. Batson made to gross anatomy and to anatomical investigative methodology. The opening sentence of his Caldwell Lecture, delivered before the American Roentgen Ray Society in Los Angeles in 1962, expressed his research orientation: "Living anatomy is slowly editing and replacing the anatomy of the dead room." Indeed, in much of his research he utilized radiological methods on living animals to understand questions he had formulated about human gross anatomical structures. He also published papers in which he utilized methods to restore mummified organs, other techniques to study capillaries, bone, and connective tissue, and injection methods to study blood flow in the vessels of the heart. Dr. Batson introduced to American anatomists the use of latex emulsions to demonstrate the extent of fields of vascular distribution or drainage of vessels. This often was combined with methods to create corrosion specimens. Among the subjects about which Dr. Batson wrote illuminating articles were the flow of blood in the cardiac veins; the anatomy of the maxillary sinus; the temporomandibular joint; the veins draining the mucosa of the nasal cavity; the lymphatic drainage of the head and neck; the cricopharyngeus muscle; the temporalis muscle; the anatomy for incisions used in gallbladder surgical procedures; and anomalies of importance to the otolaryngologist. The field of otolaryngology was of special interest to Batson because he had completed postgraduate training in that field, and he became a certified otolaryngologist in 1933. As interesting and important as these subjects were, however, his work on the vertebral system of veins became his most important contribution to medical science and the one for which anatomists and clinicians alike throughout the world recall his name. His interest in this latter field actually developed when he was formulating his educational program of courses in surgical anatomy for his students in the various surgical specialties. As early as 1926, while Dr. Batson was still in Cincinnati, he had an interest in the diploic veins of the skull. As described in his Caldwell Lecture (Batson, 1957), he asked Professor Artur Schüller, a neurologist from Vienna who had done elegant neuroradiological studies and who at the time was a Visiting Professor in Cincinnati, if he could give him literature leads on the diploic veins. Professor Schüller reportedly said, "Read Breschet, nothing significant has been done since." According to Batson, had he asked Schüller "about the spinal veins the answer would have been the same" and yet Breschet's monograph had been written in 1819, more than a century before Batson's inquiry.

The brilliance of Baston's studies was not only related to his anatomical observations but also to his interpretation of the importance of this venous system physiologically and especially pathologically in the spread of disease. Although it was true that Breschet had beautifully and accurately described the anatomy and continuity of the veins in the spinal column with those of the skull, these vessels had been known to exist since the great works of Andreas Vesalius in the 16th century and Thomas Willis in the 17th century. Batson, by the use of both corrosion specimens of the human vertebral column and skull and x-ray observations of the spread of injected opaque substances in live animals and cadavers, demonstrated how remarkably extensive the vertebral plexiform network of veins was and the fact that it bypassed the caval, pulmonary, portal, and lumbo-azygos systems of veins that drained the thoracic and abdominal cavities. The vertebral-diploic veins constituted a venous system "outside" of these cavities, and venous blood could be shunted through them before returning to the heart and lungs. For decades it was not understood how metastatic spread of tumor cells from pelvic organs would at times allow tumors to appear in the brain before the lungs. Venous drainage of pelvic organs was thought to be only by way of the caval and lumbo-azygos systems. Batson, however, observed that upon compression of the thoracic and abdominal cavities, such as might occur during coughing, lifting with the upper extremities, or defecation, pelvic blood (and even blood from the breast and other organs in the thorax) could drain into the vertebral plexus of veins. Since these veins had no valves and communicated freely with those in the cranial vault, spread of tumor cells into the central nervous system through this route finally explained metastatic paradoxes that had puzzled pathologists and many other physicians including the great William Osler. Professor Osler (1903) published a detailed report of a case of complete thrombosis of the superior vena cava, and he sketched a diagram showing the supposed routes for the collateral circulation of blood from the head and upper extremities into the inferior vena cava. The vertebral system of veins was not included. It is interesting that Dr. Batson's first manuscript on this subject was rejected by the editor of a national medical journal; however, it was soon published in the *Annals of Surgery* (Batson, 1940).

Dr. Batson received many awards, citations, and medals for his research on the vertebral veins. These included the Gold Medal from the American Medical Association in 1953 and the Henry Gray Award of the American Association of Anatomists in 1975. He was made an Honorary Fellow of the International College of Surgeons, and the university from which he received his medical degree (St.

Fig. 13.4.   Barry Joseph Anson (1894–1974).

Louis University) awarded him an honorary LLD in 1964. Dr. Batson continued to live in Philadelphia following his retirement in 1965. On November 11, 1979, one day after his 85th birthday, Dr. Batson died following a short cardiovascular illness.

BARRY JOSEPH ANSON (Fig. 13.4) was born in Muscatine, Iowa, on March 21, 1894. At the age of 17 he matriculated at the University of Wisconsin in Madison; he was a biology major and graduated in 1917. Dr. Anson served as a sergeant in the 213th U.S. Army Engineer Corps during World War I. His interests in biology were stimulated by spending his summers during college working as a scientific aide in the laboratories of the U.S. Bureau of Fisheries at Fairport, Iowa. Following graduation from college he received a full-time appointment as a Scientific Assistant, a position he maintained in the Bureau for 5 years. It was during this period that he met Dr. Leslie B. Arey, and a lifelong friendship developed (Arey, 1975). Professor Arey was to be instrumental in Anson receiving a National Research Council Fellowship in Medicine, which allowed him to pursue graduate studies at Harvard Medical School. Anson received the M.A. in 1923 and the Ph.D. in Anatomy in 1926 at Harvard, under the direction of Professor Frederick T. Lewis. His first appointment was Instructor in Anatomy at Northwestern University Medical School where Dr. Arey was now departmental chairman. Dr. Anson spent the next 36 years at Northwestern and was promoted through the ranks to Professor of Anatomy in 1942; in 1956 he became the Robert Loughlin Rea Professor and Chairman of Anatomy, a post he held until his retirement from

Northwestern at the age of 68 in 1962. The last 12 years (1962–1974) of his life were spent as a Research Professor in the Department of Otology and Maxillofacial Surgery at The University of Iowa.

Dr. Anson's earliest publications were in the field of parasitology while he was still a Scientific Assistant at the U.S. Fisheries Biological Station in Fairport. These studies involved observations on the larval and parasitic (glochidium) stage of freshwater mussels in the *Unionidae* family (Howard and Anson, 1922). As a result of his research as a graduate student in the Anatomy Department at Harvard, Dr. Anson next published a series of papers on the comparative anatomy of the villous-like outgrowths found on the inner surfaces of lips in many vertebrate species as well as in the human newborn. His definitive paper on this subject (Anson, 1929) describes the characteristics of lips and homologous structures from the cyclostomes to man. His examination of 825 specimens along with over 300 other specimens in sagittal sections in this study was indicative of the thoroughness that could be expected in future research from this young anatomist who was now in the Anatomy Department at Northwestern University Medical School.

During his career Dr. Anson published over 300 papers. By far the greatest number were in the field of gross anatomy, and although many of his articles related to the structures of the ear and its development and the anatomy of the temporal bone, in fact, he wrote on at least 50 other anatomical subjects! Usually in collaboration with students, articles appeared on such subjects as the surgical anatomy of the inguinal and hypogastric regions as well as inguinal and obturator herniae. Other subjects included the pelvic and urogenital diaphragms, female pelvis, uterine tube and round ligament of the uterus, blood supply to the ureter, and renal abnormalities such as pelvic kidney, horseshoe kidney, and retrocaval ureter. He also published articles on the fascial planes in the femoral, perineal, and abdominal regions and on the rectus adbominis muscle, rectus sheath, and epigastric vessels. He discussed abnormal viscera *in situ*, the anatomy of the hepatic hilum, the gallbladder, and bile ducts. He wrote articles on the branches of the aortic arch, the visceral branches of the aorta, subclavian artery and its vertebral branch, as well as the blood supply to the breast. Other vessels on which articles appeared were the inferior phrenic, bronchial, and esophageal arteries, renal arteries, vasculature of the small intestine, lumbar arteries, internal iliac (hypogastric), obturator artery, brachial and antebrachial arteries, and vasculature of the hand. Articles on at least 12 different muscles and the courses of eight different nerves were also published by Dr. Anson.

Dr. Anson was also the author of *An Atlas of Human Anatomy,* into which went much of the material he gathered in the gross anatomy laboratory with his students. In addition he was a coauthor of several other books, including the treatise, *Callander's Surgical Anatomy* (with W.G. Maddock), and monographs on *The Temporal Bone and Ear* (with J.H. Bast); *The Surgical Anatomy of the Temporal Bone and Ear;* and *The Anatomy and Surgery of Hernia* (with L.M. Zimmermann). He also was the editor of the 12th edition of *Morris' Human Anatomy.*

Another of Dr. Anson's interests was the history of medicine, and at Northwestern he lectured on this subject also to the medical students. His favorite historic figures included the great Flemish anatomist of the Renaissance, Andreas Vesalius, who worked at Padua in the 16th century; Thomas Willis, the English physician; and especially Ambroise Paré, the French surgeon. His subject for the

XXV Wherry Memorial Lecture before the American Academy of Ophthalmologists and Otolaryngologists was "The Ear and Eye in the Collected Works of Ambroise Paré, Renaissance Surgeon to Four Kings of France." Dr. Anson also wrote on the general subject of medieval medicine and on the great plague in London. There is little question, however, that his most important studies were in the field of developmental and adult anatomy of the ear. He was introduced to studies in otology by Dr. J. Gordon Wilson, a Professor of Otolaryngology at Northwestern, shortly after Dr. Anson was appointed in the late 1920s, and some of his earliest papers were published with Professor Wilson. These included brief descriptions of the utricular fold, the utriculo-endolymphatic valve, and the fossula ante fenestrum. Many of Anson's subsequent otological studies were reported in clinical journals of otology and otolaryngology, and many of his other gross anatomical studies appeared in the more general surgical journals such as *Surgery, Gynecology and Obstetrics.*

A larger number of his articles on the history of medicine, as well as certain surgically interesting papers in gross anatomy (generally written with students), appeared in the *Quarterly Bulletin of the Northwestern University Medical School,* a publication of which Dr. Anson was editor for about 20 years.

Anson's work at The University of Iowa following his retirement from Northwestern was done as a Visiting Professor in the Department of Otolaryngology and Maxillofacial Surgery. During these last 12 years of his life (1962–1974), he published many papers with residents and younger faculty colleagues on such subjects as the surgical anatomy of the facial nerve, the vascular channels in the auditory ossicles, the vestibular and cochlear aqueducts, the surgical anatomy of the endolymphatic sac and perilymphatic duct, and the anatomical consideration in the management of Menière's disease. In a tribute published in 1975 in the *Annals of Otology, Rhinology and Laryngology,* Dr. Brian F. McCabe wrote:

> Barry Anson was in many respects a renaissance man. Besides being a renowned anatomist, he was a prodigious talent in the English language, an authority on the history of medicine, a chronicler of St. George and Ambroise Paré, and a world traveler. He also collected unicorns and oriental art.
>
> It was a rare privilege to know Barry Anson. He was not only a kind, gentle and scholarly man but an indefatigable worker. At the age of 80 he was actively working on revisions of two of his surgical anatomy monographs and had commenced a new project on the vascularization of ossicular homografts. A basic scientist, he realized sooner than most that medical research is enriched by clinical relevance. A symbiotic relationship has developed between basic scientists and otolaryngologists the country wide. Barry fostered this and was a marvelous example of it. This is probably his greatest legacy.

In addition to the endowed chair that Northwestern University awarded him in 1956, Dr. Anson was recognized by several other distinctions. He served as President of the American Association of Anatomists (1957–1958) and he was elected an honorary member of the Los Angeles Society for the History of Medical Sciences, the Association of Medical Illustrators, and the American Academy of Ophthalmology and Otolaryngology. He was an honorary medalist of the American Otological Society. Combining a career of teaching gross anatomy to medical students and reporting anatomical information of surgical relevance, Dr. Anson probably had no superior in the history of our Association.

JACOB PARSONS SCHAEFFER (Fig. 13.5), born and raised on a small farm near Shamokin Dam, Pennsylvania, on August 20, 1878, rarely used his first name publicly, preferring instead to use the initial J. His parents, George Keyser Schaeffer and Elizabeth Long Schaeffer, encouraged him to learn a profession, and young J. Parsons developed an abiding interest in the human body by working as a youngster with his uncle, who was an undertaker. By the time he was 22 in 1900, he had graduated from the United States School of Embalming in New York. Prior to attending embalming school, Dr. Schaeffer helped his family financially by passing a teaching examination for primary school and then even teaching in a one-room schoolhouse for a period of time before his 21st birthday. His dedication to teaching persisted, however, and in 1901 he received a Bachelor of Education degree from the Key State Normal School (later renamed Kutztown State College), and in 1903 he received a master's degree. That same year he married Mary Mabel Bobb, whose father was a doctor. His father-in-law encouraged Schaeffer to go to medical school and, in fact, even helped support his medical education (Gibbon, 1971). In 1907, Dr. Schaeffer graduated from the University of Pennsylvania School of Medicine, and following an internship year he pursued graduate studies in anatomy at Cornell where he received the Master of Arts degree in 1909 and the PhD in 1910.

It was while he was at Cornell that he began his research on the nose and paranasal sinuses. Dr. Schaeffer stated in the preface of his famous monograph, *The Embryology, Development, and Anatomy of the Nose, Paranasal Sinuses, Nasolacrimal Passageways, and Olfactory Organ in Man* (1920), that his research in this field was performed "at intervals at Cornell University (1907–11), at Yale University (1911–14), and at the Jefferson Medical College since 1914." Indeed,

Fig. 13.5. Jacob Parsons Schaeffer (1878–1970).

Dr. Schaeffer was appointed Assistant Professor of Anatomy at Cornell in 1910. He became Assistant Professor of Anatomy at Yale in 1911, and only one year later in 1912 he was made Professor of Anatomy at Yale. In 1914 he left New Haven to return to Philadelphia as Professor of Anatomy and Director of The Daniel Baugh Institute of Anatomy at the Jefferson Medical College.

At Cornell University Dr. Schaeffer was trained by Professors Simon H. Gage, A.T. Kerr, and B.F. Kingsbury. It was early in 1914 that the Chairman of Pathology at Jefferson (W.M.L. Coplin, after whom the Coplin staining jar was named), charged with the task of finding a successor to the famous Professor of Anatomy, Edward Anthony Spitzka, visited with Schaeffer at Yale and prevailed upon him to accept the position vacated by the sudden death of Spitzka. From 1914 until his retirement 34 years later in 1948 he remained at Jefferson, and upon retirement he was appointed Emeritus Professor of Anatomy (Ramsey, 1970).

Nearly all of Dr. Schaeffer's publications dealt with the upper respiratory system and especially with the walls of the nasal cavity and with the paranasal sinuses. His monograph, published in 1920, was probably the finest treatise on the development, maturation, and adult anatomy of these structures that had ever been written to that time, and it is questionable whether anyone in the 66 years since has made as significant a contribution on this subject. It is of interest that he dedicated this most important work to his wife's father, who had largely been responsible for Dr. Schaeffer becoming a physician. Schaeffer was a contributing editor and author of the chapter "The Respiratory System" in the 6th to the 12th editions of the large systemic treatise on gross anatomy, *Morris' Human Anatomy*. Further, he was Editor-in-Chief of the 10th (1942) and 11th (1953) editions of this book and served as an Advisory Editor for the 12th edition, for which Dr. Barry J. Anson was the principal editor. Among the contributors to the 11th edition were many outstanding 20th-century anatomists, including Leslie B. Arey (Northwestern University), Raymond F. Blount (University of Texas), Eliot Round Clark (University of Pennsylvania), Harold Cummins (Tulane University), John C.B. Grant and C.G. Smith (University of Toronto), Frederick Gudernatsch (Cornell University), Ernest Lachman (University of Oklahoma), Olof Larsell and Richard E. Scammon (University of Minnesota), Joseph E. Markee (Duke University), Bradley M. Patten (University of Michigan), and Robert J. Terry and Mildred Trotter (Washington University at St. Louis). In addition to the many other contributions to the literature, such as his studies on variations of the optic chiasma in relation to problems dealing with the pituitary gland and altered visual fields, Dr. Schaeffer coauthored (with Henry K. Pancost and Eugene P. Pendergrass) an excellent radiological textbook that went through several editions, *The Head and Neck in Roentgen Diagnosis* (Pancost et al., 1940).

Recognition for his research and other scholarly achievements came to Dr. Schaeffer from many sources. In 1931 he received the Gold Medal of the American Medical Association for his basic studies on the paranasal sinuses and lacrimal duct, in 1944 the Philadelphia County Medical Society presented him with the Strittmatter Award for his contributions to medicine, and four academic institutions recognized his work: Saint Joseph's College awarded him the Clarence E. Shaffrey medal, Yale University conferred on him an honorary MA, Susquehanna University awarded him an honorary ScD, and the Jefferson Medical College gave him an honorary LittD. In 1946 Dr. Schaeffer was elected to serve as President of the College of Physicians in Philadelphia for a term of 3 years. He was a member of the AAA for 61 years (from 1909 until his death in 1970), he served on the Executive Committee from 1924 to 1929, was Vice President in 1942–1943, and he was Acting President for 3 years (from 1943 to 1946) during World War II. Because of his distinguished academic accomplishments and his creative scholarship, Dr. Schaeffer was elected to membership in the American Philosophical Society, one of the most prestigious scholarly societies in the United States.

It is well known that the medical students at the Jefferson Medical College had a deep respect and admiration for Dr. Schaeffer. In fact, when Dr. Schaeffer would enter the lecture amphitheater he was always greeted by affectionate applause. According to Gibbon (1971), "he (Schaeffer) was never sarcastic to his students, according them the dignified treatment which he commanded himself. There was an Old World courtliness about him which made improper language or coarse jokes quite impossible in his presence. Anatomy was a serious subject to him and no student of his could treat it lightly. With all these qualities he was one of the most beloved professors that I have ever encountered. There were many fine teachers among his colleagues, but few were his equal." In 1948, 24 years after assuming the headship of the Anatomy Department at The Jefferson Medical College, Dr. Schaeffer retired at the age of 70. He was, however, to enjoy a long retirement of more than 22 years. His death on February 9, 1970, at the age of 91 ended the career of a distinguished educator who, especially in his early years, contributed truly significant research.

REFERENCES

Anson, B.J. 1929 The comparative anatomy of the lips and labial villi of vertebrates. J. Morphol. Physiol., 47:335–414.

Arey, L.B. 1975 Barry Joseph Anson, 1894–1974. Anat. Rec., 183:128–130.

Batson, O.V. 1940 The function of the vertebral veins and their role in the spread of metastases. Ann. Surg., 112:138–149.

Batson, O.V. 1957 The vertebral vein system. Caldwell Lecture, 1956. Am. J. Roentgenol. Rad. Therapy 78:195–212.

Boyden, E.A. 1922 The development of the cloaca in birds, with special reference to the origin of the bursa of Fabricius, the formation of the urodaeal sinus, and the regular occurrence of a cloacal fenestra. Am. J. Anat., 30:163–202.

Boyden, E.A. 1923 The gallbladder in the cat—its development, its functional periodicity, and its anatomical variation as recorded in 2500 specimens. Anat. Rec., 24:388 (abstr.).

Boyden, E.A. 1926 A study of the behavior of the human gall-bladder in response to the ingestion of food; together with some observations on the mechanism of the expulsion of bile in experimental animals. Anat. Rec., 33:201–256.

Boyden, E.A. 1932 Congenital absence of the kidney. An interpretation based on a 10 mm human embryo exhibiting unilateral renal agenesis. Anat. Rec., 52:325–350.

Boyden, E.A. 1953 Humoral vs. neural regulation of the extra-hepatic biliary tract. Minn. Med., 36:720–723.

Boyden, E.A. 1970 The developing bronchial arteries in a fetus of the twelfth week. Am. J. Anat., 129:357–368.

Boyden, E.A. 1975 Development of the human lung. In: Practice of Pediatrics. V.C. Kelley, ed. Harper & Row, Hagerstown, Vol. IV, pp. 1–17.

Boyden, E.A. 1976 The development of the lung in the pig-tail monkey (Macaca nemestrina, L.). Anat. Rec., 186:15–38.

Boyden, E.A., and H.W. Rand 1913 Inequality of the two eyes in regenerating planarians. Zool. Jahrb. Abt. Zool. Physiol., 34:69–80.

Boyden, E.A., and L.J. Wells 1954 The development of the bronchopulmonary segments in human embryos of Horizons XVII to XIX. Am. J. Anat., 95:163–203.

Breschet, G. 1819 Essai sur les Veines du Rachis. Méquignon-Marvis, Paris.

Brooks, W.K. 1907 Joseph Leidy. Anat. Rec., 5:109–111.

Chapman, H.C. 1891 Memoir of Joesph Leidy, M.D., L.L.D. (with bibliography). Proc. Acad. Natur. Sci., Philadelphia, 42:342–388.

Deuschle, F.M. 1980 Oscar Vivian Batson, 1894–1979. Anat. Rec., 198:297–299.

Everett, J.W. 1975 Proceedings, American Association of Anatomists. Anat. Rec., 183:111–113.

Gibbon, Jr., J.H. 1971 Memoir of J. Parsons Schaeffer. Trans. Coll. Physicians, Philadelphia, 38 (4th Series):249–251.

Goss, C.M., ed. 1954. Edward Allan (sic) Boyden. Anat. Rec., 118:1–18.

Howard, A.D., and B.J. Anson 1922 Phases in the parasitism of the Unionidae. J. Parasitol., 9:68–82.

Ivy, A.C., and E. Oldberg 1928 Hormone mechanism for gall bladder contraction and evacuation. Am. J. Physiol., 86:599–613.

Leidy, J. 1861 An Elementary Treatise on Human Anatomy. J.B. Lippincott Co., Philadelphia.

Leidy Commemorative Meeting 1924 Proc. Acad. Natur. Sci., Philadelphia, 76:1–87.

McCabe, B.F. 1975 Barry J. Anson, 1894–1974. Ann. Otol. Rhinol. Laryngol., 84:131.

Minot, C.S. 1904 Genetic interpretations in the domain of anatomy. Presidential address before the Association of American Anatomists. Am. J. Anat., 4:245–263.

Osborn, H.F. 1913 Biographical Memoir of Joseph Leidy, 1823–1891. Biog. Mem. Nat. Acad. Sci., 7:335–396.

Osler, W. 1903 On obliteration of the superior vena cava. Bull. Johns Hopkins Hosp., 14:169–175.

Pancost, H.K., E.P. Pendergrass, and J.P. Schaeffer 1940 The Head and Neck in Roentgen Diagnosis. Charles C Thomas, Springfield.

Ramsey, A.J. 1970 J. Parsons Schaeffer, 1878–1970. Anat. Rec., 168:246–248.

Schaeffer, J.P. 1920 The Embryology, Development, and Anatomy of the Nose, Paranasal Sinuses, Nasolacrimal Passageways, and Olfactory Organ in Man. P. Blakiston's Son and Co., Philadelphia.

Smith, F.R. 1977 Edward Allan (sic) Boyden, 1886–1976. Anat. Rec., 189:300–302.

Chapter 14

THE RESEARCH CORRELATES OF HUMAN GROSS ANATOMY TEACHING. ORGANISMAL MORPHOLOGY: FUNCTIONAL ANATOMY, PRIMATE EVOLUTION, AND HUMAN VARIATION

Charles E. Oxnard

A history of research cognate with the teaching area of human gross anatomy requires a preamble. This is because, although the teaching of microscopic, cellular, ultrastructural, and neurobiological areas of anatomy has direct associations with equivalent modern research lines, that is not, today, the case for human gross anatomy. Human gross anatomy is, nowadays, chiefly a systematic body of knowledge important for the education of medical and other health professionals. There are probably no more major discoveries to be made in human gross anatomical research. This was not the case in much earlier times when teachers of gross anatomy were often truly carrying out new investigations into the gross anatomy of humans and related species using dissection and observation. As, however, the seam of information came to be worked out well, then teachers of human gross anatomy either relinquished claims to carrying out research at all or (most of them) moved into areas of microscopic, ultrastructural, molecular, and neurological anatomy where new problems were being generated by the advances described in most of the other chapters in this book. This led to a long decline in research cognate with the human gross anatomical teaching area.

The era of decline in research was also partly related to a teaching decline as programs of human gross anatomy teaching were reduced. Some of those reductions were necessary—human gross anatomy for too long occupied too great a proportion of the modern medical curriculum. But this decline eventually went too far, as is now known, and it was naturally associated with severe reductions in faculty. This was, equally naturally, paralleled by an almost complete void in the production of new teachers of gross anatomy. The true causal relationships in these changes are not entirely clear. The research decline probably occurred in advance of the teaching decline. Indeed, the research decline may have been a major factor initially responsible for the teaching decline, rather than the reverse, even though the eventual teaching decline had its own, secondary effect upon research. Thus, the initial problem was the reduced intellectual content of what was being carried out as research in the area cognate, at that time, with human gross anatomical teaching. For though knowledge of, say, the many variations of the maxillary artery in humans has applied implications for maxillofacial surgery, it can scarcely take a place alongside the major new ideas of the biological sciences today.

Gross anatomical research was mainly observationally oriented and used the simplest and most self-sufficient techniques: dissection of soft tissues, observation of bones, and verbal and pictorial comparisons of the anatomies so revealed. The results were a most important backbone for knowledge in anatomy during the early years of this century, certainly the whole of the past century. Indeed, such knowledge was the mainstay of the entire field of the life sciences during earlier millennia. But more recently, research in human gross anatomy was not much more than the placement of the final stitches in the tapestry woven so magnificently in skeletal form by the ancients, fleshed out by Vesalius and others during the Renaissance and later, and essentially fully clothed in the 18th, 19th, and early 20th centuries by a large number of acute anatomical observers.

This is not the total story, of course. Studies of human gross anatomy were still capable of advancing even in the middle of this century. Thus, the gross anatomical structure of the bronchial tree was not realized until a few decades ago. Gross anatomical observations of major import were still being made upon relatively rare animals (e.g., tree shrews, tarsiers, aye-ayes). And to some degree, this process continues; important new advances in medical imaging, for instance, have led to a resurgence of research correlations with an older cross-sectional anatomy that had all but disappeared. Of course, classical information and interpretation of the skeleton will always be important for paleontology, as new fossils are found that must be compared with old fossils and with well-known extant species. We may note, in parentheses, that should a living yeti, or big-foot, or other such abominable creature ever actually be discovered, we may find that the investigators knowing enough about human soft tissue anatomy to dissect the creature may have beaten it into extinction.

For the aforementioned and other reasons, therefore, most investigators who remained interested in whole organism structure have concentrated their efforts upon different facets of the subject. They can be subsumed under the general rubric of whole organism morphology. They encompass a range of topics including functional vertebrate anatomy and evolution, primate and human evolutionary morphology, and human population variation. They are expressed by the only living honorary member of our society who has written in this field, J.Z. Young. Although in his own research a neurobiologist, Young has produced three seminal texts: *The Life of Vertebrates, The Life of Mammals,* and *An Introduction to the Study of Man.*

As the numbers of gross anatomists declined, although a few older investigators remained in anatomy, many took their training and research expertise to join colleagues in the above subjects in other departments (e.g., physical anthropology, biology, paleontology, zoology). Many new investigators in these research areas were completely trained in these other departments, some of them by the transplanted anatomists. It is only today, partly as a result of pressures forcing individuals out of college science departments (especially whole organism biology) and partly as a result of a vacuum sucking individuals back into anatomy departments because of the renewal in human gross anatomy teaching, that these disciplines are once more growing in anatomy. A small but increasing cadre of teachers in human gross anatomy have found for themselves a new intellectual excitement in research into the structure of whole organisms.

WHOLE ORGANISM MORPHOLOGY—THE EARLY YEARS

Although research on humans and their relationships within the biological world is indeed ancient, the work of Darwin and Wallace and others introduced the beginnings of the modern concepts of evolution and especially of human evolution. The rediscovery of the work of Mendel and the establishment of the foundations of genetics by Morgan set up the conditions necessary for understanding evolutionary mechanisms, and they were applied to vertebrate and human evolution specifically. This was further elucidated by Huxley's synthetic theory of human evolution, which took the principles of Darwinism and considered them in the light of Morgan's new genetic concepts. The chief proponents here, many Americans, although few anatomists, included Wright, Dobzhansky, Romer, Simpson, and Mayr. Such studies continue with the developments in evolutionary theory made by J. Cracraft, S.J. Gould, N. Eldredge, T.H. Frazetta, T.J.M. Schopf, and many others.

At the same time, studies in organismal anatomies broadly defined, as well as human structure specifically, were being pursued. For many years, these studies were based upon the premise that morphology provided, directly, information about evolution. But a number of earlier anatomists were always aware that anatomical structure was primarily a pointer to function. The earliest functional anatomists stemmed then from a long line of anatomists of an older school: in the last century, Huxley, Owen, and others, and in this century, Wood Jones, Elliot Smith, Le Gros Clark, A.J.E. Cave, and others. Many distinguished American anatomists participated, e.g., S.G. Morton, Jeffries Wyman, L.A. Adams, A. Hrdlička, A.B. Howell, R.A. Miller, E.A. Hooton, William L. Straus, Jr., and many others in later times. They all depended upon acute powers of observation and thinking: functional inference from anatomical structure. However, such contributions have gradually slowed as investigations have reached toward the limits of the method. It should, nevertheless, be pointed out that there are certain untilled regions of that field (for example, the comparative anatomy of joints and fasciae with especially interesting biomechanical implications) that are so difficult that they have been but little studied.

The more specific study of human and primate evolution developed vigorously both inside and outside of anatomy and anatomy departments. Especially notable earlier contributions were those of E.A. Hooton, W.K. Gregory, R.M. Yerkes, C.R. Carpenter, W.L. Straus, Jr., S.L. Washburn, A.H. Schultz, and W. Montagna, together with a host of investigators from Europe and elsewhere. Their findings, too, led from evolutionary considerations derivable solely from structure to assessments related to the inclusion of behavior, both as one of the functional correlates of structure and in its own right. In this regard the name of S.L. Washburn is particularly important. He made many of the earlier observations and was responsible for the training of many of the new investigators.

From these auspicious beginnings, but following a considerable dry period, stemmed a whole series of developments. So complex did they become that rapid disciplinary splitting occurred, and they are now carried out by many different groups of investigators in many different departments. In anatomy departments these developments first have mainly been aligned along functional and evolutionary morphology, not only of humans and related forms, but of the entire span of the vertebrates (indeed, the principles extend to the structures of all whole organisms). A second alignment speaks to quantitative ways of describing and comparing anatomical structures. A third relates to developments more specifically in human and primate evolution, and a fourth encompasses a more rigorous view of variation in humans alone.

FUNCTIONAL MORPHOLOGY

The new functional morphology depended upon new understandings of extrinsic determinants of biological design related to environmental correlates and mechanical principles, and internal determinants of design related to phylogenetic and developmental constraints. Much of this was glimpsed by the earlier workers, but it has required developments of recent years, particularly 1) such structural investigations as the engineering properties of biological materials (especially bone), mechanical activities of muscles (especially as derivable from electromyography), and engineering aspects of joint structure and function, indeed, the entire bone/joint/muscle complex; and 2) such functional investigations as the biomechanics of gaits, of walking, running, leaping, swimming, and flying, and analyses of the physiological, ecological, and environmental milieu within which they occur. The modern end of this story is told in the recent book *Functional Vertebrate Morphology* by Hildebrand et al. (1985). Examples of the earlier functional dissectional studies include those of R.A. Miller, B. Campbell, and D.D. Davis.

In the anatomy of bone and bones, some of the first of the new studies included the work of F.G. Evans (both through his own earlier investigations and his book *Stress and Strain in Bones*, 1957). Although principally of applied import, his book not only documented the history of the earlier work (which reaches back to Galileo and before) but also introduced findings (including those of his colleagues, such as E.S. Gurdjian and H.R. Lissner) involving new engineering ideas and methods. It followed P.D.F. Murray's seminal *Bones: A Study in the Development and Structure of the Vertebrate Skeleton* (1934), and has been itself followed by more recent studies such as R. McN. Alexander's *Animal Mechanics* (1967, new edition, 1984), *Mechanical Design in Organisms* by S.A. Wainright et al. (1975), and, most recently of all, J.D. Curry's *The Mechanical Adapations of Bones* (1984). Other important contributors in this area included C.A.L. Bassett, D.H. Enlow, M.L. Moss, and B.C. Sarnat.

Similar developments have taken place in the area of muscle structure and function at the organ and organismal level. These are well described by J.V. Basmajian [through his earlier researches, and his later books, *Muscles Alive*, 1967, and *Muscles and Movements* (with M.A. MacConaill), 1969]. J.E. Pauly and L.E. Scheving also contributed at this stage. Earlier investigators included P.J. Rasch and R.K. Burke; and an especially seminal collaboration was that of V.T. Inman et al. (1944) on the shoulder. Indeed, their paper was one of the very first involving electromyography to include the evolutionary perspective. In its turn, however, it was based upon the evolutionary studies of R.A. Miller (1932) on the shoulder. Since then, although most electromyography has been clinical, Basmajian himself has used it for functional and evolutionary morphology, through studies of non-human primates with R.L. Tuttle. At about the same time, major new contributions have been introduced by a new generation of workers who have taken this technique, further refined it, associated it with a number of other approaches, not only simultaneous cinematography and videotaping, but also cineradiography, force plate and strain gauge analyses, surgical interference, kinematics and kinetics, computer graphics, and so on, in a variety of animal groups (e.g., non-human primates: J.T. Stern, Jr., J.G. Fleagle, W.L. Jungers, R. Sussman, F. Anapol, and J.W. Wells; mammals: F.R. Jenkins, Jr., S.W. Herring, and L.E. Lanyon; lower tetrapods: C. Gans, D.B. Wake, and D.M. Bramble; and fish: K. Liem, G.V. Lauder, and many, many others).

In the area of joint biomechanics and movement, again a single book provides both the earlier history and the modern developments. *Synovial Joints: Their Structure and Mechanics* by C.H. Barnett et al. (1961) gives the early history. Later studies have used these ideas in the functional anatomy of primates, e.g., E.C.B. Hall-Craggs, O. Lovejoy, and colleagues. Many of the advances here have related to the skull and its dynamics, especially the temporomandibular joint and the jaws and teeth, and the problems posed in food gathering, mastication, transport, and swallowing. H. Barghusen, A.W. Crompton, E.L. DuBrul, K.W. Hiiemae, S. Herring, A. English, W.S. Greaves, W.L. Hylander, C.L.B. Lavelle, R.P. Scapino, and many others have been major contributors. The recent book *The Mammalian Skull* (1981) by W.J. Moore provides an excellent synopsis of all aspects of this topic. It particularly emphasizes the modern synthesis, in skull and jaw studies, of combining evolutionary, developmental, functional, and growth approaches.

In all of these areas, the principal advances recognized the much greater complexity that exists than was ever before realized. The earlier biomechanics were based upon simpler theoretical engineering ideas. They needed to be replaced by concepts from new advances in engineering itself. Much of the earlier work, often dating from the past century and important though it was, confused stress, strain, and architecture; the new investigations do not. The old studies followed older strength-of-materials traditions by presenting biological materials, especially bone, as though they were homogeneous, isotropic, and perfectly elastic bodies; the new approaches acknowledge that, like many new engineering materials, bone and other living tissues are inhomogeneous and nonisotropic with imperfectly elastic, poroelastic, and plastic-elastic properties. The old stress studies used infinite beam theory; the new use finite element analysis, with improvements of almost an order of magnitude. Similar changes are evident in each of the other areas of this new functional anatomy.

ANALYSIS OF FORM AND PATTERN

A second contribution to the study of animal structure relates to the development of morphometrics for describing and comparing animal shapes. Again, the original advances were not in anatomy; indeed, they were not in biology at all. But the concept of comparing forms and patterns quantitatively is an old biological idea [e.g., E. S. Russell's *Form and Function* (1916) and D'Arcy W. Thompson's

On Growth and Form (1917)]. Embryologists also participated early [e.g., L. von Bartalanffy and J.H. Woodger's *Modern Theories of Development* (1933) and much of C.H. Waddington's early work as expressed posthumously recently in his *Tools for Thought* (1977)]. But most of these developments were stymied because the statistical thinking had not at that point been done and because, in any case, the computations could not be achieved with pencil and paper. Indeed, it is for these reasons that the earlier ideas were expressed geometrically (e.g, Thompson's coordinate transformations and Woodger's interorganismal mapping).

The modern usages, then, depend mainly upon advances in statistics together with the development of electronic computers. The base was the work of statisticians: R.A. Fisher in England, H. Hotelling in the United States, and P.C. Mahalanobis in India, in the 1930s. These studies stood, in their turn, upon the yet older work of individuals such as K. Pearson and F. Galton at the turn of the century. Newer developments were worked out by statisticians such as C.R. Rao, F. Yates, M.G. Kendall, and, of course, the present day dean of American statisticians, J.W. Tukey. The techniques were first applied in anatomy by individuals such as J.C. Trevor, E.H. Ashton, W.W. Howells, and C.E. Oxnard, working at first with statistical collaborators and consultants (e.g., C.R. Rao, F. Yates, M.J.R. Healy, and J.C. Gower). Excellent descriptions of applications in evolutionary morphology generally are to be found in R.E. Blackith and R.A. Reyment's (now R.A. Reyment, R.E. Blackith, and N.A. Campbell's) *Multivariate Morphometrics* (1971, 1984). Most recent usages in human and primate evolution are given in C.E. Oxnard's *The Order of Man; A Biomathematical Anatomy of the Primates* (1984) and *Fossils, Teeth and Sex: New Perspectives in Human Evolution* (1986).

The most widely used morphometric methods to date have been the various multivariate statistical approaches. Many workers are currently involved (e.g., W.W. Howells, E.H. Ashton, C.E. Oxnard, G.H. Albrecht, N. Creel, R.S. Corruccini, H.W. Crompton, M.R. Feldesman, B.R. Gelvin, H.M. McHenry, S.S. Lieberman, J.W. Moore, B.A. Wood, and so on). The developments have taken several different directions. The first involved simply quantifying resemblances and differences between biological shapes. When is one form intermediate between others? When is one form uniquely different from others? These studies have given rise to new views of the relationships of extant primates and fossils specifically through the morphometrics of the cranium and postcranium. A second direction came from the realization that the process of rendering many complex anatomical variables into a small number of statistical descriptors sometimes provided information about the underlying biology. The earliest of these studies involved animals other than vertebrates (e.g., painted turtles, P. Jolicoeur and J.E. Mosimann; mirid bugs, N. Waloff); and statistical axes were related to factors like overall size, sexual dimorphism, and geographic variation. Later studies in primates supplemented direct biomechanical investigations by suggesting functional factors underlying structure. They suggested that the apparently myriad anatomical features that make up the structure of a given anatomical region such as the shoulder, for example, might be related to a small number of underlying biomechanical factors. A third direction was early obvious but could not be attained until sufficient data had been amassed. That is the notion that morphometric analyses of large numbers of measures, representing a synopsis of the structure of the entire body, might allow assessment of morphological similarities, speaking directly to evolutionary relationships. For example, the first morphological data supporting the molecular view (see below) of the close relationship between humans and African apes, and the wide separation of these from the Asian orang-utans, have come from morphometrics. Most recently of all, such all-encompassing analyses have been used to examine behavioral, ecological, and dietary data, thus giving a new "niche metrics." Niche metrics are allowing highly detailed associations to be drawn between the overall anatomies that animals display and the complex lifestyles that they adopt.

Superimposed upon the multivariate statistical approaches to morphometrics are a series of yet newer morphometric tools for looking at form and pattern. Again, early studies showing how these could be employed were not in the field of human anatomy and anthropology. Curiously enough, however, many used anthropological data as exemplars, e.g., sagittal sections of human, ape, and fossil skulls, as in D'A.W. Thompson's coordinate transformations, P.H.A. Sneath's trend surface analyses, and F.L. Bookstein's biorthogonal grids. *Morphometrics in Evolutionary Biology* by Bookstein et al. (1985) outlines many of these developments. P. Lestrel has pioneered one-dimensional Fourier analysis (a method that is far more useful than generally realized) for the study of bone outlines (e.g., the lower end of the humerus). This is being extended by J.W. Moore and P. O'Higgins and colleagues for studying hominoid skulls including fossils, and for comparison with multivariate statistical morphometric methods. The author has used two-dimensional Fourier transforms (derived optically) for analyzing differences in cancellous vertebral patterns in the great apes and humans; J. Gunn has studied the complex forms of stone tools with the same method; and R.F. Kay has adopted it for characterizing microwear patterns on teeth. Even more complex imaging methods are available, and some are described in the next chapter by R.R. Peterson; but their application within this field is likely to be most important. Thus G.C. Conroy and M.W. Vannier (1984) are using high-resolution computer-aided tomography for a variety of studies of fossil skulls that allow visualization and measurement of internal structures that are not only hidden but still embedded in matrix. G. Sperber is employing modern advances in radiology in his studies of enamel in living and fossil teeth. Undoubtedly these computer-linked, noninvasive, radiological imaging techniques will become of greater and greater importance in functional and evolutionary anatomy as the equipment and technologies, at present expensive and mostly limited to clinical disciplines, come to be available to anatomists. We can expect to see a related method, computer graphics, employed in helping us understand yet further the complex changes in whole organisms that occur during both development and evolution.

MOLECULAR EVOLUTION

The above morphological studies of whole organisms have been enormously impacted in recent years by a wholly different field of investigation: molecular evolution. From the viewpoint of anatomists, this has related particularly to the molecular evolution of the primates. It is usual to refer to the names of E. Zuckercandl and L. Pauling for the expression of the basic idea. But an early discussion of implications for evolution was given by S. Zuckerman in his *Functional Affinities of Man, Monkeys and Apes* (1934). The concept was mooted at the turn of the century (e.g., by G.H.F. Nuttall in England and H. Friedenthal in Germany). It was even glimpsed by Darwin himself:

> Nevertheless, all living things have much in common, in their chemical composition, their cellular structure, . . . and their liability to injurious influences.

How much closer could Darwin have come, given the language of his day, to the concepts of molecular, ultrastructural, and immunological evolution of our times?

Within anatomy, anthropology, and related fields, however, the modern development of these studies rapidly came to include workers such as M. Goodman, R.E. Tashian, J. and V. Buettner-Janusch, W.M. Fitch, V.M. Sarich, and A.C. Wilson, together with, even more recently, a large number of other investigators. Again, a considerable number of these discoveries were made in departments of anatomy. The results depended upon the development of a wide variety of techniques including immunodiffusion, radioimmunoassay, electrophoresis, microcomplement fixation, amino acid sequencing, nucleic acid, hybridization, nucleotide sequencing, restriction endonuclease mapping, cytogenetics, and DNA-DNA hybridization. They have been carried out by a wide range of individuals, such as E.H.Y. Chu, N.A. Barnicott, J.M. Beard, W.M. Fitch, M. Goodman, H.M. Dene, W. Prychodko, G.W. Moore, P. Nute, V. Sarich, J.E. Cronin, A.C. Wilson, F.J. Ayala, E.J. Bruce, A.E. Romero-Herrara, K.A. Joysey, and C.G. Sibley, among many others. These techniques have been applied, of course, very widely throughout the life sciences. The results that are most pertinent to anatomists are in the primates. Recent key books here are from Wayne State University's Department of Anatomy: M. Goodman and R.E. Tashian's (1976) *Molecular Anthropology: Genes and Proteins in the Evolutionary Ascent of the Primates* and M. Goodman's (1982) *Macromolecular Sequences in Systematics and Evolutionary Biology*. The findings are of two main types.

The first finding relates to patterns of relationships. Thus, the evolutionary linkages that are generally thought to exist among vertebrates (based mainly upon morphological and fossil information) are usually confirmed by the new molecular studies. But there are disagreements, and these tend to pertain to relationships at lower systematic levels where convergences, parallels, and radiations may be more difficult to disentangle. For example, the ancient opinion, derived primarily from anatomical studies, that the relationships among the living hominoids are expressible as a division between the Hominidae (represented today only by humans) and the Pongidae (represented today by the living great apes: bonobos, chimpanzees, gorillas, and orang-utans) is not supported by the biomolecular information. Molecular studies of many kinds show that the real division is between 1) the large Asian ape (the orang-utan, perhaps together with the lesser apes, gibbons, depending upon the levels at which groups are defined) and 2) the combined group of humans, chimpanzees, and gorillas. It is almost a cliche now to note that the African apes and humans may share as much as 98% of their DNA.

Although this result is directly contrary to the long-held anatomical view, the last decade has seen it accepted by most morphologists. It is, therefore, of considerable interest that primate morphology, when studied using quantitative data covering most regions of the body and analyzed using morphometric techniques capable of taking account of redundant information, gives patterns of relationship that mirror those obtained from the molecules (C.E. Oxnard, 1983), a perhaps surprising anatomical confirmation of the molecular findings. And it is possible that the cladistic method (which basically also allows for a degree of redundant information in anatomies, although in a different manner) also shows similar results (e.g., B.A. Wood).

The second finding or concept relates to the timing of evolution, the idea of the "molecular clock." For example, such studies suggest that the time of divergence between humans and African apes has been extremely short. But this idea has a checkered history. In the 1960s the estimates were subject to wide variation (e.g., from approximately 1 to more than 10 million years ago). Continued study settled in recent years on a figure of 4 to 6 million years ago (e.g., V. Sarich, A.C. Wilson, W.M. Fitch; this is enormously short compared to what was generally believed by paleontologists). Even more recently, however, more cautious assessments, applications of newer techniques, and more sophisticated views about evolutionary rates (e.g., M. Goodman, J.E. Cronin, C.G. Sibley, J.E. Ahlquist, D. Read, and P.D. Gingerich) have again lengthened the estimates for the upper limit of the human/chimpanzee divergence time. Within this last year dates as wide apart as 1, 5, 8, 10, and 13 million years have all been posited. The molecular clock concept is, itself, undergoing much evolution and modification. It is likely that we shall end up with the notion that, just as there is no one morphological clock that can be used to measure rates of morphological evolution, so, too, there is no single molecular clock for timing the evolution of the molecules.

HUMAN VARIATION

From functional and evolutionary studies of species distantly or closely related to humans, we move on to investigations of humans themselves. These studies only rarely involved anatomical variations of particular human subjects (the subject of so much earlier anatomical work), but rather a whole series of new investigations of human variation in a population mode. Again, although starting in anatomy and in anatomy departments, this subject has split many times; and many of the more recent advances have come in disciplines other than anatomy. Nevertheless, a few investigators remained in anatomy, and others have returned to anatomy with the renewal that has been described. The topic is extremely broad, with many different investigators, and is perhaps best described as several different concepts.

The most fundamental of these concepts is the genetic basis of variation. It relates quite directly to the application, to humans, of the new findings in genetics stemming from the work at the turn of the century: human population genetics. Once again, growth in this area was largely due to the development of a series of techniques and procedures. These included, among others, electrophoresis for study of enzymes and blood proteins; cytological techniques for the cultivation, banding, and analysis of human chromosomes; cellular hybridization studies carried out *in vitro;* methods for the detection at birth (and, more recently still, before birth) of errors of metabolism, together with, again more recently, detection of other diseases and conditions at birth and *in utero;* and, finally, electronic computer modeling and data handling. A very large number of individuals have been responsible for these developments, but the names of J.V. Neel, N.E. Morton, J.F. Crow, H.J. Muller, R.C. Lewontin, and W.J. Schull must be mentioned.

Another element of human population research involved the study and interpretation of the concept of race. Early contributors were C.B. Davenport, E.W. Count, A.C. Haddon, E.A. Hooton, H.L. Shapiro, and M.J. Herskovits. Books by S.M. Garn (1961) and C.S. Coon (1962) have been of great influence. W.W. Howells and M. Trotter have investigated problems of morphological variation. Several American scientists raised the matter of erroneous racial concepts and racial discrimination: E.E. Hunt, G.W. Lasker, and M. Ashley Montagu have been particularly powerful voices in this regard. A.M. Brues and F.B. Livingstone developed models to understand the distribution of genetic traits. W.S. Pollitzer provided quantitative analyses of racial admixture of North American populations.

The description and analyses of human growth have also been extensive. The study of growth is most important for the elucidation of mechanisms of evolution because changes in morphological characters necessarily occur through alteration in the inherited pattern of this process. Growth also occupies an important place in the study of individual differences, for many of these also arise through differential growth of a part of the body relative to others. Despite many surveys and descriptive studies, details of this process are yet imperfectly understood. The subject has been traditionally investigated in the United States. Some of the seminal early work was done by T. Wingate Todd, A. Hrdlička, H.V. Meredith, W.W. Greulich, and W.M. Krogman. The extensive work of S.M. Garn should be mentioned, as well as other work of the Fels Research Institute, now being performed by A.F. Roche, F. Falkner, and many others.

Human variation also encompasses human ecology and physiological adaptation. This is the complex interaction of biology and culture in diverse situations and especially in relation to conditions of stress. Workers include P.T. Baker, W.S. Laughlin, F.A. Milan, A.T. Steegman, and many others. The demographic aspects of human biology have been investigated by R. Pearl. G.W. Lasker, J.N. Spuhler, and F.S. Hulse, among many others. Specifically, medical and dental anthropologies have resulted from the works of individuals such as A. Damon, A.A. Dahlberg, and C.F.A. Moorrees.

CONCLUSION: HOW THE RENEWAL DEVELOPED

Part of the story of a research renewal cognate with the renewal of the teaching of human gross anatomy stems from a different set of advances in recent years that should be documented here. With the gradual realization that there still was a need for human gross anatomy as a systematic body of knowledge for health professionals, there was also a realization that this could best be achieved if it could be taught by investigators whose research was somehow cognate with the teaching. This is not to decry the fine efforts of molecular biologists, cell biologists, and neurobiologists who, as part of their teaching commitment, have undertaken courses in human gross anatomy. Nor is it to denigrate the excellent contributions made by the large number of individuals who happened to be more interested in part-time careers as adjuncts and lecturers. Perhaps most of all, it is not to forget the most valuable services to human gross anatomical teaching supplied by a cadre of postretirement anatomists. These last have, often with an enormous fund of applied anatomical information and delightful approaches to teaching, contributed most importantly in ways that might otherwise have been lost to modern human anatomical teaching.

The teaching of human gross anatomy would clearly benefit if there were a solid group of teachers who were, like other medical school teachers, also faculty investigators at the cutting edge of a cognate subject like those described in this review. This has been achieved, in a small but growing number of departments of anatomy, through the far-sightedness of individuals, usually chairmen of departments, who understood the problem. It has been an especially altruistic development because, almost without exception, these individuals were cellular or molecular biologists who could well have been expected to cannibalize faculty positions for their own areas of anatomical investigation.

The University of Chicago was early in the field here through the efforts of H.S. Bennett, a distinguished cell biologist, who nevertheless understood the necessity of appointing gross anatomists doing cognate research to carry out the major part of human gross anatomy teaching. This led to the appointment of R. Singer as chairman of that department, and he has been, in his turn, most vocal over the years in support of this concept. He started functional and evolutionary morphology in Chicago (with the appointment of D.B. Wake, R.H. Tuttle, C.E. Oxnard, J. Hopson, L. Radinsky, E. Lombard, R. Wassersug, and others); and he supported a cadre of graduate students in evolutionary morphology who were eventually appointed all around the country as teachers of human gross anatomy. A somewhat similar pattern occurred at the State University of New York at Stony Brook through the efforts of M. Dewey. He, too, is a cellular and molecular biologist, not a gross anatomist; but he supported the appointment of human gross anatomy teachers who were full participants in research in human and primate functional anatomy and evolution (e.g., J.T. Stern, Jr., J.G. Fleagle, N. Creel, W. Jungers, R. Sussman, and so on). Likewise at Duke University, J.D. Robertson (also a cellular biologist, but similarly percipient about the problem of "gross anatomy") together with, at that time, J. Buettner-Janusch, developed a strong primate evolution group through the appointment of such individuals as M. Cartmill, W. Hylander, R. Kay, and others. Anatomy at Johns Hopkins participated in this type of development through the percipience of cell biologist T. Pollard, who appointed A.C. Walker and supports Walker's efforts in strengthening functional and evolutionary morphology. The University of Texas Health Sciences Center, through the actions of R.E. Billingham (yet another distinguished cellular biologist—and likewise altruistic), has been able to appoint functional anatomists W. Gonyea and G.T. Throckmorton in strengthening the area of human gross anatomy. Harvard has had a long tradition in this regard, and continues to keep it going by appointing individuals like F.A. Jenkins, Jr., Karel Liem, and T.A. McMahon. D.E. Kelly (also a cell biologist) has started such a development at the University of Southern California. The departments I have named are not by any means the only ones where such developments have been tried. But they are a representative selection.

It also should be documented that some attempts to start such developments have not succeeded. Lubert Stryer, a distinguished molecular anatomist at Stanford University, discussed this some years ago. But at Stanford, they were put into place in a different manner, through the development of "human biology" outside anatomy (the Department of Biological Structure), by D. Kennedy, D. Hamburg, and others. It is possible that interactions between undergraduate colleges and medical schools thus may also result in advances in both teaching and research in organismal morphology, especially as related to humans. This follows from the importance of whole organism studies for general and pre-professional education, as well as for more advanced medical and other health-related careers. It is certainly the case that teachers of human gross anatomy come, more and more frequently, to have joint appointments in anthropology, biology, and related college departments.

We can summarize by noting that the renaissance in research studies cognate with the teaching of human gross anatomy, although small, is growing. It is producing new views of whole organism structure that can be placed alongside new investigations in other aspects of the biology of whole organisms: physiology, evolution, ecology, population biology, ethnology, environmental biology, biogeography, paleontology, and so on. This level of investigation, in turn, is setting a new stage on which advances in cellular biology, ultrastructural biology, molecular biology, and neurobiology can be seen in the light of difference and change due to both the uniqueness and diversity of living things.

It may be of interest for the Association to realize that very few of the research gross anatomists mentioned in this review are Association members, even though most research gross anatomists are also teachers of anatomy in one of its various guises. Indeed, most of the individuals mentioned are members of our closest sister societies: the section of vertebrate anatomy of the American Zoologists, the American Association of Physical Anthropologists, the American Society of Primatologists, the American Association of Biomechanics, and others.

It is inevitable that a short review spanning vertebrates from hagfish to humans, and primates from bush-babies to human babies, can mention only a few of the many important contributions. It is inevitable, too, that it possesses biases (albeit completely nonmalignant) of which I am keenly aware but for which I do not apologize.

REFERENCES

Alexander, R. McN. 1967 Animal Mechanics. Washington University Press, Seattle.

Barnett, C.H., D.V. Davies, and M.A. MacConaill 1961 Synovial Joints: Their Structure and Mechanics. Charles C Thomas, Springfield.

Basmajian, J.V. 1967 Muscles Alive. Williams & Wilkins, Baltimore.

Blackith, R.E., and R.A. Reyment 1971 Multivariate Morphometrics. Academic Press, London.

Bookstein, F.L., B. Chernoff, R.L. Elder, J.M. Humphries, G.R. Smith, and R.E. Strauss 1985 Morphometrics in evolutionary biology. Acad. Nat. Sci. Phil., *15*:1–277.

Campbell, B. 1937 The shoulder muscles of the platyrrhine monkeys. J. Mammal., *18*:66–71.

Conroy, G.C., and M.W. Vannier 1984 Noninvasive three-dimensional computer imaging of matrix filled fossil skulls by high-resolution computed tomography. Science, *226*:456–458.

Coon, C.S. 1962 The Origin of Races. Knopf, New York.

Curry, J.D. 1984 The Mechanical Adaptations of Bones. Princeton University Press, Princeton.

Evans, F.G. 1957 Stress and Strain in Bones. Charles C Thomas, Springfield.

Garn, S.M. 1961 Human Races. Charles C Thomas, Springfield.

Goodman, M. 1982 Macromolecular Sequences in Systematics and Evolutionary Biology. Plenum, New York.

Goodman, M., and R.E. Tashian 1976 Molecular Anthropology: Genes and Proteins in the Evolutionary Ascent of the Primates. Plenum, New York.

Hildebrand, M., D.M. Bramble, K.F. Liem, and D.B. Wake 1985 Functional Vertebrate Morphology. Harvard University Press, Cambridge.

Inman, V. T., J. B. DeC. M. Saunders, and L. C. Abbott 1944 Observations on the function of the shoulder joint. J. Bone Joint Surg., 26:1–30.

MacConaill, M.A., and J. V. Basmajian 1969 Muscles and Movements. Williams & Wilkins, Baltimore.

Miller, R.A. 1932 Evolution of the pectoral girdle and forelimb in the primates. Am. J. Phys. Anthropol. 17:1–56.

Moore, J.W. 1981 The Mammalian Skull. Cambridge University Press, Cambridge.

Murray, P.D.F. 1936 Bones: A Study in the Development and Structure of the Vertebrate Skeleton. Cambridge University Press, London.

Oxnard, C.E. 1983 Anatomical, biomolecular and morphometric views of the primates. Prog. Anat., 3:113–142.

Oxnard, C.E. 1984 The Order of Man: A Biomathematical Anatomy of the Primates. Yale University Press, New Haven.

Oxnard, C.E. 1986 Fossils, Teeth and Sex: New Perspectives in Human Evolution. Washington University Press, Seattle.

Reyment, R.A., R.E. Blackith, and N. A. Campbell 1984 Multivariate Morphometrics. Academic Press, London.

Russell, E.S. 1916 Form and Function. John Murray, London.

Thompson, D'A.W. 1917 On Growth and Form. Cambridge University Press, London.

von Bartalanffy, L., and J.H. Woodger 1933 Modern Theories of Development. Oxford University Press, London.

Waddington, C.H. 1977 Tools for Thought. Basic Books, New York.

Wainright, S.A., W.D. Biggs, J.D. Curry, and J.M. Gosline 1975 Mechanical Design in Organisms. Wiley, New York.

Young, J.Z. 1950 The Life of Vertebrates. Oxford University Press, Oxford.

Young, J.Z. 1957 The Life of Mammals. Oxford University Press, Oxford.

Young, J.Z. 1971 An Introduction to the Study of Man. Oxford University Press, Oxford.

Zuckerman, S. 1934 Functional Affinities of Man, Monkeys and Apes. Kegan Paul, London.

Chapter 15

CROSS-SECTIONAL ANATOMY: FROM ESOTERIC TO ESSENTIAL

Roy R. Peterson

Thomas Dwight published *Frozen Sections of a Child,* the first cross-sectional anatomy in this country, one year before he was named chairman of the anatomy department at Harvard Medical School (Dwight, 1881). Nine years later, Robert Terry (Fig. 15.1) of Washington University in St. Louis presented a paper at the 13th meeting of the Association of American Anatomists describing a method for making sections of the whole, decalcified body with a knife (Terry, 1900). Some of the sections he prepared in this manner are still on display in the Washington University anatomical museum. A major contribution to understanding the body from this point of view came from the anatomy department at St. Louis University School of Medicine, when Adloph Eycleshymer (Fig. 15.2) and Daniel Schoemaker (Fig. 15.3) published their book of cross sections drawn by medical illustrator Tom Jones (Eycleshymer and Schoemaker, 1911). Although this classic was reprinted many times, it was allowed to go out of print in 1970, just a few years before radiologists everywhere started clamoring for more information about cross-sectional anatomy.

The period between 1911 and the 1970s was one of decreasing interest in cross-sectional anatomy. Dudley Morton, Raymod Truex, and Carl Kellner tried to rekindle interest and provide a method for studying anatomy from sections when they published their *Manual of Cross-Section Anatomy* (Morton et al., 1941). Although there was to be a long hiatus in serious study of the subject, interest smoldered in various anatomy departments around the country. Paul Roofe, at the University of Kansas, hired a technician to embed cross sections of a cadaver in plastic from 1950 to 1953. About the same time, anatomists who were also using the process at the UCLA Medical School developed it to a fine art. They eventually built a superbly equipped laboratory for plastic embedding that became a mecca for those who wanted to learn the technique. In more recent years, Robert Gregg at the University of Louisville started a commercial enterprise to supply the

Fig. 15.1. Robert J. Terry, Chairman, Department of Anatomy, Washington University School of Medicine, 1900–1941. In 1899, Dr. Terry made cross sections of entire decalcified human cadavers using a knife.

Fig. 15.2. Adolph Eycleshymer, Chairman, Department of Anatomy, St. Louis University School of Medicine, 1903–1913. Coauthor of the classic atlas of cross-sectional anatomy that was in print from 1911 to 1970.

Fig. 15.3. Daniel Schoemaker, Chairman, Department of Anatomy, St. Louis University School of Medicine, 1930–1946. Coauthor of the classic atlas of cross-sectional anatomy that was in print from 1911 to 1970.

great demand by other medical schools for durable, plastic-embedded specimens and sections.

The advent of such computer-assisted imaging techniques as ultrasound scanning (US), computed tomography (CT), positron emission tomography (PET), and magnetic resonance imaging (MRI) within the past 20 years has been a diagnostic boon. Inasmuch as these machines provide images of the body in section, the physicians reading their output must have a thorough understanding of the three-dimensional anatomy of the human body. Gross anatomy by dissection provides the basic framework on which such understanding is built. Knowledge of cross-sectional anatomy is essential to round out that framework.

In the early 1970s, the computer-assisted imaging modalities of ultrasound scans and computed tomography became widely used. To help interpret the images shown on a cathode ray tube screen as sections of the body, radiologists searched frantically for copies of *A Cross-Section Anatomy* (Eycleshymer and Schoemaker, 1911) in any condition. Even when they could find dog-eared copies, they were still frustrated. In order that the orientation of organs would conform to their standard convention for viewing radiographs, radiologists had elected to view the images produced by the CT scanners from below rather than from above, as anatomists previously had viewed cross sections. The gymnastics of mentally flipping images, as well as translating the Latin BNA names into more modern anatomical terminology, led many radiologists to consult with anatomists to help resolve their doubts about the structures they were seeing and to ease their frustrations at not having helpful reference books available.

In the spring of 1975, a neuroradiologist at Washington University asked the author if it would be possible to make CT scans of the head of a cadaver with the recently installed EMI head scanner and then cut sections to correspond to the scans. Working after patient hours we scanned the heads of two unembalmed cadavers. They were frozen in a Dry Ice chamber, and with a band saw we cut slices in the planes marked on the heads at the time they were scanned. The sections subsequently were photographed while still frozen. The comparisons between scans and photographs were precise and became helpful teaching material for residents and visiting radiologists. A year later, while the author was a visiting professor at Stanford University, a radiologist there asked to do a similar study for the trunk of the body using a prototype body scanner being developed by the Varian Corporation. Shortly afterward an EMI body scanner was installed at Washington University. The radiologists in the thorax and abdomen divisions there were anxious to improve their understanding of cross-sectional anatomy. In order to obtain the best possible CT images, we scanned several cadavers using radiation levels that were impossible to use on patients. The cadavers were then frozen, sectioned, and photographed. This became the nucleus of an atlas of cross-sectional anatomy.

Anatomists and radiologists at a number of medical schools were obviously doing very similar studies at about the same time. Beginning in 1977, books began to appear that correlated computerized tomography and ultrasound images in various ways with cross sections of cadavers. One of the first of these (Carter et al., 1977) was based on reduced drawings from Eycleshymer and Schoemaker (1911) with the names of structures brought up-to-date by the anatomist among the authors, James Morehead of Tufts. Lyons' *Color Atlas of Sectional Anatomy* (1978) was directed principally toward ultrasonography and showed the body in transverse, sagittal, and frontal sections. Contributions to this book by anatomists Keith Moore, Ruth Grahame, and T.V.N. Persaud were generously acknowledged by Dr. Lyons. In like manner, anatomists Faustino Suarez at Georgetown, Richard Snell at George Washington, Henry DiStefano at SUNY Upstate, and Paul McMillan and Walter Roberts at Loma Linda made significant contributions to books on cross-sectional anatomy (Ledley et al., 1977; Wyman et al., 1978; Kieffer and Heitzman, 1979; Thompson and Hasso, 1980) emanating from the radiology departments at their respective medical schools.

It was not until 1980 that books began to appear in which the major emphasis was anatomical rather than radiological in character. One reason for this was that most of the earlier books had identified little more anatomy than could be discerned in the computer-generated images. Unfortunately, by the time these books were published, the imaging techniques had progressed to the extent that the previous images were obsolete and much more anatomical detail could be seen and needed to be identified. Anatomists Walter Bo and Wayne Krueger teamed up with a radiologist at Bowman Gray Medical School and produced an atlas of cross-sectional anatomy that stressed the clinical importance of anatomical structures and relationships, and made CT images of secondary importance (Bo et al., 1980).

It became obvious to anatomists and radiologists alike that, armed with a knowledge of anatomical relationships gained from a study of serial cross sections of the body, it is possible to reason one's way through the anatomy revealed in the computed images generated by any type of imaging modality. It was on this basis that the author (Peterson, 1980) published a cross-sectional atlas that was entirely anatomical. This book stressed the need to adopt a systematic approach—learning anatomy from sections by following a single system at a time through a series of adjacent sections and relating each system to those previously studied. The use of this approach was made easier with the subsequent publication of a color slide set (Peterson, 1982a) and a workbook (Peterson, 1982b) based on the atlas.

Donald Cahill of the Mayo Medical School stimulates understanding of cross-sectional anatomy in his atlas (Cahill and Orland, 1984) by making each sheet of paper represent a single section, with the upper surface seen on one side and the lower surface on the opposite side. As the page is turned, one captures the feeling of turning the section over to follow specific structures through the thickness of the section. The illusion is heightened by the effective use of shading and dotted lines to indicate the course of some structures within the section. Marvin Wagner of the Medical College of Wisconsin, because of his surgical background, was able to contribute a different clinical flavor and impetus for understanding what he called "segmental" anatomy in his excellent book (Wagner and Lawson, 1982). Schnitzlein at South Florida added correlations of both gross and microscopic anatomy to his atlas, *Computed Tomography of the Head and Spine: A Photographic Color Atlas of CT, Gross, and Microscopic Anatomy* (Schnitzlein et al., 1983).

Anatomists at several schools have published workbooks for use by students: Jamie Estavillo at SIU Carbondale (Estavillo et al., 1981), Mary Jane Showers and Roger Crafts at the University of Cincinnati (Showers and Crafts, 1982), the author at Washington University (Peterson, 1982b), and Lowell Sether at the Medical College of Wisconsin (Sether, 1985). Some of these workbooks are available to in-house students only and others are available commercially.

During the summer of 1985, a week-long continuing education course was given at Temple University School of Medicine by Carson Schneck, Gail Crouse, J. Robert Troyer, and other members of the departments of anatomy and radiology. In addition to the basic physics of the various imaging techniques, this course presented lectures and demonstrations on the important topographic, sectional, and developmental anatomy of specific regions of the body. Problem-solving conferences also were held to cement the newly gained information into useful units of understanding.

Anatomists have been direct participants in research projects with their radiologist colleagues in attempts to clarify the understanding of particularly difficult regions of the body, and to help distinguish between the images of normal and pathological structures in specific "tight spots." Vernon Yeager of St. Louis University has collaborated on papers relating the anatomy and CT images of such diverse regions as the knee (Archer and Yeager, 1978) and the larynx (Archer et al., 1981). A study at Washington University has shown that a structure seen in CT scans between the arch of the aorta and the right pulmonary artery, often mistakenly identified as an enlarged lymph node, is a normal variation in the size of a part of the pericardial cavity named the superior sinus, in which fluid tends to become trapped, even in the absence of clinically detectable pericardial effusion (Aronberg et al., 1984).

The field of three-dimensional reconstruction from CT images is an intersection of anatomy, radiology, and computer science that has become clinically important, particularly in reconstructive surgery. Anatomists at the Pennsylvania College of Podiatric Medicine (Hirsch et al., 1983) and at the University of South Florida (Hilbelink et al., 1985) have presented posters at AAA meetings demonstrating the usefulness of this type of study in the foot and ankle and the wrist, respectively. Still another fertile area for applying this technique to anatomical research was demonstrated by Conroy and Vannier (1984). Their three-dimensional computer images of matrix-filled fossil skulls provide a method for obtaining measurements from fossils that could never before have been made without employing invasive, possibly destructive, means.

More recently, nuclear magnetic resonance has become a clinically useful imaging modality. Radiologists prefer to drop the term "nuclear" and call it magnetic resonance imaging or MRI. This removes any connotation of radioactivity or ionizing radiation being used in the process, one of its important advantages. Although MRI of a cadaver is quite different from that of a living patient, the need for making cadaver studies has become apparent and is being pursued at several institutions, one important reason being that MRI can produce images of the body in sagittal and frontal as well as transverse planes. Images in oblique planes are easily produced also and provide useful information. The increasing importance of cross-sectional anatomy is emphasized by the appearance of a special poster session at the 98th meeting of the American Association of Anatomists in Toronto by John Basmajian, Robert Chase, Roy Schwarz, and Charles Bridgeman titled, " 'Teaching Anatomy in the 21st Century.' An Anatomical Correlation of Cadaver Cryosections and Magnetic Resonance Images, presented for the Radiological Society of North America by James Holiday and Richard Saxon."

In this brief and incomplete historical account, the author has traced the transformation of one small field of anatomical study from an esoteric specialty into an *essential ingredient* in the understanding of human anatomy.

REFERENCES

Archer, C.R., S.S. Sagel, V.L. Yeager, S. Martin, and W.H. Friedman 1981 Staging of carcinoma of the larnyx: Comparative accuracy of CT and laryngography. A.J.R., *136*:571–575.

Archer, C.R., and V.L. Yeager 1978 Internal structures of the knee visualized by computed tomography. J. Comput. Tomogr., *2*:181–183.

Aronberg, D.J., H.S. Glazer, R.R. Peterson, and S.S. Sagel 1984 The superior sinus of the pericardium: CT appearance. Radiology, *153*:489–492.

Bo, W.J., I. Meschan, and W.A. Krueger 1980 Basic Atlas of Cross-Sectional Anatomy. Saunders, Philadelphia.

Cahill, D.R., and M.J. Orland 1984 Atlas of Human Cross-Sectional Anatomy. Lea & Febiger, Philadelphia.

Carter, B.L., J. Morehead, S.M. Wolpert, S.B. Hammerschlag, H.J. Griffiths, and P.C. Kahn 1977 Cross-Sectional Anatomy: Computed Tomography and Ultrasound Correlation. Appleton-Century-Crofts, New York.

Conroy, G.C., and M.W. Vannier 1984 Noninvasive three-dimensional computer imaging of matrix-filled fossil skulls by high resolution computed tomography. Science, *226*:456–458.

Dwight, T. 1881 Frozen Sections of a Child. Wood, New York.

Estavillo, J.A., W.D. Moore, and J.L. Masse 1981 Manual of Cross-Sectional Anatomy. Dept. of Anatomy, SIU Carbondale, Carbondale, IL.

Eycleshymer, A.C., and D.M. Schoemaker 1911 A Cross-Section Anatomy. Appleton-Century Co., New York.

Hilbelink, D.R., J.M. Garmendia, H.N. Schnitzlein, S.A. Stenzler, and R. Belsole 1985 Cross-sectional anatomy of the human carpus. Anat. Rec., *211*:84A (abstr.).

Hirsch, B.E., D. Roberts, K.J. Upuda, and H. Kressel 1983 Computerized three-dimensional reconstructions from C.T. scans. Anat. Rec., 205:83A (abstr.)

Kieffer, S.A., and E.R. Heitzman 1979 An Atlas of Cross-Sectional Anatomy: Computed Tomography, Ultrasound, Radiography, Gross Anatomy. Harper & Row, Hagerstown.

Ledley, R.S., H.K. Huang, and J.C. Mazziotta 1977 Cross-Sectional Anatomy: An Atlas for Computerized Tomography. Williams & Wilkins, Baltimore.

Lyons, E.A. 1978 Color Atlas of Sectional Anatomy: Neck, Chest, Abdomen, C.V. Mosby, St. Louis.

Morton, D.J., R.C. Truex, and C.E. Kellner 1941 Manual of Cross-Section Anatomy. Williams & Wilkins, Baltimore.

Peterson, R.R. 1980 A Cross-Sectional Approach to Anatomy. Year Book, Chicago.

Peterson, R.R. 1982a Cross-Sectional Anatomy: A Full Color Slide Presentation. Year Book, Chicago.

Peterson, R.R. 1982b Workbook for a Cross-Sectional Approach to Anatomy. Roy R. Peterson, St. Louis.

Schnitzlein, H.N., E.W. Hartley, F.R. Murtagh, L. Grundy, and J.T. Fargher 1983 Computed Tomography of the Head and Spine: A Photographic Color Atlas of CT, Gross, and Microscopic Anatomy. Urban & Schwarzenberg, Baltimore.

Sether, L. 1985 NASCO's Cross-Sectional Anatomy Workbook. NASCO, Ft. Atkinson, WI.

Showers, M.J., and R.C. Crafts 1982 Selected Cross Sections of the Human Body. University of Cincinnati College of Medicine, Cincinnati.

Terry, R.J. 1900 A method of sectioning the whole decalcified body with a knife. Proc. Assoc. Am. Anat. 13:8–10.

Thompson, J.R., and A.N. Hasso 1980 Correlative Sectional Anatomy of the Head and Neck: A Color Atlas. C. V. Mosby, St. Louis.

Wagner, M., and T.L. Lawson 1982 Segmental Anatomy: Applications to Clinical Medicine. Macmillan, New York.

Wyman, A.C., T.L. Lawson, and L.R. Goodman 1978 Transverse Anatomy of the Human Thorax, Abdomen, and Pelvis: An Atlas of Anatomic, Radiologic, Computed Tomographic, and Ultrasonic Correlation. Little, Brown, Boston.

Chapter 16

ENDOCRINOLOGY AND REPRODUCTIVE BIOLOGY

John W. Everett

Charles H. Sawyer

The histories of endocrinology and reproductive biology are closely intertwined. For background, it seems appropriate to review briefly their status early in the decade 1910–1920, a period heralding rapid increase of experimental approaches to biological questions. H.H. Donaldson, in his Presidential Address to this Association in 1916, welcomed the emerging broad interpretation of anatomy, considering that as "the animal body is in a continual state of flux and change . . . the inevitable tendency is to determine how such change occurs." Because structural changes are especially evident during embryological development, reproductive processes received major attention. Amphibia were favorite experimental subjects because of ready access to the embryo and the distinctive event of metamorphosis. Sexual cycles of mammals drew special interest for the practical reasons of timing ovulation and developmental processes and for studying cyclic changes in the reproductive system. The concept of "hormone" had been well established by Bayliss and Starling (1904).

Seasonal effects on reproduction had been discussed at length by Marshall in his *Physiology of Reproduction* (1910). Effects of gonadectomy, especially of males, were familiar from ancient times. In capons, effects of castration could be overcome by implanting testicular tissue (Berthold, 1849) and the same had recently been seen in frogs and rats. Interstitial tissue in both testis and ovary was thought to be the source of hormones responsible for the respective sexual characteristics (Bayliss, 1915). Mammalian corpora lutea were already known to support gestational growth of the endometrium.

The dual origin and complex composition of the pituitary were recognized. Posterior lobe substances had been extracted that caused milk discharge and contraction of smooth muscle, and effects of the anterior lobe promoting growth and metabolic functions were known (Cushing, 1912). Acromegaly was related to pituitary tumors, while eunuchoid effects accompanied absence of the gland. Fichera (1905) reported that gonadectomy results in enlargement of the anterior lobe, and signet-ring castration cells had been described in rats.

The suprarenal medulla and cortex were recognized as distinct entities. Epinephrine was already known as an active principle of the medulla and a mixture of its two isomers had been synthesized. The functional relationship of the medulla to the sympathetic nervous system was well known. It was evident that deficiency of the cortex produces the symptoms of Addison's disease. Cortical hypertrophy seemed related to sexual precocity.

The thyroids and parathyroids were also recognized as separate glands. Clinical signs of thyroid disease were well known. The presence in the thyroid of large amounts of iodine combined with protein had been shown, and crystalline thyroxin had been prepared from extracts. A classical experiment by Gudernatsch (1912) demonstrated the metamorphosis of tadpoles exposed to thyroid substance.

The existence of a pancreatic hormone regulating carbohydrate metabolism was clear, and islets of Langerhans appeared to be the source. Selective stainability of islet cells had been demonstrated by Bensley (1911).

Among presentations at meetings of the Association from 1916 to 1920, several had special importance for endocrinology as we know it today. Addison (1916) identified the signet-ring castration cells in the rat pituitary as derived from basophiles. B.M. Allen (1917) and P.E. Smith (1916 ff.) independently described hypophysectomy and its effects in amphibian larvae and adults. Smith (1920) also reported on parabiosis of normal and hypophysectomized tadpoles, both partners metamorphosing; thyroids and adrenals in the hypophysectomized partner were stimulated. Stockard and Papanicolaou (1916) gave the preliminary account of the vaginal smear technique for interpreting the guinea pig estrous cycle. Long and Evans (1919–1920) introduced their monumental study of reproduction in the rat, as disclosed by the vaginal smear and other procedures. Stages of the typical 4- to 5-day vaginal cycle were correlated with events in the ovary, uterus, and mammary glands. Pseudopregnancy was induced by stimulation of the cervix; lactation pseudopregnancy was recognized. Methods for producing deciduomata were shown. In pregnant rats, vaginal bleeding on days 13–16 was a characteristic sign. Intraperitoneal injection of anterior pituitary (AP) substance increased growth and suppressed estrous cycles. M.G. Freyer (1920) demonstrated pseudopregnancy in rats whose ovaries had been transplanted, concluding that the effect involved nerve impulses from the cervix, followed by "humoral changes" influencing the ovaries. Edgar Allen (1920) described the estrous cycle of the mouse, based on the vaginal smear technique. G.W. Corner (1916–1920) discussed the estrous cycle and spontaneous ovulation in swine, and demonstrated that the swine corpus luteum derives from both granulosa and theca interna. Atwell (1916–1920) described pituitary development in rabbits and man.

This cluster of reports and the full publications to which they led proved to be a fountainhead from which issued an ever widening stream of basic studies in

Fig. 16.1. Anatomy Department at the University of California at Berkeley around 1916. From left: Philip E. Smith, Felix Hurni, Catherine Scott (later Catherine Scott-Bishop), Herbert M. Evans, Robert O. Moody and George W. Corner. (Courtesy of Leslie L. Bennett.)

endocrinology and reproductive biology. Within that stream several principal currents can be recognized, each propelled by (and propelling) efforts of members of this Association.

GRAAFIAN FOLLICLE. THE SEARCH FOR AN ESTROGENIC HORMONE

The vaginal smear method for determining the estrous cycle of guinea pigs (Stockard and Papanicolaou, 1917) was the breakthrough making possible the eventual isolation and synthesis of estrogenic hormones (Figs. 16.1 and 16.2). In that study and subsequent investigations in rats (Long and Evans, 1922) and mice (E. Allen, 1922), occurrence of cornified cell masses in the vagina during estrus was consistently related to the presence of large vesicular follicles in the ovaries. Allen and Doisy (1923) made use of that fact in determining that oily extracts of porcine follicular fluid injected into spayed mice would produce vaginal cornification. This simple procedure in either rats or mice became the Allen-Doisy test, basic to biochemical studies that followed. The definitive article by Allen et al. appeared in 1924. Although isolation of hormone from follicular extracts was hindered by the presence of other lipids, Doisy et al. (1929) were able to isolate and cystallize estrone ("theelin") from human pregnancy urine. These findings were promptly confirmed by others. Eventually came the important announcement from Doisy's laboratory (1935) of the isolation from porcine ovaries of estradiol, now judged to be the primary ovarian estrogen.

CORPUS LUTEUM. THE SEARCH FOR A HORMONE OF GESTATION

The story of this search is masterfully told by George Corner (1942), one of its central figures. (Fig. 16.3). Once the corpus luteum was observed structurally to resemble a gland of internal secretion, several workers began experimentally to test its function. Leo Loeb (1909–1911, 1917) established in the guinea pig that: 1) corpora lutea sensitize the endometrium, resulting in the decidual reaction to a blastocyst or even to mechanical irritation, and 2) corpora lutea suppress ovulation, since their removal in either pregnant or non-pregnant animals shortens the time to the next ovulation. This effect in non-pregnant guinea pigs was later confirmed with greater precision by Papanicolaou (1923). Loeb's work was paralleled abroad by demonstration in rabbits that luteectomy interferes with pregnancy and that corpora lutea are essential for specific progestational changes of the endometrium.

Corner (1928) examined in rabbits the effects on early embryos of the deficiencies resulting from ovariectomy or selective elimination of the corpora lutea. When progestational proliferation of the endometrium was prevented, the embryos failed to survive. The rabbit progestational reaction and the deciduoma response in guinea pigs and rats became important tests as physiological and biochemical studies of corpora lutea proceeded. Weichert (1928) reported deciduomata in spayed guinea pigs treated with an alcoholic extract of porcine corpora lutea. Soon afterward, Corner and W.M. Allen (1929) obtained with the rabbit test a depend-

Fig. 16.2. Members of Herbert M. Evans' Institute of Experimental Biology in 1947. From left: Joseph A. Long (zoologist); Herman Becks (professor of oral biology); Marjorie Nelson (nutritionist); Herbert M. Evans; Miriam E. Simpson (anatomist); Choh Hao Li (chemist); and Leslie L. Bennett (physiologist). In the foreground, sitting directly in front of Marjorie Nelson, is Alexis A. Koneff (anatomist). (Courtesy of L.L. Bennett.)

Fig. 16.3. From left: Edgar Allen, 1892–1943 (courtesy of Williams & Wilkins); George W. Corner, 1889–1981 (courtesy of G.E. Erikson); Philip E. Smith, 1884–1970 (courtesy of Hadley Kirkman).

ably active "progestin" from similar extracts. By 1934, W.M. Allen and Wintersteiner and several other chemists had isolated and crystallized chemically pure progesterone. The availability of pure estrogen and progesterone greatly facilitated studies of ovarian steroid interaction with anterior pituitary function.

ANTERIOR PITUITARY

Remarkably, in the short span of years from 1925 to 1935 the anterior lobe of the hypophysis "advanced from a state of mystery and obscurity and from an object of curiosity to the head of the family of internally secreting glands" (Greep, 1974). Many American anatomists were in the forefront of that advance, including E.T. Engle, H.M. Evans, F.L. Fevold, R.O. Greep, F.L. Hisaw, S.L. Leonard, W.R. Lyons, J.A. Long, R.K. Meyer, C.R. Moore, W.O. Nelson, F.L. Reichert, M.E. Simpson, and P.E. Smith. The studies by Smith and B.M. Allen have already been mentioned regarding effects of hypophysectomy in amphibia: atrophy of thyroids and adrenals and failure to metamorphose. These losses were counteracted by intraperitoneal injection of bovine AP substance (Smith and Smith, 1921). Although the monograph by Long and Evans (1922) on the rat estrous cycle made no mention of the pituitary, they reported elsewhere that same year the marked effects of crude extracts chronically injected into intact female rats: gigantism, ovarian enlargement, masses of corpora lutea, and suppression of estrous cycles. This was the first demonstration of AP growth-promoting and gonadotropic substances. Smith's (1926) technique for parapharyngeal hypophysectomy in rats was the necessary breakthrough for differentiating the several AP trophic hormones and their eventual characterization.

Following AP ablation, maintenance or repair of gonads was achieved by repeated intramuscular implants of fresh AP tissue (Smith and Engle, 1927). Independently from Zondek and Aschheim, Smith and Engle noted that similar AP treatment of immature rats promoted sexual maturity. In an immature monkey Edgar Allen (1928) produced ovarian enlargement and follicle growth, reddening of the sex skin, and mammary gland stimulation by multiple implants of monkey

Fig. 16.4. From left: Roy O. Greep, 1905–   (courtesy of Dr. Greep); Frederick L. Hisaw, 1891–1972 (courtesy of R.O. Greep); Alden B. Dawson, 1892–1968 (courtesy of G.E. Erikson).

pituitaries. Similar effects were shown by Hartman (1930) from implants of pig pituitaries.

Separation of growth-promoting material from gonadotropic AP fractions was accomplished by Evans et al. (1933). Greep (1935) (Fig. 16.4) separated a thyrotropic principle from gonadotropic material. Distinction among gonadotropic agents, on the other hand, was delayed by faulty interpretation of the luteinizing hormone of pregnancy urine (Prolan B) as of pituitary origin. Several years elapsed before its placental origin was proved. Furthermore, the distinction between luteinization *per se* and corpus luteum maintenance (luteotropic action) was clarified only later when prolactin (PRL) was shown to be the principal luteotropin in rats. The progressive purification and chemical analysis of growth hormone (GH), follicle-stimulating hormone (FSH), luteinizing hormone (LH), thyroid-stimulating hormone (TSH), PRL, and adrenocorticotropic hormone (ACTH) required not only increased sophistication of *in vitro* methodology, but at the same time progressively refined definition of the respective biological actions of the several hormones. The dramatic story of this adventure into the unknown is told in the above-cited review by Greep, one of its leading protagonists.

The idea of a reciprocal functional relationship between the AP and its target organs arose from early reports that postcastration enlargement of the AP and formation of signet-ring basophiles could be prevented by implanting gonadal substance. This was confirmed by Haterius and Nelson (1932), who also showed lack of sex specificity in the effect. Wolfe (1935) and others counteracted castration-cell formation by estrogen injection. Whereas gonadectomy increases AP gonadotropic potency (Engle, 1929; Evans and Simpson, 1929), administration of estrin (Meyer, Leonard, Hisaw, and Martin, 1930, 1932) prevented the increase; in intact female rats treated for 30 days, the AP gonadotropin content was greatly reduced. Moore (1930) and Moore and Price (1932) formally stated the hypothesis of reciprocal AP-gonadal influence as an approximate explanation of the female sexual cycle. They were aware of modifying factors, nevertheless, as in the case of seasonal breeders.

Reciprocity between the AP and thyroids was shown in rats by the formation of vacuolated basophile cells after thyroidectomy, differing in form from castration cells (Guyer and Claus, 1935). Hoskins (1949) formulated the AP-thyroid relationship as a "servo" mechanism. Feedback actions of adrenal cortical secretion were eventually shown after long delay.

Lack of space prevents full discussion of work on *pituitary cytology* paralleling the biochemical and physiological investigations. Diversity of AP cell types had been recognized for over 30 years when Smith and Smith (1923) made the momentous discovery that in the bovine gland basophile and "chromophobe" cells predominate in an anteromedial region, while surrounding tissue is predominantly acidophilic. Implanted into tadpoles, tissue from the basophilic region induced metamorphosis through stimulation of the thyroids, whereas implants of the acidophilic zone stimulated body growth. Absence of acidophiles from the pituitaries of dwarf mice (Smith and McDowell, 1930) was further clear evidence of growth hormone secretion by this cell class. P. Bailey and L.M. Davidoff (1925) emphasized the correlation of acromegaly with acidophilic pituitary tumors, a relationship noted 25 years earlier by Benda. Attempts to correlate staining reactions and other features of specific granules with function were to occupy pituitary cytologists for the following 30–40 years.

As the cytological studies gained momentum internationally, American anatomists continued to make important contributions along the way. In addition to workers already mentioned, a partial list follows: B.L. Baker, H.R. Catchpole, A. Costoff, R. Cleveland, A.B. Dawson, M.G. Farquhar, N.S. Halmi, H. Kirkman, W.H. McShan, E.G. Rennels, A.E. Severinghaus, M. Shiino, E. Steinberger, L.A. Sternberger, and J.M. Wolfe. Differential staining methods have gradually been supplanted by immunocytochemical techniques, often combined with electron microscopy. Methods have been developed for separating secretory granules, cell organelles, and even cell types by density gradient centrifugation, as well as for enzymatic dispersion of cells and monolayer tissue culture. Much has been learned, yet old questions remain, dressed in new clothes. How specific are the agents (antibodies) used? Are there specific cells for each hormone, or can a given cell produce more than one hormone? Are the hormones always present as granules or may they exist unpackaged in the cytoplasm?

Neural Mechanisms Regulating the Anterior Pituitary

The importance of brain-pituitary interactions was slow to gain general recognition, although long implied by the influence of environmental factors on reproduction in many species of animals. It was known that some female mammals (rabbits, cats, and ferrets) will ovulate only in response to genital stimulation and that in rats pseudopregnancy can be induced by stimulating the uterine cervix. Searches for nerve fibers reaching the AP via the pituitary stalk failed; Rasmussen (1938) convincingly demonstrated in rabbits that the only nerves entering the gland are destined for blood vessels. Yet Swedish workers had proved that the ovulation reflex requires integrity of the stalk. The solution to the puzzle lay in the peculiarities of the pituitary *blood supply*.

The presence of prominent *portal vessels* on the human pituitary stalk had been recognized for several years when similar vessels in the rabbit, cat, and

Fig. 16.5. From left: John D. Green, 1917–1964 (courtesy of Dr. Green); Geoffrey W. Harris, 1913–1971 (courtesy of Dr. Harris); George B. Wislocki, 1892–1956 (courtesy of G.E. Erikson).

monkey were described by Wislocki and King (1936) and Wislocki (1937) (Fig. 16.5). They concluded on histological grounds that the direction of blood flow in the vessels is "downward" toward the AP, not toward the brain. In fact, that had already been seen directly in an amphibian by Houssay et al. It was later corroborated in several amphibia (J.D. Green, 1947), the rat (Green and Harris, 1947, 1979), the mouse (Worthington, 1955), and others. A comparative study allowed Green (1951) to state that "the portal circulation or its equivalent is a constant feature of vertebrates." A crucial finding by Harris (1950) established that the portal vessels regenerate rapidly and that to isolate the gland from the brain an inserted barrier must be impenetrable. This at once explained discrepancies that had arisen from pituitary stalk sectioning. Green and Harris (1947) proposed that liberation of AP hormones is governed by a substance or substances transmitted from the median eminence to the gland by the portal vessels. Regeneration of the vessels was the obvious explanation of Greep's (1936) functional grafts of AP tissue placed in the emptied "sella"; the only question about those experiments lay in the inability to prove that the initial hypophysectomies had been complete. To avoid that problem, Harris and Jacobsohn (1952) hypophysectomized rats parapharyngeally and made transplants transtemporally into contact with the median eminence. Such grafts into female rats from either newborn donors or adult males or females were often rapidly vascularized and fertile estrous cycles restored. Significantly the infantile grafts quickly acquired adult function and there was lack of sex specificity in the grafted tissue. Nikitovitch-Winer and Everett (1958) added information with a two-stage operation, first autotransplanting the AP to the kidney; weeks later, when gonadotropic, thyrotropic, and corticotropic powers had largely disappeared, the gland was retransplanted to the median eminence or under the temporal lobe. In spite of the double insult, grafts revascularized from the median eminence quickly restored fertile estrous cycles. Thyroids and adrenal cortex were moderately restored. The final chapter in that story was written, appropriately, by P.E. Smith (1961, 1963). Rats hypophysectomized ~40 days of age developed the typical apituitary syndrome. After 23 to 375 days, the original site of the gland was reopened and a homograft of AP was inserted. Significantly improved thyrotropic, corticotropic, and somatotropic functions followed, males became sexually potent, and females recovered fertile cyclicity. Essential stimulative effects on these several functions were established beyond all doubt. Several hypothalamic releasing hormones are now well characterized.

Evidence for *inhibition* of prolactin secretion by the hypothalamus was shown by Everett (1954, 1956). AP autografts to the kidney capsule on the day after ovulation in female rats maintained corpus luteum secretion of progesterone while the other trophic secretions largely disappeared. This luteotropic function persisted for months except when grafts were replaced close to the median eminence as noted above. Nikitovitch-Winer (1965) demonstrated similar selective increase of luteotropic action by pituitary stalk section with barrier inserted; massive lesions destroying the median eminence had the same effect.

Although the neural apparatus regulating the endocrine system is outside the province of this chapter, mention of certain pioneer contributions seems to be appropriate. P. Bailey and F. Bremer (1921) and P.E. Smith (1927) described genital atrophy as the result of hypothalamic lesions. Induction of ovulation by hypothalamic stimulation was accomplished in rabbits by Harris (1937), Haterius and Derbyshire (1937), and Markee, Sawyer, and Hollinshead (1946). These last authors showed the pituitary gland to be electrically inexcitable by stimuli that were effective when applied to the basal hypothalamus, a finding confirmed by Harris (1948) with a remote control system in alert rabbits and used by him as supporting evidence for the portal system's role in controlling AP secretion. First to induce ovulation by brain stimulation of spontaneous ovulators were Critchlow (1957–1958) and Bunn and Everett (1957), normal ovulation being blocked by either Nembutal (see below) or continuous light (Browman, 1937; Dempsey and Searles, 1943), respectively.

Steroid Feedback in Regulation of the Ovarian Cycle

Although early study with ovarian extracts and purified hormones emphasized suppression of gonadotropin secretion, under certain conditions they stimulate, as in advancing puberty (Engle, 1931). A more acute positive action was first described by Hohlweg and Chamorro, who induced corpora lutea in immature rats by estrogen treatment. In adults, induction of ovulation by estrogen injection in sheep was confirmed by Casida (1946). J. Everett (1941–1944) discovered positive feedback by progesterone. Daily injection of small amounts in anovulatory persistent-estrous rats restored ovulatory cycles instead of suppressing estrus; the treatment was important primarily during proestrus. In normal rats, progesterone could advance ovulation 24 hr. Injection of estrogen at an appropriate time caused similar advance. Estrogen-progesterone interaction was shown by ovulation induced by estrogen treatment in early pregnancy.

A further, indirect effect of estrogen was cholesterol accumulation in the pregnancy corpora lutea (Everett, 1945). This was actually due to the LH surge and, like ovulation, was preventable by hypophysectomy the day after the estrogen treatment. It could also be overridden by excess PRL. Cholesterol accumulation in corpora lutea of the estrous cycle was evidence that they are not totally inactive as commonly supposed.

There is now general agreement that the preovulatory release of LH and FSH is promoted and primarily determined by estrogen. Even in species that do not ovulate spontaneously, the reflexive process is facilitated by estrogen (Sawyer, 1949). The extent to which progesterone and other steroids normally participate is less clear (Fig. 16.6).

Fig. 16.6. From left: Burton L. Baker, 1912–1978 (courtesy of G.E. Erikson); Richard J. Blandau, 1911–   (courtesy of Dr. Blandau); William C. Young, 1899–1965 (courtesy of R.J. Blandau).

The Time of Ovulation

In rabbits, the interval between coitus and ovulation is around 10–11 hr (Smith and White, 1931; Waterman, 1943; and others). Meanwhile, the Graafian follicles display characteristic maturation changes: thecal hyperemia, secondary liquor folliculi, loosening of the cumulus, prominence of corona radiata, and first polar body (Pincus and Enzmann, 1935). These events depend on the induced surge of LH secretion. Hypophysectomy at different times after coitus showed that adequate gonadotropin for ovulation is discharged within 60 min as first shown by Fee and Parkes (confirmed by Smith and White, 1931; Hill, 1934). Hilliard, Hayward, and Sawyer (1964) estimated from indirect evidence that LH secretion rises rapidly and is largely completed within 2 hr post coitum. Modern radioimmunoassay evidence essentially confirms this.

In spontaneously ovulating mammals including humans, it is now well known that ovulation is preceded by a large and time-limited surge of LH analogous to that in rabbits and likewise essential for follicle maturation. In retrospect, this fact is inherent in early information on follicle volumes during the guinea pig cycle (Dempsey, 1937). A steady rise in volume during the luteal phase is succeeded by a rapid growth spurt as estrus approaches. Removal of the corpora lutea results in a premature similar spurt. The preovulatory maturation changes occur only in connection with this rapid growth. Myers, Young, and Dempsey (1936) concluded that the maturation processes correspond in time to onset of behavioral estrus. In the rat, Boling, Blandau, Soderwall, and Young (1941) somewhat similarly related follicle maturation to the occurrence of heat. Since rats' activity rhythms are strongly governed by environmental light and darkness, it is not surprising that their ovulation time is similarly influenced by lighting. Dependence of ovulation in rats on an acute spontaneous surge of LH on the preceding day was indicated by a series of pharmacological studies comparing rabbits and rats (Sawyer, Markee, Hollinshead, Townsend, and Everett, 1947–1953; Everett, Sawyer, and Markee, 1949–1953).

In rabbits the ovulation reflex was blocked by rapid intravenous injection of Dibenamine (antiadrenergic) within 1 min after coitus. Atropine (anticholinergic) also blocked if injected even sooner. The possibility that these same drugs could block ovulation in rats was tested and found true. On the afternoon of proestrus, intravenous injection of Dibenamine around 1400 hr usually prevented the ovulation expected early next morning. Massive subcutaneous injection of atropine at 1400 hr also blocked. Postponed injection of either drug until 1600 hr failed to block, thus delimiting a 2-hr "critical period" for a spontaneous event analogous to that provoked reflexly in rabbits. Dibenamine and atropine also prevented induction of ovulation by progesterone in cyclic rats and by estrogen in pregnant rats. Blockade of cyclic ovulation was also accomplished with Nembutal during the proestrous critical period; this led to demonstration of 24-hr periodicity in the "LH-release apparatus" of this species. Several other drugs were later shown to be effective ovulation blockers, notably morphine, chlorpromazine, and reserpine (Barraclough and Sawyer, 1955, 1957).

Ovulation time in the human menstrual cycle was for a long time a great enigma, chiefly because of the absence of behavioral estrus and the misconception that menstruation corresponds to proestrus. Critical investigation by E. Allen, G.W. Corner, C.G. Hartman, F.L. Hisaw, G. van Wagenen, and others resolved the problem, with strong evidence for ovulation near midcycle. Menstruation was seen to result from withdrawal of estrogen or progesterone secretion, not their increase (Bartelmez, 1937; Hisaw et al., 1937; Markee, 1940) (Fig. 16.7). The rhesus monkey was especially useful in this work. Both the biological evidence and assays of blood and urine established the marked rise of estrogen in advance of ovulation (E. Allen et al., 1936, for example). Modern evidence shows clearly that the rising estrogen promotes the great preovulatory surge of gonadotropins in primates as in other animals.

THE TESTIS

A partial list of American anatomists contributing fundamentally to biology of the testis includes J.M. Bedford, A.V. Boccabella, A.K. Christensen, Y. Clermont, D.W. Fawcett, C.W. Hooker, R.O. Greep, J.H. Leathem, C.P. Leblond, C.R.

Fig. 16.7. From left: George W. Bartelmez, 1867–1956 (courtesy of G.E. Erikson); Joseph E. Markee, 1904–1970 (courtesy of Mrs. Markee); Carl G. Hartman, 1879–1968 (courtesy of G.E. Erikson).

Fig. 16.8. From left: Warren O. Nelson, 1906–1964 (courtesy of D.J. Patanelli); James H. Leathem, 1911–1978 (courtesy of D. Matt); Yves W. Clermont, 1926–   (courtesy of Dr. Clermont).

Moore, W.O. Nelson, D. Price, E.C. Roosen-Runge, M.E. Simpson, P.E. Smith, E. Steinberger, L.J. Wells, and W.C. Young (Fig. 16.8).

The dual function of the testis in producing sperm and maintaining masculine characteristics was long recognized. The early view that the interstitial (Leydig) cells produce the male hormone has been fully documented. Histological modifications in these cells with age and functional changes were reported by Hooker (1944, 1948) in bull testes and by Nelson and Heller (1945) in human biopsies. Electron microscopy disclosed fine structure of the cells to be typical of steroid-secreting tissue (Christensen and Fawcett, 1961, 1963; Fawcett and Burgos, 1960). By separating living seminiferous tubules and interstitial tissue, Christensen and Mason (1960) showed that while the tubules have some ability to produce androgen from precursor, the capacity for this is much greater in Leydig cells.

For the cytological details and dynamics of spermatogenesis in the seminiferous tubules, we are indebted to Clermont and Leblond (1955), Clermont (1962), and Roosen-Runge (1956).

A series of studies by C.R. Moore and associates (1919 ff.) established several fundamentals of testis physiology. Effects of castration and administration of testis extracts on both soma and psyche were noted. Study of the biology of the scrotum disclosed that elevated temperature as in cryptorchidism inhibits spermatogenesis. On the other hand, relatively little impairment followed ligation of the duct system. Several assay methods were devised that became useful in subsequent purification of testis hormones. Evaluation of the effects of testis extracts in intact and hypophysectomized animals led Moore and Price (1932) to their hypothesis of pituitary-gonad reciprocity.

Differential effects of urinary gonadotropins on androgen secretion and spermatogenesis were noted in rats by Smith et al. (1934). Evans et al. (1934) and Greep et al. (1936) determined that FSH stimulates the seminiferous tubules selectively, while LH (interstitial cell-stimulating hormone, ICSH) acts on the Leydig cells. Direct action of androgens in support of spermatogenesis was explored by Nelson and Merkel (1937). The process could be sustained for months in hypophysectomized rats (Nelson, 1941), although the age at the time of the operation was important (Leathem, 1942). Smith (1944) confirmed the effect in hypophysectomized monkeys.

SEXUAL DIFFERENTIATION

Gonad Development, Origin of Germ Cells, and Determination of Gonadal Sex

The literature in this area includes the names of many American anatomists: T.H. Bissonette, R.J. Blandau, R.K. Burns, A. Buyse, L.V. Domm, K.L. Duke, N.B. Everett, M.J. Guthrie, G.T. Hargitt, R.R. Humphrey, F.R. Lillie, H.W. Mossman, D.L. Odor, B.H. Willier, and E. Witschi (Fig. 16.9). Although primordial germ cells have been traced from the embryonic gut wall to definitive locations in the gonads, the fundamental question remains as to whether germ cells may later arise anew from somatic cells (cf. N.B. Everett, 1945; Mossman and Duke, 1973).

The effect of sex hormones on differentiation of sex characteristics is illustrated by a remarkable experiment of nature, the free-martin in cattle. Lillie (1916–1917) was among the first to draw attention to this condition, in which vascular anastomosis between male and female twins results in transformation of ovaries into testes with accompanying male ducts. Lillie (1923), Bissonnette (1924–1928), and Willier (1921) examined the developmental history of the free-martin. Sex reversals were studied in other species (notably by Burns (1930 ff.), Humphrey (1929 ff.), Willier (1924 ff.), and Witschi (1927 ff.) (Fig. 16.10). Techniques used were parabiosis of amphibian larvae, chorioallantoic grafts of gonads in birds, or injection of hormones of the opposite sex (cf. Burns, 1961).

Sexual Differentiation of CNS-AP System

Functional differences of male and female pituitaries reported by many workers include a much greater gonadotropic potency of the male gland and certain

Fig. 16.9. From left: Frank R. Lillie, 1870–1947 (courtesy of National Academy of Sciences); Carl R. Moore, 1892–1955 (courtesy of National Academy of Sciences); George T. Hargitt, 1881–1971 (courtesy of K. Duke).

Fig. 16.10. From left: Emil Witschi, 1890–1971 (courtesy of D.C. Johnson); Benjamin H. Willier, 1890–1972 (courtesy of National Academy of Sciences); Harland W. Mossman, 1898– (courtesy of Dr. Mossman).

differences of cytology. Ovaries transplanted into adult male hosts rarely, if ever, luteinize (Goodman, 1934; Moore, 1919; Smelser, 1933). C.A. Pfeiffer (1936) in a classic paper demonstrated that the rat AP at birth is bipotential, its adult status depending on the presence at the time of an ovary or testis. Males castrated at birth were able as adults to luteinize ovarian transplants, while testis transplants to newborn females made them unable to luteinize, the ovaries becoming poly-follicular and the vaginas continuously cornified. This phenomenon was later analyzed by Barraclough and Gorski (1961), demonstrating that the masculinizing ability of androgen is confined in rats to the perinatal period, that its influence is on the hypothalamus rather than on the AP, and that it involves aromatization of testosterone. The perinatal steroid action leads to the development of a sexually dimorphic nucleus in the preoptic area, larger in the male rat brain than in the female (Gorski, 1980).

It has been necessary arbitrarily to omit consideration of several areas of the biology of reproduction and general endocrinology. Much more could have been written about the areas that were included, especially the luteal phase of the ovarian cycle, the special phenomenon of pseudopregnancy, and control of the pregnancy corpus luteum. A survey of the literature on the functional anatomy of the endometrium would include the contributions of G.W. Bartelmez, G.H. Daron, and J.E. Markee. Blandau's work on ovum transport is classic. The placenta and mammary gland received much attention from F.J. Agate, E.W. Dempsey, A.C. Enders, H.W. Mossman, H.A. Padykula, E.M. Ramsey, and G.B. Wislocki. Out-standing work on the thyroid was contributed by N.J. Nadler and C.P. Leblond. Investigators of the parathyroid include B.L. Baker, E. De Robertis, and R.O. Greep. The cytophysiology of pancreatic islets owes much to P.E. Lacy, A. Lazarow, and T.B. Thomas, as well as to the pioneer study by R.R. Bensley. Among those contributing importantly to the histophysiology of the suprarenal gland were H.S. Bennett, H.W. Deane, R. Gaunt, R.D. Yates, and R.L. Zwemer.

REFERENCES

Allen, E. 1922 The oestrous cycle of the mouse. Am. J. Anat., *30*:297–371.

Corner, G.W. 1942 The Hormones in Human Reproduction. Princeton University Press, Princeton.

Everett, J.W. 1956 Functional corpora lutea maintained for months by autografts of rat hypophysis. Endocrinology, *58*:786–796.

Everett, J.W., and C.H. Sawyer 1950 A 24-hour periodicity in the "LH-release apparatus" of female rats, disclosed by barbiturate sedation. Endocrinology, *47*:198–218.

Green, J.D., and G.W. Harris 1947 The neurovascular link between the neurohypophysis and adenohypophysis. J. Endocrinol., *5*:136–146.

Greep, R.O. 1974 History of research on anterior hypophysial hormones. Handbook of Physiology, Sec. 7, Endocrinology, Vol. IV, Part 2. American Physiological Society, Washington, D.C., pp. 1–27.

Loeb, L. 1917 The relation of the ovary to the uterus and mammary gland from the experimental aspect. Surg. Gynecol. Obstet., *25*:300–315.

Long, J.A., and H.M. Evans 1922 The Oestrous Cycle in the Rat and Its Associated Phenomena. Memoirs of the University of California, Vol. 6. University of California Press, Berkeley.

Markee, J.E. 1940 Menstruation in intraocular endometrial transplants in the rhesus monkey. Contrib. Embryol., *177*:219–308.

Moore, C.R., and D. Price 1932 Gonad hormone functions and the reciprocal influence between gonads and the hypophysis, with its bearing on sex hormone antagonism. Am. J. Anat., *50*:13–71.

Pfeiffer, C.A. 1936 Sexual differences of the hypophyses and their determination by the gonads. Am. J. Anat., *58*:195–225.

Sawyer, C.H., J.E. Markee, and B.F. Townsend 1949 Cholinergic and adrenergic components in the neurohumoral control of the release of LH in the rabbit. Endocrinology, *44*:18–37.

Smith, P.E. 1936 Postponed pituitary homotransplants into the region of the hypophysial portal circulation in hypophysectomized female rats. Endocrinology, *73*:793–806.

Smith, P.E., and E.T. Engle 1927 Experimental evidence regarding the role of the anterior pituitary in the development and regulation of the genital system. Am. J. Anat., *40*:159–217.

Stockard, C.R., and G.N. Papanicolaou 1917 The existence of a typical oestrous cycle in the guinea-pig with a study of its histological and physiological changes. Am. J. Anat. *22*:225–283.

Wislocki, G.B., and L.S. King 1936 The permeability of the hypophysis and hypothalamus to vital dyes, with a study of the hypophyseal portal supply. Am. J. Anat., *58*:421–472.

Chapter 17

NEUROENDOCRINOLOGY

B. Scharrer

Neuroendocrinology, i.e., the study of the close interaction between the two systems of integration, the nervous and the endocrine, became established as a discipline in its own right in the early 1960s. Its origins may be traced back to two morphological studies, one by Carl C. Speidel (1919) on "gland cells of internal secretion" in the caudal spinal cord of skates, and one by Ernst Scharrer (1928) (Fig. 17.1) on "neurosecretory cells" in the hypothalamus of a teleost fish. The special significance of Scharrer's contribution was that, at the outset, he proposed an endocrine role for these unusual hypothalamic neurons in relationship with the activity of the pituitary gland, and formulated the rationale for what later was referred to as the neuroendocrine axis.

However, the bold conclusion, drawn from a cytological discovery, that certain neurons may signal to other cells by means of hormonal, i.e., blood-borne messenger substances, quite understandably met with considerable opposition. For the great majority of contemporary investigators, among them S. W. Ranson, who with his collaborators (J.C. Hinsey, W.R. Ingram, H.W. Magoun, and others) was engaged in an intensive study of diabetes insipidus experimentally induced by hypothalamic lesions and severance of the hypothalamo-hypophyseal tract, this revolutionary concept was "apparently too much" (Ingram, W.R. 1975 A personal neuroscientific development with remarks on other events and people. In: Pioneers in Neuroendocrinology I. J. Meites, B.T. Donovan, S.M. McCann, eds. Plenum Press, New York, pp. 175–191).

Speidel did not pursue his initial discovery any further, but for E. and B. Scharrer the search for the functional role of the phenomenon of neurosecretion became a lifetime endeavor; and for many years they had the territory practically to themselves. In the early phase of this search, a broadly based comparative approach revealed the universality of peptide-producing neurosecretory centers throughout the animal kingdom and laid to rest recurrent criticisms suggesting their putative pathological nature. Moreover, these studies on cytophysiological correlates in vertebrates (E. Scharrer) and invertebrates (B. Scharrer) demonstrated a remarkable degree of analogy between two neuroendocrine organ complexes, the hypothalamic-hypophyseal system of vertebrates and the brain-corpus cardiacum-corpus allatum system of insects. The heuristic value of the analysis of such parallelisms continued to be apparent also in subsequent ultrastructural, physiological, and biochemical studies.

Initial experimental attempts to probe into the functional role of neurosecretion suffered from the inadequacy of the methods then available, and progress was slow. However, in due course, stepwise advances resulting from the combined efforts of an increasing number of investigators led to the solution of the enigma and firmly established the central role of blood-borne neuropeptides in providing a link between the brain and the endocrine system. By the same token, the existence and functional significance of afferent hormonal signals to the central nervous system were clarified.

As the annals of this Association illustrate, many of these contributions were made by anatomists, and it is fascinating to contemplate where this field of research would stand today without the essential knowledge of the structural parameters of neuroendocrine interactions. In keeping with its specific objective, this brief retrospective narrative will focus on contributions by members of the Association dealing with the elucidation of neuroglandular function and neuroendocrine interaction. No comprehensive historical treatment of the subject should be expected, and some overlap with the material covered in the chapter entitled "Endocrinology and Reproductive Biology" by Everett and Sawyer will be unavoidable.

Fig. 17.1. Ernst Scharrer.

Several approaches used in the search for structure-function relationships in neurosecretory systems have yielded much significant information. The first, exemplified by the early work of E. Scharrer and his collaborators (D.C. Billenstien, J.P. Hagedoorn, T.F. Leveque, S.L. Palay, and A.B. Rothballer) at the light-microscopic level, revealed distinctive cytological changes in hypothalamic neurosecretory cells correlated with different physiological and experimentally altered states (e.g., castration, section of the hypophyseal stalk, water deprivation, stress, explantation of neurosecretory tissue). The results provided persuasive indirect evidence for a role of neurosecretion in the control of reproductive function and of water metabolism.

The next approach, made possible by the advent of electron microscopy, added much to the structural and functional characterization of neurosecretory neurons of vertebrates and invertebrates. S.L. Palay was one of the first to examine the sites of synthesis and release of their secretory products at the ultrastructural level. His results, and those of W. Bargmann, D. Bodian, E. De Robertis, and D. Duncan in various vertebrates, as well as those obtained in insects (B. Scharrer), showed the neurosecretory material to consist of strikingly electron-dense, membrane-bounded granules, easily identified and localized. The subsequent demonstration of their origin in packaged form from the Golgi apparatus (E. Scharrer, H. Bern) and their axonal release by exocytosis (e.g., B. Scharrer among others) provided further evidence in support of a close similarity with the products of protein-secreting gland cells. Other studies were concerned with the examination of structural correlates of degeneration and regeneration of neurosecretory neurons and of the axonal transport of their secretory products (H.D. Dellmann).

A further, equally rewarding step forward in the analysis of peptide-secreting neurons and their distribution in the nervous system occurred with the development of histochemical procedures. R.J. Barrnett (1954) demonstrated protein-bound disulfide (cystine) in neurosecretory products and used its presence for their identification in tissues fixed under varying experimental conditions, e.g., following stress. The more recent pioneering contributions of L.A. Sternberger (Fig. 17.2) to the development and refinement of immunocytochemical methods resulted in major advances in the chemical identification of a number of neuronal peptides as well as their sites of origin and action. His peroxidase-antiperoxidase method has proved very productive in the hands of numerous investigators, among them F.E. Bloom, R.P. Elde, E.O. Eränkö, H.J. Karten, K.M. Knigge, H. Kobayashi, G.P. Kozlowski, P. Petrusz, A.J. Silverman, and their coworkers. The demonstration, by such techniques, of the wide distribution of vertebrate-type neuropeptides in the neuroendocrine systems of invertebrates (e.g., B. Scharrer, in collaboration with B.L. Hansen and G.N. Hansen) has revealed their long evolutionary history and structural stability.

HYPOTHALAMIC-NEUROHYPOPHYSEAL SYSTEM

It is interesting to underscore at this point that the first breakthrough revealing hormonal functions attributable to certain hypothalamic neurosecretory cells was made possible, if not by immunochemistry, at least by an advance in the selective stainability of proteinaceous cellular products. In 1949, W. Bargmann (Fig. 17.3), using the chrome-alum hematoxylin phloxin technique introduced by W. Gomori for other purposes, was able to trace neurosecretory material from its perikaryonal site of origin in the hypothalamus to its site of release into the circulation in the posterior lobe of the pituitary gland (Bargmann and Scharrer, 1951). The correct interpretation of this topographic relationship established the hypothalamic origin of the "posterior lobe hormones" oxytocin and vasopressin, introduced a new class of neurochemical mediators (neurohormones), and assigned to the posterior lobe the rank of a neurohemal storage and release center (Bargmann and Scharrer, 1951). Experimental documentation for the intraneuronal transport of such neuron-derived hormonal messengers to their release sites in analogous neurohemal organs located outside of the brain was provided by W. Hild (Fig. 17.4) in vertebrates and by B. Scharrer in invertebrates. In both cases, the material became accumulated proximal and depleted distal to the level of surgical interruption of the neurosecretory pathway. Hild further showed a clear correlation between the functional potency of tissue extracts determined by pharmacological tests and the amount of selectively stainable neurosecretory material present in the tissues under investigation.

Exciting as these developments were, they did not provide a satisfactory answer to the long-debated question as to why neurons should deviate so profoundly from the norm to function as gland cells of internal secretion. The type of direct control over "terminal target cells" exemplified by the antidiuretic effect of vasopressin began to make sense when information on the evolutionary history of neuropeptides became available. Such first-order neurosecretory activities seem to be carryovers from a time in the distant past, when organisms lacking "regular" glands of internal secretion had to rely on neurons for supplying all of the chemical signals required for integrative control.

HYPOTHALAMIC-ADENOHYPOPHYSEAL SYSTEM

A new and far-reaching phase in the elucidation of the raison d'être for neurosecretory phenomena in higher forms began with the realization that the existence of an endocrine apparatus proper requires mechanisms for its effective

Fig. 17.2.   Ludwig A. Sternberger.

Fig. 17.3.   Wolfgang Bargmann.

neural control (Scharrer and Scharrer, 1963). As projected by E. Scharrer (1952), the dual (neural and glandular) properties of neurosecretory neurons make them eminently suited for this task. Intensive examination of their mode of operation in bridging the gap between neural and endocrine regulatory centers now became a major concern of the emerging discipline of neuroendocrinology (Szentágothai et al., 1962). Stimulatory and inhibitory neurohormones ("releasing" or "regulating factors") governing gonadotropic, thyrotropic, adrenocorticotropic, and other mechanisms were identified and their sites of production localized in hypothalamic centers, e.g., the arcuate nucleus. The median eminence was recognized as the neurohemal release organ for these hypophysiotropic neurohormones [R.A. Gorski, J.P. Hagedoorn, K.M. Knigge, H. Kobayashi, B.S.G. Monroe, and J. Szentágothai (Fig. 17.5)] and the hypophyseal portal system, analyzed by G. Wislocki, E.W. Dempsy, J.W. Everett, J.C. Hinsey, and others, as their "semiprivate" pathway.

Much of the credit for the elucidation of this vascular hypothalamic-adenohypophyseal link is due to the work of G.W. Harris, who, in collaboration with J.D. Green and D. Jacobsohn, demonstrated in 1955 that reproductive function is interrupted by stalk section and restored after the regeneration of the portal vessels. Further advances in the clarification of the neuroendocrine control of reproductive phenomena, including the rich contributions by J.W. Everett and C.H. Sawyer and their collaborators, are reported in greater detail in their chapter in this volume.

Hypophysiotropic factors were shown to play an essential role also in the control of other adenohypophyseal, incuding thyrotropic, adrenocorticotropic, and metabolic, functions (K.M. Knigge, H. Kobayashi). Many of these contributions concern neuroendocrine control systems in non-mammalian vertebrates, e.g., birds (A. Oksche, C.L. Ralph) and amphibians (S.A. D'Angelo, W. Etkin). Detailed studies on the brain-pituitary-thyroid system in the control of amphibian metamorphosis were contributed by W. Etkin and S.A. D'Angelo. The inhibitory neural control of the tadpole pars intermedia observed by W. Etkin was shown to be paralleled by that of the corpus allatum of insects by B. Scharrer. The dependency of corticotropic as well as thyrotropic hypophyseal activities on neurohormonal signals was demonstrated in elegant experiments by M. Nikitovitch-Winer in which hypophyseal homotransplants, placed close to the brain, regained their functional capacity following revascularization.

An unforeseen variant by which peptidergic neural signals may address endocrine cells at close range was observed in the mammalian pars intermedia (W. Bargmann) and in the corpus allatum of insects (B. Scharrer). This close "synaptoid" relationship ("neurosecretomotor junction," H. Bern) led Bargmann to introduce the term "peptidergic neuron," which has now acquired a much larger dimension. What these and additional ultrastructural observations indicated was that neurosecretory neurons are able to communicate by several alternate, non-neurohormonal mechanisms, some of which come very close to the pattern of classical synaptic intervention.

Fig. 17.4. Walther Hild.

Fig. 17.5. János Szentágothai.

A number of studies dealt with the variety of exteroceptive and interoceptive signals determining the activity of hypophysiotropic hypothalamic centers. The analysis of the pathways transmitting this information was carried out, for example, by electrical stimulation of discrete hypothalamic centers (S.A. D'Angelo, C.H. Sawyer), by small lesions or deafferentation (R.A. Gorski, N. Halmi), and by implantation of endocrine tissue or hormone crystals into certain brain areas (R.A. Gorski, K.M. Knigge, C.H. Sawyer, J. Szentágothai, among others). Important examples of exteroceptive factors contributing to the body of information which, in integrated form, determines the nature and degree of hypophysiotropic activity are olfactory and photic stimuli. The rhinencephalic pathway conveying olfactory stimuli to the hypothalamus was examined by J.D. Green and C.H. Sawyer.

The general concept of photoneuroendocrine systems operating in the control of a number of autonomic functions, and the involvement of a component of the optic system distinct from the apparatus for vision, were introduced by E. Scharrer (1964). The influence of photoperiodic stimuli on a number of physiological activities was demonstrated by several investigators, e.g., B.V.Critchlow, J.W. Everett, R. Greep, and H. Kobayashi. As carefully recorded by A. Oksche (Fig. 17.6), such stimuli may be received via a retino-hypothalamic projection to the suprachiasmatic nucleus by the pineal organs and by deep encephalic photoreceptive areas. Major contributions to the structural and functional characterization of the pineal gland in its relation to the hypothalamic-hypophyseal system were made by W. Bargmann, W. Hild, D.E. Kelly, A. Oksche, W.B. Quay, and E. Scharrer.

AFFERENT HORMONAL SIGNALS TO THE NERVOUS SYSTEM

As to the second channel of communication correlating the activities of the two systems of integration, that between the endocrine apparatus and the nervous system, several important functional relationships have been demonstrated. Afferent directives to neural centers by circulating hormones play an important role in early development and continue to operate throughout adult life.

The presence or absence of androgen at the perinatal stage was demonstrated to be the determining factor for the differentiation of the sex-related patterns of hypophyseal gonadotropin release as early as 1936 by C.A. Pfeiffer. Subsequently, the primary effector site for this permanent organizational effect of gonadal steroids was recognized to be the hypothalamus (R.W. Goy, C. H. Phoenix, W. C. Young). The hormone-controlled functional differentiation into male versus female systems also applies to the establishment of sex-related behavior patterns, and is paralleled by the development of morphological differences (D.W. Pfaff, C.D. Toran-Allerand). A striking example is the sexually dimorphic nucleus in the preoptic region of the rat, discovered by R.A. Gorski.

A number of additional studies have demonstrated an effect of thyroid hormones and corticosteroids on neurogenesis and on the maintenance of certain neural structures, e.g., the mesencephalic nucleus of the trigeminal nerve (M. Hamburgh, J.J. Kollros, J.M. Lauder, I. Pesetsky, P. Weiss). The perinatal presence of thyroid hormone was shown to be required also for the development of certain behavioral responses, e.g., home orientation in rats (M. Hamburgh and co-workers).

In the adult animal, afferent signals reaching the brain by circulating hormones have two distinctive roles to play. 1) They are part of the three-step feedback mechanism by which their release from their sites of production is controlled. This form of biological regulation permits the integration of information on hormone

Fig. 17.6.   Andreas Oksche.

Fig. 17.7.   Mary Weitzman.

titers in the circulation with other, e.g., exteroceptive, signals so as to result in coordinated hypophysiotropic directives (R.A. Gorski, C.H. Sawyer, J. Szentágothai, and their collaborators). This regulatory system operates in concordance with the simpler (two-step) negative feedback system, exemplified by the reciprocal signaling between gonads and pituitary, discovered by D. Price in 1930 and generally referred to as the Moore-Price theory. 2) The second, temporary (i.e., activational) type of effect of circulating hormones is that on behavior. Much has been learned about the mode of operation by which steroid signals result in sexual as well as sex-determined behavior, e.g., aggressiveness and certain learning skills (E.W. Dempsey, R.A. Gorski, R.W. Goy, D.W. Pfaff, C.H. Phoenix, C.H. Sawyer, W.C. Young). Receptor sites that bind steroids to specific neurons (where interconversion may occur) have been identified (e.g., D.W. Pfaff, W. Stumpf).

The caudal neurosecretory center in the spinal cord, discovered by Speidel, has attracted renewed attention from some "second-generation neurosecretionists," among them H. Bern, who, with his collaborators, made a series of contributions to the structural and functional characterization of the urophysis.

This overview of the history of neuroendocrinological research would be incomplete without grateful acknowledgment of the painstaking efforts of M. Weitzman (Fig. 17.7), who, during the period 1964 to 1980, compiled and distributed *Bibliographia Neuroendocrinologica,* a reference resource of great value to investigators in this field.

The insights gained with accelerating speed in recent years have culminated in discoveries that reach beyond the confines of neuroendocrinology and challenge the tenets of classical neurobiology. Neurohormones and a growing number of additional neuropeptides have been demonstrated in almost every part of the nervous sytem, as well as in several non-neural tissues (e.g., F.E. Bloom, H.J. Karten, P. Petrusz). Recognition of their multiple modes of operation (hormonal, transmitter-like, modulatory) mediated by specific receptors (e.g., G.B. Stefano and B. Scharrer) and of their coexistence with nonpeptidergic neurotransmitters in one and the same neuron (V. Chan-Palay, T. Hökfelt) has widened the spectrum of neurochemical communication. Transitional forms of intercellular signaling have removed the once sharply drawn borderline between "conventional" neurons and other cellular species, especially endocrine cells.

REFERENCES

Bargmann, W., and E. Scharrer 1951 The site of origin of the hormones of the posterior pituitary. Am. Sci., *39*:255–259.

Bloom, F.E., ed. 1980 Peptides: Integrators of Cell and Tissue Function. Society of General Physiologists Series, Raven Press, New York, Vol. 35.

Gainer, H., ed. 1977 Peptides in Neurobiology. Plenum Press, New York.

Meites, J., B.T. Donovan, and S.M. McCann, eds. 1975 Pioneers in Neuroendocrinology I. Plenum Press, New York.

Meites, J., B.T. Donovan, and S.M. McCann, eds. 1978 Pioneers in Neuroendocrinology II. Plenum Press, New York.

Scharrer, B. 1978 Peptidergic neurons: Facts and trends. Gen. Comp. Endocrinol., *34*:50–62.

Scharrer, E. 1952 The general significance of the neurosecretory cell. Scientia, *46*:177–183.

Scharrer, E. 1966 Principles of neuroendocrine integration. In: Endocrines and the Central Nervous System. Res. Publ. Assoc. Nerv. Ment. Dis., *43*:1–35.

Scharrer, E., and B. Scharrer 1963 Neuroendocrinology. Columbia University Press, New York.

Szentágothai, J., B. Flerkó, B. Mess, and B. Halász 1962 Hypothalamic Control of the Anterior Pituitary. An Experimental Morphological Study. Akadémiai Kiadó, Budapest.

Chapter 18

ANATOMISTS' CONTRIBUTIONS TO TISSUE CULTURE

Sergey Fedoroff

In 1953, it was my good fortune to attend the Tissue Culture Course in Cooperstown, New York, offered by the Tissue Culture Association, and to meet most of the American pioneers of tissue culture. At that time only a handful of people were in the field, and they knew each other well. In fact, as we shall see, tissue culture grew out of the work of a tangled web of teachers and their students, husband-wife teams, and friends of friends in other laboratories—a productive network of contacts that spread the technique from one place to another and from one discipline to many. Now, 30-odd years later, tissue culture is no longer black magic but a powerful technique for the study of cells and tissues, the propagation of viruses, cytogenetics, and production of biologically active substances—its uses limited only by the imagination of investigators.

Anatomists played a seminal role in the birth of tissue culture, which can be traced back to the Department of Anatomy in Johns Hopkins Medical School, Baltimore. In 1893, Franklin Paine Mall, a student and lifelong friend of the famous German embryologist and neurohistologist Wilhelm His, became the first Professor of Anatomy at Johns Hopkins. He gathered around him an outstanding group of anatomists: Ross Harrison, Warren and Margaret Lewis, Lewellys Barker, and Florence Sabin.

Soon after arriving at the department in 1896, Ross Harrison (Fig. 18.1) began a series of experiments on the development of nerve fibers, using tadpoles. A vigorously debated question at that time was whether or not the nerve fiber is a product of many cells, as proposed by Schwann, or is an outgrowth of a neuron, the view advanced by Wilhelm His, August Forel, and S. Ramón y Cajal. To resolve the argument, Harrison devised some simple experiments using surgically fragmented frog embryos (Harrison, 1908). Cut pieces were reunited in altered relationships, and the resulting structures were studied. These experiments were based on the observation of Gustav Born (1894) of Breslau that cut parts of a frog embryo would reunite in any manner, provided the freshly cut surfaces were held together for a few hours. First, Harrison demonstrated by removal of the neural crest that Schwann cells are not necessary for the development of nerve fibers; then he showed that if the neural tube is removed, nerve fibers do not develop, although the Schwann cells are left intact. By removing a piece of spinal cord and allowing the gap to be filled with mesenchyme, he showed that nerve fibers could grow into the mesenchyme, that is, into an alien environment.

Although all these experiments indicated that nerve fibers were related to neurons, they did not dissuade believers in Victor Henson's syncytial theory that protoplasmic bridges are left everywhere between dividing cells of the embryo so that at the time when nerves begin to differentiate, a complex system of protoplasmic connections already exists between various parts of the body; those that function as conduction paths are presumed to differentiate into nerve fibers while the rest ultimately disappear. The matter was finally settled by Harrison, who took pieces of embryonic nerve tissue, embedded them in clotted fresh lymph on a coverslip, inverted the coverslip over a hollow slide, and sealed it with paraffin, all done aseptically. He observed the tissue fragments under the microscope from day to day and kept them alive for more than 5 weeks. After 2 days of culturing, he observed fibers extending out from the tissue fragments into the lymph clot. He made sketches of the fibers and observed that in one case the same fiber stretched 20 μm during an interval of 25 min. The end of the fiber resembled the growth cone that he and others had previously observed at the ends of nerve fibers in sections of young embryos. Harrison's interpretation of these observations was ". . . that the nerve-fiber begins as an outflow of hyaline protoplasm from a cell situated within the central nervous system . . . [and] . . . it extends farther and farther from

Fig. 18.1. Ross Granville Harrison (1870–1959). Credited with performing first experiment using tissue culture (1907).

Fig. 18.2.   Montrose Thomas Burrows (1884–1947). Acted as catalyst in early development of tissue culture.

its cell of origin. Retaining its pseudopodia at its distal end, the protoplasm is drawn out into a thread, which becomes the axis-cylinder of a nerve fiber." This rather simple experiment firmly established the neuron theory and at the same time stimulated other scientists to study cells outside the body in tissue culture.

In the conclusion of Harrison's paper (1907), in which he reported his observations on the outgrowth of nerve fibers, he wrote: "The possibility becomes apparent of applying the above method to the study of the influences which act upon a growing nerve. While at present it seems certain that the mere outgrowth of the fibers is largely independent of external stimuli, it is of course probable that in the body of the embryo there are many influences which guide the moving end and bring about contact with the proper end structure. The method here employed may be of value in analyzing these factors." Harrison was interested in tissue culture only inasmuch as it helped him solve the controversy related to the development of the nerve fibers. He must have been surprised that his single experiment eventually catalyzed an enormous expansion in biological experimentation with tissue culture as a fundamental technique.

At the time when Harrison was working on the development of nerve fibers, there was a medical student in Johns Hopkins, Montrose Thomas Burrows (Fig. 18.2), who had become interested in tissue regeneration in Kansas. He had been told that Mall was one of the greatest men in American medicine, and so he had headed for Johns Hopkins, where he frequented the Department of Anatomy, had discussions with Mall, and learned about Harrison's work. When he graduated in 1909, at Mall's suggestion he went to the Rockefeller Institute in New York to work on tissue regeneration. Simon Flexner, at that time Director of the Institute and, incidentally, brother of Abraham Flexner, who revolutionized medical education, heard about Burrows' observation that when he grafted pieces of tissue, cells grew out from the graft and eventually connected it to the rest of the body, indicating that fragments of tissue have the potential of independent growth when separated from the body. Flexner saw the importance of the observation and put Burrows to work with Alexis Carrel, the famous French surgeon who received the Nobel Prize in 1912 for his work in vascular microsurgery. Flexner also arranged for Burrows to spend the summer of 1910 with Ross Harrison, by then Bronson Professor of Comparative Anatomy at Yale University.

Burrows recorded his recollections about his experience at Yale in a letter[1] written to Frederick M. Allen in New York in 1942: "The problem before me was to reproduce the exudate as it occurs in a wound. I must prepare blood plasma first. Then I must add tissue extracts which occur in the wound exudate. Harrison did not uphold my ideas but finally consented to let me repeat his nerve experiment using a warm-blooded animal. . . . When I showed the growing and dividing cells to Harrison he was astonished. Flexner was overjoyed."

While at Yale, Burrows showed that cells of the chick embryo can grow and divide in cultures where they can be observed under the highest powers of the microscope. Burrows worked with Carrel at the Rockefeller Institute for only 2 years (1909–1911), but during this time they cultured various tissues from embryos and adult animals including chickens, rats, mice, dogs, cats, and man. They also observed growth in cultures of malignant tumors (Burrows, 1913).

Burrows then went to Cornell University Medical School where he was Instructor of Anatomy from 1911 to 1915 and eventually settled in private practice in Pasadena, California. There he became interested in cancer and performed complex surgery without formal qualifications in surgery. He was a controversial figure but admired by many.

In 1908 Margaret Reed (Fig. 18.3) was working in Berlin with Dr. Rhoda Erdmann, a pioneer in cell biology and founder of the *Archiv für Experimentelle Zellforschung,* who was cultivating amebas on nutrient agar made with physiological salt solution. Margaret Reed explanted small pieces of bone marrow from a guinea pig into a tube of this medium. She observed that after a few days in the incubator the bone marrow cells formed a membrane-like growth on the surface of the agar and that some nuclei exhibited mitotic figures. Probably this was the first *in vitro* culture of mammalian cells.

Warren Lewis (Fig. 18.4) was a member of Mall's Department of Anatomy in Johns Hopkins Medical School. When Ross Harrison left Hopkins in 1907, Lewis became Mall's senior colleague. In 1910 he married Margaret Reed and they began to work together on the growing of bone marrow in cultures, a continuation of the work that Margaret Reed Lewis had begun in Berlin with Rhoda Erdmann. This was at the same time that Burrows was working at Yale. While others in the field of tissue culture concentrated on growing tissues from various sources, the Lewises concentrated on the study of single cells and to do so they needed special media in which cells would be clearly visible. They tried salt solutions and found that connective tissue cells, endothelium, and other cells would spread out into the

[1] M. T. Burrows, copy of January 26, 1942, letter to Dr. Frederick M. Allen, New York, R. G. Harrison Papers, Archives and Manuscript Department, Sterling Library, Yale University, New Haven, CN.

Fig. 18.3.   Margaret Reed Lewis (1881–1970). First to culture mammalian cells and observe cell division (1908).

fluid from explanted tissue fragments. The Lewises laid the groundwork for chemically defined media, but it was not until 1950 that the first such medium was developed by Joseph F. Morgan and Helen J. Morton in Raymond Parker's laboratory in Toronto, Canada. Parker had been an early coworker of Carrel at the Rockefeller Institute and was a member of the American Association of Anatomists.

Excerpts from two letters give insight into the rather elusive story of the birth of tissue culture. Burrows, in a letter[2] to Dr. Frederick M. Allen, January 26, 1942, wrote: "Mall had the idea that nerves could be grown *in vitro*. He told me that he had planned these experiments in detail and had had Harrison do them. They succeeded as he planned but the cells would not grow and divide in these cultures." In a letter[3] to Professor William Seifriz, October 20, 1928, Harrison had written: "In the year 1907, when I was deeply interested in the study of the development of nerve fibers, I hit upon the idea of growing embryonic tissues outside of the body and thereby was able to show that embryonic nerve cells formed long protoplasmic processes which could be identified with nerve fibers within the embryo. This has often been stated to have been the origin of tissue

---

[2] See Footnote 1.

[3] R. G. Harrison, copy of October 20, 1928, letter to Professor William Seifriz, Philadelphia, R. G. Harrison Papers, Archives and Manuscript Department, Sterling Library, Yale University, New Haven, CN.

culture." Further along he wrote: "Of course others before me had the idea of isolating tissues and studying their behavior. The botanist Haberlandt did, however, publish in 1902 a remarkable paper based on the study of plant cells isolated in culture media. This was unknown to me at the time my work was published . . .". There is no doubt that it was the logical progression of Harrison's work on the development of nerve fibers that led him to the crucial experiment on growing nervous tissue in cultures. It is possible that Mall, who was deeply interested in nervous tissue, and who was a student and friend of Wilhelm His, the original postulater of the neuron theory, had some suggestions for Harrison's work; but it was the whole environment and interest in nervous tissue in Mall's department that led to the birth of tissue culture, in which Harrison, Margaret and Warren Lewis, and Burrows participated (Bang, 1977).

In addition to individuals, mostly anatomists, who contributed to tissue culture's origins, the AAA played an important role in providing a forum for the early papers and eventually for nurturing and encouraging the formation of the Tissue Culture Association (TCA).

During World War II, AAA suspended its annual meetings for 3 years; the meetings were resumed in 1946 at Western Reserve University in Cleveland. Nine

Fig. 18.4. Warren Harmon Lewis (1870–1964). A colleague of Ross Harrison. Pioneer in chemically defined nutrients in tissue culture.

Fig. 18.5. Keith Porter (left) receiving Medal of Merit from Don Fawcett (right) during dedication ceremonies of the W. Alton Jones Cell Science Center on June 9, 1971.

papers dealing with tissue culture were presented, and they were purposely grouped in one session. Among the papers, one by Keith Porter (Fig. 18.5) stood out. Porter was at that time working with cultures of chick embryo in the Rockefeller Institute. He realized that tissue culture preparations are ideal for electron-microscopic examination of cell structure, particularly in areas where the cytoplasm is flattened. Using one of the first electron microscopes in the United States, he obtained micrographs of the ultrastructure of various cell organelles. The micrographs had exceptional clarity, unobtainable with the light microscope. In addition, his micrographs showed new structural detail in the cytoplasm, including the netlike pattern of extremely fine canals or chains of vesicles now known as endoplasmic reticulum. George O. Gey (Fig. 18.6), a longtime associate of Warren and Margaret Lewis, who was directing a tissue culture laboratory in the Department of Surgery at Johns Hopkins Medical School, heard Porter's paper during that AAA meeting. He was excited by Porter's observations and, on returning home, wrote a letter to Charles Pomerat (Fig. 18.7), Professor of Anatomy, University of Texas, Medical Branch at Galveston, proposing that a submission be made to the Committee on Growth of the National Research Council advocating establishment of a panel on tissue culture. Pomerat sent Gey's letter to Keith Porter who then wrote to Pomerat suggesting that to avoid the panel being controlled by the Committee on Growth, perhaps they should ask for an outright grant from the Committee. Porter wrote that he would be in favor of a new society provided it would disseminate information and techniques, prepare a bibliography, and assume responsibility for standardization and quality of salt solutions and frozen dried plasma and serum; in other words, he wanted an organization similar to the Commission of Biological Stains.

As a result of negotiations, a conference organized by the Committee on Growth was held at Hershey, Pennsylvania, November 11–13, 1946, attended by 40 people, including tissue culturists and experts on the growth and nutritional requirements of microorganisms, unicellular organisms, parasites, and higher animals. The conference opened with an address by Harrison entitled, "The Historical Development of Tissue Culture." After the conference, a group of participants established an informal group, the Tissue Culture Commission, having as its purpose assistance to workers in tissue culture. Its chairman was Keith Porter; secretary was Margaret R. Murray; and the executive consisted of George O. Gey, Duncan C. Hetherington, and Charles M. Pomerat. All five were members of AAA. Murray was Professor of Anatomy at the College of Physicians and Surgeons, Columbia University, and Hetherington was Professor of Anatomy at Duke University.

Pomerat arranged with Eliot R. Clark, secretary-treasurer of AAA, for papers on tissue culture to again be grouped in one program at the 1947 meeting, and he suggested loose ties with AAA. After that meeting Pomerat wrote to Wilton Earle, a member of AAA and head of a tissue culture laboratory at the National Institutes of Health, that he had been remiss about organizing and circulating information to tissue culturists; only four papers, one demonstration, and one time-lapse movie on tissue culture had been presented at the AAA meeting at McGill University in Montreal in 1947.

On September 15, 1947, Pomerat[4] wrote to Dr. Normand Hoerr, the new secretary-treasurer of AAA:

Fig. 18.6. George Otto Gey (1899–1970). Enthusiastic and energetic contribution to science of tissue culture, organization of TCA, establishment of W. Alton Jones Cell Science Center, and development of HeLa cell line.

---

[4]C.M. Pomerat, copy of September 15, 1947, letter to Dr. Normand Hoerr, Cleveland, Tissue Culture Archives, Tissue Culture Association, Gaithersburg, MD.

Fig. 18.7. Charles Marc Pomerat (1905–1964). Pioneer of tissue culture. Master of time-lapse cinematography of nervous tissue cultures.

Two years ago, a group of workers who regularly employ tissue culture techniques in their researches, gathered at the Cleveland meetings of the Association of Anatomists and presented their papers as a group during one of the regular sessions. The kindness of the Association's officers in permitting this arrangement was in part responsible for subsequent events in this field. As you may know, a Tissue Culture Commission has been born which gives great promise of helping with developments in the study of "living anatomy". It is hoped that the Association will again be willing to permit a grouping of papers from the tissue culture field within a section or adjacent sessions. Dr. Murray has discussed the question with Dr. Detwilder, who urged that we communicate with you. She has also suggested that all of the members of the Tissue Culture Commission's executive committee are members of the Association of Anatomists. Of the 94 American and Canadian members of the Commission as a whole, 30 are members of the Association. It is expected that the majority of the group would attend the Madison meetings in any case.

In discussions regarding similar arrangements in previous years, tissue culture workers agreed that it would not be advisable in future planning to segregate tissue culture reports from their proper fields within the wide scope of functional anatomy. However, at this time a sort of renaissance is going on in the tissue culture field and it does seem that profit might be derived from joint discussion leading to standardisation of techniques and basic principles. Should the Association be willing to shepherd the group during this phase of development, the Commission would certainly agree that in time tissue culture studies directed toward neurological, haematological, and other fields be presented in their proper sections.

I do hope that the executives of the committee may see fit to help the Commission in evolving solid foundations.

In this letter Pomerat envisaged the future course of tissue culture. It had begun as a technique and had quickly permeated all fields of biological sciences. His idea was that tissue culture would for a time be the focus of meetings of various groups with common interests in the new technique, then the groups would disperse to their various disciplines in which tissue culture was used. He probably didn't foresee the blossoming of a new organization centered on tissue culture itself.

The American Association of Anatomists agreed to have all tissue culture papers in one session at its meeting in Madison, Wisconsin, in 1948. Twelve papers and two demonstrations on tissue culture were presented. The Tissue Culture Commission again met in conjunction with AAA, and its first general meeting was held with about 30 members attending. Various committees were set up, among them a summer course committee and a testing laboratory committee. Subsequently, the Constitution Committee recommended that the organization be known as the Tissue Culture Association. Its purpose was "to foster the collection and dissemination of information concerning the maintenance and experimental use of tissue cells *in vitro* and the evaluation and development of procedures therefore."

The next general meeting, still as the Tissue Culture Commission, was held at the AAA meeting in Philadelphia on April 14, 1949. A year later during the AAA meeting in New Orleans, two sessions were devoted to tissue culture; 19 papers and two demonstrations were presented. The Tissue Culture Association, as such, held its first business meeting and elected officers: President, George O. Gey; Vice President, Dale R. Coman; Secretary-Treasurer, Duncan C. Hetherington; Corresponding Secretary, Mary S. Parshley; Member-at-large, Charles M. Pomerat; and Retiring President of the Commission, Keith R. Porter. Again, all but one member of the executive belonged to AAA. The TCA continued to meet with AAA until 1957. The early work on tissue culture was presented at AAA meetings, and many scientists from non-anatomical fields were drawn to the meetings and became members.

When the Tissue Culture Commission was formed, it had three major objectives: to take steps to provide common tissue culture media of guaranteed quality, which could be distributed from a central source; to prepare a comprehensive bibliography of published works on tissue culture, with thorough cross-indexing; and to establish a course to teach tissue culture. Members of AAA played key roles in fulfilling these aims. Keith Porter was instrumental in negotiating for space at the Sloan-Kettering Institute in New York for a tissue culture media testing laboratory. Its first supervisory committee consisted of three AAA members: Gey; Porter; and Mary S. Parshley, Research Associate, Department of Pathology, College of Physicians and Surgeons, Columbia University. The laboratory functioned with varying degrees of success and at the end of 3 years (1952) moved to the Department of Anatomy at Duke University with Professor Duncan Hetherington as director. Hetherington developed a method for freeze-drying components of culture media. The work of this laboratory was gradually taken over by the ever-growing biological industry. At present the TCA maintains a committee on standards that works closely with industry and keeps a watchful eye on standards of quality.

At the same time Margaret Murray, Professor of Anatomy, had a laboratory in the Department of Surgery at the College of Physicians and Surgeons at Columbia University. She assumed responsibility for preparing a bibliography of tissue culture literature, and in 1953 Academic Press published two volumes that covered tissue culture literature from 1884 to 1950 and contained 15,000 citations of original articles and 86,000 entries. The explosion of tissue culture literature was so rapid that Margaret Murray with her very limited staff could hardly cope. She and her group continued to catalogue references until 1960; these were never published but were, however, recorded on 11 reels of film that are now in the possession of TCA.

Right after the second decennial Conference of TCA in Bedford, Pennsylvania, in 1956, the executive made an arrangement with the National Library of Medicine to prepare the bibliography, and it was published beginning with the literature of 1965 and continuing until 1980. In 1978 Keith Porter presided over the meeting of the executive of the TCA at which it was decided to discontinue publication of the bibliography. By that time tissue culture had become such an integral part of all biomedical disciplines, and retrieval and indexing of literature had so far advanced, that a separate tissue culture bibliography had, in fact, outlived its usefulness.

The dispersal of the art, then the science, of tissue culture from a small group of cognoscenti to an increasing number of scientists who saw its potential is an important part of this story. The first formal course in tissue culture was offered in Raymond Parker's laboratory in Toronto, Canada, in July 1948. Sixteen persons participated and among them was Don Fawcett (Fig. 18.5), later to become Professor of Anatomy in Harvard Medical School. Of the 16 faculty members, 11 belonged to AAA. From Toronto the course moved to Cooperstown, New York. It was held at the Mary Imogene Bassett Hospital, affiliated with Columbia University, and was directed by John Hanks, Professor of Microbiology, Harvard University. In 1950, Don Fawcett assisted Hanks with the course and remained closely associated with it during subsequent years. By the end of the 1954 course, the hospital could no longer provide the space required; therefore the course was moved to the University of Colorado in Denver, where it was given from 1956 to 1959, and then to the University of Wisconsin in Madison, where it was given from 1960 to 1964. Throughout these years Charles Pomerat and William G. Cooper, Professor of Anatomy, University of Colorado, were primarily responsible for the success of the course.

It was the dream of George Gey that one day the course would have a permanent home somewhere in the New England States, and he was a vociferous and enthusiastic promoter of the idea. At the conclusion of the course in Madison in 1964, Gey and a few of us who had taught the course determined to find a permanent place for it. The dream began to come true when Patricia Edgerton, who worked in Gey's laboratory, introduced him to her mother, Mrs. W. Alton Jones. Mrs. Jones was looking for a project to provide a suitable memorial to her husband who had died in an air crash in New York. Eventually, TCA received a gift from Mrs. Jones of 34 acres of land at Lake Placid, New York, and a beautiful new building planned by members of the Association. The dedication ceremonies of the W. Alton Jones Cell Science Center at Lake Placid were held on June 9, 1971. Sadly, George Gey did not live to see that day; but to recognize his part in the realization of the Center and to pay tribute to the never-ending help of his wife, the library there is named the George and Margaret Gey Library. The Center was committed to offer courses in tissue culture, but the program was discontinued in 1982 when Gordon H. Sato was appointed Director. He reasoned that tissue culture is now used so widely that the training of tissue culturists should be done at universities.

Anatomists had in fact pioneered university courses in tissue culture. Raymond H. Kahn, Professor of Anatomy at the University of Michigan at Ann Arbor, together with Donald Merchant, Professor of Microbiology and later the first Director of the W. Alton Jones Cell Science Center, began a tissue culture course at Ann Arbor in 1952. Later, they prepared teaching kits on tissue culture for biology courses in high schools. A graduate course in tissue culture was begun by the Department of Anatomy, University of Saskatchewan, Canada, in 1954. It has been offered continuously ever since. Now graduate and undergraduate courses, as well as short courses in specialized fields of tissue culture, are offered in many universities.

The idea of tissue culture was born in the Department of Anatomy in Johns Hopkins Medical School. The AAA nurtured the early tissue culturists, and members of the Association further developed and perfected tissue culture and trained hundreds of young people in their own laboratories and at specifically designed courses.

In addition, members of AAA made major contributions to modern knowledge through tissue culture. It is impossible to list all of these, but major contributions before the field completely exploded in scope include Gey's development of the HeLa cell line, initiated from a human cervical carcinoma (Bang, 1977). This cell line and chemically defined media developed in Parker's laboratory were essential elements in the production of the poliomyelitis vaccine. The first neoplastic transformation in cultures was observed in W.R. Earle's laboratory in the National Cancer Institute, Bethesda, and it was there that the first cell line was developed from a single cell. Pomerat's laboratory made major contributions to visualization of neural cells through time-lapse cinematography (Kasten, 1966). In that laboratory, T.C. Hsu discovered how to spread chromosomes with hypotonic solution, a technique that revolutionized cytogenetics; and the laboratory became the training place for future cytogeneticists. Margaret Murray's laboratory became the school of early neurobiologists (Murray, 1977).

REFERENCES

Bang, F.B. 1977 History of tissue culture at Johns Hopkins. Bull. Hist. Med., *51*:516–537.

Burrows, MT. 1913 The tissue culture as a physiological method. Congr. Am. Phys. Surg. Trans., *9*:77–90.

Harrison, R.G. 1907 Observations on the living developing nerve fiber. Soc. Exp. Biol. Med. Proc., *4*:140–143.

Harrison, R.G. 1908 Embryonic transplantation and the development of the nervous system. Harvey Lect., *3*:199–222.

Kasten, F.H. 1966 Charles Marc Pomerat—Experimental biologist and humanist. Med. Biol. Illus. *16*:78–88.

Murray, M.R. 1977 Introduction. In: Cell, Tissue and Organ Cultures in Neurobiology. S. Fedoroff and L. Hertz, eds. Academic Press, New York, pp. 1–8.

PART IV

APPENDIX

A STATISTICAL AND GRAPHICAL ARRAY OF DATA AND THEIR ANALYSES BEARING ON THE HISTORY OF THE AMERICAN ASSOCIATION OF ANATOMISTS

G. E. Erikson

With a running commentary intended to highlight signal persons and events and to aid in extracting significance and perspective from these reference sources on the present status and development of the Association.

1. INTRODUCTORY NOTE

Numbers and statistics are arid stuff—remote abstractions from the world we know and care about. But when related through a process of creative imagination back to the sources they represent, they can help us to perspectives and insights that enrich and guide.

No learned society in the world has evolved a set of records and numerical analyses to fairly represent its present status, trace past development, or illuminate even its most immediate future. Armies of dedicated workers for many organizations have labored mightily to produce the needed resources, only to be frustrated by the enormity of the labor, the exhausting expense of time and money, and the indifference of many whose active cooperation is a *sine qua non* for even moderate success.

The simple tabular and graphical arrays presented here have been derived from some decades of exploration in biomedical science and among biomedical scientists, as part of my role as archivist and erstwhile historian for the Association—and in similar official and unofficial roles for several other learned societies. Similar reports have been and are being prepared for other organizations, and it is a pleasure to share my harvests, as others have shared theirs with me.

It is important that readers appreciate the heterogeneity in the quality of these data. Some sectors are complete and reliable, within the bounds of inevitable human error. Others are incomplete and tentative, though useful, approximations. Some faults of omission and commission are remediable with continued research. Others are almost certainly irremediable—from limitations of time, energy, and resources or from the simple, stark fact that the evidence is lost forever—a painfully poignant realization for anyone researching the past.

One source of confusion, and a possible source of real error, is simple misidentification: people, institutions, and geographic entities undergo changes in name and may appear in the records in two or more guises. Until discovered they can, particularly in the case of dual or even multiple institutional names, significantly skew the data. It can be hoped that errors of these sorts are by now minimal.

Another source is more invidious and not so easily set right— that stemming from the twin ambiguities of classification and coding. This is a particular plague in the much vexed area of specialty field names and codes and, to a much lesser extent, in that of institutions and departments. There is not only the fundamental problem of neatly categorizing the quintessential nature of one's own or one's department's work—with the inevitably subjective components of conservative or *avant garde* tendencies, exacerbated by motives of image projection—but, swept along by the vagaries of changing fashion, some institutions, departments, and specialty fields suffer a sea change, including fission and fusion, and present difficult problems in categorization and code assignment.

One especially embroiled area is that of institutions with more than one campus. Records frequently cite only the parent university in giving degree or rank data; students, faculty, and administrators commonly share or change assignments between branches; and names are sometimes changed. To complicate this already difficult problem, we are in the terminal stages of elaborating our coding system for these separate divisions of large universities and must beg the indulgence of users of these data for some temporary inconsistencies.

One important note: a plea for help. Such archives and data as we have—and they are in some elements remarkably superior to those at the command of any other learned society in the world—exist in their present quantity, quality, and availability as a direct consequence of the hard work and generous cooperation of a large number of past and present good-spirited members and their families and associates. Via telephone, mail, and many visits over four decades (including those to every medical school in Canada and all but a few in the United States) I have had supportive help in every institution. But we badly need more, especially in two ways:

1. Continued and additional research on the local scene—on individuals, departments, institutions, and specialty fields.

2. Help in gathering career data on younger members and non-members of the profession who are not listed in the standard biographical publications. The C.V.'s sent by individual anatomists or department chairmen, or given to me by individuals at meetings or in my travels, have been our only source of data on our younger members. We badly need to fill out the picture on this important contingent of our profession.

Our association deserves a full, thoroughly researched, and well-written history of its first century. The present volume of essays, which goes to press more than two years before the arrival of our one hundredth birthday, while not that, is a very fitting celebration of our one hundredth meeting. (The discrepancy in anniversaries is explained in the notes to the Table of Meetings and Officers included in this appendix.) Repeated attempts by a series of individuals and committees to produce even a conventional summary volume have resulted in nothing more than Dr. Nicholas Michels' thirty-page brochure distributed at the Philadelphia meeting in 1955. In the absence of any other historical account, this has served a useful purpose, and Dr. Bas-majian has assimilated it into his two-chapter historical review here. Dr. Michels' sources were nearly exclusively the published proceedings and the not very extensive sprinkling of historical records preserved in the secretary's files (at that time in Phila-delphia—most of them have since been lost).

As Dr. Michels fully realized, since he was a member of one of the abortive historical committees, the kind of research needed to produce a thoroughgoing history would have to be of a different kind and magnitude than that for his pamphlet. The beginning of such researches were undertaken by Dr. Frederic T. Lewis of Harvard. As his presidential address in 1938 in Pittsburgh, he presented a review of the history of the Association. Sadly, it was never published, there is but the barest mention of it in our annals, and not a trace of the manuscript has been found. Interestingly, the very slides he used are among the hundreds on the history of medicine that I inherited from him after his death in 1951. I have since discovered some of his research notes on original sources. I am pleased to be continuing in a quest begun by that extraordinary scholar into the origin and early development of our Association—and beyond that into the endeavor to put the growth of our field into wider academic, geographic, and historical perspective.

There are two general conceptions of a history of a learned society. In the nar-rower view the main concerns are intrinsic and the story line chronological. Research and writing entail gathering, organizing, and digesting the published and manuscript records bearing on the origin and development of the society, distilling those elements essential to record the official chronicle and to give some flavor of the times, some humanity to the actors in the drama, and some picture of the developing science as seen in their careers, insofar as they intersect the affairs of the society. It should be expected to provide a clear, organized reference source on the meetings, on the offi-cers and other distinguished members, on awards to the members from inside and out-side the association, and to set forth statistical and graphical summaries on the mem-bership through a galaxy of parameters. It would be hoped that any such treatise would inevitably make some excursions into comparisons with relevant matters in other fields and other learned societies, but the overriding concern would be to tell the story of the society at hand. The result should be a useful source for a posterity inter-ested in that organization. There are a goodly number of such histories of various learned societies—most of them, their authors would confess, in spite of their best efforts, hardly exemplary. They attract few readers. Scholars of quality are unlikely to devote themselves to their production. Their quintessence, too often, is provincial-ism.

A broader conception of a history of a learned society encompasses all that the narrower one comprises because it builds on the basic records and expands out from them in time, place, persons, and fields and reaches out into other societies. In a true sense there can be no meaningful treatment of any entity without a modicum, at least, of broad setting and relevance. One step in such extension of relevance is that to the status and development of other professional associations. To paraphrase Goethe's famous, telling remark on knowing one's own language, we don't know our own association until we know another—or, better, until we see it in comparison with a set of related societies. Biological scientists know the stimulating and guiding value of the comparative.

The difference between the more limited and the broader ranging conception is not unlike the difference between explaining, or, at least, portraying, an organism through an account of its juvenile and adult structure versus an exposition of its full biology in all its developmental, functional, and ecological aspects. The full panoply of possible ramifications for this project, while enticing and richly rewarding, is, at the same time, overwhelming in challenge and responsibility. The details are infinite, the issues are prolix, the available resources, both scholarly and financial, are woefully inadequate. The world of modern information-handling offers bountiful contributions coupled with an infinite capacity to fail. And time is always running out.

My own conception of the right aims and methods for this study have evolved too fast and far for the maintenance of patience by a succession of rosters of the Executive Committee—who have quite simply looked for nothing more than a history of the more narrowly conceived sort. Recent officials, like their predecessors when earlier attempts failed, look on any more ambitious schemes as thinly disguised procrastination. But it should have surprised none of these decades of critics that attempts to date have been so unproductive. There simply has been no adequate foundation for the solid building of a history. We now do have rich and accessible resources—of manuscripts, photographs, books and reprints, tape-recorded interviews, richly detailed databases, and a potent armamentarium of software. Classifying, coding, and deploying the parameters for this large enterprise, now maintained on-line, has been an enormous and often ignored element in these continuing labors. Currently we are analyzing over 85,000 careers of relevance in general intellectual history—over 50,000 of them are biomedical scientists. The roles of the latter group in the membership and administration of more than 25 learned societies, and their incidental participation in more than 100 others, are being recorded and intricately inter-related. Unfortunately, at this juncture this sector is too enmeshed in a transition to a new system to make it advisable to risk in this publication a presentation of the rich nexus of interrelations.

The following reference section is to be regarded as a source of data and perspectives on the present status of the Association and as containing some elements of its history in outline. When these materials, and others like them, are perfected and the fleshed-out narrative version is completed, it could be a very appropriate tribute to a century of progress, when our centenary is attained in September 1988. These historical endeavors, it should be explicitly stated, are personal contributions to the Association, independent of my role as archivist.

2. CONCISE HISTORY OF THE AMERICAN ASSOCIATION OF ANATOMISTS

The American Association of Anatomists (until 1908, the Association of American Anatomists) was organized, through the initiative of its first secretary-treasurer, Alexander H. P. Leuf of Philadelphia, when fourteen men gathered in the Medical Department of Georgetown University in Washington, D.C., on September 17, 1888, elected the country's foremost anatomist, Joseph Leidy of the University of Pennsylvania, as their first president, and dedicated themselves to the "advancement of the anatomical sciences." The immediate occasion was the convening in Washington for the following three days of the first Congress of Physicians and Surgeons, with which the Association was to be formally affiliated until 1906, reflecting the dominant role of the medical school anatomists in the early years of the Association. Broader biological interests were well represented in this founding group and among the eighty-four charter members, and were furthered especially by Harrison Allen of the University of Pennsylvania and Burt G. Wilder of Cornell, the second and fifth presidents. Neither the medical nor the biological theme dominated the first decade of the Association's existence, but by the turn of the century the younger, European-trained, scientific anatomists provided the leadership that transformed it from the nearly exclusive domain of the nineteenth-century surgeon-anatomists of the medical schools to the broader field of anatomy, wherever taught or investigated. The three dominant figures in this movement were George S. Huntington, Ph.D., of Columbia, Charles S. Minot, S.D., of Harvard, and Franklin P. Mall, M.D., of Johns Hopkins—all in medical departments of anatomy, but all with enlightened university perspectives. Critical roles in this transformation were played by the Wistar Institute of Anatomy and Biology, the Journal of Anatomy (founded in 1901), and the Anatomical Record (established as a section of the Journal in 1906 and elevated to independent status in 1908.) By the time of the publication of the influential Flexner Report in 1910, the best of the anatomy departments could be cited for quality, most particularly Mall's department at the Hopkins. By the outbreak of the First World War, membership had grown to over 300, and there was a marked increase in attendance at meetings and in the number of scientific papers. More important was the striking improvement in the quality of teaching, research, and publication—reflecting the transition from older, part-time, clinically based surgeon-teachers to the younger, full-time professional teacher-researchers using the newer, microscopic and experimental techniques, and imbued with the broader and deeper perspectives from the German universities.

Members of the Association have done the lion's share in laying the groundwork for the the modern joint enterprise of teaching and research in the full range of morphological fields in the United States and Canada—not only in the expected medical areas of gross, microscopic, neuroanatomical, and developmental human anatomy, but in the biological fields of comparative anatomy, paleontology, physical anthropology, embryology, cytology, genetics, cell biology, neurobiology, and endocrinology, wherever treated throughout the university and beyond. It should also be more widely appreciated how significant have been the contributions of anatomists in a variety of contingent fields of biology and medicine and that a series of daughter fields, with their own organized societies, have budded off from the parent field of anatomy. This process of generating offspring societies, a phenomenon shared with other parent learned societies founded about the same time, has had a noticeable influence on the size and composition of the membership and its roles in the scientific community. Through adaptive changes the Association has increased in membership steadily, though at a slowly dwindling growth rate, until about three years ago when we experienced the first annual net loss since the mid-twenties.

In ninety-eight years the Association has enrolled 5,381 members, of whom 4,153 (77%) are still living and 2,792 (52%) are active members; 508 (18%) are women; 620 (22%) have an M.D. and 2,447 (88%) a Ph.D. (the M.D./Ph.D. proportion having approximately reversed over a century) and 324 (12%) have both of these doctorates. Doctorates in dental, osteopathic, or veterinary medicine are held by 6%, or 170 members. The overwhelming preponderance of the membership (87%) live in the United States, another 6% in Canada,and a third of the remainder live in the 6 next highest ranking countries—Japan, United Kingdom, Israel, Taiwan, China, and

Australia—overwhelmingly Oriental. In fact, of the twenty-five top ranking foreign countries, twelve are in the Eastern Hemisphere.

Quite expectedly, though not as predominately as many would estimate, the majority of the members teach and do research in departments of anatomy— 61% in medical school departments of anatomy in the United States and Canada. An additional 4% work in anatomy departments of schools of dental, osteopathic, or veterinary medicine in both countries—but the analyses here are complex, due to intermingling of departmental categories, and the composite elements must be carefully defined to assure clear perspectives. Biology and zoology, with 141 members (6% of those who assign themselves to departments), make-up a second, smaller category. Then follow four departments, each with about a 2% segment: surgery, pathology, physiology, and neuroscience, in that order.

Three-quarters of the present members are between the ages of 35 and 65 years—a not unexpected finding—and it is reassuring to note the faithful cadre of 17% over 65. But it is worrisome to see that only 6% of the members are under thirty-five years of age, that for the first time since the mid-twenties our membership is decreasing, and that the losses are largely from the younger contingent.

3. SUMMARY OVERVIEW OF MEMBERSHIP

On the 1986 Membership roster there are:

2792		**Members**	1286	(46%)	**Full Professors**
508	(18%)	**Women**	694	(25%)	**Assoc. Professors**
2284	(82%)	**Men**	451	(16%)	**Asst. Professors**
620	(22%)	**M.D.'s**	49	(2%)	**Instructors**
2447	(88%)	**Ph.D.'s or D.Sc.'s**	203	(7%)	**Emeriti or Retired**
324	(12%)	**Both Degrees**	312	(11%)	**Appt. Unknown or Other**
170	(6%)	**Dent., Osteo., & Vet. Degrees**	1726	(62%)	**In US Depts. of Anatomy**
15	(1%)	**Degree Data Unrecorded**	128	(5%)	**In Canadian Depts. of Anatomy**
2416	(87%)	**Live in the United States**			
154	(6%)	**Live in Canada**			

STATISTICAL OVERVIEW IA -- AAA CUMULATIVE MEMBERSHIP
DISTRIBUTION IN USA AND CANADA

AAA CUMULATIVE 5381

Male	4565	84.8%
Female	816	15.2%
MD	1615	30.0%
PhD	4049	75.2%

USA 4604 — 85.6%

Male	3857	83.8%
Female	747	16.2%

	MD 1243 — 27.0%	PhD 3634 — 78.9%	Both 446 — 9.7%	Other 200 — 4.3%
Male	1159 — 93.2%	2959 — 81.4%	403 — 90.4%	192 — 96.0%
Fem.	84 — 6.8%	675 — 18.6%	43 — 9.6%	8 — 4.0%

CANADA 269 — 5.0%

Male	234	87.0%
Female	35	13.0%

	MD 109 — 40.5%	PhD 187 — 69.5%	Both 50 — 18.6%	Other 18 — 6.7%
Male	101 — 92.7%	164 — 87.7%	49 — 98.0%	15 — 83.3%
Fem.	8 — 7.3%	23 — 12.3%	1 — 2.0%	3 — 16.7%

AAA ACTIVE 2792

Male	2284	81.8%
Female	508	18.2%
MD	620	22.2%
PhD	2447	87.6%

USA 2416 — 86.5%

Male	1949	80.7%
Female	467	19.3%

	MD 428 — 17.7%	PhD 2172 — 89.9%	Both 219 — 9.1%	Other 124 — 5.1%
Male	382 — 89.3%	1725 — 79.4%	189 — 86.3%	118 — 95.2%
Fem.	46 — 10.7%	447 — 20.6%	30 — 13.7%	6 — 4.8%

CANADA 154 — 5.5%

Male	129	83.8%
Female	25	16.2%

	MD 54 — 35.1%	PhD 129 — 83.8%	Both 33 — 21.4%	Other 10 — 6.5%
Male	49 — 90.7%	110 — 85.3%	32 — 97.0%	8 — 80.0%
Fem.	5 — 9.3%	19 — 14.7%	1 — 3.0%	2 — 20.0%

STATISTICAL OVERVIEW 1B -- AAA CUMULATIVE MEMBERSHIP DISTRIBUTION IN USA AND CANADA

AAA LIVING FORMER 1361

Male	1142	83.9%
Female	219	16.1%
MD	361	26.5%
PhD	1007	74.0%

USA 1111 81.6%

Male	912	82.1%
Female	199	17.9%

	MD 262 23.6%	PhD 912 82.1%	Both 129 11.6%	Other 51 4.6%
Male	242 92.4%	740 81.1%	120 93.0%	49 96.1%
Fem.	20 7.6%	172 18.9%	9 7.0%	2 3.9%

CANADA 75 5.5%

Male	68	90.7%
Female	7	9.3%

	MD 34 45.3%	PhD 40 53.3%	Both 13 17.3%	Other 8 10.7%
Male	32 94.1%	38 95.0%	13 100%	7 87.5%
Fem.	2 5.9%	2 5.0%	0 0.0%	1 12.5%

AAA DEAD FORMER 1228

Male	1139	92.8%
Female	89	7.2%
MD	634	51.6%
PhD	595	48.5%

USA 1077 87.7%

Male	996	92.5%
Female	81	7.5%

	MD 553 51.3%	PhD 550 51.1%	Both 98 9.1%	Other 25 2.3%
Male	535 96.7%	494 89.8%	94 95.9%	25 100%
Fem.	18 3.3%	56 10.2%	4 4.1%	0 0.0%

CANADA 40 3.3%

Male	37	92.5%
Female	3	7.5%

	MD 21 52.5%	PhD 18 45.0%	Both 4 10.0%	Other 0 0.0%
Male	20 95.2%	16 88.9%	4 100%	0 0.0%
Fem.	1 4.8%	2 11.1%	0 0.0%	0 0.0%

ASSOCIATION MEETINGS, OFFICERS, AND MEMBERS OF THE EXECUTIVE COMMITTEE[1]

No	Year	City	Inst	Dy	Dates	President	Vice-President	Secretary-Treasurer	Executive Committee
1	1888	Wash	Grgt	Mo	Sep17-18	Leidy, Joseph 1888-1891 [Leuf presided?]	88-Baker, Frank (1)-91 88-Weisse, Faneuil (2)-91	Leuf, Alexander 1888-1890	88-Towles, W.B.-89 88-Allen, H.-91 88-Wilder, B.G.-92
2	1889	Phil	UPa	Th	Dec26-28	(Leidy and Baker) (Presided)			
3	1890	Bost	Hrvd	Mo	Dec29-30	(Weisse presided)		(Dwight served)	89-Dwight, T.-94
4	1891	Wash	[GArH]	We	Sep23-25	(Baker presided)		Lamb, Daniel S. 1890-1901	
5	1892	Prmc	Prmc	Tu	Dec27-29	Allen, Harrison 1891-1894	91-Heitzmann, Charles (1)-94 91-Gill, Theodore N. (2)-94		91-Spitzka, E.C.-94
*	1893 NO MEETING								
6	1894	Wash	GeWa	Tu	May29-Jun1				92-Gerrish, F.H.-95
7	1894	NYor	Clmb	Fr	Dec28-29	Dwight, Thomas 1894-1895	94-Wilder, Burt Green (1)-97 94-Shepherd, Francis J. (2)-97		94-Gill, T.N.-97
8	1895	Phil	UPa	Fr	Dec27-28				94-Huntington, G.S.-97
*	1896 NO MEETING								
9	1897	Wash	GeWa	Tu	May4-6	Baker, Frank 1895-1897			95-Bevan, A.D.-98
10	1897	Itha	Crnl	Tu	Dec28-30				97-Gerrish, F.H.-99
11	1898	NYor	Clmb	We	Dec28-30	Wilder, Burt Green 1897-1899	97-Piersol, George A. (1)-99 97-Keiller, William (2)-99		97-Shepherd, F.J.-00
12	1899	NHav	Yale	We	Dec27-28				98-Holmes, E.W.-01

[1] This is a chart of MEETINGS, not a roster of officers. Therefore, all officers appear aligned with the dates of the first meeting at which they served. As indicated by the dates of their terms of office, they usually were elected in the previous year.

No	Year	City	Inst	Dy	Dates	President	Vice-President	Secretary-Treasurer	Executive Committee
13	1900	Wash	[NrmH]	Tu	May1-2	Huntington, George S. 1899-1903	99-Gerrish, Frederic H. (1)-01 99-Huber, Gotthelf Carl (2)-01		99-Minot, C.S.-02
14	1900	Balt	JnHo	Th	Dec27-28				
15	1901	Chic	UChi	Tu	Dec31-Jan2				00-Mall, F.P.-03
16	1902	Wash	GeWa	Tu	Dec30-31		01-Lamb, Daniel S. (1)-03 01-Piersol, George A. (2)-03	Huber, G. Carl 1901-1913	01-Hamann, C.A.-04 01-Barker, L.F.-05 01-Gerrish, F.H.-06
17	1903	Phil	Wist	Tu	Dec29-31				02-Minot, C.S.-03
18	1904	Phil	Wist	Tu	Dec27-29	Minot, Charles S. 1903-1905	03-Piersol, George A. (1)-05 03-Flint, J. Marshall (2)-05		03-Mall, F.P.-05 03-Huntington, G.S.-08
19	1905	Genv	1stICA	Su	Aug6-10				
20	1905	AnnA	UMi	We	Dec27-29				04-Bardeen, C.R.-09
21	1906	NYor	Clmb	Th	Dec27-29	Mall, Franklin P. 1905-1908	05-Piersol, George A. (1)-08 05-Bensley, Robert R. (2)-08		05-McMurrich, J.P.-08 05-Minot, C.S.-08
22	1907	Madi	UWi	Th	Mar28-29				06-Gage, S.H.-11
23	1908	Chic	UChi	We	Jan1-3				
24	1908	Balt	JnHo	Tu	Dec29-31	McMurrich, James P. 1908-1909	08-Miller, William S. (1)-09 08-Sabin, Florence R. (2)-09		08-Lee, T.G.-10 08-Bensley, R.R.-12
25	1909	Bost	Hrvd	Tu	Dec28-30				08-Donaldson, H.H.-13
26	1910	Brus	2ndICA	Su	Aug7-11				
27	1910	Itha	Crnl	We	Dec28-30	Piersol, George A. 1909-1911	09-McClure, C.F.W.-11		09-Hardesty, I.-10 09-Lewis, W.H.-11 09-Terry, R.J.-12 09-Lewis, F.T.-13
28	1911	Prnc	Prnc	We	Dec27-29				10-Jackson, C.M.-14 10-Kerr, A.T.-14

No	Year	City	Inst	Dy	Dates	President	Vice-President	Secretary-Treasurer	Executive Committee
29	1912	Clev	CWRs	Tu	Dec31-Jan2	Harrison, Ross G. 1911-1913	11-Lee, Thomas G.		11-Hardesty, I.-15 11-Knower, H.McE.-15
30	1913	Phil	UPa	Mo	Dec29-31				12-McClure, C.F.W.-16 12-Meyer, A.W.-16
31	1914	StLo	WaU	Mo	Dec28-30	Huber, Gotthelf Carl 1913-1915	13-Lewis, Frederic T.-15	Stockard, Charles 1913-1921	13-Herrick, C.J.-17 13-Lewis, W.H.-17
32	1915	NHav	Yale	Tu	Dec28-30				14-Bremer, J.L.-19 14-Schulte, H.V.W.-19
33	1916	NYor	[MSch]	We	Dec27-29	Donaldson, Henry H. 1915-1917	15-Jackson, Clarence M.-17		15-Clark, E.R.-19 15-Strong, R.M.-19
34	1917	Minn	UMn	Th	Dec27-29				16-Mall, F.P.-17 16-McMurrich, J.P.-20
**	1918	NO MEETING							
35	1919	Pitt	UPit	Th	Apr17-19	Bensley, Robert R. 1917-1920	17-Bardeen, Charles R.-20		17-Streeter, G.L.-20 17-Jordan, H.E.-21 17-Huntington, G.S.-21
36	1920	Wash	USNM	Th	Apr1-3				19-Evans, H.M.-23 19-Poynter, C.W.-23
37	1921	Phil	Wist	Th	Mar24-26	McClure, C.F.W. 1920-1921	20-Todd, T. Wingate-21		20-Weed, L.H.-21 20-Huber, G.C.-23
38	1921	NHav	Yale	We	Dec28-30				21-Ranson, S.W.-24 21-Terry, R.J.-24
**	1922	NO MEETING							
39	1923	Chic	UChi	We	Mar28-30	Jackson, Clarence M. 1921-1924	21-Senior, Harold D.-24	Weed, Lewis Hill 1921-1930	21-Hardesty, I.-25 21-Hooker, D.-25 21-Kingsbury, B.F.-25
40	1924	Bflo	SUNY	We	Apr16-19				23-Warren, John A.-24 23-Scammon, R.E.-26

No	Year	City	Inst	Dy	Dates	President	Vice-President	Secretary-Treasurer	Executive Committee
41	1925	Clev	CWRs	Th	Apr9-11	Sabin, Florence R. 1924-1926	24-Meyer, Arthur W.-26		24-Knower, H.McE.-26 24-Jackson, C.M.-28 24-Stockard, C.R.-28
42	1926	NHav	Yale	Th	Apr1-3				25-Schaeffer, J.P.-29 25-Todd, T.W.-29
43	1927	Nash	Vand	Th	Apr14-16	Streeter, George L. 1926-1928	26-Ranson, Steven W.-28		26-Corner, G.W.-30 26-Cowdry, E.V.-30
44	1928	AnnA	UMi	Th	Apr5-7				27-Coghill, G.E.-31 27-Danforth, C.H.-31
45	1929	RocN	Roch	We	Apr27-30	Stockard, Charles R. 1928-1930	28-Scammon, Richard E.-30		28-Boyden, E.A.-32 28-Macklin, C.C.-32
46	1930	Char	UVa	Th	Apr17-19				29-Burr, H.S.-33 29-Hartman, C.G.-33
**	1930	Amst	3rdICA	Mo	Aug4-9				
47	1931	Chic	Nthw	Th	Apr2-4	Evans, Herbert M. 1930-1932	30-Allen, Edgar-32	Corner, George W. 1930-1938	30-Arey, L.B.-34 30-Detwiler, S.R.-34
48	1932	NYor	Clmb	Th	Mar24-26				31-Malone, E.G.-35 31-McKibben, P.A.-35
49	1933	Cinc	UCin	Th	Apr13-15	Coghill, George E. 1932-1934	32-Kingsbury, B.F. (1)-34 32-Bartelmez, George W. (2)-34		32-Cunningham, R.S.-36 32-Pohlman, A.G.-36
50	1934	Phil	UPa	Th	Mar29-31				33-Bremer, J.L.-37 33-Senior, H.D.-37
51	1935	StLo	WaU	Th	Apr18-20	Lewis, Warren H. 1934-1936	34-Cowdry, Edmund V. (1)-36 34-Patten, Bradley, M. (2)-36		34-Rasmussen, A.T.-38 34-Smith, P.E.-38
52	1936	Durh	Duke	Th	Apr9-11				35-Scammon, R.E.-39 35-Weed, L.H.-39
**	1936	Mila	4thICA	Th	Sep3-8				
53	1937	Trto	Trto	Th	Mar25-27	Lewis, Frederic T. 1936-1938	36-Jordan, Harvey E. (1)-38 36-Danforth, Charles H. (2)-38		36-Bartelmez, G.W.-40 36-Cummins, H.-40

No	Year	City	Inst	Dy	Dates	President	Vice-President	Secretary-Treasurer	Executive Committee
54	1938	Pitt	UPit	Th	Apr14-16				37-Atwell, W.J.-41 37-Wislocki, G.B.-41
55	1939	Bost	Hrvd Tuft BstU	Th	Apr6-8	Ranson, S. Walter 1938-1940	38-Todd, T. Wingate (1)-39 38-Kuntz, Albert (2)-39	Clark, Eliot R. 1938-1942	38-Corner, G.W.-42 38-Larsell, O.-42
56	1940	Loui	ULou	We	Mar20-22		39-Kuntz, Albert (1)-40 39-Chambers, Robert (2)-40		39-Boyden, E.A.-46 39-Guild, S.R.-46
57	1941	Chic	UChi	We	Apr9-11	Smith, Philip E. 1940-1942	40-Hartman, Carl G. (1)-42 40-Hooker, Davenport (2)-42		40-Hinsey, J.C.-47 40-Speidel, C.C.-47
58	1942	NYor	Crnl	We	Apr1-3				41-Craigie, E.R.-48 41-Sullivan, W.E.-48
**	1943-1945		NO MEETINGS			Allen, Edgar 1942-1943	42-Schaeffer, J.P. (1)-46 42-Arey, Leslie B. (2)-46	Swett, Francis H. 1942-1943 Clark, Eliot R. 1943-1946	42-Clark, S.L.-49 42-Kornhauser, S.I.-49
59	1946	Clev	CWRs	Th	Apr4-6	Schaeffer, J. Parsons (Acting President) 1943-1946	Clark, Eliot Round 1943-1946		
60	1947	Mtrl	McGl	Th	Apr3-5	Corner, George W. 1946-1948	46-Boyden, Edward A. (1)-48 46-Hines, Marion (2)-48	Hoerr, Normand L. 1946-1956	46-Bloom, W.-50 46-Greulich, W.W.-50
61	1948	Madi	UWi	We	Apr21-23				47-Goss, C.M.-51 47-Nicholas, J.S.-51
62	1949	Phil	Tmpl	We	Apr13-15	Bartelmez, George W. 1948-1950	48-Wislocki, George B. (1)-50 48-Rasmussen, Andrew T. (2)-50		48-Gardner, W.U.-52 48-Ingram, W.R.-52
63	1950	NOrl	LaSU	We	Apr5-7				49-Scott, G.H.-50 49-Papez, J.W.-53
**	1950	Oxfd	5thICA	Tu	Jul25-28				
64	1951	Detr	Wyne	We	Mar21-23	Clark, Sam L. 1950-1952	50-Scott, Gordon Halter (1)-52 50-Grant, J.C. Boileau (2)-52		50-Flexner, L.B.-53 50-Duncan, D.-54 50-Simpson, M.E.-54

No	Year	City	Inst	Dy	Dates	President	Vice-President	Secretary-Treasurer	Executive Committee
65	1952	Prov	Brwn	We	Mar19-21				51-Markee, J.E.-55 51-Mossman, H.W.-55
66	1953	Cbus	OHSU	We	Mar25-27	Arey, Leslie B. 1952-1954	52-Detwiler, Samuel R. (1)-54 52-Bloom, William (2)-54		52-Figge, F.H.J.-56 52-Mason, K.E.-56
67	1954	Galv	UTx	We	Apr7-9				53-Dawson, A.B.-57 53-Magoun, H.W.-57
68	1955	Phil	Jeff	We	Apr6-8	Detwiler, Samuel R. 1954-1956 (Boyden presiding)	54-Sullivan, Walter E. (1)-56 54-Stone, Leon S. (2)-56	Jones, O.P. Program Secretary 1954-1966	54-Adams, A.E.-58 54-Leblond, C.P.-58
**	1955	Pari	6thICA	Mo	Jul25-30				
69	1956	Milw	UWi	We	Apr4-6	Boyden, Edward A. 1956-1957			55-Blandau, R.J.-59 55-Woodburne, R.T.-59
70	1957	Balt	UMd	We	Apr17-19		56-Greulich, William W. (1)-58 56-Batson, Oscar V. (2)-58	Flexner, Louis B. 1956-1964	56-Hooker, C.W.-60 56-Roofe, P.G.-60
71	1958	Bflo	SUNY	We	Apr2-4	Hoerr, Normand Louis 1957-1958 Anson, Barry Joseph 1958			57-Dempsey, E.W.-59 57-Windle, W.F.-61
72	1959	Seat	UWa	We	Apr1-3	Hooker, Davenport 1958-1959	58-Fawcett, Don Wayne (1)-60 58-Bennett, H. Stanley (2)-59		58-Bensley, S.H.-62 58-Wells, L.J.-62
73	1960	NYor	7thICA	Mo	Apr11-16	Bennett, H. Stanley 1959-1960	59-Cummins, Harold (2)-60		59-Truex, R.C.-61 59-Bodian, D.-63 59-Knisely, M.H.-63
74	1961	Chic	UIl	Tu	Mar21-24	Dempsey, Edward W. 1960-1961	60-Duncan, Donald (1)-62 60-Mortensen, Otto A. (2)-62		60-Bassett, D.L.-64 60-Johnson, R.J.-64
75	1962	Minn	UMn	Tu	Mar20-23	Cummins, Harold 1961-1962			61-Pease, D.C.-65 61-Thompson, I.M.-65
76	1963	Wash	Grgt	Tu	Apr9-11	Leblond, Charles P. 1962-1963	62-Mason, Karl E. (1)-64 62-Reynolds, Samuel R. (2)-64		62-Kollros, J.J.-66 62-Scharrer, E.-66

No	Year	City	Inst	Dy	Dates	President	Vice-President	Secretary-Treasurer	Executive Committee
77	1964	Denv	UCo	Tu	Mar31-Apr3	Magoun, Horace W. 1963-1964			63-Lazarow, A.-67 63-Ramsey, E.M.-67
78	1965	Miam	UMia	Tu	Apr20-23	Goss, Charles Mayo 1964-1965	64-Blandau, Richard J. (1)-66 64-Huber, John F. (2)-66	Woodburne, R. T. 1964-1972	64-Baker, B.L.-68 64-Palade, G.E.-68
**	1965	Wies	8thICA	Su	Aug8-13				
79	1966	SanF	UCSF	We	Apr6-8	Fawcett, Don Wayne 1965-1966			65-Hollinshead,W.H.-66 65-Barr, M.L.-69
80	1967	KCit	UKs	Tu	Apr4-7	Duncan, Donald 1966-1967	66-Windle, William F. (1)-68 66-Hollinshead, W.H. (2)-68	Finerty, John C. Program Secretary 1966-1974	66-Sawyer, C.H.-68 66-Ward, J.W.-69 66-Pearson, A.A.-70
81	1968	NOrl	Tlne	Tu	Apr9-12	Mason, Karl E. 1967-1968			67-Alden, R.H.-68 67-Kimmel, D.L.-71
82	1969	Bost	BstU Hrvd Tuft	Tu	Apr1-4	Blandau, Richard J. 1968-1969	68-Sawyer, Charles H. (1)-70 68-Leathem, James H. (2)-70		68-Bodian, D.-70 68-Elftman, H.O.-70 68-Luft, J.H.-71 68-Whitlock, D.G.-72 68-Clark, S.L.,Jr.-72
83	1970	Chic	Nthw	Tu	Mar31-Apr3	Alden, Roland H. 1969-1970			69-Clemente, C.D.-70 69-Trotter, M.-73
**	1970	Leni	9thICA	Mo	Aug17-23				
84	1971	Phil	Hahn	Mo	Apr19-22	Truex, Raymond Carl 1970-1971	70-Clemente, Carmine D. (1)-72 70-Clermont, Yves W. (2)-72		70-Swan, R.C.,Jr.-73 70-Hay, E.D.-73 70-Friedman, S.M.-74 70-Palay, S.L.-74
85	1972	Dall	UTx	Mo	Apr3-6	Bodian, David 1971-1972			71-Sprague, J.M.-74 71-Greulich, R.C.-75
86	1973	NYor	Crnl	Mo	Apr9-12	Gardner, William U. 1972-1973	72-Clermont, Yves W. (1)-73 72-Langman, Jan (2)-73	Pauly, John E. 1972-1980	72-Ladman, A.J.-76 72-Nauta, W.J.H.-76

No	Year	City	Inst	Dy	Dates	President	Vice-President	Secretary-Treasurer	Executive Committee
87	1974	Clev	CWRs	Mo	Apr1-4	Everett, John W. 1973-1974	73-Langman, Jan (1)-74 / 73-ITO, Susumu (2)-74		73-Anderson, E.-77 / 73-Padykula, H.A.-77
88	1975	LAng	UCLA	Su	Mar23-27	Woodburne, Russell T. 1974-1975	74-Ito, Susumu (1)-75 / 74-Ramsey, Elizabeth M. (2)-75	Hess, Melvin Program Secretary 1974-1978	74-Scharrer, B.V.-75 / 74-Kelly, D.E.-78 / 74-Wood, J.G.-78
**	1975	Toky	10thICA	We	Aug25-30				
89	1976	Loui	ULou	Tu	Apr20-23	Finerty, John C. 1975-1976	75-Ramsey, Elizabeth M. (1)-76 / 75-Hay, Elizabeth D. (2)-76		75-Basmajian, J.V.-79 / 75-Slautterback. D.-79
90	1977	Detr	Wyne	Mo	May2-5	Clemente, Carmine D. 1976-1977	76-Hay, Elizabeth D. (1)-77 / 76-Sprague, James M. (2)-77		76-Bunge, R.P.-80 / 76-Lavail, J.H.-80
91	1978	Vanc	UBC	Mo	Apr3-6	Everett, Newton B. 1977-1978 (Sprague presiding)	77-Sprague, James M. (1)-78 / 77-Clark, Sam L., Jr. (2)-78		77-Low, F.N.-81 / 77-Sutin, J.-81
92	1979	Miam	UMia	Mo	Apr2-5	Scharrer, Berta V. 1978-1979	78-Clark, Sam L., Jr. (1)-79 / 78-Padykula, Helen (2)-79	Schwarz, M. Roy Program Secretary 1978-1982	78-Goodman, D.C.-82 / 78-Osmond, D.G.-82
93	1980	Omah	UNe	Mo	Apr28-May1	Pease, Daniel C. 1979-1980	79-Padykula, Helen (1)-80 / 79-Enders, Allen C. (2)-80		79-Christensen.A.K.-83 / 79-Revel, J. P.-83
**	1980	Mex	C11thICA	Su	Aug17-23				
94	1981	NOrl	LSU	Su	Apr19-23	Palay, Sanford 1980-1981	80-Enders, Allen C. (1)-81 / 80-Ladman, Aaron J. (2)-81	Jollie, William 1980-1988	80-Leak, L.V.-84 / 80-O'Steen, W.K.-84
95	1982	Indi	InU	Su	Apr04-08	Hay, Elizabeth D. 1981-1982	81-Ladman, Aaron J. (1)-82 / 81-Bunge, R.P. (2)-82		81-Hitchcock, K.R.-85 / 81-Zimny, M.L.-85
96	1983	Atla	Emry	Su	Apr3-7	Pauly, John E. 1982-1983	82-Bunge, R.P. (1)-83 / 82-Brightman, M.W. (2)-83	Slonecker, C.E. Program Secretary 1982-1990	82-Tennyson, V.M.-86 / 82-Willis, W.D.-86
97	1984	Seat	UWa	Su	Apr8-12	Enders, Allen C. 1983-1984	83-Brightman, M.W. (1)-84 / 83-Anderson, Everett (2)-84		83-Black, V.H.-87 / 83-Neutra, M.R.P.-87

No	Year	City	Inst	Dy	Dates	President	Vice-President	Secretary-Treasurer	Executive Committee
98	1985	Trto	Trto	Su	May5-9	Christensen, A. Kent 1984-1985	84-Anderson, Everett (1)-85 84-Sutin, J. (2)-85		84-Sladek, John R.-88 84-Ross, Leonard L.-88
**	1985	Lond12thICA		Tu	Aug6-16				
99	1986	Reno	UNe	Su	Apr6-10	Basmajian, John 1985-1986	85-Sutin, J. (1)-86 85-Guth, Lloyd (2)-86		85-Fallon, John F.-89 85-Holbrook, Karen A.-89
100	1987	Wash	GeWa	Su	May10-14	Kelly, Douglas E. 1986-1987	86-Guth, Lloyd (1)-87 86-Hitchcock, Karen R.(2)-87		86-Landis, Story C.-90 86-Peters, Alan-90
101	1988	Cinc	UCin	Su		Ralston, Henry J. 1987-1988	87-Hitchcock, Karen R.(1)-88		
102	1989	NOrl	Tlne						

WORLD WAR II SUPPLEMENT[1]

No	Year	City	Inst	Dy	Dates	President	Vice-President	Secretary-Treasurer	Executive Committee
*	1943	NO MEETING				Allen, Edgar 1942-1943 Schaeffer, J. Parsons (Acting President)	42-Schaeffer, J.P. (1)-46 42-Arey, Leslie B. (2)-46	Swett, Francis H. 1942-1943 (Deceased) Clark, Eliot Round (Acting Secretary)	
*	1944	NO MEETING				"	42-Arey, Leslie B. (2)-46	Clark, Eliot Round	
*	1945	NO MEETING				"	42-Arey, Leslie B. -46	"	
*	1946	Clev				"	42-Arey, Leslie B. -46	"	

[1] This is a chart of MEETINGS, not a roster of officers. Therefore, all officers appear aligned with the dates of the first meeting at which they served. As indicated by the dates of their terms of office, they usually were elected in the previous year.

TABLE OF MEETINGS, OFFICERS, AND MEMBERS OF THE EXECUTIVE COMMITTEE

— ANNOTATION AND EXPLICATION —

The accompanying table is intended to be readable without explanatory apparatus, except, perhaps, for a few less mnemonic codes for cities and institutions. Help in their interpretation will be found in the appropriate rank lists, where parallel lists of codes and names are given.

This table should not be dismissed as a mere array of dates and names to be resorted to only for quick reference. With some concentrated attention and a little historical imagination—prompted by the narrative section of this volume—the reader can get a bird's-eye-view of the prime official events and trends in the history of the Association. Some of these reflect important contemporary changes in the world-at-large, and also trace some segments of the interweaving life courses of 212 officers and members of the executive committee, as they proceed in and out of 370 offices in 98 years of the Association's history to date. Some of these happenings are treated in the course of the main body of the volume, but gain added significance as seen here in the context of the grand pattern.

THE NUMBERING OF "ANNUAL" MEETINGS AND THE DESIGNATIONS OF ANNIVERSARY CELEBRATIONS.

One might have expected the system of numbering to show an inevitable lockstep of years with the numbers assigned to "annual sessions,"—an expectation encouraged by the regular system in recent decades, and the fact that in 1987, in Washington, we are scheduled to hold our one-hundredth meeting and begin our one hundredth year (actually on September 17th).

That this is sheer coincidence will be made clear by noting in the table that such neat matching did not occur when some earlier milestones were passed. While the tenth meeting was indeed held in 1897, the twentieth came in 1905, the thirtieth in 1913 (4 years "early"), the fiftieth in 1934 (three years "early," but four years before the year selected for the 50-year celebration meeting, 1938.) That is, when President Frederic T. Lewis, on April 15, 1938, in Pittsburgh, reviewed the history of the Association, he was actually officiating at our fifty-fourth meeting and celebrating the forthcoming completion of fifty years of existence, still five months away. The system slipped back into neat alignment in 1946, when the three years of advance on the calendar was cut back by the cancellation of three successive meetings in the wartime years of 1943-1945. Since the fifty-ninth meeting in 1946 the system has been regular—i.e., the decade celebrations have fallen in the seventh year of each decade.

But what is the proper date for the observance of a centenary? At first glance the answer seems clear and unequivocal: the date of the completion of one hundred years of existence. We have the familiar example of our human birthdays in mind. But the model is inexact, and comparisons with it set a pattern of calculations that boggle the mind. While the centenarian is feted on his hundredth birthday as he completes his hundredth year, a learned society completes its ninety-ninth year as it holds its one-hundredth meeting. If we reckoned birthdays as the Chinese do, and as Dr. Corner was fond of commending them for doing, we would look on our natal day as our first birthday and count the day of transition to our second year as our second birthday. Or the same adjustment would be made if, conversely, a learned society regarded its first gathering as its Founding Meeting, and one year later held its first annual meeting. Then the system of milestones for the human organism and an organization would be the same and illuminate each other.

As it is, the American Association of Anatomists will be one hundred years old on September 17th, 1988. Since fall meetings were abandoned in 1891, the celebration of this birthday's safe attainment will have to wait until the following spring, in May 1989, with the holding of the one-hundred and second meeting. The preceding meeting, in May 1988, will be our one hundred and first, and we could, with forgivable confidence, look forward to the upcoming centenary date. The Executive Committee, in its wisdom (and some impatience with such historiographic niceties), elected to plan the celebration of our centenary for May 1987, when we will hold our one-hundredth meeting, though we will be only ninety-eight years, seven months, and some days old, and it will be somewhat premature to congratulate ourselves with a survey of a century of progress. Individual members of the Association, of course, are free to celebrate as they will. Some, perhaps, like their Archivist, will sometime on September 17, 1988, turn their visages and thoughts toward Washington and, while regretting the lack of a shrine (since Georgetown University's Medical Department has long since departed from its original site) rejoice that the science of anatomy yet endures and steadily advances.

THE CANCELLATION OF CERTAIN MEETINGS AND THE ABSENCE OF MEETINGS IN CERTAIN OTHER YEARS.

Reference to the leftmost columns of the table will show that no meetings were held in the years 1893, 1896, 1918, 1922, 1943, 1944, and 1945. Only four of these represent real cancellations—1918, 1943, 1944, and 1945 being casualties of two world wars. The other three cases represent lacunae resulting from the postponements of meetings that would have been held in December of these years—1893, 1896, and 1922—but were put off until the Spring. In the first two instances, meetings were also held in the following December (1894 and 1897), resulting in two meetings being held in those years. The meeting that would have been held in December 1922 was postponed until the end of March 1923. The intervening gap of fifteen months stands as the longest in the history of the Association—except, of course, for the two wartime periods. These postponements fit into the pattern of adjustments of schedules of meetings that permitted joint meetings with affiliated societies, as explained in the following paragraph.

DOUBLE MEETINGS IN CERTAIN YEARS.

In fifteen of the ninety-nine years being reviewed, two annual meetings were convened. Ten of these represent years in which International Congresses of Anatomy were held in Europe, and these did not replace the usual annual meetings. The remaining one of the eleven I.C.A.'s—the one that was held in New York City in April 1960—served also as the regular meeting for that year, the seventy-third. The first two international meetings, those of 1905 and 1910, were given numbers (19 and 26) in the annual series, but they did not take the place of the regular December meetings. This accounts for 10 of 15 years with two meetings each. Two more (1894 and 1897) were accounted for in the preceding paragraph. The remaining double meetings (1900, 1908, and 1921) are likewise specious, in the sense that the first meeting in each pair represents a postponement from the preceding December. In the long perspective there was no aberration in the regular average of one meeting per year.

THE FABRIC OF HISTORY OUTLINED IN THIS TABLE.

Interested scanners of this table can make out the traces of significant events and trends in our history. With the help of two accompanying tables, "Career Summaries—Officers and Members of the Executive Committee" and "Membership Statistics—Year By Year," and reference to other elements in this appendix, such an exploration can be even more informing. To cite a few examples: among the *dramatis personae*, two of the venerable heroes have a very brief run in the drama. Joseph Leidy, while universally seen as the pioneer anatomist in nineteenth-century America and unrivalled for selection as our first president, was not present at the first meeting in Washington, though he presided with Baker at the second meeting at Philadelphia, was too unwell to attend the third meeting in Boston, and died in July 1891, prior to the fourth meeting in Washington. Alexander Leuf, a virtual unknown in the annals of the society, deserves full tribute for his unique role in convoking the first meeting , writing a constitution, coining our motto, for "the advancement of anatomical sciences," and, I believe, presiding at the first meeting. Yet he is given no credit for these services and is memorialized only through a few brief listings. We will never know the full story of the shift of influence to other hands, but persistent research is revealing a good deal about this idiosyncratic first secretary, and something of the maneuvers to shift from his more essentially clinical to a more academic and biological focus. Similarly, our second secretary, Daniel Lamb, who served so faithfully through the difficult early decade of the nineties, and will always be honored for his central role in developing the medical school of Howard University, might have been expected to have attained to the presidency around the turn of the century (a repeated pattern of secretary-to-president elevation that commenced with the next secretary, Carl Huber), but by that time he had become one of the old guard, standing aside for the sweep of the young turks who succeeded to the presidency.

The Table of Membership Statistics shows that the first dozen years of the Association's existence had been precarious, and there was general despair for its survival. The membership increased by only fifty members throughout the 1890s—on the average ten new members enrolled each year, while another five resigned. But under the new leadership it came into its own.

Further on, one sees the record of two presidents prevented by fatal illness from presiding—Detwiler in 1955 and Ben Everett in 1978—and one prevented by the war, Edgar Allen.

The various routes to the presidency through lower office would make a fascinating story in itself. While the common pattern has involved service on the executive committee and in the vice presidency, some have had a more direct ascendency. The interesting phenomena of two presidents (Minot and Huntington) returning after their terms as president to serve again on the executive committee is reminiscent of John Quincy Adams's return to Congress after his presidency of the nation. Is it conceivable that some energetic, ever-loyal past president might be drafted for such return to service? There are 20 instances of second terms on the executive committee and four of third terms.

The pattern of women's participation in the general membership and governance since Mary Blair Moody was enrolled in 1894, deserves a special study. The growth of the proportion of women in the general membership has been excruciatingly slow. At the end of the Second World War it was edging above the 11 percent level. Twenty-five years later, in the early seventies, it was barely one percent higher. In the eighties there has been a clearly perceptible rise—to a level at present of just over 18% of the general membership. In certain sectors—especially in the lower ranks of various departments in the medical schools in the United States— the figure may rise to just under 30 percent.

Our first woman officer was, of course, the inimitable Dr. Florence Sabin. Of the 212 officers elected in the full course of our history, 18 have been women. All but four are still alive—Elizabeth Adams, Sylvia Bensley, Marion Hines, and Florence Sabin.

The geographic element in our history is intriguing—the "where" of our birth, education, work, and residence. The chronological development of the pattern of our meeting sites begins, of course, with the well-worn path along the Washington-Boston axis—a sortie into the wilds of Ithaca being the only break in the series: Washington, Philadelphia, Boston, Princeton, New York, New Haven, and Baltimore in the nineteenth century. Chicago (1901), Ann Arbor (1905), Madison (1907), St. Louis (1914), and Minneapolis (1917) opened the Midwest to us. Toronto in 1937 was a well-remembered host for our first meeting in Canada. Younger members will, perhaps, be suprised to learn that we did not venture west of St. Louis until we selected Galveston in 1954, and did not break through to the West Coast until 1959, when we met in Seattle, and that, while Nashville (1927), Charlottesville (1930), and Durham (1936) were our hosts fairly early, it was only in 1950 that we ventured into the Deep South—to New Orleans.

It is interesting to note—by reference to the rank lists of regions, states, provinces, cities, and institutions in the following sections of this appendix—how large a part anatomists along the Boston-Washington axis (and on a few spur tracks) still play in our profession and in our Association. Note, for example, that in the rank list of the cities where our members reside, the top eight cities contain a total number of members equivalent to just under one-fifth of our entire active membership, and that six of these eight (accounting for 15 of the 20 percent) are those same east coast centers—the other two being, of course, Los Angeles and Chicago. Rank lists and some distribution maps assign the membership to their proper countries, regions, states, provinces, cities, institutions, departments, and specialty fields.

Limitations of space prevent my offering further introductory commentary. The reader is invited to continue the quest for themes and patterns discernible throughout this reference appendix.

A final note of acknowledgement and thanks—and a plea for further help. A learned society is not likely to develop a better archive or a more meaningful historical perspective than its membership deserves. The present array demonstrates that we have made a creditable start, with the excellent help of hundreds of concerned members—including those who, with varying degrees of tolerance and understanding, point out the inevitable host of errors of omission and commission such work entails. Though many are corrected, many remain in this shifting world. Over each of the tables in this appendix should hang a prominent caveat: "Provisional Version". All of this would improve if: 1.) the membership would heed the appeals from our hardworking Secretary to keep his office notified of changes to all the items he includes in his annual membership list; and 2.) there could be prepared a new edition of his very useful *Directory of Anatomy Departments* (the present one is based on information gathered in 1982.) When we attempt our next review, on the occasion of our Centennial, we can hope for more detail, greater accuracy, and truer insight.

Joseph Leidy
1888

Harrison Allen
1892

Thomas Dwight
1894

Frank Baker
1897

James P. McMurrich
1908

George A. Piersol
1910

Ross G. Harrison
1912

Gotthelf Carl Huber
1914

Florence R. Sabin
1925

George L. Streeter
1927

Charles R. Stockard
1929

Herbert M. Evans
1931

Philip E. Smith
1941

Edgar Allen
1942

J. Parsons Schaeffer
1943

George W. Corner
1947

Edward A. Boyden
1956

Normand Louis Hoerr
1958

Barry Joseph Anson
1958

Davenport Hooker
1959

Burt Green Wilder
1898

George S. Huntington
1900

Charles S. Minot
1904

Franklin P. Mall
1906

Henry H. Donaldson
1916

Robert R. Bensley
1919

C. F. W. McClure
1921

Clarence M. Jackson
1923

George E. Coghill
1933

Warren Harmon Lewis
1935

Frederic T. Lewis
1937

S. Walter Ranson
1939

George W. Bartelmez
1949

Sam L. Clark
1951

Leslie B. Arey
1953

Samuel R. Detwiler
1955

H. Stanley Bennett
1960

Edward W. Dempsey
1961

Harold Cummins
1962

Charles P. Leblond
1963

Horace W. Magoun
1964

Charles Mayo Goss
1965

Don Wayne Fawcett
1966

Donald Duncan
1967

David Bodian
1972

William U. Gardner
1973

John W. Everett
1974

Russell T. Woodburne
1975

Daniel C. Pease
1980

Sanford Palay
1981

Elizabeth D. Hay
1982

John E. Pauly
1983

Henry J. Ralston
1988

Karl E. Mason
1968

Richard J. Blandau
1969

Roland H. Alden
1970

Raymond Carl Truex
1971

John C. Finnerty
1976

Carmine D. Clemente
1977

Newton B. Everett
1978

Berta V. Scharrer
1979

Allen C. Enders
1984

A. Kent Christensen
1985

John Basmajian
1986

Douglas E. Kelly
1987

MEMBERSHIP STATISTICS — YEAR BY YEAR

		ANNUAL CHANGES IN MEMBERSHIP										MD & PhD DEGREES						APPOINTMENTS				
Year	City	Cum	Act	Inact	Dead	Start	End	Died	Net	No.	%	MD	MD%	PhD	PhD%	Both	Both%	Instr	Asst	Assoc	Full	Full%
1888	Wash	19	19	0	0	19	0	0	19	0	0.00	16	84.21	2	10.53	1	5.26	0	0	0	13	68.42
1889	Phil	28	28	0	0	9	0	0	9	0	0.00	22	78.57	3	10.71	1	3.57	0	0	0	22	78.57
1890	Bost	83	83	0	0	55	0	0	55	0	0.00	60	72.29	15	18.07	5	6.02	0	0	0	58	69.88
1891	Wash	98	94	3	1	15	3	1	11	0	0.00	69	73.40	18	19.15	6	6.38	1	1	0	62	65.96
1892	Prnc	109	103	5	1	11	2	0	9	0	0.00	74	71.84	21	20.39	5	4.85	2	1	0	66	64.08
1893		109	101	4	4	0	0	2	-2	0	0.00	72	71.29	21	20.79	5	4.95	2	1	0	65	64.36
1894	Wash	130	105	19	6	21	15	2	4	1	0.95	80	76.19	21	20.00	5	4.76	2	1	2	66	62.86
1894	NYor	130	105	19	6	21	15	2	4	1	0.95	80	76.19	21	20.00	5	4.76	2	1	2	66	62.86
1895	Phil	142	110	25	7	12	7	0	5	1	0.91	87	79.09	21	19.09	5	4.55	2	1	2	70	63.64
1896		142	108	25	9	0	0	2	-2	1	0.93	85	78.70	21	19.44	5	4.63	4	1	2	69	63.89
1897	Wash	164	120	32	12	22	7	3	12	1	0.83	96	80.00	22	18.33	5	4.17	4	0	2	82	68.33
1897	Itha	164	120	32	12	22	7	3	12	1	0.83	96	80.00	22	18.33	5	4.17	4	0	2	82	68.33
1898	NYor	182	136	32	14	18	1	1	16	2	1.47	111	81.62	23	16.91	6	4.41	5	1	2	90	66.18
1899	NHav	183	130	37	16	1	5	2	-6	2	1.54	108	83.08	21	16.15	6	4.62	5	1	2	86	66.15
1900	Wash	203	136	50	17	20	13	1	6	2	1.47	116	85.29	21	15.44	7	5.15	4	2	3	91	66.91
1900	Balt	203	136	50	17	20	13	1	6	2	1.47	116	85.29	21	15.44	7	5.15	4	2	3	91	66.91
1901	Chic	225	143	62	20	22	13	2	7	3	2.10	117	81.82	26	18.18	8	5.59	4	2	3	99	69.23
1902	Wash	244	160	63	21	19	2	0	17	5	3.13	130	81.25	29	18.12	8	5.00	4	2	4	112	70.00
1903	Phil	268	179	67	22	24	4	1	19	8	4.47	143	79.89	32	17.88	9	5.03	5	3	5	127	70.95
1904	Phil	307	211	72	24	39	6	1	32	8	3.79	163	77.25	47	22.27	11	5.21	9	4	6	152	72.04
1905	Genv	358	250	78	30	51	8	4	39	10	4.00	182	72.80	67	26.80	18	7.20	11	6	7	180	72.00
1905	AnnA	358	250	78	30	51	8	4	39	10	4.00	182	72.80	67	26.80	18	7.20	11	6	7	180	72.00
1906	NYor	358	248	78	32	0	0	2	-2	10	4.03	180	72.58	67	27.02	18	7.26	11	6	7	178	71.77
1907	Madi	381	255	92	34	23	15	1	7	11	4.31	182	71.37	73	28.63	18	7.06	13	6	9	187	73.33
1908	Chic	419	279	105	35	38	13	1	24	11	3.94	190	68.10	83	29.75	19	6.81	14	6	12	208	74.55
1908	Balt	419	279	105	35	38	13	1	24	11	3.94	190	68.10	83	29.75	19	6.81	14	6	12	208	74.55
1909	Bost	436	281	118	37	17	14	1	2	11	3.91	188	66.90	87	30.96	20	7.12	13	5	13	213	75.80
1910	Brus	466	310	114	42	30	0	1	29	11	3.55	201	64.84	103	33.23	22	7.10	13	6	14	238	76.77
1910	Itha	466	310	114	42	30	0	1	29	11	3.55	201	64.84	103	33.23	22	7.10	13	6	14	238	76.77
1911	Prnc	475	301	131	43	9	17	1	-9	9	2.99	194	64.45	106	35.22	23	7.64	11	8	14	233	77.41
1912	Clev	475	300	130	45	0	0	1	-1	9	3.00	194	64.67	105	35.00	23	7.67	11	7	14	233	77.67
1913	Phil	519	313	156	50	44	28	3	13	11	3.51	194	61.98	119	38.02	28	8.95	16	6	16	240	76.68
1914	StLo	540	318	167	55	21	15	1	5	12	3.77	193	60.69	123	38.68	30	9.43	16	7	17	239	75.16
1915	NHav	582	339	180	63	42	16	5	21	14	4.13	200	59.00	137	40.41	30	8.85	16	8	17	255	75.22
1916	NYor	618	366	185	67	36	7	2	27	17	4.64	207	56.56	154	42.08	34	9.29	19	6	17	271	74.04

Meetings		Statistics for stated year				Changes from preceding year				Women		MD & PhD DEGREES						APPOINTMENTS				
Year	City	Cum	Act	Inact	Dead	Start	End	Died	Net	No.	%	MD	MD%	PhD	PhD%	Both	Both%	Instr	Asst	Assoc	Full	Full%
1917	Minn	649	389	191	69	31	7	1	23	19	4.88	217	55.78	164	42.16	36	9.25	19	6	18	284	73.01
1918		649	382	185	82	0	0	7	-7	19	4.97	214	56.02	160	41.88	35	9.16	19	6	18	280	73.30
1919	Pitt	677	399	189	89	28	7	4	17	20	5.01	223	55.89	166	41.60	35	8.77	19	7	18	289	72.43
1920	Wash	708	411	200	97	31	15	4	12	20	4.87	221	53.77	175	42.58	35	8.52	18	6	17	300	72.99
1921	Phil	769	453	211	105	61	15	4	42	24	5.30	237	52.32	200	44.15	38	8.39	16	8	22	339	74.83
1921	NHav	769	453	211	105	61	15	4	42	24	5.30	237	52.32	200	44.15	38	8.39	16	8	22	339	74.83
1922		769	448	210	111	0	0	5	-5	24	5.36	232	51.79	200	44.64	38	8.48	16	8	22	335	74.78
1923	Chic	785	443	223	119	16	18	3	-5	26	5.87	219	49.44	207	46.73	37	8.35	13	8	22	334	75.40
1924	Bflo	801	440	230	131	16	12	7	-3	27	6.14	216	49.09	211	47.95	39	8.86	13	8	24	331	75.23
1925	Clev	814	444	225	145	13	4	5	4	30	6.76	218	49.10	215	48.42	40	9.01	14	7	26	333	75.00
1926	NHav	828	443	233	152	14	10	5	-1	31	7.00	214	48.31	220	49.66	41	9.26	14	7	28	335	75.62
1927	Nash	846	452	231	163	18	4	5	9	35	7.74	215	47.57	232	51.33	44	9.73	14	7	34	341	75.44
1928	AnnA	865	458	235	172	19	5	8	6	34	7.42	217	47.38	235	51.31	44	9.61	16	7	35	346	75.55
1929	RocN	888	471	234	183	23	7	3	13	35	7.43	224	47.56	247	52.44	49	10.40	16	6	36	357	75.80
1930	Char	905	482	234	189	17	5	1	11	35	7.26	226	46.89	259	53.73	50	10.37	16	8	37	367	76.14
1930	Amst	905	482	234	189	17	5	1	11	35	7.26	226	46.89	259	53.73	50	10.37	16	8	37	367	76.14
1931	Chic	928	497	230	201	23	6	2	15	37	7.44	231	46.48	274	55.13	54	10.87	19	8	42	373	75.05
1932	NYor	945	499	232	214	17	9	6	2	37	7.41	233	46.69	278	55.71	56	11.22	19	10	41	381	76.35
1933	Cinc	975	518	233	224	30	7	4	19	40	7.72	238	45.95	297	57.34	59	11.39	18	12	46	398	76.83
1934	Phil	994	527	225	242	19	1	9	9	41	7.78	240	45.54	307	58.25	61	11.57	17	13	47	403	76.47
1935	StLo	1029	554	224	251	35	6	2	27	47	8.48	248	44.77	335	60.47	68	12.27	16	16	52	423	76.35
1936	Durh	1061	577	223	261	32	5	4	23	52	9.01	257	44.54	356	61.70	73	12.65	18	18	55	436	75.56
1936	Mila	1061	577	223	261	32	5	4	23	52	9.01	257	44.54	356	61.70	73	12.65	19	18	55	436	75.56
1937	Trto	1103	609	217	277	42	3	7	32	56	9.20	273	44.83	388	63.71	88	14.45	20	20	60	463	76.03
1938	Pitt	1145	635	222	288	42	8	8	26	63	9.92	276	43.46	419	65.98	93	14.65	22	23	63	483	76.06
1939	Bost	1184	661	220	303	39	3	10	26	64	9.68	288	43.57	444	67.17	102	15.43	24	25	67	502	75.95
1940	Loui	1218	686	218	314	34	2	7	25	68	9.91	294	42.86	464	67.64	105	15.31	24	29	72	516	75.22
1941	Chic	1262	717	218	327	44	5	8	31	76	10.60	303	42.26	492	68.62	111	15.48	29	32	72	535	74.62
1942	NYor	1304	752	212	340	42	4	3	35	83	11.04	315	41.89	526	69.95	120	15.96	31	33	77	561	74.60
1943		1321	761	208	352	17	2	6	9	84	11.04	314	41.26	536	70.43	120	15.77	32	35	79	564	74.11
1944		354	1784	203	367	33	1	9	23	85	10.84	320	40.82	557	71.05	122	15.56	32	36	83	582	74.23
1945		382	1805	200	377	28	2	5	21	91	11.30	328	40.75	577	71.68	126	15.65	33	37	86	600	74.53
1946	Clev	1414	818	190	406	32	3	16	13	92	11.25	331	40.46	588	71.88	125	15.28	33	37	90	611	74.69
1947	Mtrl	1460	847	188	425	46	5	12	29	98	11.57	340	40.14	610	72.02	129	15.23	32	40	92	635	74.97
1948	Madi	1499	873	185	441	39	4	9	26	103	11.80	348	39.86	633	72.51	134	15.35	33	42	96	655	75.03
1949	Phil	1536	898	182	456	37	6	6	25	110	12.25	359	39.98	653	72.72	141	15.70	33	41	96	677	75.39
1950	NOrl	1569	920	169	480	33	5	6	22	111	12.07	361	39.24	672	73.04	142	15.43	33	40	96	694	75.43
1950	Oxfd	1569	920	169	480	33	5	6	22	111	12.07	361	39.24	672	73.04	142	15.43	33	40	96	694	75.43
1951	Detr	1606	940	168	498	37	4	13	20	115	12.23	372	39.57	688	73.19	149	15.85	33	43	96	709	75.43

Meetings		Statistics for stated year				Changes from preceding year				Women		MD & PhD DEGREES						APPOINTMENTS				
Year	City	Cum	Act	Inact	Dead	Start	End	Died	Net	No.	%	MD	MD%	PhD	PhD%	Both	Both%	Instr	Asst	Assoc	Full	Full%
1952	Prov	1660	973	177	510	54	11	10	33	115	11.82	395	40.60	710	72.97	159	16.34	35	42	97	735	75.54
1953	Cbus	1711	1016	176	519	51	2	6	43	120	11.81	406	39.96	747	73.52	165	16.24	36	44	99	767	75.49
1954	Galv	1747	1039	174	534	36	3	10	23	122	11.74	414	39.85	764	73.53	168	16.17	36	46	104	783	75.36
1955	Phil	1817	1089	177	551	70	5	15	50	125	11.48	433	39.76	806	74.01	177	16.25	35	49	110	820	75.30
1955	Pari	1817	1089	177	551	70	5	15	50	125	11.48	433	39.76	806	74.01	177	16.25	35	49	110	820	75.30
1956	Milw	1889	1146	175	568	72	4	11	57	134	11.69	448	39.09	857	74.78	187	16.32	37	52	115	861	75.13
1957	Balt	1983	1212	183	588	94	15	13	66	144	11.88	458	37.79	909	75.00	189	15.59	37	50	126	914	75.41
1958	Bflo	2065	1271	188	606	82	10	13	59	153	12.04	465	36.59	966	76.00	197	15.50	37	53	134	960	75.53
1959	Seat	2126	1308	190	628	61	10	14	37	156	11.93	473	36.16	992	75.84	199	15.21	39	51	138	990	75.69
1960	NYor	2195	1354	189	652	69	6	17	46	164	12.11	480	35.45	1031	76.14	204	15.07	37	57	148	1015	74.96
1961	Chic	2282	1415	192	675	87	8	18	61	172	12.16	489	34.56	1083	76.54	211	14.91	37	61	155	1053	74.42
1962	Minn	2363	1479	190	694	81	3	14	64	181	12.24	514	34.75	1125	76.06	220	14.87	40	66	161	1091	73.77
1963	Wash	2448	1534	193	721	85	10	20	55	192	12.52	521	33.96	1169	76.21	225	14.67	40	68	181	1113	72.56
1964	Denv	2534	1593	196	745	86	8	19	59	201	12.62	537	33.71	1216	76.33	232	14.56	40	69	193	1153	72.38
1965	Miam	2643	1674	205	764	109	13	15	81	210	12.54	557	33.27	1283	76.64	240	14.34	41	71	209	1211	72.34
1965	Wies	2643	1674	205	764	109	13	15	81	210	12.54	557	33.27	1283	76.64	240	14.34	41	71	209	1211	72.34
1966	SanF	2753	1757	208	788	110	8	19	83	214	12.18	573	32.61	1343	76.44	242	13.77	43	78	223	1258	71.60
1967	KCit	2857	1831	220	806	104	17	13	74	216	11.80	587	32.06	1414	77.23	254	13.87	44	81	237	1309	71.49
1968	NOrl	3005	1941	239	825	148	22	16	110	227	11.69	619	31.89	1498	77.18	262	13.50	44	87	267	1369	70.53
1969	Bost	3137	2034	261	842	132	23	16	93	245	12.05	651	32.01	1572	77.29	282	13.86	44	100	288	1410	69.32
1970	Chic	3296	2146	280	870	159	23	24	112	262	12.21	676	31.50	1666	77.63	298	13.89	43	104	323	1463	68.17
1970	Leni	3296	2146	280	870	159	23	24	112	262	12.21	676	31.50	1666	77.63	298	13.89	43	104	323	1463	68.17
1971	Phil	3416	2188	328	900	120	52	26	42	272	12.43	687	31.40	1714	78.34	310	14.17	41	113	357	1471	67.23
1972	Dall	3520	2241	352	927	104	28	23	53	273	12.18	686	30.61	1777	79.29	316	14.10	38	119	384	1495	66.71
1973	NYor	3642	2310	379	953	122	31	22	69	290	12.55	694	30.04	1850	80.09	322	13.94	40	133	421	1512	65.45
1974	Clev	3761	2362	419	980	119	44	23	52	310	13.12	689	29.17	1908	80.78	323	13.67	42	143	457	1516	64.18
1975	LAng	3885	2417	451	1017	124	40	29	55	324	13.41	689	28.51	1972	81.59	326	13.49	42	152	510	1509	62.43
1975	Toky	3885	2417	451	1017	124	40	29	55	324	13.41	689	28.51	1972	81.59	326	13.49	42	152	510	1509	62.43
1976	Loui	4088	2564	479	1045	203	34	22	147	366	14.27	705	27.50	2114	82.45	337	13.14	45	196	584	1528	59.59
1977	Detr	4242	2640	543	1059	154	66	12	76	393	14.89	700	26.52	2207	83.60	339	12.84	48	221	634	1521	57.61
1978	Vanc	4369	2699	590	1080	127	49	19	59	407	15.08	704	26.08	2276	84.33	349	12.93	51	242	682	1504	55.72
1979	Miam	4492	2744	644	1104	123	55	19	45	422	15.38	706	25.73	2330	84.91	355	12.94	51	271	710	1486	54.15
1980	Omah	4615	2771	724	1120	123	80	16	27	437	15.77	697	25.15	2367	85.42	356	12.85	49	302	733	1462	52.76
1980	MexC	4615	2771	724	1120	123	80	16	27	437	15.77	697	25.15	2367	85.42	356	12.85	49	302	733	1462	52.76
1981	NOrl	4730	2803	779	1148	115	57	26	32	452	16.13	685	24.44	2411	86.01	350	12.49	48	343	742	1443	51.48
1982	Indi	4881	2862	861	1158	151	83	9	59	476	16.63	684	23.90	2475	86.48	356	12.44	52	391	751	1419	49.58
1983	Atla	5069	2917	980	1172	188	121	12	55	498	17.07	678	23.24	2536	86.94	357	12.24	53	419	753	1399	47.96
1984	Seat	5203	2921	1095	1187	134	116	14	4	512	17.53	664	22.73	2556	87.50	348	11.91	53	445	743	1376	47.11
1985	Trto	5303	2854	1227	1222	100	137	30	-67	511	17.90	640	22.42	2507	87.84	337	11.81	50	464	724	1323	46.36
1986	Reno	5381	2792	1361	1228	78	136	4	-62	508	18.19	620	22.21	2447	87.64	324	11.60	49	450	694	1288	46.13

CAREER SUMMARIES — OFFICERS AND MEMBERS OF THE EXECUTIVE COMMITTEE[1]

Names/Membs/Offs	Birth	Death	Position	Bach/Mast	MD/PhD	Instructor	Asst Prof	Assoc Prof	Full Prof	Chrmn
Adams, A. Elizabeth f @ 1925+ E5458	NJ 1892	1962	MtHo 1957 SHad Ma USA01075	MtHo 1914 Clmb 1918	Yale 1923	MtHo 1915		MtHo 1919	MtHo 1928	Zo4753
Alden, Roland H. A 1943 P6970 E6768	Il 1914		ETnM 1982 JnsC Tn USA37614	Stnf 1936	Yale 1941	YalM 1941 ETnM 1942	ETnM 1944	ETnM 1946	ETnM 1949	An5161
Allen, Edgar @ 1921+ P42 V3032	Co 1892	1943	YalM 1943 NHav Ct USA06510	Brwn 1915 Brwn 1916	Brwn 1921	WaU 1919			UMoC 1923 YalM 1933	An2333 An3343
Allen, Harrison @ 1888+ P9194 E8891	Pa 1841	1897	Wist 1897 Phil Pa USA19104		UPa 1861				UPaM 1865 PaDC 1866 UPa 1875	
Anderson, Everett A 1958 V8385 E7377	Tx 1928		HrvB Bost Ma USA02115	Fisk 1949 Fisk	Ula 1955	HwrM 1957	TxSU 1952 UlaM 1958		UMa 1961 HrvB 1972	
Anson, Barry Joseph @ 1925+ P5858	Ia 1894	1974	UIaM 1962 Iowa Ia USA52240	UWi 1917 Hrvd 1923	HrvC 1927	NthM 1926		NthM 1930	NthM 1942 UIaM 1962	An5662
Arey, Leslie B. g A 1915 P5254 V4246 E3034	Me 1891		NthM 1956 Chic Il USA60611	Clby 1912	HrvC 1915	NthM 1915		NthM 1917	NthM 1919	An2456
Atwell, Wayne Jason @ 1914+ E3741	Ne 1889	1941	Bflo 1941 Bflo NY USA14240	NeWs 1911 UMi 1915	Bflo 1934 UMi 1917	UMiA 1914			Bflo 1918	An1841
Baker, Burton Lowell @ 1943+ E6468	Mi 1912	1978	UMiA 1978 AnnA Mi USA48104	Kzoo 1933 KsSC 1935	ClmM 1941	ClmM 1936 UMiA 1941	UMiA 1945	UMiA 1947	UMiA 1952	
Baker, Frank @ 1888+ P9597 V8891	NY 1841	1918	GrgM 1918 Wash DC USA20013	Grgt 1888	GeWa 1880 Grgt 1890				GrgM 1883	
Bardeen, Charles R. @ 1900+ V1720 E0409	Mi 1871	1935	UWMd 1935 Madi Wi USA53703	HrvC 1893	JnHo 1897		JnHo 1897	JnHM 1901	UWMd 1904	An0435

[1] See note at end of this table explaining the significance of certain symbols and abbreviations.

Names/Membs/Offs	Birth	Death	Position	Bach/Mast	MD/PhD	Instructor	Asst Prof	Assoc Prof	Full Prof	Chrmn
Barker, Lewellys F. @ 1898-1911 E0105	*On 1867	1943	JnHM 1921 Balt Md USA21233	Trto 1890				JnHM 1897	Rush 1900 JnHM 1905 JnHM 1914	An0005
Barr, Murray L. A 1949 E6569	*On 1908		UWOM 1978 LonO On CanN6A 5C1	UWOn 1930 UWOn 1938	UWOn 1933	UBCM 1936 UWOM 1936		UWOM 1945	UWOM 1951	An5267
Bartelmez, George W. @ 1913+ P4850 V3234 E3640	NY 1885	1967	UCHM 1950 Chic Il USA60637	NYU 1906	UChi 1910	UCHM 1910		UCHM 1919	UCHM 1929	
Basmajian, John V. A 1954 P8586 E7579	Tur 1921		McMM 1977 Hami On CanL8N 3Z5		Trto 1945	TrtM 1946	TrtM 1951	TrtM 1954	TrtM 1956 QuOM 1957 EmrM 1969 McMM 1977	An5769
Bassett, David Lee @ 1944+ E6064	Ca 1913	1966	UWaM 1966 Seat Wa USA98101	Stnf 1934	Stnf 1939	StnM 1940	StnM 1944	StnM 1950	StnM 1956 UWaM 1959	
Batson, Oscar V. g 1917+ V5658	Mo 1894	1979	UPaM 1965 Phil Pa USA19104	UMo 1916 UMo 1918	StLo 1920	StLM 1919 UWMd 1920	UCnM 1921 UPaM 1942	UCnM 1924	UCnM 1927 UPaM 1928	
Bennett, H. Stanley A 1940 P5960 V5859	Jap 1910		UNCM 1981 Chap NC USA27514	Obln 1932	HrvB 1936	HrvB 1939	MaIT 1945	HrvB 1941	UWaM 1948 UCHM 1961 UNCM 1969	BS4860 An6977
Bensley, Robert R. @ 1901+ P1720 V0508 E0812	*On 1867	1956	UCHM 1933 Chic Il USA60607	Trto 1889	Trto 1892		UCHM 1901	UCHM 1905	UCHM 1907	An0533
Bensley, Sylvia H. f @ 1935+ E5862	Ind 1903	1972	TrtM 1969 Trto On CanM5S 1A8	MtHo 1925	UChi 1930	UCHM 1930	UCHM 1942	TrtM 1948	TrtM 1964	
Bevan, Arthur Dean @ 1891+ E9598	Il 1861	1943	Rush Chic Il USA60612	Yale 1879	Rush 1883			Rush 1898	Rush 1888 Rush 1902	An8802 Sr0943
Black, Virginia H. f A 1972 E8387	Mi 1941		NYUM NYor NY USA10016	Kzoo 1963 Sacr 1966	Stnf 1968	NYUM 1967	NYUM 1970	NYUM 1973		

Names/Membs/Offs	Birth	Death	Position	Bach/Mast	MD/PhD	Instructor	Asst Prof	Assoc Prof	Full Prof	Chrmn
Blandau, Richard J. g A 1950 P6869 V6466 E5559	Pa 1911		UWaM 1982 Seat Wa USA98195	Lnfd 1935	Roch 1948 Brwn 1939	HrvB 1942 Roch 1943	Roch 1948	UWaM 1949	UWaM 1951	
Bloom, William @ 1928 + V5254 E4650	Md 1899	1972	UCHM 1965 Chic Il USA60637	JnHo 1919	JnHo 1923		UCHM 1929	UCHM 1933	UCHM 1941	An4146
Bodian, David A 1937 P7172 E5963 E6870	Mo 1910		[home] 1982 Balt Md USA21218	UChi 1931	UChi 1937 UChi 1934		CWRM 1940 JnHM 1942	JnHM 1945	JnHM 1957	An5775
Boyden, Edward Allen g A 1913 + P5657 V4648 E2832 E3946	Ma 1886	1976	UMNM 1954 Minn Mn USA55455	HrvC 1909 HrvB 1911	HrvB 1916	HrvB 1916	HrvB 1919	UIIM 1926	UIIM 1929 UAIM 1929 UMNM 1931 UWaM 1954	An4054
Bremer, John Lewis @ 1901 + E1419 E3337	NY 1874	1959	HrvB 1941 Bost Ma USA02109	HrvC 1896	HrvB 1901	HrvB 1902	HrvB 1912	HrvB 1915	HrvB 1931	
Brightman, Milton W. A 1955 V8284	*On 1923		NIH Beth Md USA20892	Trto 1945 Trto 1948	Yale 1954			GeWM 1971		
Bunge, Richard Paul A 1962 V8183 E7680	SD 1932		WaUM StLo Mo USA63110	UWi 1954 UWi 1956	UWi 1960	UWMd 1957	ClmM 1962	ClmM 1966	WaUM 1970	
Burr, Harold Saxton @ 1915 + E2933	Ma 1889	1973	YalM 1958 NHav Ct USA06510	Yale 1911	Yale 1915	YalM 1914	YalM 1919	YalM 1926	YalM 1929	
Chambers, Robert, II @ 1915 + V3940	Tur 1881	1957	NYU 1947 NYor NY USA10016	Robt 1900 QuOn 1902	Muni 1908	Trto 1909 Crnl 1915	UCin 1912 Crnl 1919		Crnl 1922 NYU 1928	
Christensen, A. Kent A 1962 P8485 E7983	DC 1927		UMiA AnnA Mi USA48109	BrYg 1953 Hrvd 1956	HrvC 1958	HrvB 1960	StnM 1961	StnM 1968	TmpM 1971 UMiA 1978	An7178 AC7882
Clark, Eliot Round @ 1908 + S3842 S4346 E1519	Ma 1881	1963	UPaM 1949 Phil Pa USA19104	Yale 1903	JnHo 1907	JnHM 1908	JnHM 1908	JnHM 1911	UMoC 1914 MCGa 1922 UPaM 1926	An1422 An2226 An2647

Names/Membs/Offs	Birth	Death	Position	Bach/Mast	MD/PhD	Instructor	Asst Prof	Assoc Prof	Full Prof	Chrmn
Clark, Sam L. @ 1927+ P5052 E4249	Tn 1898	1960	VndM 1960 Nash Tn USA37202	Vand 1922 Nthw 1924	Vand 1930 WaUM 1926	NthM 1923 WaUM 1924	WaUM 1926 NthM 1927 VndM 1930	VndM 1931	VndM 1937	An3760
Clark, Sam L.Jr. A 1954 V7779 E6872	Mo 1926		UMaW Worc Ma USA01605	Duke VndM	HrvB 1949	WaUM 1954	WaUM 1957	WaUM 1963	UMaW 1968	An6877
Clemente, Carmine D. A 1953 P7677 V7072 E6970	NJ 1928		UCLM LAng Ca USA90024	UPa 1948 UPa 1950	UPa 1952	UCLM 1952	UCLM 1954	UCLM 1959	UCLM 1963	An6373
Clermont, Yves W. A 1956 V7073	*PQ 1926		McGM Mtrl PQ CanH3G 1Y6	Mtrl 1949	McGM 1953		McGM 1956	McGM 1960	McGM 1963	An7585
Coghill, George E. 1904+ P3234 E2731	Il 1872	1941	Wist 1935 Phil Pa USA19104	Brwn 1896 UNM 1899	Brwn 1902		UNMM 1899	UKsK 1913	Paci 1902 Wlmt 1906 Dnsn 1907 UKsK 1916	
Corner, George W. g @ 1913+ P4648 S3038 E2630 E3842	Md 1889	1981	JnHo Balt Md USA21205	JnHo 1909	JnHo 1913		UCa 1915	JnHM 1919	RchM 1923	An2340
Cowdry, Edmund V. @ 1913+ V3436 E2630	*Ab 1888	1975	WaUM 1960 StLo Mo USA63155	Trto 1909	UChi 1912				Pekg 1917 WaUM 1928 WaUM 1941	
Craigie, E. Horne A 1917 E4148	Sco 1894		[home] 1962 Toro On CanM4N 1B9	Trto 1916	Trto 1920		Trto 1925	Trto 1933	Trto 1945	
Cummins, Harold @ 1916+ P6162 V5960 E3640	In 1893	1976	TlnM 1964 NOrl La USA70112	UMi 1916	Tlne 1925	VndM 1916 TlnM 1919	VndM 1918 TlnM 1920	TlnM 1926	TlnM 1932	An4659
Cunningham, Robert S. @ 1913+ E3236	SC 1891	1963	AlbM 1952 Alba NY USA12208	Dvds 1911 Dvds 1911	JnHo 1915 Unio	JnHM 1915		JnHM 1922	VndM 1925 AlbM 1937	
Danforth, Charles H. @ 1910+ V3638 E2731	Me 1883	1969	StnM 1949 Stnf Ca USA94304	Tuft 1908 Tuft 1910	WaU 1941s	WaUM 1908 TftB 1910		WaUM 1916 StnM 1922	StnM 1923	An2349

Names/Membs/Offs	Birth	Death	Position	Bach/Mast	MD/PhD	Instructor	Asst Prof	Assoc Prof	Full Prof	Chrmn
Dawson, Alden B. @ 1919 + E5357	*PE 1892	1968	HrvC 1959 CamM Ma USA02109	Acda 1915	HrvC 1918		LoyC 1919	LoyC 1923 NYU 1925 Hrvd 1929	MtAl 1918 NYU 1928 Hrvd 1938	Bi4045
Dempsey, Edward W. @ 1938 + P6061 E5759	Ia 1911	1975	ClmM NYor NY USA10001	Mrta 1932 HrvC 1946	Brwn 1937	HrvB 1938	HrvB 1942	HrvB 1946	WaUM 1950 ClmM 1966	An5066 An6674
Detwiler, Samuel R. @ 1915 + P5456 V5254 E3034	Pa 1890	1957	ClmM 1957 NYor NY USA10032	Yale 1914 Yale 1916	Yale 1918	YalM 1917	Hrvd 1923	HrvB 1926	ClmM 1927	An2757
Donaldson, Henry H. @ 1901 + P1517 E0813	NY 1857	1938	UCHM 1930 Chic Il USA60637	Yale 1879	JnHo 1885	JnHM 1883	Clrk 1889		UCHM 1892 Wist 1906	Nr9206
Duncan, Donald g A 1929 P6667 V6062 E5054	Mn 1903		StnM 1982 Stnf Ca USA94304	Crlt 1923 UMNM 1927	UMNM 1929		UUtM 1929 Bflo 1930	UTxG 1932	UTxG 1941 Bflo 1942 LaSN 1943 UTxG 1946	An4243 An4668
Dwight, Thomas @ 1889 + P9495 E8994	Ma 1843	1911	HrvB 1911 Bost Ma USA02109	HrvC 1866 HrvC 1872	HrvB 1867	HrvB 1872 HrvB 1874			Bwdn 1873 HrvB 1883	
Elftman, Herbert O. A 1938 E6870	Mn 1902		ClmM 1971 NYor NY USA10032	UCBk 1923 UCBk 1925	Clmb 1929	ClmM 1940	ClmM 1929	ClmM 1948	ClmM 1961	
Enders, Allen Coffin A 1958 P8384 V7981	Oh 1928		UCDM Davi Ca USA95616	Swth 1950 Hrvd 1952	HrvC 1955		Rice 1955	Rice 1960 WaUM 1963	WaUM 1969 UCDM 1975	An7580
Evans, Herbert M. @ 1907 + P3032 E1923	Ca 1882	1971	UCBk 1952 Berk Ca USA94704	UCa 1904	JnHo 1908	JnHM 1909		JnHM 1912	UCBk 1915	
Everett, John W. g A 1935 P7374	Mi 1906		DukM 1976 Durh NC USA27710	Oliv 1928	Yale 1932	Gchr 1930 DukM 1932	DukM 1939	DukM 1947	DukM 1950	
Everett, Newton B. @ 1944 + P7778	Tx 1916	1978	UWaM Seat Wa USA98195	NTxS 1937 NTxS 1938	UMi 1942	NTxS 1939 UMiA 1942	UWaM 1946	UWaM 1948	UWa 1957	BS5778

Names/Membs/Offs	Birth	Death	Position	Bach/Mast	MD/PhD	Instructor	Asst Prof	Assoc Prof	Full Prof	Chrmn
Fallon, John F. A 1969 E8589	Ma 1938		UWi Madi Wi USA53706	Mrqt 1961	Mrqt 1966	UWi 1970	UWi 1969		UWi 1981	
Fawcett, Don Wayne g A 1947 P6566 V5860	Ia 1917		HrvB 1982 Bost Ma USA02115	HrvC 1938	HrvB 1942	HrvB 1946	HrvB 1951	HrvB 1948	CrnN 1955 HrvB 1959	An5559 An5981
Figge, Frank H.J. @ 1934+ E5256	Co 1904	1973	WdHl 1973 WdHl Ma USA02543	CoC 1927	UMd 1934	UMdB 1930	UMdB 1935	UMdB 1936	UMdB 1947	An571
Finerty, John C. A 1945 P7576 PS6674	Il 1914		[home] Hous Tx USA77018	Kzoo 1937 KsSC 1939	UWi 1942	UMiA 1943	WaUM 1946	WaUM 1949 UTx 1949	UTx 1952 UMiM 1956 LaSN 1966	An5666
Flexner, Louis B. A 1931 S5664 E5053	Ky 1902		UPaM 1967 Phil Pa USA19104	UChi 1923	JnHo 1927	JnHM 1930		JnHM 1930	UPaM 1951	An5167
Flint, J. Marshall J. @ 1900–1921 V0305	Il 1872	1944	YalM 1921 NHav Ct USA06510	UChi 1895 Prmc 1900	JnHo 1900				UCa 1901 YalM 1907	An0107
Friedman, Sydney M. A 1942 E7074	*PQ 1916		UBCM Vanc BC CanV6T 1W5	McGl 1938 McGl 1941	McGl 1940 McGl 1946		McGM 1944	McGM 1948	UBCM 1950	An5081
Gage, Simon Henry @ 1889+ E0611	NY 1851	1944	Crnl 1908 Itha NY USA14850	Crnl 1877			Crnl 1881	Crnl 1889	Crnl 1896	
Gardner, William U. A 1935 P7273 E4852	Mn 1907		YalM 1974 NHav Ct USA06477	SDSU 1930 UMo 1931	SDSU 1960s	YalM 1933	YalM 1936	YalM 1938	YalM 1943	AG4366
Gerrish, Frederic H. @ 1890–1914 V9901 E9295 E9799 E0106	Me 1845	1920	Bwdn 1911 BruM Me USA04011	Bwdn 1866	Bwdn 1869				Bwdn 1873 UMiM 1874 Bwdn 1882 Bwdn 1905	
Gill, Theodore N. @ 1890–1900 V9194 E9497	NY 1837	1914	GeWa 1910 Wash DC USA20013	GeWa 1865	GeWa 1866				GeWa 1884	

Names/Membs/Offs	Birth	Death	Position	Bach/Mast	MD/PhD	Instructor	Asst Prof	Assoc Prof	Full Prof	Chrmn
Goodman, Donald C. A 1956 E7882	Il 1927		ETnM JnsC Tn USA37614	Ull 1949 Ull 1950	Ull 1954	UPaM 1954 UMiA 1956	UFlM 1956	UFlM 1959	UFlM 1963 SNSy 1968 ETnM 1982	An6568 An6882 An82
Goss, Charles Mayo @ 1929+ P6465 E4751	Il 1899	1981	GeWM Wash DC USA20005	Yale 1921	Yale 1926	YalM 1926 ClmM 1929	ClmM 1931		UAlM 1938 LaSN 1947 GeWM 1961	An3847 An4765
Grant, J.C. Boileau @ 1920+ V5052	Sco 1886	1973	TrtM 1956 Trto On CanM5S 188	Ednb	Ednb 1909				UMbM 1919 TrtM 1930	An1930 An3056
Greulich, Richard C. A 1954 E7175	Co 1928		NlAg Md Balt USA21224	Stnf 1949	McGl 1953	UCLA 1953	UCLA 1955	UCLA 1961	UCLA 1964	
Greulich, William W. A 1935 V5658 E4650	Oh 1899		StnM 1964 Stnf Ca USA94305	Knyn 1926 Denv 1927	Stnf 1934	UCo 1928	Yale 1936	Yale 1939	CWRs 1940 StnM 1944	
Guild, Stacy Rufus @ 1913+ E3946	Ks 1890	1966	JnHM 1957 Balt Md USA21205	Wshb 1910 UMiA 1914	UMi 1918	UMiA 1913	UMiA 1918	UMiA 1923 JnHM 1932		
Hamann, Carl A. @ 1892+ E0104	Oh 1868	1930	CWRM 1930 Clev Oh USA44106		UPa 1890				CWRM 1893	
Hardesty, Irving @ 1901+ E0910 E1115 E2125	NC 1866	1944	TlnM 1933 NOrl La USA70113	WkFs 1892	UChi 1899	UCa 1900	UCa 1903	UCa 1907	TlnM 1909	An0933
Harrison, Ross G. @ 1898+ P1113	Pa 1870	1959	Yale 1938 NHav Ct USA06510	JnHo 1889	Bonn 1899 JnHo 1894	JnHo 1896		JnHo 1899	Yale 1907	Zo2738
Hartman, Carl G. @ 1921+ V4042 E2933	Ia 1879	1968	[Res] 1958 NYor NY USA10001	UTx 1902 UTx 1904	UTx 1915	UTx 1912			SHSU 1909 Ull 1941	Zo4147
Hay, Elizabeth D. f A 1954 P8182 V7577 E7073	Fl 1927		HrvB Ma Bost USA02115	Smth 1948	JnHo 1952	JnHM 1953	HrvB 1956 CmN 1957 HrvB 1960	HrvB 1964	HrvB 1969	An75

Names/Membs/Offs	Birth	Death	Position	Bach/Mast	MD/PhD	Instructor	Asst Prof	Assoc Prof	Full Prof	Chrmn
Heitzmann, Charles @ 1890+ V9194	Hun 1836	1896	[PPct] NYor NY USA10001		Vien 1859					
Herrick, C. Judson @ 1894+ E1317	Mi 1868	1960	UCHM 1937 Chic Il USA60637	UCin 1891 Dnsn 1895	Clmb 1900	Dnsn 1893	Dnsn 1897		OtKs 1892 Dnsn 1898 UCHM 1907	
Hess, Melvin @ 1953+ PS7478	NY 1925	1979	LaSN 1976 NOrl La USA70112	UOk 1948 WaU 1949	UTx 1952	EmrM 1952	EmrM 1953 UPtM 1956	UPtM 1960	LaSN 1965	An6576
Hines, Marion f @ 1917+ V4648	Mo 1889	1982	EmrM Atla Ga USA30322	Smth 1913	Smth 1943s	UCHM 1918	UCHM 1924	JnHM 1930	EmrM 1947	
Hinsey, Joseph C. @ 1928+ E4047	Ia 1901	1981	Crnl 1967 Itha NY USA14853	Nthw 1922 Nthw 1923	WaUM 1927	CWRs 1923 WaUM 1924	WaUM 1927 NthM 1928 Stnf 1929	Nthw 1929	StnM 1930 CrnN 1936 CrnN 1939	Ph3639 cA3953
Hitchcock, Karen R. f A 1971 V8688 E8185	NY 1943		TxTM Lubb Tx USA79430	StLa 1964	Roch 1968		TftB 1970	TftB 1975	TftB 1980 TxTM 1985	AC7885
Hoerr, Normand Louis @ 1933+ P57 S4656	Il 1902	1958	CWRM 1958 Clev Oh USA44101	JnHo 1923	UChi 1931 UChi 1929	UCHM 1926	UCHM 1933		CWRM 1939	An3958
Holbrook, Karen Ann f A 1975 E8589	Ia 1942		UWaM Seat Wa USA98195	UWi 1963 UWi 1966	UWaM 1972	Ripn 1966 UWaM 1972	UWaM 1975	UWaM 1979	UWaM 1984	
Hollinshead, W. Henry A 1933 V6668 E6566	Tn 1906		UNC Chap NC USA27514	Vand 1926 Vand 1927	Vand 1932	VndM 1927 DukM 1930	DukM 1939	DukM 1944	DukM 1946 Mayo 1947	
Holmes, Edmund Wales @ 1890+ E9801	SAf 1851	1905	UPaM Phil Pa USA19104	Yale 1872	UPa 1880					
Hooker, Charles W. a 1938-1985 E5660	Va 1910		UNCM 1982 Chap NC USA27514	Duke 1930 Duke 1932	Duke 1933	TlnM 1936 YalM 1937	YalM 1942	YalM 1946	EmrM 1948 UNCM 1949	

Names/Membs/Offs	Birth	Death	Position	Bach/Mast	MD/PhD	Instructor	Asst Prof	Assoc Prof	Full Prof	Chrmn
Hooker, Davenport @ 1909 + P5859 V4042 E2125	NY 1887	1965	UPtM 1956 Pitt Pa USA15261	Yale 1908 Yale 1909	Yale 1912	YalM 1909	UPtM 1914 YalM 1915		UPtM 1919	An1956
Huber, Gotthelf Carl @ 1897 + P1315 V9901 S0113 E2023	Ind 1865	1934	UMiA 1914 AnnA Mi USA48106		UMi 1887	UMiA 1889	UMiA 1891	UMiA 1898	UMiA 1903	An0314
Huber, John Franklin a 1937-1983 V6466	Mi 1904		TmpM 1972 Phil Pa USA19140	UMi 1925 UMi 1928	UMi 1929 UMi 1933	UMiA 1929	UMiA	TmpM 1936	TmpM 1944	An4471
Huntington, George S. @ 1892 + P9903 E9497 E0308 E1721	Ct 1861	1927	ClmM 1927 NYor NY USA10032	TrCt 1881 TrCt 1883	ClmM 1884				ClmM 1890	An9027
Ingram, Walter R. @ 1931 + E4852	Eng 1905	1978	UIaM 1973 Iowa Ia USA52240	Grnl 1926 Ula 1928	Ula 1929		NthM 1932 UlaM 1936	UlaM 1937	UlaM 1940	An4066
Ito, Susumu A 1961 V7375	Ca 1919		HrvB Bost Ma USA02115	Fenn 1950 CWRs 1951	CWRs 1954	CrnN 1956 HrvB 1960	HrvB 1963	HrvB 1966	HrvB 1968	
Jackson, Clarence M. @ 1901 + P2124 V1517 E1014 E2428	Ia 1875	1947	UMNM 1941 Minn Mn USA55401	UMo 1898 UMo 1899	UMo 1900	UMoC 1899	UMoC 1900		UMoC 1902 UMNM 1913	An1341
Johnson, Robert J. A 1952 E6064	Wa 1915		UPaM 1985 Phil Pa USA19104	IaSU 1937	Ula 1943	UWaM 1946	UWaM 1947	UWaM 1951	WVMC 1957 UPaM 1963	AG5763
Jollie, William P. A 1961 S8088	NJ 1928		MCVa Rich Va USA23298	Lhgh 1950 Lhgh 1952	HrvC 1959		TlnM 1961	TlnM 1965	TlnM 1968 MCVa 1969	An69
Jones, Oliver Perry 1937 PS5466	Pa 1906		SNBM 1976 Bflo NY USA14214	Tmpl 1929	SUNY 1956 UMn 1935	UMNM 1935	SNSM 1937 UMNM 1938	SNSM 1943	SNSM 1943	AI4371
Jordan, Harvey E. @ 1908 + V3638 E1721	Pa 1878	1963	WdHI 1948 WdHl Ma USA02543	Lhgh 1903 Lhgh 1904	Prnc 1907			UVaM 1908	UVaM 1911	

Names/Membs/Offs	Birth	Death	Position	Bach/Mast	MD/PhD	Instructor	Asst Prof	Assoc Prof	Full Prof	Chrmn
Keiller, William @ 1894 + V9799	Sco 1861	1931	UTxG 1931 Galv Tx USA77550		Ednb 1888				UTxG 1891	An9131
Kelly, Douglas E. A 1964 P8687 E7478	Wy 1932		USCM LAng Ca USA90033	CoSU 1954	Stnf 1958	UCo 1958	UCo 1961 UWa 1963	UWaM 1965	UMiM 1970 USCM 1974	AC7074 AC74
Kerr, Abram Tucker @ 1897 + E1014	NY 1873	1938	CrnN 1938 NYor NY USA14850	Crnl 1895	Bflo 1897		CrnN 1900		CrnN 1904	
Kimmel, Donald L. @ 1940 + E6771	Pa 1906	1986	WVMC 1974 Morg WV USA26506	Gety 1929 UMi 1935	UMi 1938	LaSU 1938	LaSU 1943 Bylr 1943	TmpM 1944	TmpM 1950 ChMS 1957 WVMC 1966	An5766 An6674
Kingsbury, B.F. @ 1904 + V3234 E2125	Mo 1872	1946	UNC 1941 Chap NC USA27514	Bctl 1893 Crnl 1894	Frei 1903 Bwdn 1937	CrnN 1896	CrnN 1902		CrnN 1908	HE0841
Knisely, Melvin H. @ 1938 + E5963	Mi 1904	1975	MUSC 1969 Chas SC USA29401	Albn 1927	UChi 1935		UCHM 1937	UCHM 1945	MUSC 1948	An4869
Knower, Henry McE. @ 1900 + E1115 E2426	Md 1868	1940	YalM 1937 NHav Ct USA06510	JnHo 1890	JnHo 1896	Wlms 1896 JnHM 1899		AlbM 1930 JnHM 1908	UCnM 1910 UAlM 1927	An1024
Kollros, Jerry John A 1948 E6266	Ast 1917		UIaM Iowa Ia USA52242	UChi 1938	UChi 1942	UChi 1945	UIaM 1947	UIaM 1950	UIaM 1957	Zo5577
Kornhauser, Sidney I. @ 1923 + E4249	Oh 1887	1959	ULoM 1958 Loui Ky USA40202	UPit 1908 Hrvd 1910	HrvC 1912	GeWa 1908	Nthw 1914	Nthw 1917	Dnsn 1919 ULoM 1922	An2258
Kuntz, Albert @ 1910 + V3840	In 1879	1957	StLM 1957 StLo Mo USA63155	Mrng 1904	StLo 1918 Ula 1910	UIaM 1911	StLM 1913	StLM 1916	StLM 1919	An3057
Ladman, Aaron John A 1954 V8082 E7276	NY 1925		HahM Phil Pa USA19102-1	NYU 1947	InUB 1952			HrvB 1958 UTnM 1961	UNMM 1964 HahM 1981	An6481

Names/Membs/Offs	Birth	Death	Position	Bach/Mast	MD/PhD	Instructor	Asst Prof	Assoc Prof	Full Prof	Chrmn
Lamb, Daniel Smith @ 1888-1916 S9001 V0103	Pa 1843	1929	HwrM 1923 Wash DC USA20059	1859	Grgt 1867				HwrM 1873 HwrM 1877	An7722
Landis, Story C. f A 1974 E8690	NY 1945		CWRM Clev Oh USA44106	Wels 1967 Hrvd 1970	HrvC 1973	HrvB 1980				
Langman, Jan @ 1958 + V7274	Net 1923	1981	UVaM Char Va USA22903	Amst	Amst 1949 Amst 1950		Amst 1948 FUAm 1951	FUAm 1952 McGM 1957	McGM 1959 UVaM 1964	An6481
Larsell, Olof @ 1919 + E3842	Swe 1886	1964	UMn 1954 Minn Mn USA55455	Lnfd 1910 Nthw 1914	Nthw 1918	Lnfd 1910 Nthw 1915	UWi 1918	Nthw 1920	UOr 1921 Nthw 1926 UMn 1952	
Lavail, Jennifer H. f j A 1972 E7680	In 1943		UCFM SanF Ca USA94143	Trny 1965	UWi 1970	HrvB 1973	HrvB 1974	UCFM 1976	UCFM	
Lazarow, Arnold @ 1944 + E6367	Mi 1916	1975	UMNM Minn Mn USA55455	UChi 1937	UChi 1941 UChi 1941	CWRM 1943	CWRM 1946	CWRM 1948	UMNM 1954	An5475
Leak, Lee Vim A 1966 E8084	SC 1932		HwrM Wash DC USA20001	SCSC 1954 MiSU 1959	MiSU 1962	HrvB 1967	MiSM 1962 HrvB 1969		HwrM 1971	An7181
Leathem, James H. @ 1941 + V6870	Pa 1911	1978	Rtgr NBru NJ USA08903	Lebn 1932 Prnc 1936	Prnc 1937	Rtgr 1941	Rtgr 1942	Rtgr 1947	Rtgr 1948	
Leblond, Charles P. g A 1937 P6263 E5458	Fra 1910		McGM 1975 Mtrl PQ CanH3G 1YG	Nanc 1932	Pari 1934 Sorb 1945		McGM 1943	McGM 1946	McGM 1948	An5775
Lee, Thomas George @ 1890-1901 V1113 E0810	NY 1860	1932	UMNM 1929 Minn Mn USA55455	UPa 1886	UPa 1886				UMNM 1892	An9213
Leidy, Joseph @ 1888 + P8891	Pa 1823	1891	Swth 1891 Swth Pa USA19081		UPa 1844	FnkM 1846			UPaM 1853 Swth 1870	

Names/Membs/Offs	Birth	Death	Position	Bach/Mast	MD/PhD	Instructor	Asst Prof	Assoc Prof	Full Prof	Chrmn
Leuf, Alexander H. P. @ 1888-1895 S8890	NY 1861	1929	UPa Phil Pa USA19104		LICM 1881					
Lewis, Frederic T. @ 1903+ P3638 V1315 E0913	Ma 1875	1951	HrvB 1941 Bost Ma USA02115	HrvC 1897 Hrvd 1898	HrvB 1901	HrvB 1902	HrvB 1906	HrvB 1915	HrvB 1931	
Lewis, Warren Harmon @ 1901+ P3436 E0911 E1317	Ct 1870	1964	Wist 1958 Phil Pa USA19104	UMi 1894	JnHo 1900	JnHM 1901		JnHM 1904	JnHM 1913	
Low, Frank Norman A 1940 E7781	NY 1911		LaSN NOrl La USA70112	Crnl 1932	CrnN 1936	UNCM 1937	UNCM 1939 JnHM 1946	WVMC 1946 LaSU 1949 UMdB 1945	LaSU 1956 UNDM 1964	
Luft, John Herman A 1958 E6871	Or 1927		UWaM Seat Wa USA98195	UWa 1949	UWaM 1953	UWaM 1956	UWaM 1958	UWaM 1961	UWaM 1967	
Macklin, Charles C. @ 1914-1929 E2832	*On 1883	1959	UWOM 1953 LonO On CanN6A 5C1	Trto 1914 Trto 1923	Trto 1918 Trto 1923	JnHM 1915		UPtM 1918 JnHM 1920	UWOM 1921	
Magoun, Horace W. A 1935 P6364 E5357	Pa 1907		[home] 1974 Sant Ca USA90402	URI 1929 SyrU 1931	Nthw 1934	NthM 1934	NthM 1937	NthM 1941	NthM 1943 UCLM 1950	An5055
Mall, Franklin P. @ 1898+ P0508 E0005 E0305 E1617	Ia 1862	1917	JnHM Balt Md USA21205		UMi 1883	JnHM 1886			UCHM 1892 JnHM 1893	An9317
Malone, Edward Fall @ 1910+ E3135	Tn 1880	1964	UCnM 1945 Cinc Oh USA45267	Vand 1903	JnHo 1907		UCnM 1910	UCnM 1915	UCnM 1918 UCnM 1924	An2445
Markee, J. Eldridge @ 1929+ E5155	Il 1903	1970	DukM 1970 Durh NC USA27701	UChi 1925	UChi 1929	UCHM 1928 StnM 1929	StnM 1930	StnM 1936	StnM 1940 DukM 1943	An4366
Mason, Karl Ernest @ 1927+ P6768 V6264 E5256	*NS 1900	1978	RchM 1965 RocN NY USA14642	Acda 1921	Yale 1925	VndM 1926	VndM 1929	VndM 1930	RchM 1940	An4065

Names/Membs/Offs	Birth	Death	Position	Bach/Mast	MD/PhD	Instructor	Asst Prof	Assoc Prof	Full Prof	Chrmn
McClure, C.F.W. @ 1902+ V0911 E1216	Ma 1865	1955	Prnc 1934 Prnc NJ USA08540	Prnc 1888 Prnc 1892		Prnc 1891	Prnc 1895		Prnc 1901	
McKibben, Paul S. @ 1913+ E3135	Oh 1886	1941	USCM 1941 LAng Ca USA90053	Dnsn 1906	UChi 1911	UCHM 1912		UMiA 1927	UWOM 1913 USCM 1929	An1327 An2941
McMurrich, James P. @ 1888+ P0809 E0508 E1620	*On 1859	1939	UCin 1930 Cinc Oh USA45221	Trto 1879 Trto 1882	JnHo 1885	JnHM 1884 WdHl 1891	Clrk 1889		UMiA 1894 TrM 1907 Hvfd 1886 UCin 1892	An0809
Meyer, Arthur W. @ 1904+ V2426 E1216	Wi 1873	1966	StnM 1938 Stnf Ca USA94304	UWi 1898	JnHo 1905	JnHM 1906	UMNM 1907		NthM 1908 StnM 1909	cA0809 CB0938
Miller, William Snow @ 1900+ V0809	Ma 1858	1939	UWMd 1925 Madi Wi USA53703		Yale 1879 UChi 1920	UWMd 1892	UWMd 1895	UWMd 1904	UWMd 1916	
Minot, Charles S. @ 1892+ P0305 E9903 E0508	Ma 1852	1914	HrvB 1914 Bost Ma USA02109	MaIT 1872	HrvC 1878s	HrvB 1883	HrvB 1887		HrvB 1892	
Mortensen, Otto Axel @ 1935+ V6062	Wi 1902	1979	UWMd 1972 Madi Wi USA53706	UWi 1927 UWi 1928	UWi 1929	UWMd 1930	UWMd 1931	UWMd 1937	UWMd 1946 StnM 1972	An5067
Mossman, Harland W. A 1927 E5155	NY 1898		DarM 1968 Hano NH USA03756	Aleg 1920 UWi 1922	UWi 1924	Aleg 1919 UWMd 1920	UWMd 1927	UWMd 1937	UWMd 1953	An5758
Nauta, Walle Jetze H. g A 1952 E7276	Ins 1916		MaIT CamM Ma USA02139		Utre 1942 Utre 1945	Utre 1942		Leid 1946 Zurc 1947	MaIT 1964	
Neutra, Marian R. f A 1968 E8387	Il 1938		HrvB Bost Ma USA02115	UMi 1960	McGl 1966		HrvB 1973	HrvB 1980		
Nicholas, John S. @ 1921+ E4751	Pa 1895	1963	Yale 1963 NHav Ct USA06510	Gety 1916 Gety 1917	Yale 1921	UPit 1921 Gety 1915	UPit 1922 Yale 1926	Yale 1932	Yale 1935	Zo4656

Names/Membs/Offs	Birth	Death	Position	Bach/Mast	MD/PhD	Instructor	Asst Prof	Assoc Prof	Full Prof	Chrmn
O'Steen, W. Keith A 1960 E8084	Ga 1928		WkFM WinS NC USA27103	Emry 1948 Emry 1950	Duke 1958	EmrM 1950 UTxG 1958	Wffd 1951 UTxG 1960	UTxG 1963	UTxG 1967 EmrM 1968 WkFM 1977	An7786
Osmond, Dennis G. A 1966 E7882	NY 1930		McGM Mtrl PQ CanH3G 1Y6	Bris 1951	Bris 1954 Bris 1975			McGM 1965	McGM 1967	An85
Padykula, Helen Ann f A 1954 V7880 E7377	Ma 1924		UMaW Worc Ma USA01605	UMa 1946 MtHo 1948	Rdcf 1954	Wels 1948 HrvB 1953	HrvB 1959		Wels 1964 UMaW 1979	An7982
Palade, George Emil g A 1950 E6468	Ro 1912		YalM 1983 NHav Ct USA06510		Buch 1940	Buch 1933	Buch 1942	Buch 1945 RckI 1946	RckI 1958 YalM 1973	CB7383
Palay, Sanford Louis A 1945 P8081 E7074	Oh 1918		UWaM Seat Wa USA98195	Obln 1940	CWRM 1943	YalM 1949	YalM 1950	YalM 1955	HrvB 1961	
Papez, James W. @ 1914+ E4953	Mn 1883	1958	CrnN 1951 NYor NY USA14850	UMn 1909	UMn 1911		EmrM 1911 CrnN 1920	MCGa 1911	EmrM 1914 CrnN 1937	
Patten, Bradley M. @ 1921+ V3436	Wi 1889	1971	UMiA 1959 AnnA Mi USA48104	Dart 1911 Hrvd 1912	HrvC 1914	CWRs 1914	CWRs 1918	CWRs 1920	UMiA 1936	AC3658
Pauly, John Edward A 1957 P8283 S7280	Il 1927		UArM LitR Ar USA72201	Nthw 1950 LoyS 1952	LoyS 1955	ChMS 1955	ChMS 1959	TlnM 1963	UArM 1967 UArM 1978	PB7880 An6783
Pearson, Anthony A. @ 1937+ E6670	SC 1906	1981	UOrP 1972 Port Or USA97201	Frmn 1928 UMi 1930	UMi 1933	UCHM 1933	LoyS 1940	Bylr 1943	UOrP 1946	An5371
Pease, Daniel Chapin A 1952 P7980 E6265 E7880	NY 1914		UCLM 1982 LAng Ca USA90024	Yale 1936 CalT 1938	Prnc 1940	ClmM 1942 USCM 1945	USCM 1947	USCM 1949 UCLM 1951	UCLM 1955	An7380
Peters, Alan A 1967 E8690	UK 1929		BstM Bost Ma USA02118	Bris 1951	Bris 1954				BstM 1966	An66

Names/Membs/Offs	Birth	Death	Position	Bach/Mast	MD/PhD	Instructor	Asst Prof	Assoc Prof	Full Prof	Chrmn
Piersol, George A. @ 1889+ P0911 V9799 V0508	Pa 1856	1924	UPaM 1921 Phil Pa USA19104	PPly 1874	UPa 1877				UPaM 1889 UPaM 1891	An0121
Pohlman, Augustus G. @ 1900+ E3236	NY 1879	1950	CrgM Omah Ne USA68178		Bflo 1900	CrnN 1901 UCBk 1918	InUB 1904	InUB 1906 USCM 1938	InUB 1908 StLM 1913 USDM 1932 CrgM 1938	An1329
Poynter, Charles W. @ 1915+ E1923	Il 1875	1950	UNeO 1945 Omah Ne USA68105	UNe 1898	UNe 1902	UNeO 1903	UNeO 1906	UNeO 1910	UNeO 1912	An1246
Ralston, Henry James A 1966 P8788	Ca 1935		UCFM SanF Ca USA94117	UCBk 1956	UCSF 1959		StnM 1965	UWMd 1969	UCFM 1973	An73
Ramsey, Elizabeth M. f A 1947 V7476 E6367	NY 1906		CrgI Wash DC USA20007	Mils 1928	YalM 1932 MCPa 1965					
Ranson, Stephen W. @ 1908+ P3840 V2628 E2124	Mn 1880	1942	WaUM 1942 StLo Mo USA63110	UMn 1902 UChi 1903	Rush 1907 UChi 1905	WaUM 1903 NthM 1908	NthM 1909	NthM 1910	NthM 1911 WaUM 1924	cA1124
Rasmussen, Andrew T. @ 1916+ V4850 E3438	Ut 1883	1955	UMNM 1952 Minn Mn USA55401	BrYg 1909	Crnl 1916	BrYg 1909 CrnN 1914 UMNM 1916	UMNM 1918	UMNM 1919	BrYg 1911 UMNM 1925	Bil113 An2552
Revel, Jean-Paul A 1961 E7983	Fra 1930		CalT Pasa Ca USA91125	Stbg 1949	HrvC 1957	Hrvd 1961	Hrvd 1963	Hrvd 1966	Hrvd 1969 CalT 1971	
Reynolds, Samuel R. M. 1936-1983 V6264	Pa 1903	1986	UIIM 1969 Chic Il USA60612	Swth 1927 Swth 1928	UPa 1931	CWRM 1932 LICM 1933	LICM 1934	LICM 1938	UIIM 1956	An5669
Roofe, Paul Gibbons A 1935 E5660	Mo 1899		UKsK 1974 KCit Ks USA66044	KsSC 1924	UChi 1934	ULoM 1934	ULoM 1935		UKsK 1945	An4570
Ross, Leonard Lester A 1956 E8488	NY 1927		MCPa Phil Pa USA19129	NYU 1946 NYU 1949	NYUM 1954		UAIM 1952 CrnN 1957	CrnN 1961	CrnN 1971 MCPa 1973	An73

Names/Membs/Offs	Birth	Death	Position	Bach/Mast	MD/PhD	Instructor	Asst Prof	Assoc Prof	Full Prof	Chrmn
Sabin, Florence R. f @ 1902 + P2426 V0809	Co 1871	1953	RckU 1938 NYor NY USA10021	Smth 1893	JnHo 1900			JnHo 1905	JnHo 1917 RckU 1925	
Sawyer, Charles H. g A 1944 V6870 E6668	Vt 1915		UCLM LAng Ca USA90024	Midl 1937	Yale 1941	StnM 1941	DukM 1944	DukM 1948	DukM 1950 UCLM 1951	An5563
Scammon, Richard E. @ 1908 + V2830 E2326 E3539	Mo 1883	1952	UCHM 1949 Chic Il USA60637	UKs 1904 UKs 1906	HrvC 1909	UKsK 1906 HrvB 1909	UKsK 1910 UMNM 1911	UMNM 1913	UMNM 1914 UCHM 1930	
Schaeffer, J. Parsons @ 1908 + P4346 V4246 E2529	Pa 1878	1970	JefM 1948 Phil Pa USA19104	Crnl 1909	UPaM 1907 Crnl 1910	CrnN 1908	CrnN 1910 YalM 1911		YalM 1912 JefM 1914	An1448
Scharrer, Berta V. f g A 1957 P7879 E7475	Ger 1906		AEMC 1978 Brnx NY USA10461		Muni 1928	CWRM 1940	UCoD 1950		AEMC 1955	An7677
Scharrer, Ernst @ 1939 + E6266	Ger 1905	1965	Vien 1965 Vien VnC Ast		Muni 1933 Muni 1927	Vien 1930	CWRM 1940	UCoD 1946	AEMC 1955	An5565
Schulte, H.V.W. @ 1907 + E1419	NY 1876	1932	ClmM 1932 NYor NY USA10032	TrCt 1897	Clmb 1902	ClmM 1904	ClmM 1910	ClmM 1910	CrgM 1917	
Schwarz, M. Roy A 1964 PS7882	Id 1936		[Busi] Chic Il USA	PacL 1959	UWa 1963	UWa 1963	UWa 1965	UWa 1968	UWaM 1972	
Scott, Gordon Hatler @ 1926 + V5052 E4950	Ks 1901	1970	WynM 1968 Detr Mi USA48201	SweC 1922 UMn 1925	UMn 1926		LoyS 1926 WaUM 1928	WaUM 1931	USCM 1942 WynM 1945	An4245 An4550
Senior, Harold D. @ 1903 + V2124 E3337	Eng 1870	1938	NYUM 1936 NYor NY USA10001	Drhm 1894	Drhm 1918			SNSy 1907	SNSy 1908 NYUM 1910	An0810
Shepherd, Francis J. @ 1890-1914 V9497 E9700	*PQ 1851	1929	McGM 1913 Mtrl PQ CanH3G 1Y6		McGl 1873				McGM 1883	

Names/Membs/Offs	Birth	Death	Position	Bach/Mast	MD/PhD	Instructor	Asst Prof	Assoc Prof	Full Prof	Chrmn
Simpson, Miriam E. f A 1924 E5054	Wy 1894		UCBk 1961 Berk Ca USA94708	UCBk 1915 UCBk 1916	JnHo 1923 UCBk 1921	UCBk 1923	UCBk 1926	UCBk 1931	UCBk 1945	
Sladek, John R., Jr. A 1972 E8488	Il 1943		RchM RocN NY USA14642	Crth 1965 Nthw 1968	ChMS 1971		RchM 1973	RchM 1977	RchM 1979	AN81
Slautterback, David B. A 1953 E7579	In 1926		HrvB Bost Ma USA02115	UMi 1948 UMi 1949	CrnN 1952	NYUM 1954 CrnN 1955	CrnN 1959 UWiM 1959	UWMd 1961	UWMd 1967 UWiM 1982	An6782
Slonecker, Charles E. A 1969 PS8290	Wa 1938		UBCM Vanc BC CanV6T1W5	UWa 1960	UWa 1965 UWa 1967		UBCM 1968	UBCM 1971	UBCM 1976	An81
Smith, Philip E. @ 1910+ P4042 E3438	SD 1884	1970	Stnf 1952 Stnf Ca USA94305	Pmna 1908 Crnl 1910	Crnl 1912	CrnN 1911 UCBk 1912	UCBk 1917	UCBk 1921 StnM 1926	ClmM 1927	
Speidel, Carl Caskey @ 1920+ E4047	DC 1893	1982	WdHI 1964 WdHI Ma USA02543	Lfyt 1914	Prnc 1918	Akm 1917	UVaM 1920	UVaM 1922	UVaM 1931	An4959
Spitzka, Edward C. @ 1889-1902 E9194	NY 1852	1914	[PPct] 1914 NYor NY USA10001		NYU 1873				NYMC 1882	
Sprague, James M. A 1942 V7678 E7174	Mo 1916		UPaM 1983 Phil Pa USA19104	UKs 1938 UKs 1940	HrvC 1942	JnHM 1943	JnHM 1946 UPaM 1950	UPaM 1953	UPaM 1958	An6776
Stockard, Charles R. @ 1908+ P2830 S1321 E2428	Ms 1879	1939	CrnN 1939 NYor NY USA10021	MsAM 1899 MsAM 1901	Clmb 1906	CrnN 1908	CrnN 1909		CrnN 1911	An1139
Stone, Leon S. @ 1921+ V5456	NJ 1893	1980	YalM 1961 NHav Ct USA06510	Lfyt 1916	Yale 1921	YalM 1921	YalM 1925	YalM 1928	YalM 1940	
Streeter, George L. @ 1903+ P2628 E1720	NY 1873	1948	Crng 1948 Pitt Pa USA15230	Unio 1895 Clmb 1899	Clmb 1899	JnHM 1905	Wist 1906		UMiA 1907	

Names/Membs/Offs	Birth	Death	Position	Bach/Mast	MD/PhD	Instructor	Asst Prof	Assoc Prof	Full Prof	Chrmn
Strong, Reuben M. @ 1905+ E1519	Wi 1872	1964	WdHI 1946 WdHI Ma USA02543	Obln 1897 Hrvd 1899	HrvC 1901	LkFs 1897 WdHI 1902 UCHM 1907		VndM 1916	UMsJ 1914 LoyS 1918	An1846
Sullivan, Walter E. @ 1917+ V5456 E4148	Me 1885	1971	UWMd 1956 Madi Wi USA53706	Bate 1907 Brwn 1909	Brwn 1912	CWRM 1911	MrqD 1913 UWMd 1920	UWMd 1924	TftB 1915 UWMd 1925	An2650
Sutin, Jerome A 1956 V8486 E7781	NY 1930		EmrM Atla Ga USA30322	Sien 1951 UMn 1953	UMn 1954	YalM 1956	YalM 1958	YalM 1963	EmrM 1966	An66
Swan, Roy Craig, Jr. @ 1966 E7073	NY 1920		CrnN NYor NY USA10021	Crnl 1941	CrnN 1947	CrnN 1952	CrnN 1953	CrnN 1955	CrnN 1959	cA5977
Swett, Francis H. @ 1919+ S4243	Me 1893	1943	DukM 1943 Durh NC USA27701	Bate 1916 Brwn 1917	Yale 1922	TftB 1917 JnfHM 1922		VndM 1925	DukM 1930	An3043
Tennyson, Virginia M. f A 1962 E8286	1924		ClmM NYor NY USA10032	PaSU 1946 Bylr 1956	Clmb 1960				ClmM	
Terry, Robert J. @ 1897+ E0912 E2124	Mo 1871	1966	WaUM 1941 StLo Mo USA63155	WaU 1901	MoMC 1895		WaUM 1899		WaUM 1900	AN0041
Thompson, Ian M. @ 1930+ E6165	*Nf 1896	1981	UMbM 1965 Winn Mb CanR3E 0W3	Ednb 1919 Ednb 1920	Ednb 1920		McGM 1924	UCBk 1927	UCBk 1932 UMbM 1936	An3036 An3665
Todd, T. Wingate @ 1913+ E2529	Eng 1885	1938	CWRM 1938 Clev Oh USA44106		Manc 1907				CWRM 1912	An1238
Towles, William B. @ 1888+ E8889	Va 1847	1893	UVaM Char Va USA22902		UVa 1867				UVaM 1885	
Trotter, Mildred f A 1923 E6973	Pa 1899		WaUM 1967 StLo Mo USA63110	MtHo 1920 WaU 1921	WaUM 1924	WaUM 1924	WaUM 1926	WaUM 1930	WaUM 1946	

Names/Membs/Offs	Birth	Death	Position	Bach/Mast	MD/PhD	Instructor	Asst Prof	Assoc Prof	Full Prof	Chrmn
Truex, Raymond Carl @ 1940 + P7071 E5961	Ne 1911	1980	TmpM 1978 Phil Pa USA19140	NeWs 1934 StLo 1936	UMn 1939	ClmM 1938	ClmM 1942	ClmM 1945	HahM 1948 TmpM 1961	An4861
Ward, James William A 1936 E6669	Tx 1904		UMsJ 1970 Jack Ms USA39216	Vand 1930 Vand 1931	VndM 1940 VndM 1935	VndM 1937	VndM 1940	VndM 1944	VndM 1958	An6063
Warren, John A. @ 1900 + E2324	Ma 1874	1928	HrvB Bost Ma USA02115	HrvC 1896	HrvB 1899		HrvB 1908	HrvB 1915		
Weed, Lewis Hill @ 1909 + S2130 E2021 E3539	Oh 1886	1952	NRC 1952 Wash DC USA20013	Yale 1908 Yale 1909	JnHo 1912	JnHM 1914		JnHM 1916	JnHM 1919	cA1947
Weisse, Faneuil D. @ 1888 + V8891	Ma 1842	1915	NYUD 1915 NYor NY USA10001		NYU 1864				NYUM 1865 NYUD 1865	
Wells, Lemen J. a 1936-1972 E5862	Il 1907		UMNM 1969 Minn Mn USA55455	SllC 1927 Nthw 1928	UChi 1934	UMoC 1935	UMoC 1937	UMNM 1940	UMNM 1949	
Whitlock, David G. A 1953 E6872	Or 1924		UCoD Denv Co USA80262	OrSU 1946	UOr 1949 UOrP 1951	UOrP 1950	UCLM 1951 SNSM 1955	SNSM 1959	SNSM 1961 UCoD 1967	An6782
Wilder, Burt Green @ 1888-1911 P9799 V9497 E8892	Ma 1841	1925	Bwdn 1910 BruM Me USA04011	HrvC 1862	HrvB 1866				CrnN 1867 Bwdn 1875	
Willis, William D. Jr A 1964 E8286	Tx 1934		UTxG Galv Tx USA77550	TxAM 1956	UTx 1960 AusU 1963		UTx 1963		UTxG 1964	An86
Windle, William F. g 1923 + V6668 E5761	In 1898	1985	Dnsn Gran Oh USA43023	Dnsn 1921 Nthw 1923	Nthw 1926	NthM 1923	NthM 1926	NthM 1929	UWaM 1946 UPaM 1947 NYUM 1971 Dnsn 1971	An4647 An4751
Wislocki, George B. @ 1915 + V4850 E3741	Ca 1892	1956	HrvB 1956 Bost Ma USA02109	WaU 1912	JnHo 1916		JnHM 1923		HrvB 1931	An3156

Names/Membs/Offs	Birth	Death	Position	Bach/Mast	MD/PhD	Instructor	Asst Prof	Assoc Prof	Full Prof	Chrmn
Wood, Joe George A 1963 E7478	Tx 1928		UTxH Hous Tx USA77025	Hous 1953 Hous 1958	UTxG 1962	UTxH 1961 Yale 1962	UAr 1963	UTSM 1966	UTxH 1970	NA70
Woodburne, Russell T. A 1937 P7475 S6472 E5559	*On 1904		USFl 1982 Tamp Fl USA33620	UMi 1932 UMi 1933	UMi 1935	UMiA 1936	UMiA 1939	UMiA 1944	UMiA 1947	AC5873
Zimny, Marilyn L. f A 1957 E8185	Il 1927		LaSN NOrl La USA70112	UIl 1948 LoyC 1951	LoyC 1954		LaSN 1954	LaSU 1959	LaSN 1964	An76

1. Ideally, there should appear here a full key to all codes, abbreviations, and symbols used in this appendix. Space limitations prevent this. As an alternative, a key to all those assigned to countries, states, provinces, cities, institutions, and departments has been designed into the rank list for each of these categories, and these can be referred to for the translation of any codes not easily interpreted—which should be very few.

There remain the special cases used in the leftmost compartment in the table above, where there are entered under the name of each officer a symbol for his or her membership status, a span of membership years, and a code for each office held, as follows:

—On the second line, immediately below the officer's name, is a symbol indicating the membership status of that officer:

  A = active member.
  a = living former member.
  @ = deceased member.

—On the third line: the year of enrollment in the Association, followed by the year of termination of membership; a "+" in place of the latter year indicates that the officer never resigned, but was an active member until death.

—On the fourth line is a concise record of offices held, with the inclusive years of tenure represented, because of space limits, by only the last two integers of those years—the reader needing to supply the "18-" or "19-", as appropriate. The symbols designating the various offices are as follows:

  P   = President   S   = Secretary-Treasurer   E   = Executive Committee
  VP = Vice President   PS = Program Secretary

ALLTIME AAA
TABLE OF MD AND PhD DEGREES BY GENDER

Members
Percent
Row Pct

Col Pct	MD Only	PhD Only	MD & PhD	Other or Unknown	Total
Male	965	2774	555	271	4565
	17.93	51.55	10.31	5.04	84.84
	21.14	60.77	12.16	5.94	
	94.79	80.50	91.74	86.86	
Female	53	672	50	41	816
	0.98	12.49	0.93	0.76	15.16
	6.50	82.35	6.13	5.02	
	5.21	19.50	8.26	13.14	
TOTAL	1018	3446	605	312	5381
	18.92	64.04	11.24	5.80	100.00

ALLTIME AAA
TABLE OF HIGHEST
ACADEMIC APPOINTMENT BY GENDER

Members
Percent
Row Pct

Col Pct	Inst	Asst	Assoc	Full	Other or Unknown	Total
Male	106	533	858	2347	721	4565
	1.97	9.91	15.94	43.62	13.40	84.84
	2.32	11.68	18.80	51.41	15.79	
	73.61	74.23	80.71	92.22	79.14	
Female	38	185	205	198	190	816
	0.71	3.44	3.81	3.68	3.53	15.16
	4.66	22.67	25.12	24.26	23.28	
	26.39	25.77	19.29	7.78	20.86	
TOTAL	144	718	1063	2545	911	5381
	2.68	13.34	19.75	47.30	16.93	100.00

AAA ACTIVE
TABLE OF MD AND PhD DEGREES BY GENDER

Members
Percent
Row Pct

Col Pct	MD Only	PhD Only	MD & PhD	Other or Unknown	Total
Male	274	1673	295	42	2284
	9.81	59.92	10.57	1.50	81.81
	12.00	73.25	12.92	1.84	
	92.88	78.95	89.39	87.50	
Female	21	446	35	6	508
	0.75	15.97	1.25	0.21	18.19
	4.13	87.80	6.89	1.18	
	7.12	21.05	10.61	12.50	
TOTAL	295	2119	330	48	2792
	10.57	75.90	11.82	1.72	100.00

AAA ACTIVE
TABLE OF HIGHEST
ACADEMIC APPOINTMENT BY GENDER

Members
Percent
Row Pct

Col Pct	Inst	Asst	Assoc	Full	Other or Unknown	Total
Male	35	330	552	1156	211	2284
	1.25	11.82	19.77	41.40	7.56	81.81
	1.53	14.45	24.17	50.61	9.24	
	71.43	73.17	79.54	89.89	67.63	
Female	14	121	142	130	101	508
	0.50	4.33	5.09	4.66	3.62	18.19
	2.76	23.82	27.95	25.59	19.88	
	28.57	26.83	20.46	10.11	32.37	
TOTAL	49	451	694	1286	312	2792
	1.76	16.15	24.86	46.06	11.17	100.00

ACTIVE AAA
TABLE OF DOCTORAL DEGREES BY GENDER

Members
Percent
Row Pct
Col Pct

	MD	Dent	Vet	PhD	MD&Dent	Vet&PhD	MD&PhD	Dent&PhD	Ost&PhD	Unknown	Total
Male	274	21	11	1572	1	49	289	54	2	11	2284
	9.81	0.75	0.39	56.30	0.04	1.76	10.35	1.93	0.07	0.39	81.81
	12.00	0.92	0.48	68.83	0.04	2.15	12.65	2.36	0.09	0.48	
	92.88	95.45	91.67	78.17	100.00	94.23	89.20	93.10	100.00	73.33	
Female	21	1	1	439	0	3	35	4	0	4	508
	0.75	0.04	0.04	15.72	0.00	0.11	1.25	0.14	0.00	0.14	18.19
	4.13	0.20	0.20	86.42	0.00	0.59	6.89	0.79	0.00	0.79	
	7.12	4.55	8.33	21.83	0.00	5.77	10.80	6.90	0.00	26.67	
Total	295	22	12	2011	1	52	324	58	2	15	2792
	10.57	0.79	0.43	72.03	0.04	1.86	11.60	2.08	0.07	0.54	100.00

TABLE OF DEGREES BY AGEGROUP

Members Percent Row Pct	20-25	26-30	31-35	36-40	41-45	46-50	51-55	TOTAL
MD ONLY	0	3	2	7	13	35	51	299
	0.00	0.12	0.08	0.27	0.50	1.35	1.97	11.53
	0.00	1.00	0.67	2.34	4.35	11.71	17.06	
	0.00	17.65	1.46	2.06	2.99	9.41	17.00	
PHD ONLY	1	11	127	306	394	294	208	1965
	0.04	0.42	4.90	11.80	15.19	11.34	8.02	75.78
	0.05	0.56	6.46	15.57	20.05	14.96	10.59	
	100.00	64.71	92.70	90.00	90.57	79.03	69.33	
MD AND PHD	0	0	5	22	25	35	36	269
	0.00	0.00	0.19	0.85	0.96	1.35	1.39	10.37
	0.00	0.00	1.86	8.18	9.29	13.01	13.38	
	0.00	0.00	3.65	6.47	5.75	9.41	12.00	
UNKNOWN	0	3	3	5	3	8	5	60
	0.00	0.12	0.12	0.19	0.12	0.31	0.19	2.31
	0.00	5.00	5.00	8.33	5.00	13.33	8.33	
	0.00	17.65	2.19	1.47	0.69	2.15	1.67	
TOTAL	1	17	137	340	435	372	300	2593
	0.04	0.66	5.28	13.11	16.78	14.35	11.57	100.00

Members
Percent
Row Pct

	56-60	61-65	66-70	71-75	76-80	81-85	86-90	91-95	TOTAL
MD ONLY	40 1.54 13.38 13.89	41 1.58 13.71 16.94	31 1.20 10.37 24.03	22 0.85 7.36 18.80	26 1.00 8.70 26.00	16 0.62 5.35 21.92	9 0.35 3.01 26.47	3 0.12 1.00 37.50	299 11.53
PHD ONLY	199 7.67 10.13 69.10	155 5.98 7.89 64.05	73 2.82 3.72 56.59	72 2.78 3.66 61.54	56 2.16 2.85 56.00	48 1.85 2.44 65.75	18 0.69 0.92 52.94	3 0.12 0.15 37.50	1965 75.78
MD AND PHD	46 1.77 17.10 15.97	34 1.31 12.64 14.05	18 0.69 6.69 13.95	19 0.73 7.06 16.24	13 0.50 4.83 13.00	9 0.35 3.35 12.33	5 0.19 1.86 14.71	2 0.08 0.74 25.00	269 10.37
UNKNOWN	3 0.12 5.00 1.04	12 0.46 20.00 4.96	7 0.27 11.67 5.43	4 0.15 6.67 3.42	5 0.19 8.33 5.00	0 0.00 0.00 0.00	2 0.08 3.33 5.88	0 0.00 0.00 0.00	60 2.31
TOTAL	288 11.11	242 9.33	129 4.97	117 4.51	100 3.86	73 2.82	34 1.31	8 0.31	2593 100.00

AGE GROUPS BY DEGREES — ACTIVE MEMBERS

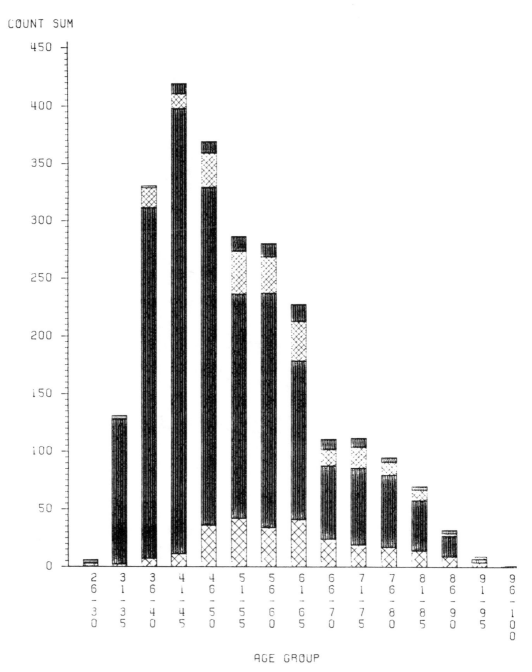

DISTRIBUTION OF ACTIVE MEMBERS IN USA

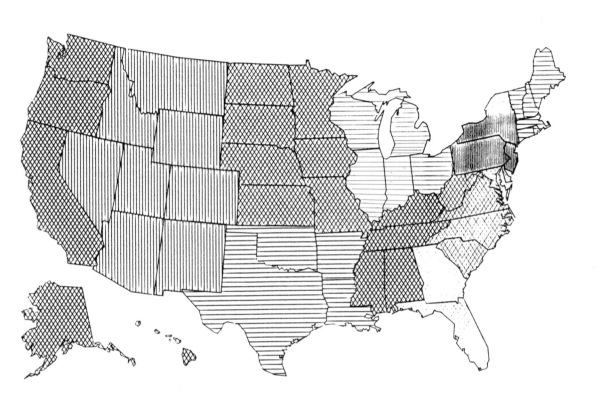

LEGEND: RESPONSE

 N.E. 187
E.N.C 429
S.A. 442
W.S.C. 247
P. 322

 M.A. 454
W.N.C 217
E.S.C. 140
M. 75

RANK ORDER OF COUNTRIES
ACTIVE MEMBERS

Rank	Code	Country	Members	Percent
01	USA	United States of America	2416	86.75
02	Can	Canada	154	5.53
03	Jap	Japan	34	1.22
04	UK	United Kingdom	16	0.57
05	Isr	Israel	13	0.47
06	Tai	Taiwan	11	0.39
07	Chn	China	10	0.36
08	Aus	Australia	9	0.32
09	Net	Netherlands	9	0.32
10	Brz	Brazil	7	0.25
11	FRG	Federal Rep. of Germany	7	0.25
12	Ind	India	7	0.25
13	Ita	Italy	6	0.22
14	Kuw	Kuwait	6	0.22
15	Fra	France	5	0.18
16	Arg	Argentina	4	0.14
17	Mex	Mexico	4	0.14
18	Swe	Sweden	4	0.14
19	Swi	Switzerland	4	0.14
20	SAr	Saudi Arabia	4	0.14
21	Thi	Thailand	4	0.14
22	BWI	British West Indies	3	0.11
23	Leb	Lebanon	3	0.11
24	NZd	New Zealand	3	0.11
25	Sgp	Singapore	3	0.11
26	SAf	South Africa	3	0.11
27	Ast	Austria	2	0.07
28	Bel	Belgium	2	0.07
29	Chl	Chile	2	0.07
30	Grc	Greece	2	0.07
31	Hun	Hungary	2	0.07
32	Jam	Jamaica	2	0.07
33	Nga	Nigeria	2	0.07
34	Nor	Norway	2	0.07
35	Pak	Pakistan	2	0.07
36	Phl	Philippines	2	0.07
37	RIr	Republic of Ireland	2	0.07
38	Spa	Spain	2	0.07
39	Ven	Venezuela	2	0.07
40	Den	Denmark	1	0.04
41	Fin	Finland	1	0.04
42	Mlt	Malta	1	0.04
43	Mly	Malaysia	1	0.04
44	Pan	Panama	1	0.04
45	Par	Paraguay	1	0.04
46	Pol	Poland	1	0.04
47	Por	Portugal	1	0.04
48	Tur	Turkey	1	0.04
49	Uru	Uruguay	1	0.04

DISTRIBUTION OF ACTIVE MEMBERS BY REGIONS OF U.S.A.

NEW ENGLAND

State	Members	Percent
Connecticut	31	18.12
Maine	5	2.92
Massachusetts	116	67.83
New Hampshire	5	2.92
Rhode Island	8	4.67
Vermont	6	3.50

MIDDLE ATLANTIC

State	Members	Percent
New Jersey	50	11.79
New York	250	58.96
Pennsylvania	124	29.24

EAST NORTH CENTRAL

State	Members	Percent
Illinois	147	33.94
Indiana	45	10.39
Michigan	82	18.93
Ohio	103	23.78
Wisconsin	56	12.93

WEST NORTH CENTRAL

State	Members	Percent
Iowa	41	20.09
Kansas	22	10.78
Minnesota	32	15.68
Missouri	67	32.84
Nebraska	24	11.76
North Dakota	9	4.41
South Dakota	9	4.41

SOUTH ATLANTIC

State	Members	Percent
Delaware	1	0.23
District of Columbia	52	12.20
Florida	59	13.85
Georgia	43	10.09
Maryland	99	23.23
North Carolina	64	15.02
South Carolina	27	6.33
Virginia	58	13.61
West Virginia	23	5.39

EAST SOUTH CENTRAL

State	Members	Percent
Alabama	35	26.31
Kentucky	29	21.80
Mississippi	14	10.52
Tennessee	55	41.35

WEST SOUTH CENTRAL

State	Members	Percent
Arkansas	14	5.80
Louisiana	66	27.38
Oklahoma	31	12.86
Texas	130	53.94

MOUNTAIN

State	Members	Percent
Arizona	15	23.43
Colorado	15	23.43
Idaho	3	4.68
Montana	3	4.68
Nevada	7	10.93
New Mexico	9	14.06
Utah	12	18.75

PACIFIC

State	Members	Percent
Alaska	1	0.32
California	227	72.99
Hawaii	5	1.60
Oregon	31	9.96
Washington	47	15.11

SUMMARY

Region	Members	Percent
East North Central	433	17.989
South Atlantic	426	17.698
Middle Atlantic	424	17.615
Pacific	311	12.921
West South Central	241	10.012
West North Central	204	8.475
New England	171	7.104
East South Central	133	5.526
Mountain	64	2.659

RANK ORDER OF CANADIAN PROVINCES

Rank	Code	Province	Members	Percent
01	On	Ontario	57	36.77
02	PQ	Province of Quebec	30	19.35
03	BC	British Columbia	22	14.19
04	Mb	Manitoba	16	10.32
05	Ab	Alberta	13	8.39
06	NS	Nova Scotia	10	6.45
07	Sk	Saskatchewan	5	3.23
08	Nf	Newfoundland	1	0.65
09	PE	Prince Edward Island	1	0.65

RANK ORDER OF US STATES, DC, PR, AND CANADIAN PROVINCES

Rank	Code	State Name	Members	Percent	Cum Percent
01	NY	New York	250	9.72	9.72
02	Ca	California	227	8.83	18.55
03	Il	Illinois	147	5.72	24.26
04	Tx	Texas	130	5.05	29.32
05	Pa	Pennsylvania	124	4.82	34.14
06	Ma	Massachusetts	116	4.51	38.65
07	Oh	Ohio	103	4.00	42.65
08	Md	Maryland	99	3.85	46.50
09	Mi	Michigan	82	3.19	49.69
10	Mo	Missouri	67	2.60	52.29
11	La	Louisiana	66	2.57	54.86
12	NC	North Carolina	64	2.49	57.35
13	Fl	Florida	59	2.29	59.64
14	Va	Virginia	58	2.26	61.90
15	On	Ontario	57	2.22	64.11
16	Wi	Wisconsin	56	2.18	66.29
17	Tn	Tennessee	55	2.14	68.43
18	DC	District of Columbia	52	2.02	70.45
19	NJ	New Jersey	50	1.94	72.40
20	Wa	Washington	47	1.83	74.22
21	In	Indiana	45	1.75	75.97
22	Ga	Georgia	43	1.67	77.64
23	Ia	Iowa	41	1.59	79.24
24	Al	Alabama	35	1.36	80.60

Rank	Code	State Name	Members	Percent	Cum Percent
25	Mn	Minnesota	32	1.24	81.84
26	Ct	Connecticut	31	1.21	83.05
27	Ok	Oklahoma	31	1.21	84.25
28	Or	Oregon	31	1.21	85.46
29	PQ	Province of Quebec	30	1.17	86.63
30	Ky	Kentucky	29	1.13	87.75
31	SC	South Carolina	27	1.05	88.80
32	Ne	Nebraska	24	0.93	89.74
33	WV	West Virginia	23	0.89	90.63
34	BC	British Columbia	22	0.86	91.49
35	Ks	Kansas	22	0.86	92.34
36	Mb	Manitoba	16	0.62	92.96
37	Az	Arizona	15	0.58	93.55
38	Co	Colorado	15	0.58	94.13
39	Ar	Arkansas	14	0.54	94.67
40	Ms	Mississippi	14	0.54	95.22
41	Ab	Alberta	13	0.51	95.72
42	Ut	Utah	12	0.47	96.19
43	NS	Nova Scotia	10	0.39	96.58
44	PR	Puerto Rico	10	0.39	96.97
45	ND	North Dakota	9	0.35	97.32
46	NM	New Mexico	9	0.35	97.67
47	SD	South Dakota	9	0.35	98.02
48	RI	Rhode Island	8	0.31	98.33
49	Nv	Nevada	7	0.27	98.60
50	Vt	Vermont	6	0.23	98.83
51	Hi	Hawaii	5	0.19	99.03
52	Me	Maine	5	0.19	99.22
53	NH	New Hampshire	5	0.19	99.42
54	Sk	Saskatchewan	5	0.19	99.61
55	Id	Idaho	3	0.12	99.73
56	Mt	Montana	3	0.12	99.84
57	Ak	Alaska	1	0.04	99.88
58	De	Delaware	1	0.04	99.92
59	Nf	Newfoundland	1	0.04	99.96
60	PE	Prince Edward Island	1	0.04	100.00

RANK ORDER OF US AND CANADIAN CITIES
WITH 15 OR MORE MEMBERS

Rank	Code	City Name	Members	Percent	Cum Percent
01	NYor	New York	115	4.14	4.14
02	Phil	Philadelphia	88	3.17	7.31
03	Bost	Boston	78	2.81	10.12
04	LAng	Los Angeles	75	2.70	12.81
05	Chic	Chicago	73	2.63	15.44
06	Wash	Washington	49	1.76	17.21
07	Beth	Bethesda	41	1.48	18.68
08	NOrl	New Orleans	41	1.48	20.16
09	Balt	Baltimore	40	1.44	21.60
10	StLo	Saint Louis	40	1.44	23.04
11	Seat	Seattle	34	1.22	24.26
12	AnnA	Ann Arbor	33	1.19	25.45
13	SanA	San Antonio	32	1.15	26.60
14	Cbus	Columbus	30	1.08	27.68
15	Hous	Houston	30	1.08	28.76
16	Iowa	Iowa City	28	1.01	29.77
17	Milw	Milwaukee	28	1.01	30.78
18	Rich	Richmond	28	1.01	31.79
19	SanF	San Francisco	28	1.01	32.79
20	Bflo	Buffalo	27	0.97	33.77
21	RocN	Rochester, NY	26	0.94	34.70
22	Chap	Chapel Hill	24	0.86	35.57
23	Port	Portland, OR	24	0.86	36.43
24	Dall	Dallas	23	0.83	37.26
25	Detr	Detroit	22	0.79	38.05
26	Madi	Madison	22	0.79	38.84
27	Mayw	Maywood	22	0.79	39.63
28	Nash	Nashville	22	0.79	40.42
29	Newa	Newark	22	0.79	41.22
30	Omah	Omaha	22	0.79	42.01
31	Atla	Atlanta	21	0.76	42.76
32	Vanc	Vancouver	21	0.76	43.52
33	Char	Charlottesville	20	0.72	44.24
34	LonO	London, ON	20	0.72	44.96
35	Mtrl	Montreal	20	0.72	45.68
36	Birm	Birmingham, AL	19	0.68	46.36
37	Galv	Galveston	19	0.68	47.05
38	Augu	Augusta, GA	18	0.65	47.70
39	Cinc	Cincinnati	18	0.65	48.34
40	ELan	East Lansing	17	0.61	48.96
41	OklC	Oklahoma City	17	0.61	49.57
42	Syra	Syracuse	17	0.61	50.18
43	Davi	Davis	16	0.58	50.76
44	Pitt	Pittsburgh	16	0.58	51.33
45	Shre	Shreveport	16	0.58	51.91
46	Winn	Winnipeg	16	0.58	52.48
47	Alba	Albany	15	0.54	53.02
48	Chas	Charleston	15	0.54	53.56
49	Loui	Louisville	15	0.54	54.10
50	Memp	Memphis	15	0.54	54.64
51	Morg	Morgantown	15	0.54	55.18
52	Tamp	Tampa	15	0.54	55.72

RANK ORDER OF INSTITUTIONS
WITH 10 OR MORE MEMBERS

Rank	Code	Institution Name	Members	Percent
1	UCLM	California, U., L.A., Sch. of Med.	43	1.78
2	HrvB	Harvard Medical School	33	1.37
3	UMiA	Michigan, U. of, Medical School	32	1.33
4	UTSM	Texas, U. of, Med. Sch. at San Antonio	30	1.24
5	UWaM	Washington, U. of, School of Medicine	29	1.20
6	UIaM	Iowa, U. of, College of Medicine	26	1.08
7	LaSN	Lousiana State U. School of Medicine	25	1.04
8	RchM	Rochester, U. of, School of Med. & Dent.	25	1.04
9	OhSM	Ohio State U., College of Medicine	24	1.00
10	USCM	California, Southern, U. of, Med. School	24	1.00
11	MCVa	Virginia, Medical College of	23	0.95
12	NJMD	New Jersey Medical School, UMDNJ	22	0.91
13	SNBM	SUNY at Buffalo School of Medicine	22	0.91
14	WaUM	Washington University School of Medicine	22	0.91
15	MCWi	Wisconsin, Medical College of	21	0.87
16	UCFM	California, U. of at SanF, Medical	21	0.87
17	UIlM	Illinois, U. of, College of Medicine	21	0.87
18	UBCM	British Columbia, U. of, Fac. of Med.	20	0.83
19	UNCM	North Carolina, U. of, Med. School	20	0.83
20	UMdB	Maryland, U. of, School of Medicine	19	0.79
21	WynM	Wayne State U. School of Medicine	19	0.79
22	ClmM	Columbia-Coll. of Physicians & Surgeons	18	0.75
23	UTxG	Texas, U. of, Medical Branch	18	0.75
24	UVaM	Virginia, U. of, School of Medicine	18	0.75
25	UWMd	Wisconsin, University of, Medical School	18	0.75
26	UWOM	Western Ontario, U., Facs. Med. & Den.	18	0.75
27	JefM	Jefferson Medical College	17	0.70
28	LoyS	Loyala U. Stritch School of Medicine	17	0.70
29	MCGa	Georgia, Medical College of	17	0.70
30	TftB	Tufts University School of Medicine	17	0.70
31	StLM	St. Louis U. School of Medicine	16	0.66
32	UCnM	Cincinnati, U. of, College of Medicine	16	0.66
33	UMbM	Manitoba, U. of, Facs. of Med. & Den.	16	0.66
34	UOkO	Oklahoma, U. of, College of Medicine	16	0.66
35	AEMC	Albert Einstein Med. Coll. at Yeshiva	15	0.62
36	ETnM	Tennessee U., East, Q-D Coll. of Med.	15	0.62
37	HwrM	Howard University, College of Medicine	15	0.62
38	MUSC	South Carolina, Medical University of	15	0.62
39	NthM	Northwestern Univ. Medical School	15	0.62
40	SNSy	SUNY Upstate, College of Medicine	15	0.62
41	ULoM	Louisville, U. of, School of Medicine	15	0.62
42	WVMC	W. Virginia U. School of Medicine	15	0.62
43	GeWM	George Washington U. School of Medicine	14	0.58
44	McGM	McGill University Facs. of Med. & Den.	14	0.58
45	MCPa	Pennsylvania, Medical College of	14	0.58

Rank	Code	Institution Name	Members	Percent
46	TmpM	Temple University School of Medicine	14	0.58
47	UTxH	Texas, U. of, Medical Sch. at Houston	14	0.58
48	YalM	Yale University School of Medicine	14	0.58
49	AlbM	Albany Medical College of Union Univ.	13	0.54
50	BstM	Boston University School of Medicine	13	0.54
51	GrgM	Georgetown Medical School	13	0.54
52	HahM	Hahnemann University Sch. of Medicine	13	0.54
53	MiSM	Michigan State College of Human Medicine	13	0.54
54	UArM	Arkansas, U. of, College of Medicine	13	0.54
55	UCIM	California, U. of at Irvine, Med. Center	13	0.54
56	UMNM	Minnesota, U. of, Medical School	13	0.54
57	CWRM	Case Western Reserve School of Medicine	12	0.50
58	EmrM	Emory University College of Medicine	12	0.50
59	LaSS	Louisiana State U. Medical at Shre	12	0.50
60	NYUD	New York Univ. College of Dentistry	12	0.50
61	Rush	Rush Medical College	12	0.50
62	TlnM	Tulane University School of Medicine	12	0.50
63	UAlM	Alabama, University of, Sch. of Medicine	12	0.50
64	UKyM	Kentucky, U. of, College of Medicine	12	0.50
65	UMsJ	Mississippi, U. of, School of Medicine	12	0.50
66	UOrP	Oregon Health Sciences University	12	0.50
67	USFM	Florida, South, U. of, Coll. of Med.	12	0.50
68	USHS	Uniformed Services Univ. of Health Sci.	12	0.50
69	UTxM	Texas, U. of, Southwestern Medical Sch.	12	0.50
70	CrnN	Cornell University Medical College	11	0.46
71	MtSi	Mount Sinai School of Medicine of CUNY	11	0.46
72	NIH	National Institutes of Health	11	0.46
73	RutM	Rutgers Medical School, UMDNJ	11	0.46
74	UKsK	Kansas, U. of, School of Medicine	11	0.46
75	UNeO	Nebraska, U. of, College of Medicine	11	0.46
76	UPtM	Pittsburgh, U. of, School of Medicine	11	0.46
77	UTnM	Tennessee, U. of, College of Medicine	11	0.46
78	VndM	Vanderbilt University School of Medicine	11	0.46
79	WkFM	Wake Forest-Bowman Gray School of Med.	11	0.46
80	DukM	Duke University School of Medicine	10	0.41
81	JnHM	Johns Hopkins Univ. School of Medicine	10	0.41
82	MCOh	Ohio, Medical College of	10	0.41
83	SAlM	Alabama, South, U. of, Sch. of Med.	10	0.41
84	SNBk	SUNY Downstate, College of Medicine	10	0.41
85	UAzM	Arizona, U. of, Medical School	10	0.41
86	UFlM	Florida, U. of, College of Medicine	10	0.41
87	UMaW	Massachussetts, U. of, Medical School	10	0.41
88	UPaM	Pennsylvania, U. of, School of Medicine	10	0.41
89	USCC	South Carolina, U. of, Sch. of Med.	10	0.41
90	UUtM	Utah, University of, School of Medicine	10	0.41

RANK LIST OF DEPARTMENTS

Though academic departments in which anatomists work have in recent decades assumed a great variety of names, they may be aggregated into 20 clusters approaching classical departments. This will permit the following ranking of those departments in which active members work.

Rank	Code	Specialty	Members	Percent
01	An	Anatomy	1594	71.61
02	Bi	Biology	146	6.56
03	DA	Dental Anatomy	81	3.64
04	VA	Veterinary Anatomy	56	2.52
05	Sr	Surgery	52	2.34
06	Pa	Pathology	50	2.25
07	Ph	Physiology	40	1.80
08	Ns	Neuroscience	38	1.71
09	CB	Cell Biology	32	1.44
10	Nr	Neurology	31	1.39
11	Ps	Psychology	21	0.94
12	OG	Obstetrics-Gynecology	16	0.72
13	Md	Medicine	12	0.54
14	Ot	Otolaryngology	11	0.49
15	PT	Physical Therapy	11	0.49
16	Ap	Anthropology	9	0.40
17	Pm	Pharmacology	9	0.40
18	Op	Ophthalmology	8	0.36
19	Pc	Psychiatry	8	0.36
20	Pn	Physical Med. and Rehab.	1	0.04

RANK LIST OF SPECIALTY FIELDS

The more than 300 specialty fields to which the members assign themselves can be generalized into these 45 specialty areas, and their 22,304 assignments arrayed in this rank list.

Rank	Code	Specialty	Members
1	Ana	Anatomy	1649
2	CBi	Cell Biology	1608
3	Hst	Histology	1059
4	Emb	Embryology	872
5	Nan	Neuroanatomy	804
6	Bio	Biology	658
7	Nbi	Neurobiology	590
8	End	Endocrinology	540
9	NCl	Neurology, Clinical	406
10	Emi	Electronmicroscopy	370
11	Phs	Physiology	316
12	Cyt	Cytology	314
13	Zoo	Zoology	313
14	AnC	Anatomy, Comparative	189
15	DAn	Anatomy, Dental	172
16	Hsc	Histochemistry	172
17	Pat	Pathology	144
18	AnA	Anatomy, Applied	142
19	Gen	Genetics	142
20	Imm	Immunology	124
21	Bic	Biochemistry	115
22	Rad	Radiology	88
23	BhS	Behavioral Science	87
24	Psc	Psychology	81
25	Mic	Microscopy	75
26	AtP	Anthropology, Physical	71
27	Hem	Hematology	69
28	Srg	Surgery	65
29	Prm	Pharmacology	53
30	AVt	Anatomy, Veterinary	51
31	Oto	Otolaryngology	28
32	Psy	Psychiatry	25
33	HSc	History of Science	23
34	Oph	Ophthalmology	22
35	Mam	Mammalology	21
36	Obs	Obstetrics	21
37	Onc	Oncology	21
38	Bie	Bioengineering	19
39	Gyn	Gynecology	19
40	Che	Chemistry, General, Theoretical	17
41	Mbi	Microbiology, Protistology	17
42	Chn	Chronobiology	15
43	Pal	Paleontology	14
44	Ped	Pediatrics	12
45	Sbi	Sociobiology	2

HONORARY MEMBERS

Year	Name	Birth	Death	Cntry	City	Inst	Dept
1892	Anderson, William A.	1842	1900	UK	Lond	Hosp	An
1984	Austin, Colin R.	1914		UK	Camb	Camb	Em
1976	Bargmann, Wolfgang L.	1906	1978	FRG	Kiel	Kiel	An
1986	Björklund, Anders	1945		Swe	Lund	Lund	Hs
1977	Brodal, Alf	1910		Nor	Oslo	Oslo	An
1900	Cleland, John	1835	1924	UK	Glas	Glas	An
1974	Couteaux, René Jean	1909		Fra	Pari	Pari	Cy
1891	Cunningham, Daniel J.	1850	1909	UK	Ednb	Ednb	An
1980	DeRobertis, Eduardo	1913		Arg	BuAi	BuAi	CB
1897	Duval, Mathias Marie	1844	1907	Fra	Stbg	Stbg	Hs
1978	Eränkö, E. Olavi	1924	1984	Fin	Hels	Hels	An
1895	Flower, William H.	1831	1899	UK	Lond	BrMu	An
1897	Gegenbaur, Karl	1826	1903	FRG	Heid	Heid	An
1903	Golgi, Camillo	1843	1926	Ita	Pavi	Pavi	Hs
1975	Gowans, James L.	1924		UK	Oxfd	Oxfd	Pa
1979	Gray, Edward George	1924		UK	Lond	Lond	An
1982	Hama, Kiyoshi	1923		Jap	Okaz	Toky	MA
1970	Harris, Geoffrey W.	1913	1971	UK	Oxfd	Muse	An
1985	Harrison, Richard J.	1920		UK	Camb	Camb	An
1905	Hertwig, Oscar	1849	1922	FRG	Brln	Brln	An
1897	His, Wilhelm	1831	1904	GDR	Leip	Leip	An
1985	Hökfelt, Tomas	1940		Swe	Stkm	Karl	CB
1895	Humphrey, George M.	1820	1896	UK	Camb	Camb	An
1981	Huxley, Hugh Esmor	1924		UK	Camb	Camb	Ml
1983	Junqueira, Luiz C.U.	1920		Brz	SaoP	SaoP	CB
1982	Kobayashi, Hideshi	1919		Jap	Toky	TohU	IM
1897	Kölliker, R. A. Von	1817	1905	FRG	Wurz	Wurz	An
1984	Le Douarin, Nicole	1930		Fra	Pari	CFra	Em
1897	Macalister, Alexander	1844	1919	UK	Camb	Camb	An
1977	Mitchell, George A.G.	1906		UK	Manc	Manc	An
1976	Nakai, Junnosuke	1918		Jap	Tsuk	Tsuk	Ad
1908	Nicolas, Adolphe	1861	1939	Fra	Pari	Pari	An
1978	Niimi, Kahee	1919		Jap	Okay	Okay	An
1908	Nussbaum, Moritz	1850	1915	FRG	Bonn	Bonn	An
1979	Oksche, Andreas	1926		FRG	Gies	Gies	An
1905	Ramón y Cajal, S.	1852	1934	Spa	Mdrd	Mdrd	Hs
1897	Ranvier, Louis A.	1835	1922	Fra	Pari	Pari	An
1903	Retzius, Gustav M.	1842	1919	Swe	Stkm	Stkm	An
1913	Roux, Wilhelm	1850	1924	GDR	Hall	Hall	Em
1986	Schiebler, Theodor H.	1923		FRG	Wurz	Wurz	An
1972	Szentagothai, Janos	1912		Hun	Bdps	Bdps	An
1903	Toldt, Carl	1840	1920	Ast	Vien	Vien	An
1894	Turner, William	1832	1916	UK	Ednb	Ednb	An
1981	Van Duijn, Pieter			Net	Leid	Leid	Hc
1903	Waldeyer, H. Wilhelm	1836	1921	FRG	Brln	Brln	An
1973	Woerdeman, Martinus W.	1892		Net	Amst	Amst	An
1983	Yamada, Eichi	1922		Jap	Fuku	Toky	An
1980	Yoffey, Joseph M.	1902		Isr	Jeru	HbUJ	An
1971	Young, John Zachary	1907		UK	Lond	UCol	An

RECIPIENTS OF ASSOCIATION AWARDS

Henry Gray Award

1970	Edward A. Boyden	1979	George W. Corner
1971	Donald Duncan	1980	W. Montague Cobb
1972	Elizabeth C. Crosby	1981	Keith R. Porter
1973	Walle Z. Nauta	1982	Berta V. Scharrer
1974	Lesley B. Arey	1983	Don W. Fawcett
1975	Oscar B. Batson	1984	Charles H. Sawyer
1976	Richard J. Blandau	1985	John W. Everett
1977	William F. Windle	1986	George E. Palade
1978	Charles P. Leblond		

Charles Judson Herrick Award

1963	W. Ross Adey	1976	Victoria Chan-Palay
1966	D. Kent Morest	1977	Carl H. Pfenniger
1967	Marc Colonnier	1978	Ann M. Graybiel
1968	Harvey J. Karten	1979	Peter L. Strick
1969	Raymond D. Lund	1980	Larry W. Swanson
1970	Thomas S. Reese	1981	Vivien O. Casagrande
1971	Peter Sterling	1982	Corey S. Goodman
1972	William C. Hall	1983	Mriganka Sur
1973	Joseph L. Price	1984	Peter Somogyi
1974	John Kelly Harting	1985	John Pinter
1975	Jennifer H. LaVail	1986	Charles J. Wilson

R.R. Bensley Award

1979	John E. Heuser	1983	Mark S. Mooseker
1980	Daniel A. Goodenough	1984	Ann L. Hubbard
1981	Elias Lazarides	1985	Jay C. Unkeless
1982	Zena Werb	1986	E.J. Rodrigues-Boulan

Jan Langman Award

1986	Gregory K. Reid

RECIPIENTS OF EXTERNAL AWARDS

American Academy of Arts and Sciences

Adey, William Ross (1965)
Barron, Donald Henry (1962)
Bennett, H. Stanley (1957)
Bigelow, Robert P. (1914)
Billingham, Rupert E. (1965)
Bloom, Floyd E. (1978)
Bodenstein, D.H.F. (1961)
Bodian, David (1968)
Boyden, Edward Allen (1924)
Brazier, Mary A. B.(1956)
Bremer, John Lewis (1916)
Briggs, Robert Wm. (1960)
Brues, Alice Moore (1957)
Bullock, Theodore H. (1958)
Carpenter, Russell L. (1963)
Cheever, David (1930)
Conklin, Edwin Grant (1914)
Corner, George W. (1961)
Councilman, William (1895)
Cowan, William M. (1976)
Dempsey, Edward W. (1949)
Detwiler, Samuel R. (1925)
Dwight, Thomas (1876)
Ebert, James David (1965)
Edds, Mac V. Jr. (1963)
Fawcett, Don Wayne (1955)
Flexner, Louis B. (1966)
Fulton, George P. (1965)
Good, Robert Alan (1974)
Goodale, George L. (1874)
Gray, William W. (1866)
Greep, Roy Orval (1950)
Hamburger, Viktor (1959)
Harrison, Ross G. (1921)
Hay, Elizabeth D. (1975)
Hertig, Arthur T. (1949)
Hisaw, Frederick Lee (1936)
Holtfreter, J. F. C. (1957)
Howell, F. Clark (1974)
Karnovsky, Morris J. (1969)
Keen, William W. (1901)
Kofoid, Charles A. (1913)
Koprowski, Hilary (1974)

Leblond, Charles P. (1970)
Leidy, Joseph (1848)
Lévi-Montalcini, R. (1966)
Lewis, Frederic T. (1916)
Little, Clarence C. (1934)
Livingston, Robert B. (1966)
Lorente de Nó, R. (1954)
Lutz, Brenton Reid (1943)
Magoun, Horace W. (1960)
Mall, Franklin P. (1901)
Mark, Edward Laurens (1884)
Marsh, Othniel C. (1875)
Minot, Charles S. (1882)
Morison, Robert S. (1960)
Nauta, Walle Jetze H. (1966)
Nicholas, John S. (1949)
Osborn, Henry F. (1901)
Palade, George Emil (1957)
Palay, Sanford Louis (1963)
Parker, George H. (1895)
Patten, William (1921)
Pincus, Gregory G. (1939)
Porter, Keith R. (1957)
Prescott, David M. Jr. (1970)
Pribram, Karl Harry (1956)
Rioch, David McK. (1958)
Romer, Alfred S. (1937)
Sawyer, Charles H. (1968)
Scharrer, Berta V. (1967)
Scheibel, Arnold B. (1981)
Schotté, Oscar Emile (1955)
Sidman, Richard Leon (1973)
Singer, Marcus J. (1958)
Soggnaes, Reidar F. (1956)
Sperry, Roger W. (1963)
Stellar, Eliot (1972)
Stryer, Lubert (1975)
Washburn, Sherwood L. (1962)
Weiss, Paul Alfred (1954)
Wilson, J. Walter (1949)
Wislocki, George B. (1938)
Woods, Frederick Adam (1915)

American Philosophical Society

Allen, Harrison (1867)
Bigelow, Henry B. (1937)
Bodian, David (1973)
Bullock, Theodore H. (1970)
Butler, Elmer G. (1948)
Cleland, Ralph E. (1932)
Coghill, George E. (1935)
Conklin, Edwin Grant (1897)
Cope, Edward Drinker (1866)
Corner, George W. (1940)
Councilman, William (1918)
Crile, George W. (1912)
Dahlgren, Ulric (1919)
Danforth, Charles H. (1944)
Darrach, William (1929)
Dercum, Francis X. (1892)
Detwiler, Samuel R. (1940)
Donaldson, Henry H. (1906)
Ebert, James David (1974)
Eigenmann, Carl H. (1917)
Flexner, Louis B. (1979)
Gill, Theodore N. (1867)
Goodale, George L. (1893)
Greenman, Milton Jay (1899)
Gregory, William K. (1925)
Harrison, Ross G. (1913)
Hisaw, Frederick Lee (1940)
Howell, F. Clark (1975)
Hrdlička, Ales (1918)
Huber, Gotthelf Carl (1912)
Jayne, Horace F. (1885)
Keen, William W. (1884)
Keith, Arthur (1931)
Kellogg, Remington (1955)
Kofoid, Charles A. (1924)
Leidy, Joseph (1849)
Lewis, Warren Harmon (1943)
Lillie, Frank R. (1916)
Loeb, Leo (1910)
Mall, Franklin P. (1906)

Mark, Edward Laurens (1907)
Marsh, Othniel C. (1868)
McClung, Clarence E. (1913)
McClure, C.F.W. (1897)
McMurrich, James P. (1907)
Meyer, Adolf B. (1899)
Minot, Charles S. (1896)
Mintz, Beatrice (1982)
Morgan, Thomas Hunt (1915)
Nauta, Walle Jetze H (1971)
Nicholas, John S. (1946)
Noble, Gladwyn K. (1933)
Oppenheimer, Jane M. (1980)
Osborn, Henry F. (1887)
Painter, Theophilus (1939)
Parker, George H. (1911)
Paton, Stewart (1914)
Pearce, Richard M. (1914)
Piersol, George A. (1897)
Porter, Keith R. (1977)
Ramón y Cajal, S. (1932)
Romer, Alfred S. (1951)
Ryder, John Adam (1886)
Schaeffer, J.Parsons (1927)
Schultz, Adolph H. (1936)
Scott, W. Berryman (1886)
Sperry, Roger W. (1974)
Spitzka, Edward A. (1908)
Stellar, Eliot (1977)
Stockard, Charles R. (1924)
Streeter, George L. (1943)
Tilney, Frederick (1930)
Warren, Charles O. (1939)
Weed, Lewis Hill (1942)
Weiss, Paul Alfred (1953)
Wilder, Burt Green (1878)
Willier, Benjamin H. (1955)
Williston, Samuel W. (1918)
Wilson, William P. (1887)

National Academy of Sciences

Bailey, Percival (1953)
Barnes, David Edward (1920)
Bartelmez, George W. (1949)
Bennett, Michael V.L. (1981)
Bern, Howard Alan (1973)
Bigelow, Henry B. (1931)
Bloom, Floyd E. (1977)
Bloom, William (1954)
Bodenstein, D.H.F. (1958)
Bodian, David (1958)
Briggs, Robert Wm. (1962)
Bullock, Theodore H. (1963)
Burns, Robert Kyle (1955)
Child, Charles M. (1935)
Clark, George (1982)
Cleland, Ralph E. (1942)
Coghill, George E. (1935)
Conklin, Edwin Grant (1908)
Cope, Edward Drinker (1872)
Corner, George W. (1940)
Councilman, William (1904)
Danforth, Charles H. (1942)
Detwiler, Samuel R. (1932)
Diamond, Irving T. (1982)
Donaldson, Henry H. (1914)
Ebert, James David (1967)
Eigenmann, Carl H. (1923)
Evans, Herbert M. (1927)
Farquhar, Marilyn G. (1984)
Fawcett, Don Wayne (1972)
Flexner, Louis B. (1964)
Gill, Theodore N. (1873)
Good, Robert Alan (1970)
Goodale, George L. (1890)
Gregory, William K. (1927)
Halsted, William S. (1917)
Hamburger, Viktor (1953)
Harrison, John M. (1965)
Harrison, Ross G. (1913)
Hartman, Carl G. (1937)
Hay, Elizabeth D. (1984)
Herrick, C. Judson (1918)
Hisaw, Frederick Lee (1947)
Hökfelt, Tomas (1984)
Holtfreter, J. F. C. (1955)
Howell, F. Clark (1972)
Hrdlička, Ales (1921)
Huntington, George S. (1924)
Kofoid, Charles A. (1922)
Koprowski, Hilary (1966)
Krogman, Wilton M. (1966)
Lacy, Eric R. (1983)
Lacy, Paul Eston (1983)
Leidy, Joseph (1863)

Lévi-Montalcini, R. (1968)
Lewis, Warren Harmon (1936)
Lillie, Frank R. (1915)
Little, Clarence C. (1945)
Loeb, Leo (1937)
Lorente de Nó, R. (1950)
MacCallum, William G. (1921)
Magoun, Horace W. (1955)
Mall, Franklin P. (1907)
Mark, Edward Laurens (1903)
Marsh, Othniel C. (1874)
McClung, Clarence E. (1920)
Minot, Charles S. (1897)
Mintz, Beatrice (1973)
Moore, Carl Richard (1944)
Morgan, Thomas Hunt (1909)
Moscona, Arthur Aron (1977)
Murphy, James B. (1940)
Nauta, Walle Jetze H (1967)
Nicholas, John S. (1949)
Osborn, Henry F. (1900)
Painter, Theophilus (1938)
Palade, George Emil (1961)
Palay, Sanford Louis (1977)
Parker, George H. (1913)
Patterson, John T. (1941)
Porter, Keith R. (1964)
Prescott, David M. Jr. (1974)
Purpura, Dominick P. (1983)
Ranson, Steven W. (1940)
Romer, Alfred S. (1944)
Rose, Jerzy Edwin (1972)
Sabin, Florence R. (1925)
Sawyer, Charles H. (1980)
Scharrer, Berta V. (1969)
Schultz, Adolph H. (1939)
Scott, W. Berryman (1906)
Sidman, Richard Leon (1979)
Smith, Philip E. (1939)
Sperry, Roger W. (1960)
Sprague, James M. (1984)
Stellar, Eliot (1968)
Stockard, Charles R. (1922)
Straus, Wm.L., Jr. 1 (1962)
Streeter, George L. (1931)
Stryer, Lubert (1984)
Waelsch, Salome G. (1979)
Washburn, Sherwood L (1963)
Weiss, Paul Alfred (1947)
Willier, Benjamin H. (1945)
Williston, Samuel W. (1915)
Wislocki, George B. (1941)

Institute of Medicine

Bloom, Floyd E. (1982)
Clemente, Carmine D. (1980)
Cobb, Jewel Plummer (1974)
Cowan, Maxwell W. (1979)
Dixon, Andrew Derart (1979)
Ebert, James David (1974)

Good, Robert Alan (1970)
Lacy, Paul Eston (1984)
Purpura, Dominick P. (1983)
Smith, Richard André (1972)
Stellar, Eliot (1983)

Nobel Laureates

Morgan, Thomas Hunt (1933)
Palade, George Emil (1974)

Sperry, Roger W. (1981)

Royal Society of London

Barr, Murray L. (1972)
Black, Davidson (1932)
Corner, George W. (1955)
Cowan, Maxwell W. (1982)
Gray, Peter (1977)

Leblond, Charles P. (1965)
Morgan, Thomas Hunt (1919)
Osborn, Henry F. (1926)
Parkes, Alan S. (1933)
Sperry, Roger W. (1976)